Studies in Diversity Linguistics

Chief Editor: Martin Haspelmath

Consulting Editors: Fernando Zúñiga, Peter Arkadiev, Ruth Singer, Pilar Valenzuela

In this series:

1. Handschuh, Corinna. A typology of marked-S languages.

2. Rießler, Michael. Adjective attribution.

3. Klamer, Marian (ed.). The Alor-Pantar languages: History and typology.

4. Berghäll, Liisa. A grammar of Mauwake (Papua New Guinea).

5. Wilbur, Joshua. A grammar of Pite Saami.

6. Dahl, Östen. Grammaticalization in the North: Noun phrase morphosyntax in Scandinavian vernaculars.

7. Schackow, Diana. A grammar of Yakkha.

8. Liljegren, Henrik. A grammar of Palula.

9. Shimelman, Aviva. A grammar of Yauyos Quechua.

10. Rudin, Catherine & Bryan James Gordon (eds.). Advances in the study of Siouan languages and linguistics.

11. Kluge, Angela. A grammar of Papuan Malay.

12. Kieviet, Paulus. A grammar of Rapa Nui.

13. Michaud, Alexis. Tone in Yongning Na: Lexical tones and morphotonology.

ISSN: 2363-5568

A grammar of Yauyos Quechua

Aviva Shimelman

language
science
press

Aviva Shimelman. 2017. *A grammar of Yauyos Quechua* (Studies in Diversity Linguistics 9). Berlin: Language Science Press.

This title can be downloaded at:
http://langsci-press.org/catalog/book/83
© 2017, Aviva Shimelman
Published under the Creative Commons Attribution 4.0 Licence (CC BY 4.0):
http://creativecommons.org/licenses/by/4.0/
ISBN: 978-3-946234-21-0 (Digital)
      978-3-946234-22-7 (Hardcover)
      978-3-946234-23-4 (Softcover)
ISSN: 2363-5568
DOI:10.5281/zenodo.376355

Cover and concept of design: Ulrike Harbort
Typesetting: Sebastian Nordhoff, Aviva Shimelman
Illustration: Sebastian Nordhoff
Proofreading: Alan Scott, Alec Shaw, Charlotte van Tongeren, Conor Pyle, Eitan Grossman, Jo-Anne Ferreira, Mario Bisiada, Martin Haspelmath, Siri Tuttle, Siva Kalyan, Tamara Schmidt
Fonts: Linux Libertine, Arimo, DejaVu Sans Mono
Typesetting software: XƎLATEX

Language Science Press
Unter den Linden 6
10099 Berlin, Germany
langsci-press.org

Storage and cataloguing done by FU Berlin

Language Science Press has no responsibility for the persistence or accuracy of URLs for external or third-party Internet websites referred to in this publication, and does not guarantee that any content on such websites is, or will remain, accurate or appropriate.

For my father

Contents

Acknowledgments		ix
Notational conventions		xi
1	**Introduction**	**1**
1.1	Location	2
1.2	Endangerment	3
1.3	Existing documentation	5
1.4	The dialects of Yauyos	5
1.5	Classification	7
1.6	Presentation	13
1.7	Fieldwork	14
1.8	A note to Quechuanists and typologists	16
1.9	Broader interest	18
	1.9.1 Semantics – evidentials	18
	1.9.2 Language contact – Aymara	18
2	**Phonology and morphophonemics**	**21**
2.1	Introduction and summary	21
2.2	Syllable structure and stress pattern	23
2.3	Phonemic inventory and morphophonemics	24
2.4	Spanish loan words	26
	2.4.1 Spanish loan word restructuring	26
	2.4.2 Loan word orthography	28
3	**Substantives**	**31**
3.1	Parts of speech	31
3.2	Substantive classes	32
	3.2.1 Nouns	32
	3.2.2 Pronouns	36
	3.2.3 Interrogative-indefinites *pi, ima, imay, imayna, mayqin, imapaq, ayka*	45

Contents

		3.2.4	Adjectives	55
		3.2.5	Numerals	59
		3.2.6	Multiple-class substantives	64
		3.2.7	Dummy *na*	64
	3.3	Substantive inflection		66
		3.3.1	Possessive (person)	67
		3.3.2	Number *-kuna*	70
		3.3.3	Case	72
	3.4	Substantive derivation		98
		3.4.1	Substantive derived from verbs	98
		3.4.2	Substantives derived from substantives	112
4	**Verbs**			**121**
	4.1	Verb stems		121
	4.2	Types of verbs		121
		4.2.1	Transitive verbs	121
		4.2.2	Intransitive verbs	123
		4.2.3	Copulative/equational verbs	124
		4.2.4	Onomatopoetic verbs	126
	4.3	Verb inflection		129
		4.3.1	Summary	129
		4.3.2	Person and number	138
		4.3.3	Tense	148
		4.3.4	Conditional	168
		4.3.5	Imperative and injunctive	181
		4.3.6	Aspect	186
		4.3.7	Subordination	191
	4.4	Verb derivation		202
		4.4.1	Suffixes deriving verbs from substantives	202
		4.4.2	Verbs derived from verbs	209
5	**Particles**			**241**
	5.1	Interjections		241
	5.2	Assenters and greetings		243
	5.3	Prepositions		244
	5.4	Adverbs		245
	5.5	Particles covered elsewhere		248

Contents

6 Enclitics — 249
- 6.1 Sequence — 250
- 6.2 Individual enclitics — 250
  - 6.2.1 Emphatic -*Yá* — 252
  - 6.2.2 Interrogation, negation, disjunction -*chu* — 253
  - 6.2.3 Restrictive, limitative -*lla* — 257
  - 6.2.4 Discontinuative -*ña* — 259
  - 6.2.5 Inclusion -*pis* — 260
  - 6.2.6 Precision, certainty -*puni* — 263
  - 6.2.7 Topic-marking -*qa* — 264
  - 6.2.8 Continuative -*Raq* — 265
  - 6.2.9 Sequential -*taq* — 267
  - 6.2.10 Emotive -*ya* — 269
  - 6.2.11 Evidence — 270

7 Syntax — 283
- 7.1 Constituent order — 283
- 7.2 Sentences — 284
- 7.3 Coordination — 284
- 7.4 Comparison — 287
- 7.5 Negation — 289
- 7.6 Interrogation — 291
- 7.7 Reflexives and reciprocals — 294
- 7.8 Equatives — 296
- 7.9 Possession — 297
- 7.10 Topic — 299
- 7.11 Focus — 300
- 7.12 Complementation (infinitive, agentive, indicative and subjunctive clauses) — 300
- 7.13 Relativization — 302
- 7.14 Subordination — 305

Appendix A: Analysis of the Southern Yauyos Quechua lexicon — 309

Appendix B: Further analysis of evidential modifiers — 317
- B.1 The EM's and the interpretation of propositions under direct -*mI* — 317
- B.2 The EM's and the interpretation of propositions under conjectural -*trI* — 319
- B.3 A sociolinguistic note — 323

Contents

References **325**

Index **329**
    Name index 329
    Language index 331
    Subject index 333

Acknowledgments

It is a joy for me to be able to acknowledge all the people and institutions who have helped me in the course of this project. I owe thanks, first, to Willem Adelaar, who read the manuscript with extraordinary care and offered me invaluable comments which saved me from numerous, numerous errors. Many thanks are due, too, to Rodolfo Cerrón-Palomino for comments and advice, as well as to Andrés Chirinos Rivera for orientation. Also offering orientation as well as generous and very enjoyable hospitality were Carmen Escalante Gutiérrez and Ricardo Valderrama Fernández. Paul Heggarty – an intrepid Andean hiker – joined me in the field in the course of his own research; he also found me much-needed support to complete this grammar as well as its accompanying lexicon. Three anonymous reviewers offered extensive, wise comments. Limitations on my time and abilities kept me from incorporating all the changes they suggested. Selfless proofreaders also offered advice for which I am very grateful. Teachers and consultants in Yauyos number more than one hundred; they are acknowledged – insufficiently – in §1.7. In addition to these, there are many, many people in Yauyos and especially in Viñac who are owed thanks for all manner of help and, above all, for friendship. Requiring special mention among these are my principal teacher, Delfina Chullukuy, my principal translator, Esther Madueño, and my *ñaña* and *turi* Hilda Quispe and Ramón Alvarado.

Thanks go, too, to Elio A. Farina for help with LaTeX.

Finally, I honestly don't know how to express my gratitude to Sebastian Nordhoff and Martin Haspelmath, above all for their wisdom and patience.

The fieldwork upon which the grammar and dictionary are based enjoyed the support of several institutions. I am grateful to San Jose State University which offered support in the form of a faculty development that enabled me to initiate the project. Support at the conclusion came from the Max Planck Institute for Evolutionary Anthropology; it is thanks to the MPI that I was able to turn a ragged draft into a publishable manuscript. Finally, I benefited extensively from two Documenting Endangered Languages fellowships from the National Endowment for the Humanities and National Science Foundation (FN-50099-11 and FN-501009-12). Any views, findings, conclusions, or recommendations expressed here do

Acknowledgments

not necessarily reflect those of the National Endowment for the Humanities or the National Science Foundation.

Errors remain, of course, for which I am entirely responsible.

Notational conventions

Table 1 lists the gloss abbreviations employed and the morphemes to which they correspond. Unless otherwise noted, all morphemes are common to all dialects.

Throughout, *Á* indicates alternation between [á] and an accent shift to the final syllable. *H, I, N, R,* and *S* indicate alternations between [ø] and [h], [i], [n], [r], and [s], respectively. *U* indicates alternation between [u] and [a]. *Y* indicates alternation between [y], [i] and [ø]. *PI* indicates an alternation between [pi] and [ø] (unique to the additive enclitic *-pis*). The first five alternations are conditioned by environment in all dialects. *R* indicates alternative realizations of */r/ – realized as [r] in all dialects except that of CH, where it is predominantly realized as [l]. Where two morphemes share the same code (as occurs, for example in the case of *-pa* and *-pi*, which both indicate both genitive and locative case) the code is subscripted with a number (*i.e.*, GEN$_1$, GEN$_2$; LOC$_1$, LOC$_2$). Where the same morpheme has two or more functions (as is the case, for example, with *-paq*, which indicates ablative, benefactive and purposive cases) the morpheme is subscripted (*i.e.*, *-paq$_1$, -paq$_2$, -paq$_3$*). In the body of the text, I do not make use of these subscripts. Unless otherwise noted, a morpheme occurs in all five dialects. Where a morpheme is exclusive to one or more dialects, that is indicated in small caps in parentheses. Tables 1 and 2 list morpheme codes and their corresponding morphemes. The former is sorted by morpheme code; the latter, by morpheme.

Table 1: Morpheme codes (sorted by code)

ø	[*none*]	zero morpheme	nominal or verbal
1$_1$	-*y*	first person (AMV, LT)	nominal inflection, possession
1$_2$	-*ni*	first person (AMV, LT)	verbal inflection
1$_3$	-:$_1$	first person (ACH, CH, SP)	nominal inflection, possession
1$_4$	-:$_2$	first person (ACH, CH, SP)	verbal inflection
1.FUT	-*shaq*	first person singular future	verbal inflection
1.OBJ	-*wa*	1P object (AMV, LT)	verbal inflection
1.OBJ	-*ma*	1P object (ACH, CH, SP)	verbal inflection
1>2	-*yki$_2$*	1P subject 2P object	verbal inflection
1>2.FUT	-*sHQayki*	1P subject 2P object future	verbal inflection

Continued on next page...

Notational conventions

Table 1: Continued from previous page.

1PL$_1$	-nchik	first person plural	nominal inflection, possession
1PL$_2$	-nchik	first person plural	verbal inflection
1PL.COND	-chuwan	first person plural conditional	verbal inflection
1PL.FUT	-shun	first person plural future	verbal inflection
2$_1$	-yki$_1$	second person	nominal inflection, possession
2$_2$	-nki	second person	verbal inflection
2.COND	-waq	second person conditional	verbal inflection
2.OBJ	-sHu	second person object	verbal inflection
2>1	-wa-nki	2P subject 1P object	verbal inflection
3$_1$	-n$_1$	third person	nominal inflection, possession
3$_2$	-N$_2$	third person	verbal inflection
3.FUT	-nqa	third person future	verbal inflection
3>1$_1$	-wan$_1$	3P subject 1P object (AMV, LT)	verbal inflection
3>1$_2$	-man	3P subject 1P obj (ACH, CH, SP)	verbal inflection
3>1PL$_1$	-wa-nchik	3P subject 1PL. obj (AMV, LT)	verbal inflection
3>1PL$_2$	-ma-nchik	3P subject 1PL. obj (ACH, CH, SP)	verbal inflection
3>2	-shunki	3P subject 2P object	verbal inflection
ABL	-paq$_3$	ablative	nominal inflection, case
ACC$_1$	-ta	accusative (ACH, AMV, LT, SP)	nominal inflection, case
ACC$_2$	-Kta	accusative (CH)	nominal inflection, case
ACMP	-sHi	accompaniment	verbal derivation, vv
ADD	-PIs	additive	enclitic
AG	-q	agentive	nominal derivation, vn
ALL	-man$_1$	allative, dative	nominal inflection, case
BEN$_1$	-paq$_2$	benefactive	nominal inflection, case
BEN$_2$	-pU	benefactive, translocative	verbal derivation, vv
CAUS$_2$	-chi	causative	verbal derivation, vv
CERT	-puni	certainty, precision	enclitic
CISL	-mu	cislocative, translocative	verbal derivation, vv
COMP	-hina	comparative	nominal inflection, case
COND	-man$_2$	conditional	verbal inflection
CONT	-Raq	continuative	enclitic
DEM.D$_1$	chay	demonstrative, distal	demonstrative (pron. & det.)
DEM.D$_2$	wak	demonstrative, distal removed	demonstrative (pron. & det.)
DEM.P	kay	demonstrative, proximal	demonstrative (pron. & det.)
DESR$_1$	-naya	desirative	verbal derivation, vv
DESR$_2$	-naya-	desirative	verbal derivation, nv
DIM$_1$	-cha$_1$	diminutive	restrictive nominal suffix
DIM$_2$	-cha$_2$	diminutive	verbal derivation, vv
DISC	-ña	discontinuative	enclitic
DISJ	-chu$_3$	disjunctive	enclitic

Continued on next page...

Table 1: Continued from previous page.

DMY$_1$	*na*	dummy noun	noun
DMY$_2$	*na-*	dummy verb	verb
DUR	*-chka*	durative-simultaneative	verbal inflection
EMPH$_1$	*-Yá*	emphatic	enclitic
EMPH$_2$	*-ARi*	emphatic	enclitic
EVC	*-trI*	evidential - conjectural	enclitic
EVD	*-mI*	evidential - direct	enclitic
EVR	*-shI*	evidential - reportative	enclitic
EXCEP	*-YkU*	exceptional	verbal derivation, vv
EXCL	*-pura*	exclusive	nominal inflection, case
F	*-a*	feminine	nominal, adjectival inflection
FACT	*-cha$_3$*	factive	verbal derivation, nv
FREQ	*-katra*	frequentive	verbal derivation, vv
GEN$_1$	*-pa$_1$*	genitive	nominal inflection, case
GEN$_2$	*-pi$_1$*	genitive	nominal inflection, case
IK	*-ik*	evidential modifier (strong)	enclitic
IKI	*-iki*	evidential modifier (strongest)	enclitic
INCEP	*-ri*	inceptive	verbal derivation, vv
INCH	*-ya$_3$*	inchoative	verbal derivation, sv
INCL	*-ntin*	inclusive	nominal derivation, nn
INF	*-y$_2$*	infinitive	nominal derivation, vs
INJUNC	*-chun*	injunctive	verbal inflection
IMP	*-y$_3$*	imperative	verbal inflection
INSTR	*-wan$_2$*	instrumental - comitative	nominal inflection, case
INTENS	*-ya$_2$*	intensifier	verbal derivation, vv
IRREV	*-tamu*	irreversible change	verbal derivation, vv
JTACT	*-pa(:)ku*	joint action	verbal derivation, vv
LIM$_1$	*-kama$_1$*	limitative	nominal inflection, case
LIM$_2$	*-kama$_2$*	limitative	verbal derivation, vv
LOC$_1$	*-pa$_2$*	locative	nominal inflection, case
LOC$_2$	*-pi$_2$*	locative	nominal inflection, case
LOC$_3$	*-traw*	locative (CH)	nominal inflection, case
M	*-u*	masculine	nominal, adjectival inflection
MULT.ALL	*-sapa*	multiple possessive	nominal derivation, nn
MUTBEN	*-puku*	mutual benefit	verbal derivation, vv
NEG	*-chu$_1$*	negation	enclitic
NONEXHST	*-kuna$_2$*	non-exhaustive	nominal derivation, nn
NMLZ	*-na$_1$*	nominalizer	nominal derivation, vn
NPST	*-sHa$_1$*	perfect	verbal inflection
PART	*-masi*	partnership	nominal derivation, nn
PASS	*-raya*	passive	verbal derivation, vv

Continued on next page...

Notational conventions

Table 1: Continued from previous page.

PASSACC	-ka	passive, accidental	verbal derivation, vv
PL$_1$	-kuna	plural	nominal inflection
POSS	-yuq	possessive	nominal derivation, nn
PERF	-sHa$_2$	perfectivizer	nominal derivation, vs
PROG	-ya$_1$	progressive	verbal inflection
PROH	ama	prohibitive	particle
PST	-RQa	past tense	verbal inflection
PURP	-paq$_3$	purposive	nominal inflection, case
Q	-chu$_2$	question marker	enclitic
REASN	-rayku	reason	nominal inflection, case
RECP	-nakU	reciprocal	verbal derivation, vv
REFL	-kU	reflexive-middle-med.passive	verbal derivation, vv
REPET	-pa$_3$	repetitive	verbal derivation, vv
RPST	-sHQa	reportative past tense	verbal inflection
RSTR	-lla	restrictive	enclitic
SEQ	-taq	sequential	enclitic
SIMUL	-tuku	simulative	verbal derivation, vv
SUBADV	-shtin	subordinator - adverbial	nominal derivation, vn
SUBDS	-pti	subordinator different subjects	nominal derivation, vn
SUBIS	-shpa	subordinator identical subjects	nominal derivation, vn
TOP	-qa	topic	enclitic
UNINT	-Ra	uninterrupted action	verbal derivation, vv
URGT	-RU	urgent, personal interest	verbal derivation, vv
VRBZ	-na$_2$	verbalizer	verbal derivation, nv

Table 2: Morphemes codes (sorted by morpheme)

-:	1$_4$	first person (ACH, CH, SP)	verbal inflection
-:	1$_3$	first person (ACH, CH, SP)	nominal inflection, possession
-a	F	feminine	nominal, adjectival inflection
-aRi	EMPH$_2$	emphatic	enclitic
-cha$_1$	DIM$_1$	diminutive	restrictive nominal suffix
-cha$_2$	DIM$_2$	diminutive	verbal derivation, vv
-cha$_3$	FACT	factive	verbal derivation, nv
-traw	LOC$_3$	locative (CH)	nominal inflection, case
-chi	CAUS	causative	verbal derivation, vv
-chka	DUR	durative-simultaneative	verbal inflection
-chu$_1$	NEG	negation	enclitic
-chu$_2$	Q	question marker	enclitic
-chu$_3$	DISJ	disjunctive	enclitic

Continued on next page...

Table 2: Continued from previous page.

-chun	INJUNC	injunctive	verbal inflection
-chuwan	1PL.COND	first person plural conditional	verbal inflection
-hina	COMP	comparative	nominal inflection, case
-ik	IK	evidential modifier (strong)	enclitic
-iki	IKI	evidential modifier (strongest)	enclitic
-ka	PASSACC	passive, accidental	verbal derivation, vv
$-kama_1$	LIM_1	limitative	nominal inflection, case
$-kama_2$	LIM_2	limitative	verbal derivation, vv
-katra	ITER	frequentive	verbal derivation, vv
-kta	ACC_2	accusative (CH)	nominal inflection, case
-kU	REFL	reflexive-middle-med.passive	verbal derivation, vv
$-kuna_1$	PL_1	plural	nominal inflection
$-kuna_2$	NONEXHST	non-exhaustive	nominal derivation, nn
-lla	RSTR	restrictive	enclitic
-ma	1.OBJ	1p object (ACH, CH, SP)	verbal inflection
$-man_1$	ALL	allative, dative	nominal inflection, case
$-man_2$	COND	conditional	verbal inflection
-ma-nchik	3>$1PL_2$	3P subject 1PL obj (ACH, CH, SP)	verbal inflection
-masi	PART	partnership	nominal derivation, nn
-mI	EVD	evidential - direct	enclitic
-mu	CISL	cislocative, translocative	verbal derivation, vv
-n	3_1	third person	nominal inflection, possession
-N	3_2	third person	verbal inflection
-ña	DISC	discontinuative	enclitic
$-na_1$	NMLZ	nominalizer	nominal derivation, vn
$-na_2$	VRBZ	verbalizer	verbal derivation, nv
-nakU	RECP	reciprocal	verbal derivation, vv
$-naya_1$	$DESR_1$	desiderative	verbal derivation, vv
$-naya_{-2}$	$DESR_2$	desiderative	verbal derivation, nv
$-nchik_1$	$1PL_1$	first person plural	nominal inflection, possession
$-nchik_2$	$1PL_2$	first person plural	verbal inflection
$-ni_1$	1_2	first person (AMV, LT)	verbal inflection
$-ni_2$	EUPH	euphonic	nominal inflection
-nki	2_2	second person	verbal inflection
-nqa	3.FUT	third person future	verbal inflection
-ntin	$INCL_1$	inclusive	nominal derivation, nn
-pa(:)kU	JTACT	joint action	verbal derivation/inflection, vv
-pakU	MUTBEN	mutual benefit	verbal derivation/inflection, vv
$-pa_1$	GEN_1	genitive	nominal inflection, case
$-pa_2$	LOC_1	locative	nominal inflection, case
$-pa_3$	REPET	repetitive	verbal derivation, vv

Continued on next page...

Notational conventions

Table 2: Continued from previous page.

-paq$_1$	ABL	ablative	nominal inflection, case
-paq$_2$	BEN	benefactive	nominal inflection, case
-paq$_3$	PURP	purposive	nominal inflection, case
-pi$_1$	GEN$_2$	genitive	nominal inflection, case
-pi$_2$	LOC$_2$	locative	nominal inflection, case
-PIs	ADD	additive	enclitic
-pti	SUBDS	subordinator different subjects	nominal derivation, vn
-pU	BEN$_2$	benefactive, translocative	verbal derivation, vv
-puni	CERT	certainty, precision	enclitic
-pura	EXCL	exclusive	nominal inflection, case
-q	AG	agentive	nominal derivation, vn
-qa	TOP	topic	enclitic
-Ra	UNINT	uninterrupted action	verbal derivation, vv
-Raq	CONT	continuative	enclitic
-Raya	PASS	passive	verbal drivation, vv
-rayku	REASN$_1$	causal	nominal inflection, case
-ri$_1$	INCEP$_1$	inceptive	verbal derivation, vv
-RQa	PST	past tense	verbal inflection
-RU	URGT	urgent, personal interest	verbal derivation, vv (inflective)
-sapa	MULT.ALL	multiple possessive	nominal derivation, nn
-sHa$_1$	NPST$_1$	narrative past	verbal inflection
-sHa$_2$	PERF$_2$	perfectivizer	nominal derivation, vn
-shaq	1.FUT	first person singular future	verbal inflection
-shI	EVR	evidential - reportative	enclitic
-sHi	ACMP	accompaniment	verbal derivation, vv
-shpa	SUBIS	subordinator - identical subjects	nominal derivation, vn
-sHQa	RPST	reportative past tense	verbal inflection
-sHQayki	1>2.FUT	1P subject 2P object future	verbal inflection
-shtin	SUBADV	subordinator - adverbial	nominal derivation, vn
-sHu	2.OBJ	second person object	verbal inflection
-shun	1PL.FUT	first person plural future	verbal inflection
-shunki	3>2	3P subject 2P object	verbal inflection
-ta	ACC$_1$	accusative (ACH, AMV, LT, SP)	nominal inflection, case
-tamu	IRREV	irreversible change	verbal derivation, vv
-taq	SEQ	sequential	enclitic
-trI	EVC	evidential - conjectural	enclitic
-tuku	SIMUL	simulative	verbal derivation, nv
-u	M	masculine	nominal, adjectival inflection
-wa	1.OBJ	1P object (AMV, LT)	verbal inflection
-wan$_1$	3>1$_1$	3P subject 1P object (AMV, LT)	verbal inflection
-wan$_2$	INSTR	instrumental - comitative	nominal inflection, case

Continued on next page...

Table 2: Continued from previous page.

-wa-nchik	3>1PL$_1$	3P subject 1PL obj (AMV, LT)	verbal inflection
-wa-nki	2>1	2P subject 1P object	verbal inflection
-waq	2.COND	second person conditional	verbal inflection
-y$_1$	1$_1$	first person (AMV, LT)	nominal inflection, possession
-y$_2$	INF	infinitive	nominal derivation, vs
-y$_3$	IMP	imperative	verbal inflection
-Yá	EMPH$_1$	emphatic	enclitic
-ya$_1$	PROG	progressive	verbal inflection
-ya$_2$	INTENS	intensifier	verbal derivation, vv
-ya$_3$	INCH	inchoative	verbal derivation, sv
-yki$_1$	2$_1$	second person	nominal inflection, possession
-yki$_2$	1>2	1P subject 2P object	verbal inflection
-YkU	EXCEP	exceptional	verbal derivation, vv
-yuq	POSS	possessive	nominal derivation, nn
[none]	∅	zero morpheme	nominal or verbal
ama	PROH	prohibitive	particle
chay	DEM.D	demonstrative, distal	demonstrative (pron. & det.)
kay	DEM.P	demonstrative, proximal	demonstrative (pron. & det.)
na	DMY$_1$	dummy noun	noun
na-	DMY$_2$	dummy verb	verb
wak	DEM.D	demonstrative, distal removed	demonstrative (pron. & det.)

Further abbreviations:

    C   consonant
    lit.   literally
    Sp   Spanish
    Spkr   Speaker
    SYQ   Southern Yauyos Quechua
    V   vowel

Notation:

    {·}   set
    [·]   phonetic form or, in case it appears inside single quotations marks, translator's insertion
    /·/   phoneme or phonemic form
    ∼   alternation
    →   transformation
    *   illicit form or, in case it appears before slashes, a proto-form

1 Introduction

Yauyos is a critically endangered Quechuan language spoken in the Peruvian Andes, in the Province of Yauyos, Department of Lima. The language counts eight dialects. These are listed below in Table 1.1. At the time I undertook my research in the area, three of these had already become extinct. The missing dialects are those formerly spoken in the north of the province: Alis-Tomas (AT), Huancaya-Vitis (HV) and Laraos (L).[1] This grammar, therefore, unfortunately, covers only the five southern dialects: Apurí-Madeán-Viñac (AMV), Azángaro-Chocos-Huangáscar (ACH), Cacra-Hongos (CH), Lincha-Tana (LT) and Liscay-San Pedro (SP).

Table 1.1: The dialects of Yauyos Quechua

Region	Dialect	Abbreviation
South		
	Apurí-Madeán-Viñac	AMV
	Azángaro-Chocos-Huangáscar	ACH
	Cacra-Hongos	CH
	Lincha-Tana	LT
	Liscay-San Pedro	SP
North		
	Alis-Tomas	AT
	Huancaya-Vitis	HV
	Laraos	L

The lacuna is highly relevant to any conclusions that might be drawn from this study and, in particular, to any conclusions that might be drawn with regard to its significance for the classification of the Quechuan languages, as two of the

---

[1] A ten-day town-to-town search undertaken in the north of the province in January 2010 failed to turn up any speakers of Yauyos Quechua. Some speakers of the Quechua of neighboring Huancayo, however, could be found yet.

1 Introduction

missing three – Alis-Tomas (AT), Huancaya-Vitis (HV) – were those that, according to previous work (Taylor 1994; 2000), most resembled the QII languages of Central Peru.

The remainder of this introduction begins with a section describing the location of the various towns where SYQ is spoken and the geography of the region (§1.1). The endangerment of the language is the topic of §1.2. §1.3 catalogs the previous research on the language. Sections §1.4 and §1.5 follow with a brief discussion of the internal divisions among the various dialects of Yauyos and then a slightly longer discussion of the classification of the language. The conventions employed in this volume are detailed in §1.6. §1.7 supplies information about the fieldwork on which this study is based. Finally, (§1.8) lists the tables and sections likely to be of particular interest to students of Andean languages, while §1.9 points to topics where the Yauyos data are potentially relevant to linguists from other subfields.

1.1 Location

The five dialects of SYQ are spoken in the ten disctricts: Apurí, Madeán, and Viñac; Azángaro, Chocos, and Huangáscar; Lincha and Tana; Cacra and Hongos; and San Pedro. The first two sets are located in the valley created by the Huangáscar River and its principal tributary, the Viñac River, as can be seen on Map 1.1. The second two are located in the valley created by the Cacra River and its principal tributaries, the Lincha and Paluche Rivers. The two valleys are separated by a chain of rather high and rocky hills. Running from east to west, these are the cerros Pishqullay, Tinco, Punta Tacana, Ranraorqo, Pishunco, Cochapata, Yanaorqo, and Shallalli.

No district except San Pedro is located more than one day's walk from any other; in the case of San Pedro, it is two.[2] The four districts that lie within the province of Yauyos center at 12°62′S and 75°7′W. The principal towns of all the districts except Chocos, Huangáscar, and Tana sit at altitudes around 3300 meters, while those of Chocos, Huangáscar, and Tana sit at just under 3000 meters. The relevant region can be contained within an area of 40 m²; its highest peak reaches 5055 m.[3]

---

[2] It is not irrelevant to the explanation of the dialect cleavages that this mountain range seems to block the movement of brides from one set of districts to another. Until very recently, newlywed women generally only moved from one town to another within the same valley.

[3] There exists a series of topographical maps prepared and published in 1996 by the U.S. Defense Mapping Agency. Southern Yauyos is covered on the section labeled Tupe and identified Series 1745, Sheet J632, Edition -1 DMA.

1.2 Endangerment

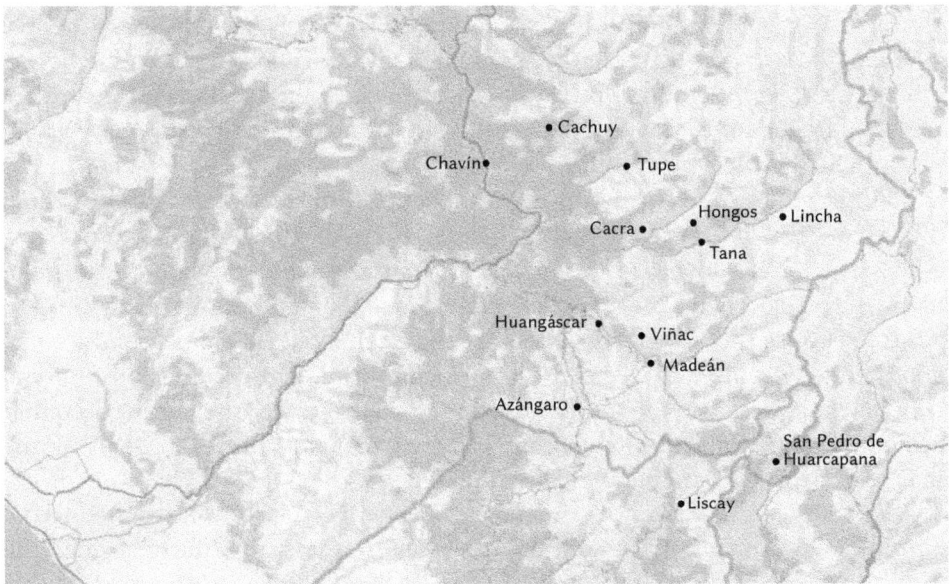

Figure 1.1: Map of Andean municipalities of southern Yauyos, Peru

1.2 Endangerment

At the date of this writing, the UNESCO classifies Yauyos as critically endangered. The 18th edition of *Ethnologue* (Lewis, Simons & Fennig 2015), however, tags it as "moribund." Although, as I see it, there is no real likelihood that any dialect of Yauyos will ever be revived, it is early yet to declare it moribund. I estimate that there are about twenty teens who understand the Viñac and San Pedro dialects, as well as many as 80 adults in their forties and fifties who can still speak it relatively fluently. Moreover, although its use is now generally restricted to the discussion of every-day and ritual activities, it is still used frequently among the oldest speakers.

The 1993 Peru census counted 1,600 speakers, 25% of them over 65 (Chirinos-Rivera 2001: 121). That census, however, did not distinguish between speakers of Yauyos and speakers of other Quechuan languages who resided in the province (Chirinos-Rivera, p.c.). This is crucial to the assessment of the data on the Quechua-speaking population of the north of the province. Although there are many Quechua-speaking migrants there – principally from Huancayo, the town with which the north has the most commercial contact – I was unable to locate any speakers of the dialects indigenous to the area. Further, population

1 Introduction

data in the province tend to be exaggerated for several reasons. First, people who emigrated from the region years or even decades ago remain, nevertheless, officially resident there for reasons of convenience. Second, death certificates are often not issued for the deceased. Less than ten years before that survey – still, to my knowledge, the most recent – electricity had yet to come to the Andean towns of southern Yauyos and the only physical connections between those towns to the rest of the world were three 40-kilometer dirt paths that wound their perilous way 2,000 meters down the canyon. Since that time, the Peruvian government has installed electricity in the region and widened the perilous dirt paths into perilous dirt roads.[4] TelMex and Claro now offer cable television, and buses come and go on alternate days. In short, the isolation that had previously preserved the Quechua spoken in the region has been broken and the language now counts, according to my estimates, fewer than 450 speakers, most over 65, and all but the most elderly fully bilingual in Spanish.

The drastic reduction in the number of speakers can also be attributed to the Shining Path. During the 1980's and early 1990's, the period during which the Maoist army terrorized the region, there was a large-scale exodus, particularly of young people, who ran to escape forced conscription. Many never returned, remaining principally in the coastal cities of Cañete and Lima. Theirs was the last generation to learn Quechua to any degree. Currently, there are a few children – those who live with their grandmothers or great-grandmothers in the most isolated hamlets – with a passive knowledge of the language. The youngest speakers, however, are in their late thirties.

Quechuan as a language family is not currently endangered, and other Quechuan languages are well-documented. Estimates of the numbers of Quechuan speakers range between 8.5 and 10 million, and, although Quechua is being pushed back by Spanish in many areas, the majority dialects of its major varieties – Ancash, Ayacucho, Bolivian, Cuzco, Ecuadorian[5] – are quite viable (Adelaar & Muysken 2004: 168). Paradoxically, however, the viability of the major varieties is coming at the expense of the viability of the minor varieties. Adelaar (2008: 14) writes: "If Quechua will survive, its speakers will probably be users of four of five of the most successful dialects, most of which belong to Quechua IIB and IIC." The dialects of southern Yauyos, classified as either QI or QIIA, and other minor Quechuan languages are rapidly disappearing.

---

[4] In the space of just one year, spanning 2012 and 2013, fourteen people died in six separate accidents in the region when their vehicles fell from the road down the canyon.

[5] It is worth noting that much of the diversity internal to these languages is being lost, as one anonymous reviewer points out.

1.3 Existing documentation

Echerd (1974) and Brougère (1992) supply some socio-linguistic data on Yauyos. There is also a book of folktales, in Spanish, collected in the region in the 1930's and 1940's: *Apuntes para el folklor de Yauyos* (Varilla Gallardo 1965). Yauyos is mentioned in the context of two dialectological studies of Quechua by Torero (1968; 1974).

With these exceptions, all that is known about Yauyos we owe to the French researcher Gerald Taylor. Taylor's PhD dissertation describes the morphology of Laraos, a northern dialect of Yauyos. This work was republished or excerpted, sometimes with revisions, in Taylor (1984; 1990; 1994; 1994b). Taylor (1987a) supplements the data on Laraos with data on Huancaya, and Taylor (1990; 2000) provides a comparison of all seven dialects on the basis of eight grammatical elements and fifty lexical items. Finally, Taylor (1987b,c; 1991) transcribes and translates several folktales into Spanish and French.

1.4 The dialects of Yauyos

Yauyos groups together various dialects that, although mutually intelligible, differ in ways that are relevant both to the classification of Yauyos as well as to the current paradigm for the classification of the Quechuan languages generally. That classification is highly contested, and, indeed, has been since the first proposals were suggested in the 1960s (See in particular Landerman 1991).

The Province is located on the border between the two large, contiguous zones where languages belonging to the two great branches of the Quechua language family are spoken: the "Quechua I" (Torero) or "Quechua B" (Parker) languages are spoken to its north; the "Quechua II" or "Quechua A" languages, to its south, as the map in Figure 1.3 shows.

For reasons detailed in §1.5, the model that divides the Quechuan family tree into two principal branches doesn't apply very well to Yauyos, as its different dialects manifest different characteristics of both of branches. Yauyos is, of course, not alone in this, not in the least because the division of the languages into two branches was, arguably, based on rather arbitrary criteria in the first place (See in particular Landerman 1991). The significance of Yauyos lies in the fact that it may represent the "missing link" between the two (See in particular Heggarty 2007). There exist three proposals in the literature – Taylor (2000); Torero (1974); Lewis, Simons & Fennig (2015) – with regard to the grouping of the province's fifteen districts into dialect bundles. Taylor (2000: 105) counts seven varieties of Yauyos

1 Introduction

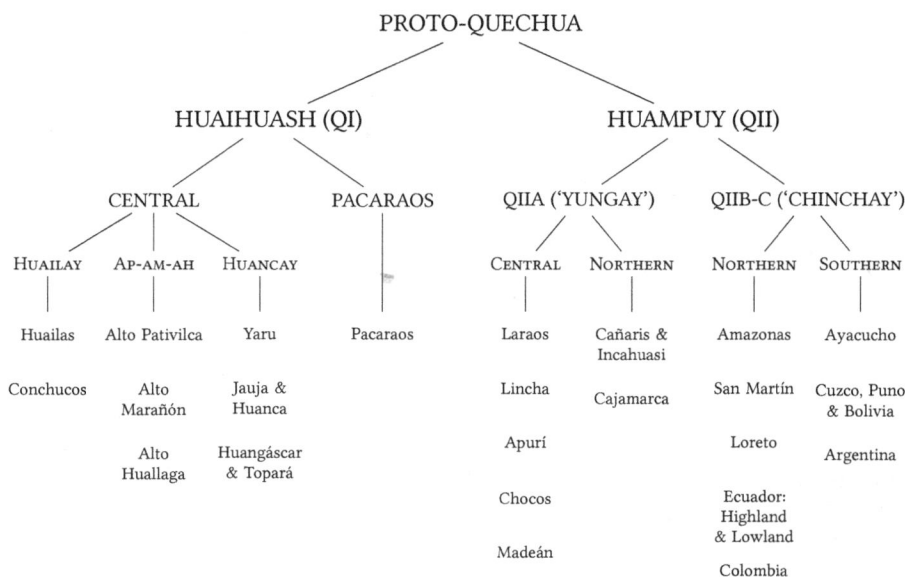

Figure 1.2: Quechuan languages family tree

Quechua, dividing these into two groups along a north-south axis. In the north are the dialects of Alis/Tomas, Huancaya/Vitis, and Laraos; in the south, those of Apurí/Chocos/Madeán/Viñac, Azángaro/Huangáscar, Cacra/Hongos, and Lincha/Tana. Taylor classes four of these dialects – the northern dialects of Alis/Tomas and Huancaya/Vitis and the southern dialects of Azángaro/Huangáscar and Cacra/Hongos – as belonging to the QI branch; he classes the remaining three – Laraos in the north as well as Apurí/Chocos/Madeán/Viñac and Lincha/Tana in the south – as belonging to QII. Torero (1974) counted only six dialects, excluding Azángaro/Huangáscar from the catalogue, classing it independently among the QI dialects along with with Chincha's Topará. Ethnologue, like Taylor, includes Azángaro/Huangascar and adds, even, an eighth dialect, that of San Pedro de Huacarpana, spoken on the Chincha side of the Yauyos-Chincha border. Ethnologue further differs from Taylor in putting Apurí in a group by itself; and it differs from both Taylor and Torero in grouping Chocos with Azángaro/Huangáscar. My research supports Taylor's grouping of Apurí with Madeán and Viñac; it also supports Ethnologue's inclusion of San Pedro de Huacarpana among the dialects of Yauyos. San Pedro is located immediately to the north-east of Madeán and Azángaro, at less than a days' walk's distance. Although formerly counted a part of the Department of Lima and the Province of Yauyos, a redrawing of

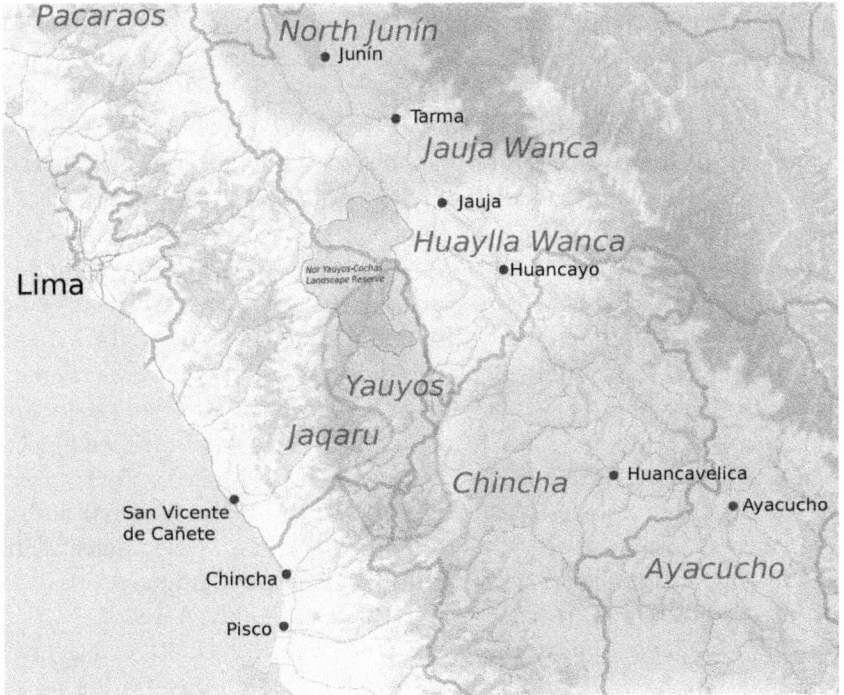

Figure 1.3: Peruvian languages map

political boundaries placed San Pedro on the Ica side of the contemporary Ica-Lima border. During the colonial period, the Province of Yauyos was larger and included parts of what are now the Provinces of Chincha and Castrovirreyna (Huancavelica) Landerman (1991: 1.1.3.2.7). Apurí, like its neighbors Viñac and Madeán, uses -*ni* and -*y* to indicate the first-person singular in the verbal and substantive paradigms; they also use -*rqa* and -*sa* to indicate the past tense and perfect. The first pair of characteristics set the Madeán/Viñac and Lincha/-Tana dialects apart from the other three; the second pair of characteristics sets Madeán/Viñac apart from Lincha/Tana. Chocos, like its neighbors Huangáscar and Azángaro, uses vowel length to indicate the first-person singular in the verbal and substantive paradigms.

1.5 Classification

Yauyos Quechua was dubbed by Alfredo Torero (1974) a "supralect" and its most careful student, Gerald Taylor, referred to it as a "mixed" language (Taylor 1990:

1 Introduction

2, Taylor 2000: 105). Indeed, the designation of Yauyos as a language may seem, at first, to be no more than a relic of the first classifications of the Quechuan languages not by strictly linguistic criteria but, rather, by geographic criteria. Yauyos is located on the border between the two large, contiguous zones where the languages of the two different branches of the Quechuan language family are spoken. QI is spoken immediately to the north, in the Department of Junín and the north of the Department of Lima; QII, immediately to the south, in the Departments of Huancavelica and Ayacucho. Yauyos manifests characteristics of both branches. Take first-person marking. Three dialects, Azángaro-Chocos[6]-Huangáscar (ACH), Cacra-Hongos (CH), and San Pedro (SP), use the same marking (vowel length) for the first person in both nominal and verbal paradigms[7] and mark the first-person object with *-ma*. These are the two characteristics that define a Quechuan language as belonging to the QI (also called Quechua B or *Huaihuash*) branch. The other two dialects, Apurí-Madeán-Viñac (AMV) and Lincha-Tana (LT), mark the first person differently in the nominal and verbal paradigms (with *-y* and *-ni*, respectively) and mark first-person object with *-wa*. These two dialects, then, sort with the QII (A/*Huampuy*) languages. Indeed, the first three are classed as QI (specifically, Central-*Huancay*) and the other two, QII (specifically *Yunagay*-Central) (Cerrón-Palomino 1987: 247). Nevertheless, the "QI" dialects, ACH, CH, and SP, manifest few of the other traits that set the QI languages apart from the QII languages. They do use *ñuqakuna* in place of *ñuqayku* to form the first person plural exclusive as well as *-pa(:)ku* to indicate the plural. Crucially, however, so do both the "QII" SYQ dialects.[8] And none of the five manifest any other of the principal traits that generally set the QI languages apart from the rest. None use *-naw* in place of *-Sina* to form the comparative, *-piqta* in place of *-manta* to form the ablative, or *-naq* in place of *-shqa* to form the narrative past; and none except for Cacra uses *-r* (realized [l]) in place of *-shpa* to form same-subject subordinate clauses. Now, the two "QII" SYQ dialects manifest several of the traits that set the QIIC (*Chínchay Meridional*) languages apart from the rest. Like the QIIC languages, the AMV and LT dialects use the diminutive *-cha*, the emphatic *-ari*, the assertive *-puni*, and the alternative conditional *-chuwan*; the AMV dialect additionally uses the alternative con-

---

[6] I am very grateful to Peter Landerman for correcting me with regard to the classification of Chocos, which I had originally misclassified with Madeán and Viñac.

[7] Crucially, though, vowel length is not distinctive anywhere else in the grammar or lexicon of these dialects. For example, these dialects use the QII *-naya*, *-raya*, and *-paya*, not the QI *-na:*, *-ra:*, and *-pa:* to mark the desiderative, passive, and continuative, respectively. And all districts but Cacra use *tiya-*, not *ta:-* 'sit', again sorting with the QII languages.

[8] The CH dialect is unique in using *-traw* in alternation with both *-pi* and *-pa* for the locative.

ditional -*waq*. Crucially, however, the three "QI" SYQ dialects, too, use three of these: -*cha*, -*ari* and -*chuwan*. Further, all five share with Ayacucho Q the unique use of the evidential modifier -*ki*. None of the five manifest any of the other defining traits of the QIIC languages: none uses -*ku* to indicate the first-person plural exclusive or the third-person plural; nor does any use -*chka*[9] to form the progressive or -*nka* to form the distributive. Further, none suffered the fusion of */tr/ with */ch/ or */sh/ with */s/. (See Cerrón-Palomino (1987: 226–248) on the defining characteristics of the various Quechuan languages) Rather, the dialects of Southern Yauyos are mutually intelligible, and they together share characteristics that set them apart from all the other Quechuan languages. With the single exception that CH uses the accusative form -*Kta* in place of -*ta*, all five dialects employ the same case system, which includes the unique ablative form -*paq* and unique locative -*pi*. All dialects use the progressive form -*ya*;[10] all employ the plural -*kuna* with non-exhaustive meaning; and all employ the same unique system of evidential modification (see §6.2.11.4). Further, with a single exception,[11] the five dialects are uniform phonologically, all employing a highly conservative system[12] that retains all those phonemes hypothesized by Parker and Cerrón-Palomino to have been included in the Proto-Quechua (see §2.3). Table 1.2, below, summarizes this information. Please note that the table presents a somewhat idealized portrait and that the characteristics it posits as belonging exclusively to QII may sometimes be found in QI languages as well. Exceptions of which I am aware are signaled in notes to the table.

The case of Azángaro-Chocos-Huangáscar requires particular attention in this context. Torero (1968: 293, 1974: 28–29) classified Azángaro and Huangáscar as forming an independent group with Topará (Chavín), placing it among the QI *Huancay* languages. Cerrón-Palomino (1987: 236), following Torero, cites five cri-

---

[9] Although all use -*chka*, unproductively except in SP, to indicate simultaneous action that persists in time.

[10] One of many attested reductions from *-*yka:* (-*yka:*, -*yka*, -*yga*, -*ycha:*, -*yya:*, -*yya-*, -*ya:*, and -*ya*) (Hintz 2011: 213–219, 260–268, 290). I am grateful to an anonymous reviewer for pointing this out to me.

[11] In the CH dialect, as in neighboring Junín, the protomorphemes */r/, */s/, and */h/ are sometimes realized as [l], [h], and [sh], respectively. I have no explanation for why these alternations occur in some cases but not in others. Indeed, it may be the case that where CH differs from the rest of the dialects in that it employs */sh/where they employ */h/, it is the former that preserves the original form.

[12] An anonymous reviewer points out that other Quechuan languages, Corongo among them, for example, are more conservative than Yauyos with respect to some features, including the preservation of the protoform *ñ in *ñi- 'say' and ña:-ña 'right now'. Sihuas, too, preserves elements of proto Quechua not found in Yauyos. In contrast, while Yauyos preserves a few proto-Quechua features not found in either Corongo or Sihuas, it also manifests others that reflect innovations likely adopted from neighboring QII languages.

1 Introduction

Table 1.2: Use of QI, QII and local structures in the five SYQ dialects

	CH	ACH	SP	AMV	LT
1Singular nominal inflection	-:	-:	-:	-y	-y
1Singular verbal inflection	-:	-:	-:	-ni	-ni
1Singular object inflection	-ma	-ma	-ma	-wa	-wa
1Plural exclusive pronoun *ñuqakuna*	yes	yes	yes	yes	yes
Fusion of */ch/ and */tr/[a]	no	no	no	no	no
Fusion of */s/ and */sh/	no	no	no	no	no
s>o inflection order NUM-O-TNS-S	yes	yes	yes	yes	yes
Vowel length distinctive elsewhere[b]	no	no	no	no	no
Same-subject subordinator *-shpa*[c]	yes	yes[d]	yes	yes	yes
Narrative past inflection *-sHQa*	yes	yes	yes	yes	yes
Comparative *-hina*	yes	yes	yes	yes	yes
Diminutive *-cha*[e]	yes	yes	yes	yes	yes
Emphatic *-ari*	yes	yes	yes	yes	yes
1Plural Altern. Conditional *-chuwan*	yes	yes	yes	yes	yes
2Singular Altern. Conditional *-waq*	no	no	no	yes	no
Assertive *-puni*	no	no	no	yes	no
Evidential modifier *-ki*[f]	yes	yes	yes	yes	yes
Locative *-pa*	yes[g]	yes	yes	yes	yes
Ablative *-paq*[h]	yes	yes	yes	yes	yes
Non-exhaustive *-kuna*	yes	yes	yes	yes	yes
Lateralization of */r/	yes[j]	no	no	no	no

Note:
[a] An anonymous reviewer points out that this is not exclusively a feature of QII languages in that the fusion of */ch/ and */tr/ is attested in Huallaga, a QI variety.
[b] With the exception of *-pa(:)ku*, where the long vowel distinguishes JTACC from BEN-REFL.
[c] An anonymous reviewer points out that, although this may originally have been posited to be a defining characteristic of QII languages, it is, in fact, far from such: *-shpa* is common in several QI dialects: in Ancash, it attested in Huaylas; it is attested, also in Pachitea in Huanuco.
[d] Cacra but not Hongos also uses *-r* (realized [l]).
[e] An anonymous reviewer points out that while diminutive *-cha* is less productive in QI than in QII, it is still is common throughout QI, e.g. Victoria-Vitucha, Cabrito-Kapcha.
[f] Also used in Ayacucho (QII).
[g] Also uses *-traw* (QI).
[h] An anonymous reviewer points out that ablative *-paq* is almost certainly derived from */-piq/ / */-pik/ via vowel harmony. The former is attested in Huaylas and the latter in Corongo. The other *-pi*-initial forms in QI (*-pita, -pi:ta, -pikta, -piqta*, among others) would have developed later via suffix amalgamation, similar to the formation of bipartite *-manta* in QII (see, e. g. , Hintz & Dávila 2000).
[j] Also occurs in Junín (QI).

Key: *: QI trait; †: QII/QIIC trait; ‡: trait shared by all SYQ dilects not characteristic of either QI or QII/QIIC.

teria for grouping Huangáscar with Topará. Both dialects, he writes, use -*pa:ku* and -*:ri* to indicate the plural; both use -*shpa* in place of -*r* to form same-subject subordinate clauses; and both use -*tamu* to indicate completed action; the two dialects, further, are alike in using unusual locative and ablative case-marking. Only three of these claims are accurate. First, Huangáscar, as Taylor (1984) already indicated, does not use -*:ri*. Second, Huangáscar and Topará may indeed both use unusual locative and ablative case marking, but, crucially, they do not use the same unusual case marking: Huangáscar uses -*pa* to indicate the locative while Topará uses -*man*; Huangáscar uses -*paq* to indicate the ablative while Topará uses -*pa* (C.-P. himself points out these last two facts). Huangáscar does indeed use -*shpa* to form subordinate clauses and -*tamu* to indicate irreversible change. Crucially, however, so do all the dialects of southern Yauyos. In sum, there is no basis for grouping Huangáscar with Topará and not with the other dialects of SYQ. Torero's data were never corroborated; indeed, the findings of Taylor and Landerman, the scholars who have most thoroughly studied Yauyos before now,[13] contradict those of Torero.

SYQ is not a jumble of dialects that, were it not for geographical accident, would not be classed together; it is, rather, a unique, largely uniform language. Although I myself do not believe that the current paradigm can be maintained, I have tried to present the data in a way that remains as neutral as possible with regard to the question of how the internal diversity within the Quechuan language family is best characterized, and, in particular, with regard to the question of whether or not the various Quechuan languages are helpfully construed as belonging to one or the other of two branches of a family tree (See in particular Adelaar 2008). I leave it to other scholars to interpret the data as they see fit. That said, as long as it is maintained, the current paradigm should be revised to more accurately reflect the relationships of SYQ with/to the languages currently named on the Quechuan family tree as it is currently drawn. That tree groups nine of the eleven districts of southern Yauyos into five sets, assigning each of these sets the status of an independent language. Moreover, two of these sets are actually singletons, as Chocos is listed independent of (Azángaro-)Huangáscar, to which it is identical, and Apurí is listed independent of Madeán(-Viñac), to which it is identical. (Cacra-Hongos, the set that would deserve independent placement, if any did, appears nowhere at all). The fact that all these "languages" are completely mutually intelligible does not justify this. It further seems un-

---

[13] An anonymous reviewer points out that Martha Hardman, Steve Echerd, Rick Floyd, Conrad Phelps – in addition to several students from Universidad San Marcos – have given Yauyos extensive attention, although they may not have added to the storehouse of data on the language.

1 Introduction

justified to place the Quechua of single villages on the level of that of whole nations – Bolivia and Ecuador. I suggest, therefore, that Chocos be joined with (Azángaro-)Huangáscar, and Apurí with Madeán(-Viñac). The first of these new triplets, Azángaro-Chocos-Hunagáscar, should be mutated to join the other "languages" of southern Yauyos, under the category *Central Yungay*. The four sets should, further, be collapsed and the resulting set called *Southern Yauyos*. The revised (pruned) tree would then be as in Figure 1.4. In the event that it be necessary to honor the internal diversity that would be obscured by this move, note may simply be made to the fact that this "new" language counts multiple dialects. In this case, Cacra-Hongos and San Pedro de Huacarpana would have to be listed among these.[14]

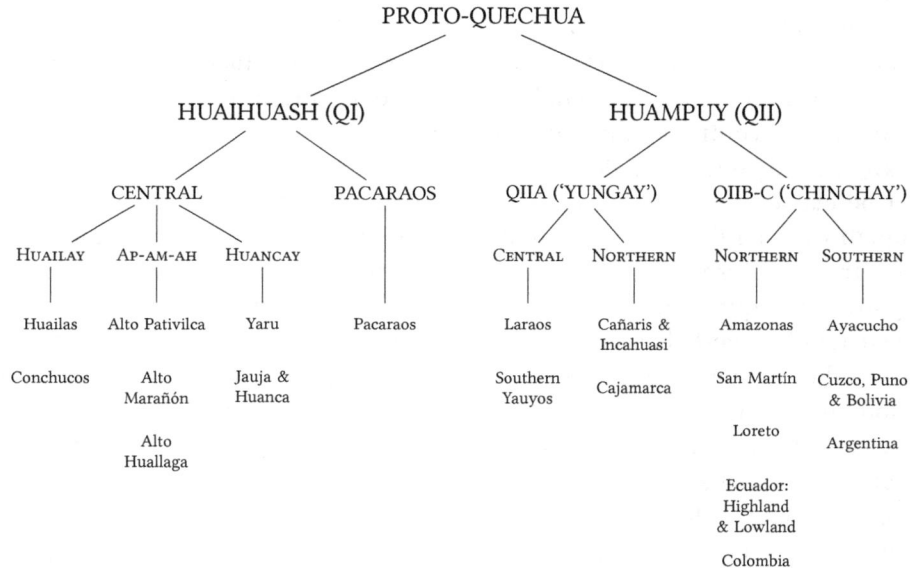

Adapted from source:

http://lingweb.eva.mpg.de/quechua/Eng/Cpv/Locations.htm#TheTraditionalQuechuaFamilyTree

Figure 1.4: Quechuan languages family tree revised

---

[14] I regret having to list Laraos independently here, as I believe it is possible to make a convincing argument for its inclusion as a dialect of Southern Yauyos. Nothing in this volume, however, directly speaks to that question. I plan to address it explicitly in a future paper.

1.6 Presentation

To facilitate comparison with other Quechuan languages, the presentation here follows the structure of the six Quechua grammars published by the Peruvian government in 1976. Readers familiar with those grammars will note the obvious debt this one owes to those: it follows not just their format, but also, in large part, their analysis. The six 1976 grammars cover the Quechuas of Ancash, Ayacucho, Cajamarca, Cuzco, Huanca and San Martín. (Parker 1976; Soto Ruiz 1976a; Quesada Castillo 1976; Cusihuamán Gutiérrez 1976; Cerrón-Palomino 1976a; Coombs, Coombs & Weber 1976). Other published grammars of Quechuan languages include Herrero & Lozada (1978) on Bolivian Quechua; Catta (1994) on Ecuadorian Quechua; Taylor (1994) on Ferreñafe; Weber (1989) on Huallaga (Huanuco);[15] Cole (1982) on Imbabura; Adelaar (1977) description of Tarma Quechua and his (1986) morphology of Pacaraos; as well as the surveys and compilations of Cerrón-Palomino (1987); Cerrón-Palomino & Solís-Fonesca (1990), and Cole, Hermon & Martín (1994).

Words and phrases appearing in italics – *like this* – are in Quechua. English and Spanish interpretations appear in single quotation marks – 'like this'. Interpretations are sometimes given in Spanish – the language I used with my consultants[16] – as well as English. Transformations (illustrations of changes indicated as a result of morphological processes referenced) are indicated with arrows – *like* → *like_this*. Quechua words are broken into component morphemes, like this: *warmi-**kuna***. It is the morpheme relevant to the topic in focus that is in bold.

Each section and major subsection begins with an account of the topic under consideration. Terminal subsections supply more extended discussion and further examples, generally about 10, often as many as 30 or even 40. All examples except those indicated with a dagger are taken from the corpus of recordings collected during the course of the documentation of the language. Those with a dagger were elicited. Transcriptions can be checked against the original recordings by downloading the compilation of recordings archived with the corpus,

---

[15] Thanks to an anonymous reviewer for pointing this out. Hintz (2011) supplies a grammar of aspect and related categories in Quechua, especially South Conchucos Quechua (Ancash).

[16] Indeed, all English glosses are my translations from the Spanish glosses my consultants originally supplied. In most cases, the Spanish translations reflected the syntax and semantics of the original Quechua. I sacrificed this in preparing the the English glosses that appear here. I made this choice because the more literal glosses are standard in Andean Spanish – in structures like the possessive 'su n de a' ('his N of a') – they would not be standard in any English dialect of which I am aware.

1 Introduction

typing a couple of words from either the example or its gloss into the search bar and following the recording title and time signature back to the original recording. I am also happy to supply this information. Source titles refer to .eaf files archived with DoBeS and AILLA. File names include three elements: the place in which the recording was made, the initials of the principal participant, and a word or two recalling the principal topic(s). For example, the file Vinac_JC_Cure was made in Viñac, has for its principal participant Jesús Centeno and for its principal topic a curing ceremony. Because of restrictions on file names, no accents are used. So, Azángaro is rendered "Azangaro" and so on.

Glosses were prepared in accord with the Leipzig glossing rules. For reasons of space, two deviations from the standard abbreviations were made: "proximal demonstrative" is not rendered "DEM.PROX" but "DEM.P"; and "distal demonstrative" is not rendered "DEM.DIST" but "DEM.D". Gloss codes are listed with the notational conventions at page xi, in the section with that name.

1.7 Fieldwork

The fieldwork upon which this document is based was conducted in June and July of 2010; January through April 2011; August through December 2011; April through September 2012; and for a total of 10 months between October 2012 and July 2014. The second of these trips was funded by a faculty development grant from San José State University; the third through sixth, by two National Endowment for the Humanities-National Science Foundation Documenting Endangered Languages fellowships (FN-50099-11 and FN-50109-12).

The corpus counts 206 distinct audio and audio-video recordings. The recordings, totaling over 71 hours, were made in the seven districts of Southern Yauyos – Apurí, Azángaro, Cacra, Chocos, Hongos, Huangáscar, Lincha, Madeán, and Viñac – as well as in the district of San Pedro de Huacarpana in Chincha. Recordings include stories, songs, riddles, spontaneous dialogue, personal narrative, and descriptions of traditional activities, crafts and healing practices. Over 28 hours of recordings were transcribed, translated and glossed. The recordings as well as the ELAN time-aligned transcriptions and accompanying videos are archived both at The DoBeS project, housed at the Max Planck Institute in Nijmegen, The Netherlands, and at the Archive of the Indigenous Languages of Latin America at the University of Texas, Austin, USA. All materials can be accessed via those institutions' websites, http://www.mpi.nl/DOBES/ and http://www.ailla.utexas.org/. The more popular video recordings – many transcribed – can also be easily accessed via endangeredlanguages.com. All examples that follow except those noted † were taken from this corpus. It is my hope that these examples will give the reader a sense of the life that supported and was supported by the language.

Unicode was used for character encoding; audio and video recordings were saved in the standard formats – PCM wav 44.1/32 bits, .mpg, and .mpeg; unstructured texts were saved as plain text; structured texts have XML-based underlying schemas. Recording equipment includes a Marantz PMD 660 solid state digital audio recorder (pre-January 2013 recordings); a Roland R-26 solid state audio recorder; an AudioTechnica 831b cardioid condenser microphone (pre-May 2012 recordings); a Sennheiser MKH 8060 cardioid condenser microphone; and a Canon Vixia HF S100 HD flash memory camcorder. Transcriptions, translations and glosses were prepared with ELAN; Audacity was used for editing audio recordings; iMovie for video recordings. All work was done on a MacBook Pro (pre-July 2011 recordings) or MacBook Air (post-July 2011 recordings).

Exactly one hundred participants contributed recordings: AA, DO, Pedro Carrún (Apurí); Victoria Díaz, Gabino Huari, Ernestina Huari, Efrén Yauri (Madeán); Isabel Chávez (Tayamarka); Dona Alvarado, Eudosia Alvarado, Pripodina Auris, Jesus Centeno, Meli Chávez, Delfina Chullukuy, Martina Guerra, Victoria Guerra, Carmen Huari, Aleka Madueño, Acención Madueño, Melania Madueño, Hilda Quispe, Angélica Romero, Saturnina Utcañe (Viñac);Margarita Madueño (Casa Blanca); Floriana Centeno, Emilia Guerra (Esmeralda); Juana Huari, Leonarda Huari, Neri Huari, Corsinia Javier, Cecilia Quispe (Florida); AB (Ortigal); Octavia Arco, Bautista Cárdenas (Llanka); Octavio Sulluchuco (Qanta); Cecilia Guerra, Emiliano Rojas (Qunyari); María Guerra, Teresa Guerra, Alejandra Quispe (Shutco); Alejandrina Centeno, Macedonia Centeno, Soylita Chullunkuy, Hida Evangelista, Soylita Huari (Tambopata); Urbana Yauri (Yuracsayhua); Anselma Caja, Filipa Postillón (Azángaro); Genoveva Rodríguez, Lucía Rodríguez (Colca); Fortunato Gutiérrez, Isak Gutiérrez (Marcalla); Alcibiada Rodríguez (Puka Rumi); Victorina Aguado, Senovia Gutiérrez (Villaflor); Honorato B., Bonifacia de la Cruz, Julia Mayta (Chocos); Benedicta Lázaro, CW, Luisa Gutiérez, PP, Victoria Quispe, Teódolo Rodríguez, Natividad Saldaña (Huangáscar); Grutilda Saldaño; Eudisia Vicente (Tapalla); Iris Barrosa, Maximina Barrosa, Regina Huamán (Cacra); Archi V., Eduardo Centeno, Dina Huamán, Leona Huamán, SA, Sabina Huamán, Senaida Oré, Hipólita Santos, Maximina Tupac, Erlinda Vicente (Hongos); Ninfa Flores, Anselma Vicente, Sofía Vicente (Lincha); Amador Flores, Gabina Flores, Lucio Flores, Dina Lázaro, Elisa Mancha, Isabel Mancha (Tana); Santa Ayllu, Edwin Fuentes, Neli Fuentes, Elvira Huamán, Sofía Huamán, Lucía Martinez, RF, Rosa O., Maximina Paloma, Juan Páucar (Liscay).

1 Introduction

For help with transcription and the lexicon, unending thanks to Benedicta Lázaro and Martina Reynoso (ACH); Mila Chávez, Delfina Chullunkuy, Esther Madueño, Hilda Quispe, and Celia Rojas (AMV); Iris Barrosa, Gloria Cuevas, Senaida Oré, Hipólita Santos, and Erlinda Vicente, (CH); Ninfa Flores and Sofía Vicente (LT); and Santa Ayllu, Elvira Huamán, Sofía Huamán, and Maximina Paloma (SP).

1.8 A note to Quechuanists and typologists

Those already familiar with Quechuan languages will likely be interested in the tables and sections listed in Tables 1.3 and 1.4 immediately below. These indicate differences between Southern Yauyos Quechua and other Quechuan languages as well as differences among the various dialects of SYQ. The footnotes appearing in these sections may be of interest as well. Those familiar with the literature on Quechuan languages will immediately recognize the presentation and analysis here as very much derivative of much previous work on those languages.

Table 1.3: Tables of more interest to Quechuanists

1.2	Use of QI, QII and local structures in the five SYQ dialects	10
2.1	Vowel inventory	25
2.2	Consonant inventory	25
3.5	Case suffixes with examples	73
4.5	Verbal inflectional suffixes with different realizations in SYQ dialects	132
4.6	Verbal inflection paradigm	133
4.7	Verbal inflection paradigm – subject-object suffixes	135
4.9	Actor-object inflectional suffixes	148
4.29	"Modal" (verb-verb derivational) suffixes, with examples	211
6.1	Enclitics, with examples	251
6.2	Evidential schema: "evidence from" by "evidence for"	273

1.8 A note to Quechuanists and typologists

Table 1.4: Sections of more interest to Quechuanists

1.5	Classification	7
1.9	Broader interest	18
1.2	Endangerment	3
2.3	Phonemic inventory	24
3.2.2.1	Personal pronouns ñuqa, qam, pay	36
3.3.1	Allocation	67
3.3.3	Case	72
3.3.3.4	Genitive, locative -pa_1, -pa_2	79
3.3.3.5	Ablative, benefactive, purposive -paq	82
3.3.3.6	Genitive, locative -pi	86
3.4.1.4	Infinitive -y	108
3.4.2.2	Accompaniment -nti(n), -kuna	113
4.2.4	Onomatopoetic verbs	126
4.3.2.1	Subject and allocation suffixes	138
4.3.2.2	Actor and object reference	138
4.3.3.3.1	Simple past -RQa	154
4.3.3.3.2	Quotative simple past tense -sHQa	159
4.3.4.1	Regular conditional -man	168
4.3.4.2	Excursis: Modality	168
4.3.4.3	Alternative conditional -waq and -chuwan	176
4.3.6.1	Progressive -ya	186
4.3.6.2	Durative, simultaneous -chka	189
4.3.6.3	Perfective -ku	190
4.4.2.3.4	Frequentive -katra	217
4.4.2.3.16	Urgency/personal interest -RU	233
5.1	Interjections	241
6.2.11	Evidence (entire subsection)	270

1 Introduction

1.9 Broader interest

Yauyos should be of particular interest to semanticists as well as to students of language contact. Semanticists may find the language's unusual evidential system of interest, while students of language contact may want to look for evidence of contact between the districts where Yauyos is spoken – that of Cacra-Hongos in particular – with the three Aymara-speaking districts in the same region of the province.

1.9.1 Semantics – evidentials

For typologists and semanticists, Yauyos' evidential system should be of interest. Evidentials, broadly speaking, are generally said to indicate the type of the speaker's source of information. SYQ, like most other Quechuan languages, employs a three-term system,[17] indicating direct, reportative, and inferred evidence (*i.e.* the speaker has personal-experience evidence for *P*, the speaker has non-personal-experience evidence for *P*, or the speaker infers *P* based on either personal- or non-personal-experience evidence). In SYQ, the three evidentials are realized *-mI*, *-shI*, and *-trI* (See Floyd (1999) on Wanka Quechua; Faller (2003) on Cuzco Quechua). The evidential system of SYQ is of particular interest because it employs a second three-term system of evidential modifiers. The evidential system of SYQ thus counts nine members: *-mI*, *-mik*, and *-miki*; *-shI*, *-shik*, and *-shiki*; and *-trI*, *-trik*, and *-triki*. The *-I* *-ik*, and *-iki* forms are not allomorphs: they receive different interpretations. §6.2.11 describes this system in detail. (For further formal analysis, see Shimelman 2012 and Shimelman 2014).

1.9.2 Language contact – Aymara

For students of language contact, it is the contact of Yauyos with Aymara that should be of particular interest.[18] The northern branch of the Aymara family is situated entirely in the province of Yauyos (Adelaar & Muysken 2004: 173): the Aymaran languages Kawki and Jaqaru are spoken in the central Yauyos municipalities of Cachuy, Aysa and Tupe. There are, further, reports dating from the beginning of the 20th century of other Aymaran-speaking communities in the

---

[17] An anonymous reviewer points out that South Conchucos has a 5-choice evidential system, and Sihuas a 6-choice system (Hintz & Hintz 2017), while Huallaga has a 4-choice system (Weber 1989).

[18] Contact of Quechuan languages with Spanish, of course, is of interest here, as it is in all Quechuan languages.

province (174).[19] I was unable to find evidence of any unusual lexical borrowing in Yauyos, *i.e.*, of words – like (*pampa-* 'bury') – not also attested in other Quechuan languages. That said, the lexicon I assembled includes only 2000 words, in large part because the vocabulary of the language has been much-reduced, as is to be expected, given that such reduction is one of the symptoms of extreme language endangerment. Those more familiar with the Aymaran languages may, however, still be able to find evidence of calquing or structural influence.

---

[19] On Aymara and the relationship of Quechua and Aymara see, among others, Adelaar with Muysken (2004: 259–317) and Cerrón-Palomino (1994; 2000). On Jaqaru, see, among others, Hardman (1966; 1983; 2000).

2 Phonology and morphophonemics

This chapter covers the syllable structure, stress pattern, phonemic inventory, and morphophonemics of Southern Yauyos Quechua.

2.1 Introduction and summary

The syllable structure, stress pattern, phonemic inventory, and morphophonemics of SYQ are not extraordinary. Indeed, what is most extraordinary about them is precisely how unextraordinary they are: SYQ is, phonologically, extraordinarily conservative,[1] with four of its five dialects essentially instantiating the systems proposed for Proto-Quechua in Landerman (1991), Cerrón-Palomino (1987: ch.4). All SYQ dialects retain contrasts between (1) [č] and [ĉ]; (2) [k], [q] and [h]; (3) [l] and [λ]; (4) [n] and [ň]; and (5) [s] and [š].

(1) While in Ecuador, Columbia, Bolivia, Argentina, the east and south of Peru, as well as in Sihuas, Ambo-Pasco, Tarma, Wanka, Lambayeque, Chachapoyas and Cajamarca,[2] */ĉ/ underwent deretroflection, SYQ retains Proto-Quechua forms like *trina* 'female', *trupa* 'tail', *katrka-* 'gnaw', and *qutra* 'lagoon'. In SYQ, *traki* 'foot' contrasts with *chaki* 'dry'.

(2) */q/ was neither velarized nor glottalized in SYQ (which is not to say that these processes are the norm). The language retains, for example, the PQ forms *qusa* 'husband', *qasa-* 'freeze', *waqa-* 'cry', *aqu* 'sand', *uqu-* 'wet', *wiqaw* 'waist', *waqra* 'horn', and *atuq* 'fox'. SYQ thus retains contrasts like those between *qiru* 'stick' and *kiru* 'tooth'; *qilla* 'lazy' and *killa* 'moon'. */h/ appears in SYQ, as in PQ, principally word-initially, as in *hapi-* 'grab', *hampi-* 'cure', and *haya-* 'be bitter'.

(4) In SYQ, [ň] did not undergo depalatalization as it did in the Quechuas of Central Peru. [ň] figures in the first-person personal pronoun *ñuqa* as well as in lexemes such as *ñaka-ri-* 'suffer', *ñaña* 'sister', *ñiti-* 'crush', *ñawsa* 'blind', and *ñañu*

---

[1] Other phonologically conservative Quechuan languages include Sihuas, which, like Yauyos, retains contrasts between */ch/ and */tr/, */ll/ and */l/, as well as */sh/ and */s/. Thanks to an anonymous reviewer for pointing this out.

[2] Thanks to an anonymous reviewer for calling my attention to the final examples here.

2 Phonology and morphophonemics

'thin'. Examples of [n]/[ñ] minimal pairs include *ana* 'mole' and *aña-* 'scold'; and *na* DMY and *ña* DISC.

(5) [š] suffered depalatalization throughout the south. SYQ, however, retains Proto-Quechua forms such as *shimi* 'mouth', *shunqu* 'heart', *shipash* 'maiden', *washa* 'back', *ishkay*, 'two', and *mishki* 'sweet'. [s]/[š] minimal pairs include *suqu* 'gray hair' and *shuqu-* 'sip'. One also finds contrasts between the native-borrowed pairs *ashta-* 'move' and *asta* 'until'; and *asha-* 'yawn' and *asa-* 'anger'.

None of the dialects includes ejectives or aspirates in its phonemic inventory.

Vowel length is contrastive in the grammars but not the lexicons of the dialects of Azángaro-Chocos-Huangáscar, Cacra-Hongos and San Pedro. In these dialects, as in all the QI (QB) languages with the exception of Pacaraos, vowel length marks the first person in both the nominal (possessive) and verbal paradigms (*wasi-:* 'my house' and *puri-:* 'I walk'). The Cacra-Hongos dialect is unique among the five in that, there, the protomorpheme */r/ is generally but not uniformly realized as [l], and word-initial */s/ and */h/ are generally but not uniformly realized as [h], and [š], respectively.[3] The first of these mutations it has in common with neighboring Junín.

A note on */l/ Cerrón-Palomino – like (Torero 1964), but unlike Parker (1969) – does not include */l/ in his catalogue of proto-phonemes. He admits, however, that the status of */l/ is controversial. While it does occur in a small number of proto-morphemes, and, indeed, both /l/ and /ll/ occur in all of the QI contemporary varieties in Ancash and Huanuco, except for Humalies and Margos (thanks to an anonymous reviewer for pointing this out), he calls it "*Un elemento marginal y parasitario*" ("a marginal and parasitic element"). He admits, however, that the hypothesis that PQ included palatal lateral (/ll/) but not a alveolar lateral (/l/) runs into the problem that the universal tendency is that the presence of /ll/ depends on the presence of /l/, but not vice versa Cerrón-Palomino (1987: 123). W. Adelaar (p.c.) writes, "In support of the controversial status of */l/ which runs against the universal tendency that /λ/ presupposes /l/, there is the case of Amuesha (Yanesha'). This language has a generalized palatal vs. non-palatal opposition in its consonant inventory, but precisely */l/ is missing (apparently an areal feature shared with Quechua)." I have postulated an /l/ for SYQ, as both [λ]

---

[3] W. Adelaar (p.c.) writes that, at least with regard to the examples given here and below, the "Cacra-Hongos development of */s/ to /h/ is found throughout Junín (with the exception of Jauja). These dialects also use *shamu-*, instead of *hamu-*. The first form [...] is typical for Quechua I, and also for Ecuador and San Martín. *shamu-* may be older than *hamu-*," he writes, "but the correspondence is largely unpredictable according to dialects." An anonymous reviewer adds that Sihuas retains */s/ in *sama-* 'rest', *saru-* 'step on', *sayta-* 'kick', and *sita-* 'hit', among others.

and [l] appear in more than just a few marginal lexemes. [λ] appears in SYQ lexemes like *llaki* 'sadness', *lluqsi-* 'exit', *allin* 'good', *allqu* 'dog', *tullu* 'bone', *ayllu* 'family', *wallqa* 'garland', and *kallpa* 'strength', among many others. As for [l], as noted in §2.3, it appears, first, as an allomorph of /r/ in the CH dialect. It also appears in exclamations like *¡alaláw!* 'how cold!' and *¡añaláw!* 'how beautiful!' (which occur in Jaqaru, a neighboring Aymara language, as well Castro 1995), as well as in onomatopoetic terms like *luqluqluqya-* 'make the sound of boiling'. Finally, crucially, [l] also appears in a non-negligible number of semantically contentful lexemes, including *lapu-* 'slap', *lapcha-* 'touch', *laqatu* 'slug', *lashta* 'snow', *lawka-* 'feed a fire', *layqa-* 'bewitch', *lani* 'penis', *lumba* 'without horns', *alpaka* 'alpaca', *almi-* 'forge a river', and *alqalli* 'testicle'. [l]/[λ] minimal pairs can be found in contemporary SYQ in the CH dialect where [l] is an allomorph of /r/. These pairs include *laki-* 'separate' and *llaki-* 'grieve'; *tali-* 'find' and *talli-* 'pour'; *lunku* 'sack' and *llunku* 'picky'; and *lulu* 'kidney' and *llullu* 'unripe'.

§2.2 treats syllable structure and stress pattern; §2.3, phonemic inventory and morphophonemics; §2.4, Spanish loan words.

2.2 Syllable structure and stress pattern

Syllable structure in SYQ, as in other Quechuan languages, is (C)V(C) except in borrowed words. That is, syllables of the form CCV and VCC are prohibited. One vowel does not follow another without an intervening consonant, *i.e.*, sequences of the form VV are prohibited. Only the first syllable of a word may begin with a vowel (*a.pa-* 'bring'; *ach.ka* 'a lot').

As in the overwhelming majority of Quechuan languages, primary stress falls on the penultimate syllable of a word (compare *yanápa-n* 'he helps' and *yanapáya-n* 'he is helping'; *awá-rqa* 'he wove' and *awa-rqá-ni* 'I wove'). The first syllable of a word with more than four syllables generally receives weak stress. There are two exceptions to this rule. First, in all dialects, exclamations often receive stress on the ultimate syllable (*¡Achachák!* 'What a fright!' *¡Achachalláw!* 'How awful!'). Second, in those dialects where vowel length indicates the first person, stress falls on the ultimate syllable just in case person marking is not followed by any other suffix (*uyari-yá-:* 'I am listening', *ri-rá-:* 'I went').[4]

---

[4] It is worth noting that this is phenomenon is far from universal: as an anonymous reviewer points out, "all of the Ancash Quechua varieties mark first person with vowel length, but stress never falls on the lengthened syllable in word-final position. The same is true for Huamalies in western Huanuco. The phenomenon [described here for Yauyos] does hold for Huallaga in central Huanuco, as described by Weber (1989)".

2 Phonology and morphophonemics

2.3 Phonemic inventory and morphophonemics

SYQ counts three native vowel phonemes: /a/, /i/, and /u/. In words native to SYQ, the closed vowels /i/ and /u/ have mid and lax allomorphs [e], [ɪ] and [o], [ʊ], respectively. That is, in words native to SYQ, no member of either of the triples {[i], [e], [ɪ]} or {[u], [o], [ʊ]}, is contrastive with any other member of the same triple. The alternations [i] ~ [e] and [u] ~ [o] are conditioned by environment: the second member of each pair appears in a syllable including /q/ (/qilla/ 'lazy' → [qeλa], /atuq/ 'fox' → [atoq]).[5]

Vowel length is contrastive in the morphologies but not the lexicons of the dialects of ACH, CH and SP. In these dialects – as in all the QI (QB) languages with the exception of Pacaraos – vowel length marks the first person in both the substantive (possessive) and verbal paradigms (*wawa-:* 'my house' and *puri-:* 'I walk' (rendered '*wawa-y*' and *puri-ni* in the AMV and LT dialects))[6].

In all dialects, the consonant inventory counts seventeen native and six borrowed phonemes. The native phonemes include voiceless plosives /p/, /t/, /ch/, /tr/, /k/ and /q/; voiceless fricatives /s/, /sh/ and /h/; nasals /m/, /n/ and /ñ/; laterals /l/ and /ll/; tap /r/; and approximants /w/ and /y/. Borrowed from Spanish are voiced plosives /b/, /d/ and /g/;[7] voiceless fricative /f/; voiced fricative /v/; and trill /rr/. In the Cacra-Hongos dialect, the protomorpheme */r/ is generally but not uniformly realized as [l] (**runa* > *luna* 'person', **ri-y* > *li-y* 'go!', **harka-* > *halka-* 'herd'), and word-initial */s/ and */h/ are generally but not uniformly realized as [h][8] and [ʃ] (**sapa* > *hapa* 'alone', **surqu-* > *hurqu-* 'take out',

---

[5] An anonymous reviewer points out that "the most complete grammars of Quechuan languages show several lexemes with mid vowels that are not conditioned by /q/. See, for example, the discussions in Cusihuamán Gutiérrez (1976: 46–51) on Cuzco and in Swisshelm (1972: xiv–xv) on Ancash. Similar mid vowel data are found in Ayacucho, Santiago del Estero, Cajamarca, San Martin, Huallaga, and Corongo, among others. It would be surprising (and noteworthy!) if SYQ has no such lexemes, in contrast to other Quechuan languages across the family." I cannot at this point confirm either that Yauyos does or does not have such lexemes.

[6] It is worth noting that in some QI varieties – Huaylas, South Conchucos and Huamalies among them – lengthened high vowels lower to mid vowels, e. g. , /wayi-:/ [waye:], /puri-:/ [pure:]. Thanks to an anonymous reviwer for pointing this out.

[7] In SYQ, */p/ */t/ and */k/ were not sonorized. SYQ retains PQ forms like *wampu* 'boat' and *shimpa* 'braid'; *inti* 'sun' and *anta* 'copper-colored'; and *punki* 'swell' and *punku* 'door, entryway'.

[8] This is hardly unique to Yauyos, occurring in notably in the lects of Yauyos' immediate neighbor to the north, Junín. In CH, as in the QB lects generally, many stems retain initial /s/: *supay* 'phantom', *sipi* 'root', *siki* 'behind', *supi* 'fart', *suwa-* 'to rob', *sinqa* 'nose', *sasa* 'hard', and *siqna* 'wrinkle'. CH also shares with Junín the mutation of r to l. CH patterns with Huanca with regard to all but one of the phonological innovations common to the lects of other QB regions. For example, CH and Huanca retain ñ and ll, ch and tr.

2.3 Phonemic inventory and morphophonemics

hamu- > shamu- 'come', **hampatu > shampatu* 'frog'). Further examples include: *saru- > haru-* 'trample', *sara > hara* 'corn', *siqa- > hiqa-* 'go up', *sira- > hila-* 'sew', *sama > hama* 'rest'. Examples of native and borrowed lexemes that resist these mutations include *riqsi-* 'become acquainted' and *riga-* 'irrigate'; *siki* 'behind' and *sapu* 'frog'; and *hapi-* 'grab'). In Lincha and Tana – Cacra and Hongos' immediate neighbors to the north-east and south-west, respectively – speakers may realize word-initial */r/ and */s/ as [l] and [h], respectively, in a few cases (**runku- > lunku-* 'bag', **sapa > hapa* 'alone'). These substitutions are not systematic, however, and remain exceptions.

Tables 2.1, 2.2, and 2.3 give the vowel inventory, consonant inventory, and morphophonemics of SYQ. If the orthographic form differs either from the usual orthographic symbol among Andean linguists or from the IPA symbol, these are noted in square brackets. Parentheses indicate a non-indigenous phoneme.

Table 2.1: Vowel inventory

	Front	Central	Back
Closed (High)	i		u
Open (Low)		a	

Table 2.2: Consonant inventory

	Bilabial	Labio-dental	Alveolar	Post-alveolar	Retroflex	Palatal	Velar	Uvular
Voiceless plosive	p		t		tr [ĉ][ʈ]	ch [č][c]	k	q
Voiced plosive	(b)		(d)				(g)	
Nasal	m		n			ñ [ň][ɲ]		
Trill			(rr)[r]					
Tap or Flap			r [ɾ]					
Voiceless fricative		(f)	s	sh [š][ʃ]			h	
Voiced fricative		(v)						
Approximant	w					y [j]		
Lateral approximant			l			ll [λ][ʎ]		

2 Phonology and morphophonemics

Table 2.3: Morphophonemics

/n/	realized as [m] before /p/; in free alternation with nasalization of the preceeding vowel before /m/; (*i.e.*, *rinanpaq* → [rinaɱpaq])
/m/	[m] is in free alternation with [n] before /w/ and /m/ (*i.e.*, *qamman* → [qan̪man])
/k/	[k] is in free alternation with [ø] before /k/ and /q/ (*i.e.*, *wakqa* → [waqa])
/q/	[q] is in free alternation with [ø] before /q/ (*i.e.*, *ruwaqqa* → [ruwaqa])
/q/	[q] is in free alternation with [g] after /n/ (*i.e.*, *rinqa* → [ringa])
/-qa/ TOP	[qa] is in free alternation with [aq] after [aj] (*i.e.*, *chay-qa* → [tʃajaq])
/u/	realized as [o] or [ʊ] when it figures in a syllable that either includes /q/ or precedes one that does (*i.e.*, *urqu* → [ɔrqo])
/i/	realized as [e] or [ɛ] when it figures in a syllable that either includes /q/ or precedes one that does (*i.e.*, *qillu* → [qeʎu])

2.4 Spanish loan words

As detailed in §1.2, SYQ is extremely endangered: all but the most elderly speakers are bilingual and, indeed, Spanish-dominant. As a result, individual speakers are not limited by the constraints of Quechuan phonology and generally pronounce loan words with something very close to their original syllable structure and phonemes, even where these do not conform to the constraints of Quechuan phonology. With that said, where restructuring does take place, it does so according to the rules detailed in §2.4.1.

2.4.1 Spanish loan word restructuring

Syllable structure violations – vowel sequences. In cases where the loaned word includes the prohibited sequence *VV, SYQ, like other Quechuan languages, generally applies one of three strategies: (a) the elimination of one or the other of the two vowels (*aceite* → *asiti* 'oil'); (b) the replacement of one of the two vowels by a semiconsonant (*cuerpo* → *kwirpu* 'body', *sueño* → *suyñu* 'dream'); or (c) the insertion of a semiconsonant between the two vowels (*cualquiera* → *kuwalkiyera* 'any').

2.4 Spanish loan words

Syllable structure violations – consonant sequences. In case the loaned word includes a syllable of the prohibited form *CCV or *VCC, SYQ, again, like other Quechuan languages, employs one of two strategies: (a) the elimination of one of the two consonants (***gringo*** → ***ringu*** 'gringo') or (b) the insertion of an epenthetic vowel (***groche*** → ***guruchi*** 'hook', 'crochet').

Stress pattern violations. Speakers vary in the extent to which they restructure borrowed Spanish terms to conform to Quechua stress pattern. Plentiful are examples of both practices:

Table 2.4: Loan word restructuring

No restructuring		Restructuring	
kanásta-wan	Sp canásta 'basket'	tirruristá-wan	Sp terrorísta 'terrorist'
fwíra-ta	Sp fuéra 'outside'	Kañití-ta	Sp Cañéte 'Cañete'
mútu-qa	Sp móto 'motorcycle'	vaká-qa	Sp váca 'cow'

Words of five or more syllables permit the preservation of the original Spanish stress pattern in the interior of a word that still adheres to the Quechua pattern of assigning stress to the penultimate syllable (*timblúr-wan-ráq-tri* 'with an earthquake, still, for sure' (Sp *temblór* 'earthquake')).

Phonemic inventory – consonants. Spanish loan words often feature consonants foreign to the SYQ inventory: voiced plosives /b/, /d/ and /g/; voiceless fricative /f/; voiced fricative /v/; and trill /rr/. It might be expected that [b] and [d] would be systematically replaced with their voiceless counterparts, [p] and [t], and that trill [r] would, similarly, be replaced by tap/flap [ɾ]. Speakers of SYQ, even the oldest, do not in fact regularly replace these or other non-native phonemes (***balde*** → ***baldi*** 'bucket'; ***doctor*** → ***duktur*** 'doctor'; ***carro*** → ***karru*** 'car'; ***fiesta*** → ***fiysta*** 'festival'; ***velar*** → ***vilaku-*** 'watch', 'hold vigil').

Phonemic inventory – vowels. The inventory of Spanish vowels includes two foreign to SYQ: /o/ and /e/ (*Dios* 'God'; *leche* 'milk'). As detailed in §2.3, in words native to SYQ, [o] and [e] are allophones of /u/ and /i/, respectively. It is to be expected, then, that speakers would systematically replace the [o] and [e] of Spanish loan words with native correlates [u] and [i], respectively (***sapo*** → ***sapu*** 'frog'; ***cerveza*** → ***sirbisa*** 'beer'). This does indeed occur. More commonly, however, [o] and [e] are either replaced by the /u/ and /i/ allophones [ʊ] and [ɪ]

2 Phonology and morphophonemics

(*cosa* → [kʊsa] 'thing', *tele* → [tɪlɪ] 'TV') or, even, not replaced at all. The realization of non-native vowels varies both among speakers and also among words: different speakers render the same word differently and individual speakers render the same phoneme differently in different words.

Special case: ado. Spanish loan words ending in -ado – with the non-native /d/ and /o/ – present a special case. -ado is generally rendered [aw] in SYQ (*apurado* → *apuraw* 'quick'; *lado* → *law* 'place'). [9]

Finally, restructuring to accommodate any of the three – stress pattern, syllable structure or phonemic inventory – does not depend on restructuring to accommodate any of the others. That is, stress pattern can be restructured to eliminate violations of SYQ constraints, while violations of constraints on syllable structure or phonemic inventory are left unrestructured, and similarly for any of the six possible permutations of the three.

2.4.2 Loan word orthography

I have chosen an orthography that makes use of all and only the letters appearing in Tables 2 and 2.1, above. Orthography rather strictly follows pronunciation in the case of consonants in both indigenous and borrowed words; in the case of vowels in borrowed words, it is something of an idealization (*i.e.*, it should not in these cases be mistaken for phonetic transcription).

This alphabet does not include the letters *c, j, z, e* or *o*, all of which occur in the original Spanish spelling of many borrowed words. Spanish *c, j* and *z* have been replaced with their SYQ phonetic equivalents: "hard" *c* is replaced with *k*; "soft" *c* with *s*; *j* with *h*; and *z* with *s*. Thus, the borrowed Spanish words *caja* ('box', 'coffin') and *cerveza* ('beer') are rendered **kaha** and **sirbisa**, with no change in the pronunciation of the relevant consonants in either case. Spanish *e* and *o*, appearing simply, are replaced with *i* and *u* (*compadre* → *kumpadri*). Spanish vowel sequences including *e* and *o* are replaced as shown in Table 2.5.

In the special case where the sequence *ue* or *ua* is preceded by *h* – generally not not necessarily silent in Spanish – *h* and *u* together are replaced by the semi-consonant [w] (**huérfano** → **wirfanu** 'orphan').

---

[9] An anonymous reviewer has brought it to my attention that "in many QI languages, such as several varieties in Ancash,-ado → /a:/, e.g, *apura:*. In fact, -la: has become a case suffix 'at, near' that competes with the semantic territory of the native locative."

2.4 Spanish loan words

I have deviated from these practices only in the case of proper names, spelling these as they are standardly spelled in Spanish. Thus, Cañete and San Jerónimo, for example, are *not* rendered, as they would be under the above conventions, *Kañiti* and *San Hirunimu*. 'Dios' ('God') is treated as a proper name.

Table 2.5: Loan word orthography

ea → iya	*solea*	→ *suliya-*	'sun'
au → aw	*autoridad*	→ *awturidad*	'official'
ía → iya	*policía*	→ *pulisiya*	'police'
ia → ya	*familia*	→ *familya*	'family'
ie → iy	*siempre*	→ *siympri*	'always'
io → yu	*invidioso*	→ *inbidyusu*	'jealous'
ío → iyu	*tío*	→ *tiyu*	'uncle'
ua → wa	*guardia*	→ *gwardya*	'guard'
ue → wi	*cuento*	→ *kwintu*	'story'
ue → uy	*sueño*	→ *suyñu*	'dream'

3 Substantives

This chapter covers the various substantives in Southern Yauyos Quechua. It surveys their different classes and describes the patterns of inflection and derivation in the various dialects of the language.

3.1 Parts of speech

The parts of speech in Southern Yauyos Quechua, as in other Quechuan languages, are substantives (*warmi* 'woman'), verbs (*hamu-* 'come'), ambivalents (*para* 'rain, to rain'), and particles (*mana* 'no, not'). Substantives and verbs are subject to different patterns of inflection; ambivalents may inflect either as substantives or verbs; particles do not inflect.

The class of substantives in Quechuan languages is usually defined as including nouns (*wasi* 'house'); pronouns (*ñuqanchik* 'we'); interrogative-indefinites (*may* 'where'); adjectives (*sumaq* 'pretty'); pre-adjectives (*dimas* 'too'); and numerals (*kimsa* 'three'). All substantives with the exception of dependent pronouns (*Sapa* 'alone') may occur as free forms.

The class of verbs in Quechuan languages is usually defined to include transitive (*qawa-* 'see'), intransitive (*tushu-* 'dance'), and copulative (*ka-* 'be') stems. A fourth class can be set apart: onomatopoetic verbs (*chuqchuqya-* 'nurse, make the sound of a calf nursing'). All verbs, with the exception of *haku!* 'let's go!', occur only as bound forms.

Ambivalents form a single class.

The class of particles is usually defined to include interjections (*¡Alaláw!* 'How cold!'); prepositions (*asta* 'until'); coordinators (*icha* 'or'); pre-numerals (*la, las*, occurring with expressions of time); negators (*mana* 'no, not'); assenters and greetings (*aw* 'yes'); adverbs (*ayvis* 'sometimes').

The remainder of this section covers substantives; verbs are covered in Chapter 4 and particles in Chapter 5.

3 Substantives

3.2 Substantive classes

In SYQ, as in other Quechuan languages, the class of substantives comprises six subclasses: nouns, pronouns, interrogative-indefinites, adjectives, pre-adjectives, and numerals. §3.2.1–3.2.5 cover each of these in turn. Multiple-class substantives and the dummy noun *na* are covered in §3.2.6 and 3.2.7, respectively.

3.2.1 Nouns

The class of nouns may be divided into four sub-classes: regular nouns (*wayta* 'flower'), time nouns (*kanan* 'now'), gender nouns (*tiya* 'aunt'), and locative nouns (*qipa* 'behind'). §3.2.1.1–3.2.1.4 cover each of these in turn.

3.2.1.1 Regular nouns

The class of regular nouns includes all nouns not included in the other three classes. Although in this sense it is defined negatively, as a kind of default class, it includes by far more members than any of the others. (1–5) give examples.

(1) ***Warmi**npis qatiparun **urqu**ta.* AMV
    warmi-n-pis   qati-pa-ru-n   urqu-ta
    woman-3-ACC follow-REPET-URGT-3 hill-ACC
    'His **wife** herded him back to the **hills**.'

(2) ***Qari**ntash wañurachin, **masha**ntash wañurachin.* AMV
    qari-n-ta-sh   wañu-ra-chi-n   masha-n-ta-sh
    man-3-ACC-EVR   die-URGT-CAUS-3   son.in.law-3-ACC-EVR
    wañu-ra-chi-n
    die-URGT-CAUS-3
    'She killed her **husband**, they say; she killed her **son-in-law**, they say.'

(3) ***Lata**wan yanushpataqshi **runa**tapis mikurura.* ACH
    lata-wan   yanu-shpa-taq-shi   runa-ta-pis   miku-ru-ra
    tin.pot-INSTR cook-SUBIS-SEQ-EVR   person-ACC-ADD eat-URGT-PST
    'They even cooked **people** in metal **pots**, they say, and ate them.'

(4) *Unaykunaqa **watu**ta ruwaq kayanchik **llama**paqpis **alpaka**paqpis.* AMV
    unay-kuna-qa watu-ta   ruwa-q   ka-ya-nchik   llama-paq-pis
    before-pl-top rope-ACC make-AG   be-PRG-1PL   llama-ABL-ADD
    alpaka-paq-pis
    alpaca-ABL-ADD
    'In the old days, we used to make **rope** from [the wool of] **llamas** and **alpacas**.'

(5) ***Ukucha**pa **trupa**llanta **paluma**qa quykun.* ACH
    ukucha-pa   trupa-lla-n-ta   paluma-qa   qu-yku-n
    mouse-GEN   tail-RSTR-3-ACC   dove-TOP   give-EXCEP-3
    'The **dove** gave them the **tail** of a **mouse**.'

3.2.1.2 Time nouns

Nouns referring to time (*kanan* 'now', *wata* 'year') form a unique class in that they may occur adverbally without inflection, as in (1–5).

(1) *Tukuy **puntraw** yatramunanchikpaq.* AMV
    tukuy puntraw yatra-mu-na-nchik-paq
    all   day   know-CISL-NMLZ-1PL-PURP
    'So we can learn all **day**.'

(2) ***Kanan** vakata pusillaman chawayanchik kabratahina.* AMV
    kanan vaka-ta   pusilla-man chawa-ya-nchik   kabra-ta-hina
    now   cow-ACC   cup-ALL   milk-PRG-1PL   goat-ACC-COMP
    '**These days** we milk a cow into just a cup, like a goat.'

(3) *Pishiparullaniñam. Kutimunki **paqarin**.* AMV
    pishipa-ru-lla-ni-ña-m   kuti-mu-nki   paqarin
    tire-URGT-RSTR-1-DISC-EVD   return-CISL-2   tomorrow
    'I'm tired already. You'll come back **tomorrow**.'

(4) *Rinrilla:pis uparura **qayna wata**qa.* ACH
    rinri-lla-:-pis   upa-ru-ra   qayna   wata-qa
    ear-RSTR-1-ADD   deaf-URGT-PST   previous   year-TOP
    'My ears went deaf **last year**.'

3 Substantives

(5) **Qayna huk wata**hina timblur yapa kaypa kaptinqa. AMV
qayna huk wata-hina timblur yapa kay-pa
previous one year-COMP earthquake again DEM.P-LOC
ka-pti-n-qa
be-SUBDS-3-TOP
'About **a year ago**, when there was an earthquake here again.'

3.2.1.3 Gender nouns

Nouns indigenous to SYQ do not inflect for gender. SYQ indicates biological gender either with distinct noun roots (*maqta* 'young man', *pashña* 'young woman') or by modification with *qari* 'man' or *warmi* 'woman' in the case of people (*qari wawa* 'boy child', *warmi wawa* 'girl child') or *urqu* 'male' or *trina* 'female' in the case of animals. A few nouns, all borrowed from Spanish, are inflected for gender (masculine /u/ and feminine /a/). (1–4) give examples.

(1) *¿Kayllata nisitanki, aw, **tiyu**, llama wirata?* AMV
kay-lla-ta nisita-nki aw tiyu llama wira-ta
DEM.P-RSTR-ACC need-2 yes uncle llama fat-ACC
'You need only this, **uncle**, llama fat?'

(2) *Chaytri **Tiya** Alejandraqa Shutcollapa yatrarqa.* AMV
chay-tri Tiya Alejandra-qa Shutco-lla-pa yatra-rqa
DEM.D-EVC Aunt Alejandra-TOP Shutco-RSTR-LOC reside-PST
'That must be why **Aunt** Alexandra lived just in Shutco.'

(3) *Wak karu purikushayta **ansyanaña** kashayta.* LT
wak karu puri-ku-sha-y-ta ansyana-ña ka-sha-y-ta
DEM.D far walk-REFL-PRF-1-ACC old.lady-DISC be-PRF-1-ACC
'There where I've walked far, an **old lady** already.'

(4) *Unay unay blusataraqchu hinam ushturayachinpis **awilitaqa**. ¡Ve!* AMV
unay unay blusa-ta-raq-chu hina-m
before before blouse-ACC-CONT-Q thus-EVD
ushtu-ra-ya-chi-n-pis awilita-qa ve
dress-UNINT-INTENS-CAUS-3-ADD grandmother-TOP look
'The **old lady** is dressed in a blouse like the olden ones. Look!'

3.2 Substantive classes

3.2.1.4 Locative nouns

Locative nouns indicate relative position (*chimpa* 'front', *hawa* 'top'). They are inflected with the suffixes of the substantive (possessive) paradigm which indicate the person – and, in the case of the first person, also the number – of the complement noun. (1–5) give examples.

(1) *Hinashpaqa hatariru:. Allqukuna **yata**npa kara.* ACH
    hinashpa-qa   hatari-ru-:   allqu-kuna   yata-n-pa   ka-ra
    then-TOP   get.up-URGT-1   dog-PL   side-3-LOC   be-PST
    'Then I got up. Dogs were **at his side**.'

(2) *Kalamina **hawa**nta pasarachisa **uku**nman saqakuykusa.* AMV
    kalamina   hawa-n-ta   pasa-ra-chi-sa   uku-n-man
    corrugated.iron   above-3-ACC   pass-URGT-CAUS-NPST   inside-3-ALL
    saqa-ku-yku-sa
    go.down-REFL-EXCEP-NPST
    'He made him go **on top of** the tin roof and he fell **inside**.'

(3) *Plantachaqa alfapa **trawpi**npa wiñan.* AMV
    planta-cha-qa   alfa-pa   trawpi-n-pa   wiña-n
    tree-DIM-TOP   alfalfa-LOC   middle-3-LOC   grow-3
    'The little plant grows in the **middle** of alfalfa [fields].'

(4) *Kalabira, tullu, wama-wamaq chay **uku**paq kakuyan.* ACH
    kalabira, tullu, wama-wamaq   chay   uku-paq   ka-ku-ya-n
    skeleton bone   a.lot-a.lot DEM.D   inside-LOC   be-REFL-PROG-3
    'Skeletons, bones – there are a lot there **inside**.'

(5) *Uma nanaypaq ... trurarunchik huk limuntam **trawpi**paq partirunchik.* AMV
    uma   nana-y-paq   trura-ru-nchik   huk   limun-ta-m   trawpi-paq
    head   hurt-INF-PURP   put-URGT-1PL   one   lime-ACC-EVD   middle-LOC
    parti-ru-nchik
    split-URGT-1PL
    'For headaches ... we put a lime – we cut it in the **center**.'

3 Substantives

3.2.2 Pronouns

In SYQ, as in other Quechuan languages, pronouns may be sorted into four classes: personal pronouns, demonstrative pronouns, dependent pronouns and interrogative-indefinite pronouns.

The personal pronouns in SYQ are *ñuqa* 'I'; *qam* 'you'; *pay* 'she/he'; *ñuqa-nchik* 'we'; *qam-kuna* 'you.PL'; and *pay-kuna* 'they'. SYQ makes no distinction between subject, object, and possessive pronouns. With all three, case marking attaches to the same stem: *ñuqa* (1) 'I'; *ñuqa-ta* (1-ACC) 'me'; *ñuqa-pa* (1-GEN) 'my' (nominative being zero-marked). Table 3.1 summarizes this information.

The demonstrative pronouns are *kay* 'this', *chay* 'that', and *wak* 'that (other)'.

The dependent pronouns are *kiki* 'oneself', *Sapa* 'only, alone', *llapa* 'all', and *kuska* 'together'. These occur only with substantive person inflection, which indicates the person and, in the case of the first person plural, number of the referent of the pronoun (*kiki-y/-:* 'I myself'; *sapa-yki* 'you alone'). One additional pronoun may appear suffixed with substantive person inflection: *wakin* 'some ...', 'the rest of ...'

§3.2.2.1–3.2.2.3 cover the personal pronouns, demonstrative pronouns, and dependent pronouns. Interrogative-indefinite pronouns are covered in §3.2.3.

3.2.2.1 Personal pronouns *ñuqa, qam, pay*

SYQ has three pronominal stems – *ñuqa, qam,* and *pay,* as in (1), (2) and (3). These correspond to the first, second and third persons. Table 3.1 lists the personal pronouns.

Table 3.1: Personal pronouns

Person	Singular	Plural
1	ñuqa	ñuqa-nchik (dual)
		ñuqa-nchik-kuna (inclusive)
		ñuqa-kuna (exclusive)
2	qam	qam-kuna
3	pay	pay-kuna

(1) *Kala: Cañetepi chaypim uyarila: ñuqapis.* CH
    ka-la-:   Cañete-pi   chay-pi-m   uyari-la-:   ñuqa-pis
    be-PST-1 Cañete-LOC DEM.D-LOC-EVD hear-PST-1   I-ADD
    'I was in Cañete. I, too, heard it there.'

(2) *Manam **ñuqa**qa Viñaqta riqsi:chu. ¿**Qam** riqsinkichu, Min?* CH
　　mana-m　ñuqa-qa　Viñaq-ta　riqsi-:-chu　　　　　　qam
　　no-EVD　I-TOP　　Viñac-ACC　be.acquainted.with-1-NEG　you
　　riqsi-nki-chu　　　　　　Min
　　be.acquainted.with-2-Q　Min
　　'**I** don't know Viñac. Do **you** know it, Min?'

(3) ***Pay**qa hatarirushañam rikaq.* LT
　　pay-qa　　hatari-ru-sha-ña-m　　　　rika-q
　　3-TOP　　get.up-URGT-NPST-DISC-EVD　see-AG
　　'**He** had already gotten up to see.'

These may but need not inflect for number as *ñuqa-kuna*, *qam-kuna*, and *pay-kuna* (4), (5) and (6).

(4) *Unay **ñuqakuna**qa manam qawarqanichu, paykunaqa alminus manam qawarqapischu.* AMV
　　unay　　ñuqa-kuna-qa　　mana-m　qawa-rqa-ni-chu,　pay-kuna-qa
　　before　I-PL-TOP　　　　no-evd　see-PST-1-NEG　　3PL-TOP
　　alminus　mana-m　qawa-rqa-pis-chu
　　at.least　no-EVD　see-PST-ADD-NEG
　　'Before, **we** didn't see, but they, at least, didn't see either.'

(5) *"**Qamkuna** ashiptikim chinkakun", ni:.* AMV
　　qam-kuna　ashi-pti-ki-m　　　　chinka-ku-n　ni-:
　　you-PL　　look.for-SUBDS-2-EVD　lose-REFL-3　say-1
　　'"When **you** looked for him, he got lost," I said.'

(6) *¿Manachu **paykuna** wakpa wasinpi mikun uqata?* AMV
　　mana-chu　pay-kuna　wak-pa　　wasi-n-pi　　miku-n　uqa-ta
　　no-Q　　　he-PL　　DEM.D-LOC　house-3-LOC　eat-3　　oca-ACC
　　'There in her house, don't **they** eat oca?'

SYQ makes available a three-way distinction in the first person plural among *ñuqa-nchik* (dual), *ñuqa-nchik-kuna* (inclusive), and *ñuqa-kuna* (exclusive) (7), (8), (4).

3 Substantives

(7) *Ishkay kashpallam, "**ñuqanchik**" nin.* AMV
   ishkay   ka-shpa-lla-m   ñuqa-nchik   ni-n
   two   be-SUBIS-RSTR-EVD   I-1PL   say-3
   'If there are only two people, they say *ñuqanchik*.'

(8) *Kaypi **ñuqanchikkuna**qa kustumbrawmi kanchik.* AMV
   kay-pi   ñuqa-nchik-kuna-qa   kustumbraw-mi   ka-nchik
   DEM.P-LOC   we-1PL-PL-TOP   accustomed-EVD be-1PL
   'Around here, **we**'re used to it.'

ñuqa-kuna is employed in all five dialects (9–11).

(9) *Manam **ñuqakuna**qa talpula:chu paypa wawinmi talpula.* CH
   mana-m   ñuqa-kuna-qa   talpu-la-:-chu   pay-pa   wawi-n-mi
   no-EVD   1-PL-TOP   plant-PST-1-NEG   he-3   baby-3-EVD
   talpu-la
   plant-PST
   '**We** haven't planted. Her children have planted.'

(10) *Chaynakunam **ñuqakuna** kwintu: kara.* SP
   chayna-kuna-m   ñuqa-kuna   kwintu-:   ka-ra
   thus-PL-EVD   I-PL   story-1   be-PST
   'That's how **our** stories were.'

(11) *Linchapi **ñuqakuna**pa kanchu.* LT
   Lincha-pi   ñuqa-kuna-pa   ka-n-chu
   Lincha-LOC   1-PL-GEN   be-3-NEG
   '**We** don't have any in Lincha.'

In practice, except in CH, *ñuqa-nchik* is employed with dual, inclusive and exclusive interpretations to the virtual complete exclusion of the other two forms. Verbs and substantives appearing with the inclusive *ñuqa-nchik-kuna* inflect in the same manner as verbs do and substantives appearing with the dual/default *ñuqa-nchik* (12); verbs and substantives appearing with the exclusive *ñuqa-kuna* inflect in the manner as those appearing with the singular *ñuqa* (13), (14).

3.2 Substantive classes

(12) *Kriyi**nchik** ñuqanchikkuna.* AMV
kriyi-nchik   ñuqa-nchik-kuna
believe-1PL   I-1PL-PL
'**We** believe.'

(13) *Familyallan **ñuqakuna** suya:* CH
familya-lla-n   ñuqa-kuna   suya-:
family-RSTR-3   I-PL   wait-1
'Only **we**, their relatives, wait.'

(14) *Puntrawyayanñam **ñuqakuna**qa lluqsiniñam.* AMV
puntraw-ya-ya-n-ña-m   ñuqa-kuna-qa   lluqsi-ni-ña-m
day-INCH-PROG-3-DISC-EVD   I-PL-TOP   go.out-1-DISC-EVD
'It's getting to be daytime – **we** leave already.'

In the verbal and nominal paradigm tables, for reasons of space, I generally do not list *ñuqa-nchik-kuna* and *ñuqa-kuna* with the other first person pronouns in the headings; it can be assumed that the first patterns with *ñuqa-nchik*, the second with *ñuqa*. In practice, where context does not adequately specify the referent, speakers of SYQ make distinctions between the dual, inclusive and exclusive first-person plural exactly like speakers of English and Spanish do, indicating the dual, for example, with *ishkay-ni-nchik* 'the two of us'; the inclusive with *llapa-nchik* 'all of us'; and the exclusive with modifying phrases, as in *ñuqa-nchik Viñac-pa* 'we in Viñac'. SYQ makes no distinction between subject, object (15) and possessive (16) pronouns. With all three, case marking attaches to the same stem; nominative case is zero-marked.

(15) ***Ñuqata** mikumuwananpaq kutimushpa traqnaruwan.* AMV
ñuqa-ta   miku-mu-wa-na-n-paq   kuti-mu-shpa
I-ACC   eat-CISL-1.OBJ-NMLZ-3-PURP   return-CISL-SUBIS
traqna-ru-wa-n
bind.limbs-URGT-1.OBJ-3
'In order to me able to eat **me** when he got back, he tied me up.'

(16) *Manam kanchu. **Ñuqapaq** puchukarun.* AMV
mana-m   ka-n-chu   ñuqa-paq   puchuka-ru-n
no-EVD   be-3-NEG   I-GEN   finish-URGT-3
'There aren't any. **Mine** finished off.'

39

3 Substantives

(17) *Huk qawaptinqa, **ñuqanchik** qawanchikchu. Almanchik puriyanshi.* AMV
huk qawa-pti-n-qa ñuqa-nchik qawa-nchik-chu alma-nchik
one see-SUBDS-3-TOP I-1PL see-1PL-NEG soul-1PL
puri-ya-n-shi
walk-PROG-3-EVR
'"Although others see them, **we** don't see them. Our souls wander around," they say.'

3.2.2.2 Demonstrative pronouns *kay*, *chay*, *wak*

SYQ has three demonstrative pronouns: *kay* 'this', *chay* 'that', and *wak* 'that (other)' (1–3).

(1) *"**Kay**qa manam balinchu mikunanchikpaq", [nishpa] allquman qaraykurqani.* AMV
kay-qa mana-m bali-n-chu miku-na-nchik-paq allqu-man
DEM.P-TOP no-EVD be.worth-3-NEG eat-NMLZ-1PL-PURP dog-ALL
qara-yku-rqa-ni
serve-EXCEP-PST-1
'"**This** is not good for us to eat," I said and I served it to the dog.'

(2) *Ollanta Humala, "Kanan **chay**kunakta wañuchishaq", niyan.* CH
Ollanta Humala kanan chay-kuna-kta wañu-chi-shaq ni-ya-n
Ollanta Humala now DEM.D-PL-ACC die-CAUS-1.FUT say-PROG-3
'[President] Ollanta Humala is saying, "Now I'll kill **those**."'

(3) *Wak mulaqa manam mansuchu. Runatam **wak** wañuchin.* AMV
wak mula-qa mana-m mansu-chu runa-ta-m wak
DEM.D mule-TOP no-EVD tame-NEG person-ACC-EVD DEM.D
wañu-chi-n
die-CAUS-3
'That mule is not tame. **That** kills people.'

chay may have both proximate and distal referents. *wak* is consistently translated in Spanish as '*ese*' ('that'), not, perhaps contrary to expectation, as '*aquel*'. The demonstrative pronouns may substitute for any phrase or clause (4). They can but need not inflect for number (2).

3.2 Substantive classes

(4) *Hinashpa achkaña wawan kayan.* **Chay***paq ñakannataqtri mikuypaq.* ACH
    hinashpa achka-ña wawa-n ka-ya-n   chay-paq
    then   a.lot-DISC baby-3 be-PROG-3 DEM.D-ABL
    ñaka-n-ña-taq-tri   miku-y-paq
    suffer-3-DISC-SEQ-EVC   eat-INF-ABL
    'Then she has a lot of babies. She'll suffer, too, a lot from **that**, from hunger.'

They can appear simultaneously with possessive inflection (5).

(5) **Kayninchik.** AMV
    kay-ni-nchik
    DEM.P-EUPH-1PL
    'These of ours.'

In complex phrases with demonstrative pronouns, case marking attaches to the final word in the phrase (6).

(6) **Kay llañutapis** *puchkani kikiymi.* AMV
    kay   llañu-ta-pis   puchka-ni kiki-y-mi
    DEM.P thin-ACC-ADD   spin-1   self-1-EVD
    'I spin **this thin one**, too, myself.'

chay may be employed without deictic meaning, in particular when it figures in sentence-initial position (7).

(7) **Chaymi** *hampichira: hukwan, hukwan.* ACH
    chay-mi   hampi-chi-ra-:   huk-wan, huk-wan
    DEM.D-EVD   heal-CAUS-PST-1   one-INSTR one-INSTR
    '**So** I had him cured with one and with another.'

In this case, it is generally suffixed with one of the evidentials *-mi* or *-shi* and indicates that the sentence it heads is closely related to the sentence that precedes it.[1] SYQ demonstrative pronouns are identical in form to the demonstrative determiners (8–10).

---

[1] As an anonymous reviewer points out, forms such as *chay-mi* and *chay-shi* are lexicalized discourse markers, and, as such "they do not take productive affixes such as *-kuna*, *-pi*, or *-man*" among others.

3 Substantives

(8) **Kay** *millwapaqmi imapis lluqsimun.* ACH
    kay   millwa-paq-mi ima-pis   lluqsi-mu-n
    DEM.P   wool-ABL-EVD   what-ADD   come.out-CISL-3
    'Anything comes out of **this** wool.'

(9) *¿Manachu **chay** qatra wambrayki rikarinraq?* AMV
    mana-chu   chay   qatra   wambra-yki   rikari-n-raq
    no-Q   DEM.D   dirty   child-2   appear-3-CONT
    'Didn't **that** dirty kid of yours appear yet?'

(10) **Wak** *trakrayqa hunta hunta kakuyan.* AMV
     wak   trakra-y-qa   hunta   hunta   ka-ku-ya-n
     DEM.D   field-1-TOP   full   full   be-REFL-PROG-3
     '**That** field of mine is really full.'

3.2.2.2.1 Determiners SYQ does not have an independent class of determiners. *huk* 'one', 'once', 'other' can be used to introduce new referents; in this capacity, it can be translated 'a' (1).

(1) **Huk** *pashñash karqa ubihira. Chaymanshi trayarushqa* **huk** *qari yuraq kurbatayuq.* AMV
    huk   pashña-sh   ka-rqa   ubihira   chay-man-shi
    one   girl-EVR   be-PST   shepherdess   DEM.D-ALL-EVR
    traya-ru-shqa   huk   qari
    arrive-URGT-SUBIS   one   man
    '**A** girl was a shepherdess. Then, they say, **a** man with a white tie arrived.'

kay 'this', *chay* 'that', and *wak* 'that (other)' can be used to refer to established referents; in this capacity, they can be translated 'the' (2).

(2) *Yuraq kurbata-yuq yana tirnuyuq* **chay** *pashñawan purirqa.* AMV
    yuraq   kurbata-yuq   yana   tirnu-yuq   chay   pashña-wan   puri-rqa
    white   tie-POSS   black   suit-POSS   DEM.D   girl-INSTR   walk-PST
    'With a white tie and a black suit, he walked about with **the** girl.'

(3) *Runa **chay** maqtata wañurachin hanay urqupa.* AMV
 runa chay maqta-ta wañu-ra-chi-n hanay urqu-pa
 person DEM.D young.man-ACC die-URGT-CAUS-3 above hill-LOC
 'People killed **the** boy up in the hills.'

3.2.2.3 Dependent pronouns *kiki-*, *Sapa-*, *llapa-*, *kuska-*

SYQ has four dependent pronouns: *kiki-* 'oneself' (1), *Sapa-* 'alone' (2), *llapa-* 'all' (3), and *kuska-* 'together' (4).

(1) ***Kiki**ypaq ruwani hukkunapaq ruwani.* AMV
 kiki-y-paq ruwa-ni huk-kuna-paq ruwa-ni
 self-1-BEN make-1 one-PL-BEN make-1
 'I make them for **myself** and I make them for others.'

(2) *Yatrarqani **sapa**llay.* AMV
 yatra-rqa-ni sapa-lla-y
 reside-PST-1 alone-RSTR-1
 'I lived all **alone**.'

(3) ***Llapa**nta apakunki.* CH
 llapa-n-ta apa-ku-nki
 all-3-ACC bring-REFL-2
 'You're going to take along them **all**.'

(4) *Mikuypaqpis wañuyanki **kuska**yki wawantin.* AMV
 miku-y-paq-pis wañu-ya-nki kuska-yki wawa-ntin
 eat-INF-ABL-ADD die-PROG-2 together-2 baby-INCL
 'You're going to be dying of hunger – you **together** with your children.'

These pronouns are dependent in the sense that they cannot occur uninflected: the suffixes of the nominal (possessive) paradigm attach to dependent pronouns indicating the person and – in the case of the first person – sometimes the number of the referent of the pronoun (*llapa-nchik* 'all of us'). Dependent pronouns function in the manner as personal pronouns do: they may refer to any of the participants in an event, subject (5) or object (6); they inflect obligatorily for case (7) and optionally for number; and they may be followed by enclitics (8).

3 Substantives

(5) *Sikya fayna kaptinmi liya: **llapa**:.* AMV
sikya   fayna   ka-pti-n-mi   li-ya-:   llapa-:
canal work.day be-SUBIS-3-EVD go-PROG-1 all-1
'When there's a community work day on the canal, we **all** go.'

(6) *Chay **kuska**nta wañurachisa chaypa.* ACH
chay   kuska-n-ta   wañu-ra-chi-sa   chay-pa
DEM.D together-3-ACC die-URGT-CAUS-NPST DEM.D-LOC
'They killed those **together** there.'

(7) *Huk runata kaballun **kiki**npi kaballun trakinta pakirusa.* AMV
huk runa-ta   kaballu-n kiki-n-pi   kaballu-n traki-n-ta
one person-ACC horse-3   self-3-GEN horse-3   foot-3ACC
paki-ru-sa
break-URGT-NPST
'A man's horse – **his own** horse – broke his foot.'

(8) ***Kikinkamatr** wañuchinakura.* ACH
kiki-n-kama-tr   wañu-chi-naku-ra
self-3-LIM-EVC die-LIM-RECP-PST
'They must have killed each other **themselves**.'

All except *kiki* may occur as free forms as well; it is, however, only as adjectives that they may occur uninflected; as pronouns (9) or adverbs (10) all still demand inflection.

(9) *Hinashpa pantyunman apawanchik **llapa** familyanchik kumpañawanchik.* AMV
hinashpa pantyun-man apa-wanchik llapa familya-nchik
then   cemetery-ALL bring-3>1PL all   family-1PL
kumpaña-wanchik
accompany-3>1PL
'Then they take us to the cemetery. Our **whole** family accompanies us.'

(10) *¿Imayna chay lluqsilushpaqa mana **kuska** lilachu?* CH
imayna chay   lluqsi-lu-shpa-qa   mana kuska   li-la-chu
why   DEM.D go.out-URGT-SUBIS-TOP no   together go-PST-NEG
'Why didn't they go **together** when they went out?'

3.2 Substantive classes

Sapa is realized *hapa* in the CH and LT dialects (11), (12); *sapa* in all others (13).

(11) *¿Imayna trankilu pulin **hapa**llan?* CH
 imayna trankilu puli-n hapa-lla-n
 how tranquil walk-3 alone-RSTR-3
 'How does she walk about calmly all **alone**?'

(12) *Pitaq atindinqa **hapa**llay kayaptiyqa.* LT
 pi-taq atindi-nqa hapa-lla-y ka-ya-pti-y-qa
 who-SEQ attend.to-3.FUT alone-RSTR-1 be-PROG-SUBDS-1-TOP
 'Who's going to take care of him if I'm all **alone**?'

(13) *Pampawanchik tardiqa diharamuwanchik **sapa**llanchikta.* AMV
 pampa-wanchik tardi-qa diha-ra-mu-wanchik
 bury-3>1PL afternoon-TOP leave-URGT-CISL-3>1PL
 sapa-lla-nchik-ta
 alone-RSTR-1PL-ACC
 'They bury us in the afternoon and then they leave us **alone**.'

One additional pronoun may appear inflected with possessive suffixes: *wakin* 'some, the rest of' (14), (15) (not attested in CH).

(14) ***Wakin**taq intindiya:. Piru **wakin**taq manam.* SP
 wakin-taq intindi-ya-: piru wakin-taq mana-m
 some-SEQ understand-PROG-1 but some-SEQ no-EVD
 'I'm catching [lit. understanding] **some** of them. But the **rest**, no.'

(15) *Mamanqa kawsakunmi **wakin**ninpaqqa.* ACH
 mama-n-qa kawsa-ku-n-mi wakin-ni-n-paq-qa
 mother-3-TOP live-REFL-3EVD some-EUPH-3-ABL-TOP
 'His mother lived thanks to [lit. from] **another** [man].'

3.2.3 Interrogative-indefinites
pi, ima, imay, imayna, mayqin, imapaq, ayka

SYQ has seven interrogative-indefinite stems: *pi* 'who', *ima* 'what', *imay* 'when', *may* 'where', *imayna* 'how', *mayqin* 'which', *imapaq* 'why', and *ayka* 'how much

3 Substantives

or how many', as shown in Table 3.2. These form interrogative (1–12), indefinite (13–21), and negative indefinite pronouns (22–29). Interrogative pronouns are formed by suffixing the stem – generally but not obligatorily – with any of the enclitics *-taq*, *-raq*, *-mI*, *-shI* or *-trI* (*pi-taq* 'who', *ima-raq* 'what'); indefinite pronouns are formed by attaching *-pis* to the stem (*pi-pis* 'someone', *ima-pis* 'something'); negative indefinite pronouns, by preceding the indefinite pronoun with *mana* 'no' (*mana pi-pis* 'no one', *mana ima-pis* 'nothing').

Table 3.2: Interrogative-indefinites

Stem	Translation	(Negative) indefinite	Translation
pi	who	(mana) pipis	some/anyone (no one)
ima	what	(mana) imapis	some/anything (nothing)
imay	when	(mana) imaypis	some/anytime (never)
may	where	(mana) maypis	some/anywhere (nowhere)
imapaq	why	(mana) imapaqpis	some/any reason (no reason)
imayna	how	(mana) imaynapis	some/anyhow (no how)
mayqin	which	(mana) mayqinpis	which ever (none)
ayka	how many	(mana) aykapis	some/any amount (none)

(1) ¿*Pitaq willamanchik?* ACH
    pi-taq   willa-ma-nchik
    who-SEQ tell-1.OBJ-1PL
    '**Who**'s going tell us?'

(2) "¿*Imatam maskakuyanki?*" "*Antaylumata maskakuya:*". SP
    ima-ta-m   maska-ku-ya-nki   antayluma-ta
    what-ACC-EVD look.for-REFL-PROG-2 antayluma.berries-ACC
    maska-ku-ya-:
    look.for-PROG-1
    '"**What** are you looking for?" "I'm looking for antayluma berries."'

(3) ¿*Imayshi riyan Huancayota?* AMV
    imay-shi   ri-ya-n   Huancayo-ta
    when-EVR go-PROG-3 Huancayo-ACC
    '**When** is he going to Huancayo, did he say?'

3.2 Substantive classes

(4) *¿**May**payá Hildapa wakchan kayan?* AMV
may-pa-yá   Hilda-pa   wakcha-n   ka-ya-n
where-LOC-EMPH Hilda-GEN   sheep-3   be-PROG-3
'**Where** is Hilda's sheep?'

(5) *Chay mutuqa, ¿**may**pitaq kayan?* ACH
chay   mutu-qa,   may-pi-taq   ka-ya-n?
DEMD   motorcycle-TOP where-LOC-TOP   be-PROG-3
'**Where** is that motorbike?'

(6) *¿**Ima**paq ... papata apamuwarqanki?* AMV
ima-paq   papa-ta   apa-mu-wa-rqa-nki
what-PURP   potato-ACC bring-CISL-1.OBJ-PST-2
'**Why** ... have you brought me potatoes?'

(7) *¿**Ima**paqtaq chayna walmilla kidalun?* CH
ima-paq-taq   chayna   walmi-lla   kida-lu-n
what-PURP-SEQ   thus   woman-RSTR   stay-URGT-3
'**Why** did just the woman stay like that?'

(8) *Llakikuyan atuqqa. "Diharuwan kumpadriy. ¿Kanan **imayna**taq kutishaq?"* AMV
llaki-ku-ya-n   atuq-qa diha-ru-wa-n   kumpadri-y kanan
be.sad-REFL-PROG-3   fox-TOP leave-URGT-1.OBJ-3   compadre-1 now
imayna-taq   kuti-shaq
how-SEQ   return-1.FUT
'The fox was sad. "My compadre left me. Now **how** am I going to get back?"'

(9) *¿**Mayqin**nin tunirun? ¿Kusinan?* AMV
mayqin-ni-n   tuni-ru-n   kusina-n
which-EUPH-3   crumble-URGT-3   kitchen-3
'**Which** of them crumbled? Her kitchen?'

3 Substantives

(10) *Lutuyuqmi kayan wak runakuna. ¿Mamanchutr ñañanchutr? ¿**Maqin**raq wañukun?* LT
lutu-yuq-mi   ka-ya-n   wak   runa-kuna   mama-n-chu-tr
mourning-POS-EVD be-PROG-EVD DEM.D person-PL mother-3-Q-EVC
ñaña-n-chu-tr   maqin-raq   wañu-ku-n
sister-3-Q-EVC which-CONT die-REFL-3
'Those people are wearing mourning. Would it be their mother or their sister? **Which** died?'

(11) *¿**Aykaña**tr awmintarun kabranqa?* AMV
ayka-ña-tr   awminta-ru-n   kabra-n-qa
how.many-DISC-EVC increase-URGT-3 goat-3-TOP
'**How much** have her goats increased?'

(12) *Chaypaqa ¿**Ayka**ktataq pagaya:?* CH
chay-pa-qa   ayka-kta-taq   paga-ya-:
DEM.D-LOC-TOP how.much-ACC-SEQ pay-PROG-1
'**How much** am I paying there?'

(13) ***Pipis** fakultaykuwananpaq.* LT
pi-pis   fakulta-yku-wa-na-n-paq
pi-ADD faciliate-EXCEP-1.OBJ-NMLZ-3-PURP
'So **someone** will help me out.'

(14) *Wak chimpata pasashpaqa **imallatapis**.* SP
wak   chimpa-ta   pasa-shpa-qa   ima-lla-ta-pis
DEM.D opposite.side-ACC pass-SUBIS-TOP what-RSTR-ACC-ADD
'When you go by there on the opposite side – [it could do] **anything**.'

(15) *Chay muquykuna **imaypis** nanaptin.* AMV
chay   muqu-y-kuna   imay-pis   nana-pti-n
DEM.D knee-1-PL   when-ADD   hurt-SUBDS-3
'**Any time** my knees hurt.'

(16) *Kay qullqita qushqayki. ¡Ripukuy **maytapis**!* AMV
kay   qullqi-ta   qu-shqayki   ripu-ku-y   may-ta-pis
DEM.P money-ACC give-3>1PL.FUT go-REFL-IMP where-ACC-ADD
'I'm going to give you this money. Get going **whereever**!'

3.2 Substantive classes

(17) *Kitrarun **imaynapis** yaykurun Lluqi-Makiqa.* AMV
 kitra-ru-n imayna-pis yayku-ru-n Lluqi-Maki-qa
 open-URGT-3 how-ADD enter-URGT-3 Lluqi-Maki-TOP
 'Strong Arm opened it **any way** [he could] and entered.'

(18) *Manam kaytaqa dihayta muna:chu. **Imaynapaqpis** hinatam ruwakulla:.* ACH
 mana-m kay-ta-qa diha-y-ta muna-:-chu imayna-paq-pis
 no-EVD DEM.P-ACC-TOP leave-INF-ACC want-1-NEG how-ABL-ADD
 hina-ta-m ruwa-ku-lla-:
 thus-ACC-EVD make-REFL-RSTR-1
 'I don't want to leave this. Like this, I just make **whichever way**.'

(19) ***Imaynapis** yatrashaqmi. Limapaqa buskaq kanmiki.* LT
 imayna-pis yatra-shaq-mi Lima-pa-qa buska-q ka-n-mi-ki
 how-ADD know-1.FUT-EVD Lima-LOC-TOP look.for-AG be-3-EVD-KI
 '**Any way** about it, I'm going to find out. In Lima, there are people who read cards.'

(20) *Chay wambra **imapaqpis** rabyarirun.* AMV
 chay wambra ima-paq-pis rabya-ri-ru-n
 DEM.D child what-PURP-ADD be.mad-INCEP-URGT-3
 'That child gets mad for **any reason**.'

(21) *Ayvis dimandakurun tiyrayuqkuna trakrakunapaq **imapaqpis**.* SP
 ayvis dimanda-ku-ru-n tiyra-yuq-kuna trakra-kuna-paq
 sometimes denounce-REFL-URGT-3 land-POSS-PL field-PL-ABL
 ima-paq-pis
 what-ABL-ADD
 'Sometimes they denounced landholders for their fields, **for any thing at all**.'

(22) ***Mana pipis** yachanchu.* AMV
 mana pi-pis yatra-n-chu
 no who-ADD know–3-NEG
 '**No one** lives here.'

3 Substantives

(23) *Puntrawqa **manam imapis** kanchu.* SP
puntraw-qa   mana-m   ima-pis   ka-n-chu
day-TOP   no-EVD   what-ADD   be-3-NEG
'In the day, there's **nothing**.'

(24) *Piru **mana imaypis** kaynaqa.* AMV
piru   mana   imay-pis   kayna-qa
but   no   when-ADD   thus-TOP
'But **never** like that.'

(25) *Kasarakura: kayllapam hinallam kay lawpa kawsaku: tukuy watan watan **manam maytapis** lluqsi:chu.* ACH
kasara-ku-ra-:   kay-lla-pa-m   hina-lla-m   kay
marry-REFL-PST-1   DEM.P-RSTR-LOC-EVD   thus-RSTR-EVD   DEM.P
law-pa   kawsa-ku-:   tukuy   wata-n   wata-n   mana-m
side-LOC   live-REFL-1   all   year-3   year-3   no-EVD
may-ta-pis   lluqsi-:-chu
where-ACC-ADD   go.out-1-NEG
'I got married right here. Just like that, here I live, year in, year out, I don't go **anywhere**.'

(26) ***Mana** talilachu **maytrawpis**.* CH
mana   tali-la-chu   may-traw-pis
no   find-PST-NEG   where-LOC-ADD
'They haven't found him **anywhere**.'

(27) *Ñakarinchikmi sapallanchikqa **manam imaynapis**.* SP
ñaka-ri-nchik-mi   sapa-lla-nchik-qa   mana-m   imayna-pis
suffer-UNINT-1PL-EVD   alone-RSTR-1PL-top   no-EVD   how-ADD
'We suffer alone **without any way** [to make money].'

(28) ***Mayqinnikipis** mana yuyachiwarqankichu.* AMV
mayqin-ni-ki-pis   mana   yuya-chi-wa-rqa-nki-chu
which-EUPH-2-ADD   no   remember-CAUS-1.OBJ-PST-2-NEG
'**Neither** of you reminded me.'

3.2 Substantive classes

(29) *Rayaqa **manam aykas** kanchu.* ACH
raya-qa mana-m ayka-s ka-n-chu
row-TOP no-EVD how.many-ADD be-3-NEG
'There is**n't even a small number** of rows.'

Indefinite pronouns may figure in exclamations (30).

(30) *¡**Ima maldisyaw** chay Dimunyu! ¡Pudirniyuq!* AMV
ima maldisyaw chay dimunyu pudir-ni-yuq
what damned DEM.D devil power-EUPH-POS
'**How damned** is the Devil! He's powerful!'

Interrogative pronouns are suffixed with the case markers corresponding to the questioned element (31).

(31) *¿Runkuwanchu qaqurushaq? ¿**Imawantaq** qaquruyman?* AMV
runku-wan-chu qaqu-ru-shaq ima-wan-taq qaqu-ru-y-man
sack-INSTR-Q rub-URGT-1.FUT what-INSTR-SEQ rub-URGT-1-COND
'Should I rub it with a sack? **With what** can I rub it?'

Enclitics generally attach to the final word in the interrogative phrase: where the interrogative pronoun completes the phrase, the enclitic attaches directly to the interrogative (plus case suffixes, if any) (32); where the phrase includes an NP, the enclitic attaches to the NP (*pi-paq-taq* 'for whom' *ima qullqi-tr* 'what money') (33), (34).

(32) *"¿**Imapaqmi** qam puka traki kanki?" nishpa.* SP
ima-paq-mi qam puka traki ka-nki ni-shpa
what-PURP-EVD you red foot be-2 say-SUBIS
'"**Why** are your feet red?" he said, they say.'

(33) *¿Ukaliptuta pitaq simbranqa? ¿**Pipaqñataq**?* AMV
ukaliptu-ta pi-taq simbra-nqa pi-paq-ña-taq
eucalyptus-ACC who-SEQ plant-3.FUT who-BEN-DISC-SEQ
'Who's going to plant eucalyptus trees? **For whom**?'

(34) *¿**Ayka watañataq** kanan nubinta i trispaq?* AMV
ayka wata-ña-taq kanan nubinta i tris-paq
how.many year-DISC-SEQ now ninety and three-ABL
'**How many years** is it already since ninety-three?'

3 Substantives

The interrogative enclitic is not employed in the interior of a subordinate clause but may attach to the final word in the clause (*¿Pi mishi-ta saru-ri-sa-n-ta qawa-rqa-nki?* 'Who did you see trample the cat?' *¿Pi mishi-ta saru-ri-sa-n-ta-ta qawa-rqa-nki?* 'Who did you see trample the cat?').

Interrogative phrases generally raise to sentence-initial position (35); they may, however, sometimes remain *in-situ*, even in non-echo questions (36).

(35) *¿Piwan tumashpatr pay hamun?* AMV
 pi-wan   tuma-shpa-tr   pay hamu-n
 who-INSTR take-SUBIS-EVC he come-3
 '**Who** did he come drinking **with**?'

(36) *¿Qaliqa likun **maytataq**?* CH
 qali-qa   li-ku-n   may-ta-taq
 man-TOP come-REFL-3 where-ACC-SEQ
 'The man went **where**?'

Interrogative indefinites are sometimes employed as relative pronouns (37), (38).

(37) *Pashñaqa **piwan** trayaramun* † AMV
 pashña-qa pi-wan   traya-ra-mu-n
 girl-TOP   who-INSTR arrive-URGT-CISL-3
 'The girl **with whom** she came'

(38) *Familyanqa qawarun **imayna** wañukusam pustapa.* AMV
 familya-n-qa qawa-ru-n imayna wañu-ku-sa-m   pusta-pa
 family-3-TOP see-URGT-3 how   die-REFL-NPST-EVD clinic-LOC
 'Her family saw **how** she had died in the clinic.'

Speakers use both *ima ura* and *imay ura* 'what hour' and 'when hour' to ask the time (39).

(39) *¿**Imay urataq** huntanqa kay yakuqa?* LT
 imay ura-taq   hunta-nqa kay   yaku-qa
 when hour-SEQ fill-3.FUT DEM.P water-TOP
 '**What time** will this water fill up?'

Interrogative pronouns may be stressed with *diyablu* 'devil' and like terms (40).

3.2 Substantive classes

(40) ***¿Ima diyabluyá** ñuqanchik kanchik?* AMV
ima diyablu-yá ñuqa-nchik ka-nchik
what devil-EMPH I-1PL be-1PL
'**What the hell** are we?'

Possessive suffixes attach to indefinites to yield phrases like 'your things' and 'my people' (41–43); attaching to *mayqin* 'which', they yield 'which of PRON' (44).

(41) **Mana imaykipis** *kaptin* ACH
mana ima-yki-pis ka-pti-n
no what-2-ADD be-SUBDS-3
'If you don't have **anything**'

(42) *Yasqayaruptiki **mana pinikipis** kanqachu.* ACH
yasqa-ya-ru-pti-ki mana pi-ni-ki-pis ka-nqa-chu
old-INCH-URGT-SUBDS-2 no who-EUPH-2-ADD be-3.FUT-NEG
'When you're old, you won't have **anyone**.'

(43) ***Mana** vakanchik **imanchik** kaptin hawkatr tiyakuchuwan.* AMV
mana vaka-nchik ima-nchik ka-pti-n hawka-tr
no cow-1PL what-1PL be-SUBDS-3 tranquil-EVC
tiya-ku-chuwan
sit-REFL-1PL.COND
'**Without** our cows and **our stuff**, we could sit [live/be] in peace.'

(44) "*¿**Mayqinninchik** pirdirishun? Kusisam kayhina silbaku:*" *nin.* SP
mayqin-ni-nchik pirdi-ri-shun kusi-sa-m kay-hina
which-EUPH-1PL lose-INCEP-1PL.FUT sew-PRF-EVD DEM.P-COMP
silba-ku-: ni-n
whistle-REFL-1 say-3
'"**Which of us** will lose? Sewed up like this, I whistle," he said.'

Imapaq 'why' is also sometimes realized as *imapa* in ACH (45).

(45) *¿**Imapam** chayta ruwara paytaq? ¿**Imaparaq**?* ACH
ima-pa-m chay-ta ruwa-ra pay-taq ima-pa-raq
what-PURP-EVD DEM.DACC make-PST he-SEQ what-PURP-CONT
'**Why** did they do that to him? **Why ever**?'

3 Substantives

Negative indefinites may be formed with *ni* 'nor' as well as *mana* (46); they may sometimes be formed with no negator at all (47), (48).

(46) *Manañam kanan chay llamatapis qawanchikchu **ni imaypis** kanan unayñam.* ACH
   mana-ña-m   kanan chay   llama-ta-pis   qawa-nchik-chu   ni
   NO-DISC-EVD now   DEM.D llama-ACC-ADD see-1PL-NEG   nor
   imay-pis   kanan unay-ña-m
   when-ADD   now   before-DISC-EVD
   'Now we don't see llamas **any more ever**. For a long time now.'

(47) *Katraykurun. ¡**Imapis** kanchu! "¡Ñuqata ingañamara!" nishpa.* SP
   katra-yku-ru-n   ima-pis   ka-n-chu!   ñuqa-ta   ingaña-ma-ra
   release-EXCEP-URGT-3 what-ADD   be-3-NEG   I-ACC   trick-1.OBJ-PST
   ni-shpa
   say-SUBIS
   '[The fox just] let it go and – **nothing**! "He tricked me!" said [the fox].'

(48) *Wakhina inutilisadu kakuyan **imapaqpis** balinchu.* LT
   wak-hina   inutilisadu ka-ku-ya-n   ima-paq-pis
   DEM.D-COMP unused   be-REFL-PROG-3 what-PURP-ADD
   bali-n-chu
   be.worth-3-NEG
   'It's unused like that. It's **not** good for **anything**.'

Suffixed with the combining verb *na-*, *ima* 'what' forms a verb meaning 'do what' or 'what happen' (49–51).

(49) *Wañuq runalla hukvidata llakikuyan. "Kananqa prisutriki ñuqaqa rikushaq. ¿**Imanashaq**?"* SP
   wañu-q   runa-lla   huk-vida-ta   llaki-ku-ya-n   kanan-qa
   die-AG   person-RSTR one-life-ACC sorrow-REFL-PROG-3 now-TOP
   prisu-tri-ki   ñuqa-qa riku-shaq   ima-na-shaq
   imprisoned-EVC-KI I-TOP   go-1.FUT   what-VRBZ-1.FUT
   'She was very sorry for the deceased person. "Now I'm going to go to jail. **What will I do**?"'

3.2 Substantive classes

(50) *"¿Karahu-ta-taq **imanaruntaq**?" qawaykushpaqa huk utrpata qapikushpa kay kunkanman pasaykurun.* AMV
karahu-ta-taq   ima-na-ru-n-taq   qawa-yku-shpa-qa   huk
jerk-ACC-SEQ   what-VRBZ-URGT-3-SEQ   look-EXCEP-SUBIS-TOP   one
utrpa-ta   qapi-ku-shpa   kay kunka-n-man   pasa-yku-ru-n
ash-ACC   grab-REFL-SUBIS   kay throat-3-ALL   pass-EXCEP-URGT-3
'She watched him then she said, "**What happened** to that bastard?" and grabbed some ashes and stuffed them down his throat.'

(51) *Wañukunmantriki.¿**Imanan**mantaq? ¿Imayna mana kutikamunmanchu?* ACH
wañu-ku-n-man-tri-ki   ima-na-n-man-taq   imayna   mana
die-REFL-3-COMP-EVC-KI   what-VRBZ-3-COND-SEQ   why   no
kuti-ka-mu-n-man-chu
return-REFL-CISL-3-COND-NEG
'He could die, of course. What could **happen**? Why can't he come back?'

In the CH dialect, *imayna* alternates with *imamish* (52).

(52) *Quni qunim ñuqa kaya:, kumadri. ¿Qam **imamish** kayanki?* CH
quni   quni-m   ñuqa   ka-ya-:   kumadri   qam   imamish
warm   warm-EVD   I   be-PROG-1   comadre   you   how
ka-ya-nki
BE-PROG-2
'I'm really warm, comadre. **How** are you?'

3.2.4 Adjectives

I follow the general practice in the treatment of adjectives in Quechuan languages and sort SYQ adjectives into two classes: regular adjectives (*puka* 'red') and adverbial adjectives (*sumaq-ta* 'nicely'). An additional class – not native to SYQ nor Quechua generally – may be distinguished: gender adjectives (*kuntinta* 'happy'). All three classes figure towards the end of the stack of potential noun modifiers, all of which precede the noun. Nouns may be modified by demonstratives (**chay** *trakra* 'that field'), quantifiers (**ashlla** *trakra* 'few fields'), numerals (**trunka** *trakra* 'ten fields'), negators (**mana** *trakra-yuq* 'person without fields'), pre-adjectives (**dimas karu** *trakra* 'field too far away'), adjectives (**chaki** *trakra*

3 Substantives

'dry field') and other nouns (*sara trakra* 'corn field'). Where modifiers appear in series, they appear in the order DEM-QUANT-NUM-NEG-preADJ-ADJ-ATR-NUCLEUS (*chay trunka mana dimas chaki sara trakra* 'these ten not-too-dry corn fields').[2]. §§3.2.4.1–3.2.4.4 cover regular adjectives, adverbial adjectives, gender adjectives, and preadjectives. Numeral adjectives are covered in §3.2.5

3.2.4.1 Regular adjectives

The class of regular adjectives includes all adjectives not included in the other two classes (*trawa* 'raw', *putka* 'turbid'). (1–2) give examples. Adjectives are often repeated. The effect is augmentative (*uchuk* 'small' → *uchuk-uchuk* 'very small'). When adjectives are repeated, the last consonant or the last syllable of the first instance is generally elided (*alli-allin* 'very good', *hat-hatun* 'very big').

(1) *Wak pishqu mikukuyan mikunayta – ¡qatra pishqu!* AMV
    wak   pishqu miku-ku-ya-n   miku-na-y-ta   qatra pishqu
    DEM.D   bird   eat-REFL-PROG-3   eat-NMLZ-1-ACC   dirty bird
    'That bird is eating my food – dirty bird!'

(2) *Wak umbruyanñatr mamanta.* **Hat hatun** *kayan.* AMV
    wak   umbru-ya-n-ña-tr   mama-n-ta   hat-hatun
    DEM.D   carry.on.shoulder-PROG-3-DISC-EVC   mother-3-ACC big-big
    ka-ya-n
    be-PROG-3
    'That one would be carrying his mother on his shoulders already – he's really big!'

3.2.4.2 Adverbial adjectives

Adjectives may occur adverbally, in which case they are generally but not necessarily inflected with *-ta* (*quyu* 'ugly' → *quyu-ta* 'awfully'). (1–2) give examples.

---

[2] Analysis and example taken from Parker (1976), confirmed in elicitation

3.2 Substantive classes

(1)   *Aburikurun sakristanqa **wama-wamaqta** kampanata suynachiptin* AMV
      aburi-ku-ru-n   sakristan-qa wama-wamaq-ta   kampana-ta
      annoy-REFL-URGT-3 deacon-TOP   a.lot-a.lot-ACC   bell-ACC
      suyna-chi-pti-n
      sound-CAUS-SUBDS-3
      'The deacon got annoyed that [Lluqi Maki] rang the bell **so much**.'

(2)   *Rupanchikta trurakunchik **qilluta**.* AMV
      rupa-nchik-ta   trura-ku-nchik   qillu-ta.
      clothes-1PL-ACC put-REFL-1PL   yellow-ACC
      'We dress **[in] yellow**.'

3.2.4.3 Gender adjectives

A few adjectives, all borrowed from Spanish, may inflect for gender (masculine /u/ or feminine /a/) (*kuntintu* 'happy', *luka* 'crazy') in case they modify nouns referring to animate male or female individuals, respectively. Some nouns indigenous to SYQ specify the gender of the referent (*masha* 'son-in-law', *llumchuy* 'daughter-in-law') (1).

(1)   ***masha**:pis qalipis walmipis wawi:kunapaq* CH
      masha-:-pis   qali-pis   walmi-pis   wawi-:-kuna-paq
      son.in.law-1-ADD   man-ADD woman-ADD baby-1-PL-GEN
      'my **son-in-law**, too, my children's sons and daughters'

Indeed, some names of family relations specify the gender of both members of the relationship (*wawqi* 'brother of a male', *ñaña* 'sister of a female') (2–4).

(2)   *Wañurachin **wawq**inñataqa, "¡Ama **wawqi**:ta!" niptin.* ACH
      wañu-ra-chi-n   wawqi-n-ña-ta-qa   ama   wawqi-:-ta
      die-URGT-CAUS-3 brother-3-DISC-ACC-TOP PROH brother-1-ACC
      ni-pti-n
      say-SUBDS-3
      'They killed his **brother** when he said, "Don't [kill] my **brother**!"'

(3)   ***Ñaña**ypis turiypis karqam piru wañukunña.* AMV
      ñaña-y-pis   turi-y-pis   ka-rqa-m   piru wañu-ku-n-ña
      sister-1ADD brother-1-ADD be-PST-EVD but   die-REFL-3-DISC
      'I had a **sister** and a **brother**, but they died already.'

57

3 Substantives

(4) *chay **ubihapa wawan**ta chay **karnirupa churin**ta* AMV
    chay   ubiha-pa   wawa-n-ta   chay   karniru-pa   churi-n-ta
    DEM.D sheep-GEN baby-3-ACC DEM.D ram-GEN   child-3-ACC
    'the **baby of that sheep**, the **baby of that ram**'

Where it is necessary to specify the gender of the referent of a noun that does not indicate gender, SYQ modifies that noun with *qari* 'man' or *warmi* 'woman' in the case of people (*warmi wawa* 'daughter' *lit.* 'girl child') and *urqu* 'male' or *trina* 'female' in the case of animals (5), (6).

(5) *"Pagashunñam rigarunanpaqmi. Balikurunki", niwara ya chay **wawi warmi**.* LT
    paga-shun-ña-m   riga-ru-na-n-paq-mi
    pay-1PL.FUT-DISC-EVD   irrigate-URGT-NMLZ-3-PURP-EVD
    bali-ku-ru-nki   ni-wa-ra   ya   chay   wawi
    request.service-REFL-URGT-2 say-1.OBJ-PST EMPH DEM.D baby
    warmi
    woman
    '"We're going to pay already to water. You're going to request someone," my **daughter** said to me.'

(6) *Wak vakanqa watrarusa. ¿Wak **urqu**chu wawan, **trina**chu?* AMV
    wak   vaka-n-qa   watra-ru-sa   wak   urqu-chu   wawa-n
    DEM.D cow-3-TOP   give.birth-URGT-NPST DEM.D male-Q   baby-3
    trina-chu
    female-Q
    'His cow gave birth. Is it a **male** or a **female**?'

3.2.4.4 Preadjectives

Adjectives admit modification by adverbs (1) and nouns functioning adjectivally; the latter are suffixed with *-ta*.

3.2 Substantive classes

(1) *Pasaypaq chanchu sapatu pasaypaq lapi chuku pasaypaqshi ritamun paypis.* LT
    pasaypaq   chanchu sapatu pasaypaq   lapi   chuku pasaypaq-shi
    completely old   shoe   completely old   hat   completely-EVR
    rita-mu-n   pay-pis
    go-CISL-3   he-ADD
    'He, too, went with **totally** old shoes and a **completely** worn hat, they say.'

3.2.5 Numerals

SYQ employs two sets of cardinal numerals. The first is native to Quechua; the second is borrowed from Spanish. The latter is always used for time and almost always for money. Also borrowed from Spanish are the ordinal numerals, *primiru* 'first', *sigundu* 'second', and so on. There is no set of ordinal numerals native to SYQ. §§3.2.5.1–3.2.5.3 cover general numerals, ordinal numerals, and time numerals in turn. §3.2.5.4 and 3.2.5.5 cover numerals inflected for possessive and the special case of *huk* 'one', respectively.

3.2.5.1 General numerals

The set of cardinal numerals native to SYQ includes twelve members: *huk* 'one'; *ishkay* 'two'; *kimsa* 'three'; *tawa* 'four'; *pichqa* 'five'; *suqta* 'six'; *qanchis* 'seven'; *pusaq* 'eight'; *isqun* 'nine'; *trunka* 'ten'; *patrak* 'hundred'; and *waranqa* 'thousand' (1–3).

(1) *Ishkay Wanka samakushqa huk matraypi.* AMV
    ishkay   Wanka   sama-ku-shqa   huk   matray-pi
    two   Huancayoan rest-REFL-NPST   one   cave-LOC
    '**Two** Huancayoans rested in a cave.'

(2) *Kimsa killam kaypaq paranqa.* AMV
    kimsa   killa-m   kay-paq   para-nqa
    three   month-EVD   DEM.P-LOC   rain-3.FUT
    'It's going to rain for **three** months here.'

3 Substantives

(3) Ingañaykun. Chay **waranqa** kwistasantam ... ACH
 ingaña-yku-n   chay   waranqa   kwista-sa-n-ta-m
 cheat-EXCEP-3   DEM.D   thousand   cost-PRF-3-ACC-EVD
 'They cheat them. That which cost one **thousand** ...'

'Twenty', 'thirty' and so on are formed by placing a unit numeral – *ishkay* 'two', *kimsa* 'three', and so on – in attributive construction with *trunka* 'ten' (4).

(4) Riganchik chay sarataqa **ishkay trunka kimsa trunka**
 puntrawniyuqtamá. AMV
 riga-nchik   chay   sara-ta-qa   ishkay   trunka   kimsa   trunka
 irrigate-1PL DEM.D   corn-ACC-TOP two   ten   three   ten
 puntraw-ni-yuq-ta-m-á
 day-EUPH-POSS-ACC-EVD-EMPH
 'We water the corn that's **twenty** or **thirty** days old.'

'Forty-one' and 'forty-two' and so on are formed by adding another unit numeral – *huk* 'one', *ishkay* 'two', and so on – using *-yuq* or, following a consonant, its allomorph, *-ni-yuq* (*ishkay trunka pusaq-ni-yuq* 'twenty-eight') (5).

(5) **Trunka ishkayniyuq**paqpis ruwanchik. AMV
 trunka   ishkay-ni-yuq-paq-pis   ruwa-nchik
 ten   two-EUPH-POSS-ABL-ADD   make-1PL
 'We make them out of **twelve** [strands], too.'

General numerals are ambivalent, and may function as modifiers and as pronouns (6).

(6) **Ishkay**llata apikunaypaq. Shantipa mana kashachu. LT
 ishkay-lla-ta   api-ku-na-y-paq   Shanti-pa   mana
 two-RSTR-ACC   pudding-REFL-NMLZ-1-PURP   Shanti-GEN no
 ka-sha-chu
 be-NPST-NEG
 'Just **two** so I can make pudding. Shanti didn't have any.'

3.2.5.2 Ordinal numerals

SYQ has no native system of ordinal numerals. It borrows the Spanish *primero segundo* and so on (1), (2).

(1) *"Chay mamakuqta siqachinki **primiru** yatrachishunaykipaq", nin.* ACH
chay   mamakuq-ta siqa-chi-nki   primiru
DEM.D old.lady-ACC go.up-CAUS-2   first
yatra-chi-shu-na-yki-paq   ni-n
know-CAUS-3>2-NMLZ-3>2-PURP   say-3
'"Make the old woman go up **first** in order to teach you," they said.'

(2) ***Kwartulla kintulla** manam puchukachiwarqapischu.* AMV
kwartu-lla   kintu-lla   mana-m   puchuka-chi-wa-rqa-pis-chu
fourth-RSTR fifth-RSTR   no-EVD   finish-CAUS-1.OBJ-PST-ADD-NEG
'They had me finish **fourth** [grade], no more, **fifth** [grade], no more.'

The expression *punta-taq* is sometimes employed for 'first' (3).[3]

(3) *Qarinman sirvirun **puntataq** hinashpa kikinpis mikuruntriki.* AMV
qari-n-man   sirvi-ru-n   punta-taq   hinashpa   kiki-n-pis
man-3-ALL   serve-URGT-3   point-SEQ   then   self-3-ADD
miku-ru-n-tri-ki
eat-URGT-3-EVC-KI
'She served her husband [the poisoned tuna] **first** then she herself must have eaten it.'

3.2.5.3 Time numerals and pre-numerals

SYQ makes use of the full set of Spanish cardinal numerals: *unu* 'one', *dus* 'two', *tris* 'three', *kwatru* 'four', *sinku* 'five', *sis* 'six', *siyti* 'seven', *uchu* 'eight', *nuybi* 'nine', *dis* 'ten', and so on. It is this set that is used in telling time. As in Spanish, time numerals are preceded by the pre-numerals *la* or *las* (1).

(1) *Puñukun tuta **a las tris** di la mañanataqa.* AMV
puñu-ku-n   tuta   a   las   tris   di   la   mañana-ta-qa
sleep-REFL-3   night   at   the   three   of   the   morning-ACC-TOP
'He went to sleep at night – at **three** in the morning.'

---

[3] An anonymous reviewer points out that "most Quechuan languages express ordinals by attaching the enclitic *-kaq* to the numeral," as in *ishkay-kaq* 'second', literally 'that which is number two'. "The *-kaq* enclitic derives historically from the copula *ka- plus agentive *-q." This structure is not attested in Yauyos.

3 Substantives

Time expressions are usually suffixed with -ta (*a las dusi-ta* 'at twelve o'clock'):

(2) *Las tris i midyata qaykuruni.* AMV
las tris i midya-ta qayku-ru-ni
the three and middle-ACC corral-URGT-1
'I threw him in the corral **at three thirty**.'

3.2.5.4 Numerals with possessive suffixes

Any numeral, NUM, may be suffixed with any plural possessive suffix – *-nchik*, *-Yki*, or *-n*. These constructions translate 'we/you/they NUM' or 'the NUM of us/you/them' (*kimsanchik* 'we three', 'the three of us') (1).

(1) ***Ishkaynin, kimsan** kashpaqa mikunyá.* AMV
ishkay-ni-n kimsa-n ka-shpa-qa miku-n-yá
two-EUPH-3 three-3 be-SUBIS-TOP eat-3-EMPH
'If there are **two of them** or **three of them**, they eat.'

In the case of *ishkay* this translates 'both of' (2).

(2) ***Ishkayninchik** ripukushun.* AMV
ishkay-ni-nchik ripu-ku-shun
two-EUPH-1PL leave-REFL-1PL.FUT
'Let's go **both of us**.'

huknin translates both 'one of' and 'the other of' (3).

(3) ***Huknin**pis **huknin**pis hinaptin sapalla: witrqarayachin.* ACH
huk-ni-n-pis huk-ni-n-pis hinaptin sapa-lla-:
one-EUPH-3-ADD one-EUPH-3-ADD then alone-RSTR-1
witrqa-ra-ya-chi-n
close-UNINT-INTENS-CAUS-3
'**One of them** then the **other of them** [leaves] and I'm closed in all alone.'

3.2.5.5 *huk*

huk 'one' has several functions in addition to its function as a numeral (1) and numeral adjective (2).

(1) *Pichqa mulla.* **Huk**, *ishkay, kimsa, tawa, pichqa.* CH
    pichqa mulla huk ishkay kimsa tawa pichqa
    five   quota one two   three four five
    'Five quotas [of water]. **One**, two, three, four, five.'

(2) *Achka ... lluqsin* **huk** *pakayllapaq.* AMV
    achka lluqsi-n   huk pakay-lla-paq
    a.lot   come.out-3 one pacay-RSTR-ABL
    'A lot [of seeds] come out of just **one** pacay.'

It may serve both as an indefinite determiner, as in (3) and (4), and as a pronoun, as in (5) and (6).

(3) **Huk** *inhiniyrush rikura. Chay ubsirvaq hinashpash ...* ACH
    huk inhiniyru-sh riku-ra chay ubsirva-q hinashpa-sh
    one engineer-EVR go-PST DEM.D observe-AG then-EVR
    '**An** engineer went. That observer, then, they say ...'

(4) *Hinaptinña* **huk** *atrqay pasan, ismu atrqay.* "**Huk** *turutam pagasayki*". SP
    hinaptin-ña huk atrqay pasa-n, ismu atrqay huk turu-ta-m
    then-DISC one eagle pass-3 grey eagle one bull-ACC-EVD
    paga-sayki
    pay-1>2.FUT
    'Then **an** eagle passed by, a gray eagle. "I'll pay you **a** bull," [said the girl].'

(5) *Puchka: paqarinninta* **huk***ta ruwa: minchanta* **huk***ta.* ACH
    puchka-: paqarin-ni-n-ta   huk-ta   ruwa-:
    spin-1   tomorrow-EUPH-3-ACC one-ACC make-1
    mincha-n-ta   huk-ta
    day.after.tomorrow-3-ACC one-ACC
    'I'll spin tomorrow and make **one**; the day after tomorrow, **another**.'

3 Substantives

(6) *Ayvis lliw chinkarun ayvis **huk**lla ishkayllata tariru:.* ACH
 ayvis lliw chinka-ru-n ayvis huk-lla ishkay-lla-ta
 sometimes all lose-URGT-3 sometimes one-RSTR two-RSTR-ACC
 tari-ru-:
 find-URGT-1
 'Sometimes all get lost; sometimes I find just **one** or two.'

With 'another' interpretation, *huk* may be inflected with plural *-kuna* (7).

(7) *Kikiypaq ruwani **hukkuna**paq ruwani.* AMV
 kiki-y-paq ruwa-ni huk-kuna-paq ruwa-ni
 self-1-BEN make-1 one-PL-BEN make-1
 'I make them for myself and I make them for **others**.'

Suffixed with allative/dative *-man*, it may be interpreted 'different' or 'differently' (8).

(8) *Waytachaypis **hukman** lluqsiruwan ishkay trakiyuqhina lluqsirun.* AMV
 wayta-cha-y-pis huk-man lluqsi-ru-wa-n ishkay
 flower-DIM-1-ADD one-ALL come.out-URGT-1.OBJ-3 two
 traki-yuq-hina lluqsi-ru-n
 foot-POSS-COMP come.out-URGT-3
 'My flower came out **differently** on me. It came out like with two feet.'

3.2.6 Multiple-class substantives

Some substantives are ambivalent. Regular nouns may appear as regular modifiers (1) and adverbial adjectives (2); interrogative pronouns as indefinite and relative pronouns (3); dependent pronouns as unit numerals (4); unit numerals as pronouns (5), (6); and dependent pronouns as adverbs (7) and quantitative (8) adjectives. Table 3.3 gives some examples.

3.2.7 Dummy *na*

na is a dummy noun, standing in for any substantive that doesn't make it off the tip of the speaker's tongue (1), (2).

3.2 Substantive classes

Table 3.3: Multiple-class substantives

(1)	*mishki*	'a sweet', 'sweet'
(2)	*tardi*	'afternoon', 'late'
(3)	*ima*	'thing', 'what', 'that'
(4)	*sapa*	'each' 'one alone'
(5)	*huk*	'one', 'I'
(6)	*ishkay*	'two[stones]' 'two[came]'
(7)	*kuska*	'we/you/they together' 'together'
(8)	*llapa*	'all of us/you/them' 'all'

(1) *Wak **na** lawkunapa Wañupisa. Yanak lawkunapatr.* ACH
    wak   na   law-kuna-pa   Wañupisa Yanak law-kuna-pa-tr
    DEM.D   DMY   side-PL-LOC   Wañupisa Yanak side-PL-LOC-EVC
    'Around that **what-is-it** – Wañupisa. Around Yanak, for sure.'

(2) *Wanqakunchik **na**kta papaktapis uqaktapis. Walmi.* CH
    wanqa-ku-nchik   na-kta   papa-kta-pis   uqa-kta-pis   walmi
    turn-REFL-1PL   DMY-ACC   potato-ACC-ADD oca-ACC-ADD   woman
    'We turn the **what-do-you-call-them** – the potatoes, the oca. [We] women.'

na inflects as does any other substantive – for case (3), number, and possession (4).

(3) *Wak **na**tatr qawanqa hinashpatr rimanqa.* AMV
    wak   na-ta-tr   qawa-nqa   hinashpa-tr   rima-nqa
    DEM.D   DMY-ACC-EVC   see-3.FUT   then-EVC   talk-3.FUT
    'She's going to look at that **thingamajig**, then she'll talk.'

(4) *Waqayan. Uray lawpa apamunki chay **na**nta.* AMV
    waqa-ya-n   uray   law-pa   apa-mu-nki   chay   na-n-ta
    cry-PROG-3 down.hill   side-LOC   bring-CISL-2   DEM.D   DMY-3-ACC
    'He's crying. Bring his **thingy** down there!'

na is ambivalent, serving also as a dummy verb (5).

3 Substantives

(5) *Chaykuna rimanqaña **narushpaqa**.* AMV
 chay-kuna rima-nqa-ña na-ru-shpa-qa
 DEM.D-PL talk-3.FUT-DISC DMY-URGT-SUBIS-TOP
 'They'll talk after **doing that**.'

3.3 Substantive inflection

Substantives in SYQ, as in other Quechuan languages, inflect for person, number and case. This introduction summarizes the more extended discussion to follow.

The substantive ("possessive") person suffixes of SYQ are *-y* (AMV, LT) or *-:* (ACH, CH, SP) (1P), *-Yki* (2P), *-n* (3P), and *-nchik* (1PL) (*mishi-y, mishi-:* 'my cat'; *asnu-yki* 'your donkey'). Table 3.4 below displays this paradigm.

The plural suffix of SYQ is *-kuna* (*urqu-kuna* 'hills').

SYQ has ten case suffixes: comparative *-hina* (*María-hina* 'like María'); limitative *-kama* (*marsu-kama* 'until March'); allative, dative *-man* (*Cañete-man* 'to Cañete'); genitive and locative *-pa* (*María-pa* 'María's' *Lima-pa* 'in Lima'); ablative, benefactive, and purposive *-paq* (*Viñac-paq* 'from Viñac', *María-paq* 'for María,' *qawa-na-n-paq* 'in order for her to see'); locative *-pi* (*Lima-pi* 'in Lima'); exclusive *-puRa* (*amiga-pura* 'among friends'); causative *-rayku* (*María-rayku* 'on account of María'); accusative *-ta* (*María-ta* 'María' (direct object)), and comitative and instrumental *-wan* (*María-wan* 'with María', *acha-wan* 'with an axe'). Table 3.5 below displays this paradigm.

All case marking attaches to the last word in the nominal phrase. When a stem bears suffixes of two or three classes, these appear in the order person-number-case (1), (2).

(1) *¡Blusallay**kuna**ta kayllaman warkurapuway!* AMV
 blusa-lla-y-kuna-ta kay-lla-man warku-ra-pu-wa-y
 blusa-RSTR-1-PL-ACC DEM.P-RSTR-ALL hang-URGT-BEN-1.OBJ-IMP
 'Hang just **my** blouse**s** up just over there for me!'

(2) *Kusasni**nchik**kunallatatr ñitinman.* AMV
 kusas-ni-nchik-kuna-lla-ta-tr ñiti-n-man
 things-EUPH-1PL-PL-RSTR-ACC-EVC crush-3-COND
 'Just **our** things would crush.'

3.3 Substantive inflection

Sections §3.3.1–3.3.3 cover inflection for possession, number and case, respectively. Most case suffixes are mutually exclusive; §3.3.3.2 gives some possible combinations.

3.3.1 Possessive (person)

The possessive suffixes of SYQ are the same in all dialects for all persons except the first-person singular. Two of the five dialects – AMV and LT – follow the QII pattern, marking the first-person singular with *-y*; three dialects – ACH, CH, and SP – follow the QI pattern, marking it with *-:* (vowel length). The SYQ nominal suffixes, then, are: *-y* or *-:* (1P), *-Yki* (2P), *-n* (3P), *-nchik* (1PL). Table 3.4 lists the possessive suffixes.

Table 3.4: Possessive (substantive) suffixes

Person	Singular	Plural
1	-y (AMV, LT) -: (ACH, CH, SP)	-nchik (dual, inclusive) -y (exclusive AMV, LT) -: (exclusive ACH, CH, SP)
2	-Yki	-Yki
3	-n	-n

Stems of the following substantive classes may be suffixed with person suffixes: nouns (*wambra-yki* 'your child') (1), general numerals (*kimsa-nchik* 'the three of us') (2), dependent pronouns (*kiki-n* 'she herself') (3), demonstrative pronouns (*chay-ni-y* 'this of mine') (4) and interrogative-indefinites (5).

(1) *Hinashpaqa pubriqa kutimusa llapa animalninwan wasinman.* AMV
    hinashpa-qa pubri-qa kuti-mu-sa   llapa animal-ni-n-wan
    then-TOP   poor-TOP return-CISL-NPST all   animal-EUPH-3-INSTR
    wasi-n-man
    house-3-ACC
    'Then the poor man returned to **his** house with all **his** animals.'

3 Substantives

(2) *"Kananqa aysashun kay sugawan", nishpa **ishkaynin** aysapa:kun sanqaman.* SP
kanan-qa aysa-shun kay suga-wan ni-shpa ishkay-ni-n
now-TOP pull-1PL DEM.P rope-INSTR say-SUBIS two-EUPH-3
aysa-pa:-ku-n sanqa-man
pull-JTACC-3 ravine-ALL
'"Now we'll pull with this rope," he said and **the two of them** pulled it toward the ravine.'

(3) *Pay **sapallan** hamuyan kay llaqtataqa.* AMV
pay sapa-lla-n hamu-ya-n kay llaqta-ta-qa
she alone-RSTR-3 come-PROG-3 DEM.P town-ACC-TOP
'She's coming to this town **all alone**.'

(4) ***Chaynikita** pristawanki.* AMV
chay-ni-ki-ta prista-wa-nki
DEM.D-EUPH-2-ACC lend-1.OBJ-2
'Lend me that [thing] **of yours**.'

(5) *Manam **mayqinniypis** wañuniraqchu.* AMV
mana-m mayqin-ni-y-pis wañu-ni-raq-chu
no-EVD which-EUPH-1-ADD die-1-CONT-NEG
'**None of us** has died yet.'

In the case of words ending in a consonant, -*ni* – semantically vacuous – precedes the person suffix (6).

(6) *¿**Maynintapis** ripunqañatr? Gallu Rumi altuntapis ripunqañatr.* AMV
may-ni-n-ta-pis ripu-nqa-ña-tr Gallu Rumi
where-EUPH-3-ACC-ADD go-3.FUT-DISC-EVC Cock Rock
altu-n-ta-pis ripu-nqa-ña-tr
high-3-ACC-ADD go-3.FUT-DISC-EVC
'**Where abouts** will he go? He'll go up above Gallu Rumi, for sure.'

The third person possessive suffix, -*n*, attaching to *may* 'where' and other expressions of place, forms an idiomatic expression interpretable as 'via' or 'around' (7).

3.3 Substantive inflection

(7) *Hamuyaq **kayninta**.* AMV
    hamu-ya-q   kay-ni-n-ta
    come-PROG-AG   DEM.P-EUPH-3-ACC
    'He used to be coming **around here**.'

In the first person singular, the noun *papa* 'father' inflects *papa-ni-y* to refer to one's biological or social father, (8).[4]

(8) *Vikuñachayta diharuni **papaniywan**.* AMV
    vikuña-cha-y-ta   diha-ru-ni   papa-ni-y-wan
    vicuña-DIM-1-ACC   leave-URGT-1   father-EUPH-1-INSTR
    'I left my little vicuña with **my father**.'

SYQ possessive constructions are formed SUBSTANTIVE-POSS *ka-* (**allqu-n ka-rqa** 'she had a dog' (lit. 'her dog was')) (9)(10).

(9) *Mana **wambrayki kan**chu mana **qariyki kan**chu.* ACH
    mana wambra-yki ka-n-chu mana qari-yki ka-n-chu
    no   child-2   be-3-NEG no   man-2   be-3-NEG
    '**You** don't **have children** and **you** don't **have a husband**.'

Finally, possessive suffixes attach to the subordinating suffix *-pti* as well as to the nominalizing suffixes *-na* and *-sa* to form subordinate (10), purposive (11), complement (12), and relative (13), (14) clauses.

(10) ***Yasqayaruptiki** mana pinikipis kanqachu.* ACH
     yasqa-ya-ru-pti-ki   mana pi-ni-ki-pis   ka-nqa-chu
     old-INCH-URGT-SUBDS-2   no   who-EUPH-2-ADD   be-3.FUT-NEG
     '**When you're old**, you won't have anyone.'

(11) ***Hampikunaykipaq** yatranki.* AMV
     hampi-ku-na-yki-paq   yatra-nki
     cure-REFL-NMLZ-2-PURP   know-2
     'You'll learn **so that you can cure**.'

---

[4] An anonymous reviewer writes, "As a loan word, most Central Quechuan languages have *papa:* with final vowel length (reinterpretation of final accent in Spanish '*papá*'). As such, *-ni* is required before a syllable-closing suffix, such as *-y*. Though *papa* does not end in a long vowel in SYQ, it probably did at one time, and the effect is retained."

3 Substantives

(12) **Atipasantatriki** ruwan. ACH
 atipa-sa-n-ta-tri-ki   ruwa-n
 be.able-PRF-3-ACC-EVC-KI make-3
 'They do **what they can**.'

(13) Chay wawqin ama **nisantas** wañuchisataq. ACH
 chay   wawqi-n   ama   ni-sa-n-ta-s   wañu-chi-sa-taq
 DEM.D brother-3 PROH say-PRF-3-ACC-ADD die-CAUS-NPST-SEQ
 'They also killed his brother **who said "No!"**'

(14) Truraykun frutachankunata – llapa **gustasan**. AMV
 trura-yku-n   fruta-cha-n-kuna-ta llapa gusta-sa-n
 save-EXCEP-3 fruit-DIM-3-PL-ACC   all   like-PRF-3
 'They put out their fruit and all – everything **they liked**.'

3.3.2 Number -*kuna*

-*kuna* pluralizes regular nouns, as in (1), where it affixes to *kabra* 'goat' to form *kabra-kuna* 'goats'.

(1) **Kabrakuna**ta hapishpa mikukuyan. AMV
 kabra-kuna-ta hapi-shpa miku-ku-ya-n
 goat-PL-ACC   grab-SUBIS eat-REFL-PROG-3
 'Taking ahold of the **goats**, [the puma] is eating them.'

-*kuna* also pluralizes the personal pronouns *ñuqa*, *qam*, and *pay* (2), demonstrative pronouns (3), and interrogative-indefinites (4).

(2) Awanmi **paykuna**pisriki. AMV
 awa-n-mi   pay-kuna-pis-r-iki
 weave-3-EVD he-PL-ADD-R-IKI
 '**They**, too, weave.'

(3) **Chaykuna**pa algunusqa pamparayan. AMV
 chay-kuna-pa algunus-qa   pampa-ra-ya-n
 DEM.D-PL-LOC some.people-TOP bury-UNINT-INTENS-3
 'Some people are buried in **those**.'

3.3 Substantive inflection

(4) *¿Imakunam ubihaykipa sutin?* AMV
   ima-kuna-m ubiha-yki-pa suti-n
   what-PL-EVD sheep-2-GEN name-3
   '**What** are your sheep's names?'

-kuna follows the stem and possessive suffix, if any, and precedes the case suffix, if any (5).

(5) *Chamisninkunata upyarin kukankunata akun.* AMV
   chamis-ni-n-kuna-ta   upya-ri-n   kuka-n-kuna-ta aku-n
   chamis-EUPH-3-PL-ACC drink-INCEP-3 coca-3-PL-ACC chew-3
   'They drink **their chamis** and they chew **their coca**.'

Number-marking in SYQ is optional. Noun phrases introduced by numerals or quantifying adjectives generally are not inflected with *-kuna* (6).

(6) *Ishkay yatrarqa, ishkay warmi.* AMV
   ishkay yatra-rqa ishkay warmi
   two   live-PST two   woman
   '**Two** lived [there], **two** women.'

-kuna may receive non-plural interpretations and, like *-ntin*, may indicate accompaniment or non-exhaustivity (7).[5]

(7) *Chay kwirpuykikuna mal kanman umaykikuna nananman.* AMV
   chay   kwirpu-yki-kuna mal ka-n-man   uma-yki-kuna nana-n-man
   DEM.D body-2-PL   bad be-3-COND head-2-PL   hurt-3-COND
   '**Your whole body** could be not well; **your head and everything** could hurt.'

Finally, words borrowed from Spanish already inflected for plural – i.e., with Spanish plural *s* – are generally still suffixed with *-kuna* (*cosas* → *kusas-ni-nchik-kuna*) (8).

---

[5] This example is, in fact, ambiguous between as reading in which *-kuna* receives a non-plural interpretation and one in which it simply pluralizes the possessed item. Thus, *kwirpu-y-kuna* could also refer to 'your (plural) bodies', as an anonymous reviewer points out.

3 Substantives

(8) *Qayashpa waqashpa purin animali**sninchikuna**qa.* AMV
    qaya-shpa   waqa-shpa-m   puri-n   animalis-ni-nchik-kuna-qa
    scream-SUBIS cry-SUBIS-EVD walk-3   animals-EUPH-1PL-PL-TOP
    'Our animals walk around screaming, crying.'

3.3.3 Case

A set of ten suffixes constitutes the case system of SYQ. Table 3.5 gives glossed examples. These are: *-hina* (comparative), *-kama* (limitative), *-man* (allative, dative), *-pa/-pi* (genitive, locative), *-paq* (ablative, benefactive, purposive), *-puRa* (exclusive), *-rayku* (reason), *-ta* (accusative), and *-wan* (comitative, instrumental). Genitive, instrumental and allative/dative may specify noun-verb in addition to noun-noun relations. *-pa* is the default form for the locative, but *-pi* is often and *-paq* is sometimes used. The CH dialect uses a fourth form, *-traw*, common to the QI languages. The CH dialect is also unique among the five in its realization of accusative *-ta* as *-kta* after a short vowel. *-puRa* – attested only in Viñac – and *-rayku* are employed only rarely. The genitive and accusative may form adverbs (*tuta-pa* 'at night', *allin-ta* 'well'). Instrumental *-wan* may coordinate NPs (*llama-wan alpaka-wan* 'the llama and the alpaca'). All case processes consist in adding a suffix to the last word in the nominal group. Most case suffixes are mutually exclusive. §3.3.3.1–3.3.3.12 cover each of the case suffixes in turn.

3.3.3.1 Simulative *-hina*

The simulative *-hina* generally indicates resemblance or comparison (*yawar-**hi**-**na*** 'like blood') (1– 7).

(1) *Ñawilla: pukayarura tutal puka. Yawar**hina** ñawi: kara.* ACH
    ñawi-lla-:   puka-ya-ru-ra   total   puka   yawar-hina ñawi-:
    eye-RSTR-1   red-INCH-URGT-PST   completely red   blood-COMP eye-1
    ka-ra
    be-PST
    'My eyes turned red, totally red. My eyes were **like** blood.'

(2) *Karsilpa**hina**m. Witrqamara wambra:kuna istudyaq pasan.* ACH
    karsil-pa-hina-m   witrqa-ma-ra   wambra-:-kuna   istudya-q   pasa-n
    prison-LOC-COMP   close.in-1.OBJ-PST   child-1-PL   study-AG   pass-3
    'It was **like** in prison. When my children went to school, they closed me in.'

3.3 Substantive inflection

Table 3.5: Case suffixes with examples

-hina	comparative	Runa-**hina**, uyqa-**hina**	'**Like** people, **like** sheep'
-kama	limitative	Fibriru marsu-**kama**-raq-tri para-nqa.	'It will rain still **until** February or march.'
-man	allative, dative	Lima runa-kuna traya-mu-pti-n siyra-n-**man**.	'When people from Lima return **to** their sierra.'
-pa₁	genitive	Algunus-**pa** puchka-n tipi-ku-ya-n-mi.	'Some people**'s** thread breaks on them.'
-pa₂	locative	Urqu-lla-**pa**-m chay-qa wiña-n.	'It grows only **in** the mountains.'
-pi	locative	Yana-ya-sa qutra-pa pata-n-**pi** qutra-pa tuna-n-**pi**.	'Blackened **on** the banks of the lake, **in** the corner of the lake.'
-paq₁	ablative	Huangáscar-**paq**-mi hamu-ra wama-wamaq polisiya-pis.	'Lots of policemen came **from** Huangáscar.'
-paq₂	benefactive	Chay qari-kuna mana ishpa-y-ta atipa-q-**paq**.	'This is **for** the men who can't urinate.'
-paq₃	purposive	Qawa-na-y-**paq** ima-wan wañu-ru-n … kitra-ni.	'**In order to** see what he died from … I opened him up.'
-puRa	reciprocal	Qam pay-wan wawqi ñaña-**pura** ka-nki.	'You and she are going to be true brothers and sisters.'
-rayku	reason	Chawa-shi-q lichi-lla-n-rayku ri-y-man-tri.	'I might go help milk **on account of** her milk.'
-ta	accusative	¿Maqta-kuna-**ta** pusha-nki icha pashña-**ta**?	'Are you going to take the boys or the girl?'
-wan₁	comitative	¿Imapaq-mi wak kundinaw-**wan** puri-ya-nki?	'Why are you walking around **with** that zombie?'
-wan₂	instrumental	Ichu-**wan**-mi chay-ta ruwa-nchik.	'We make this one **with** straw.'

in Cacra-Hongos dialect only:

-Kta   replaces *-ta* to mark accusative
-traw alternates with *-pa* and *-pi* to mark the locative

(3) *Trakin, ishkaynin trakin kayan maniyasha**hina**.* LT
    traki-n, ishkay-ni-n traki-n ka-ya-n   maniya-sha-hina
    foot-3   two-EUPH-3   foot-3   be-PROG-3 bind.feet-PRF-COMP
    'His feet, it's **like** both are shackled.'

3 Substantives

(4) *Wak**hina**llam purikuni. ¿Imanashaqmi?* LT
wak-hina-lla-m   puri-ku-ni ima-na-shaq-mi
DEM.D-COMP-RSTR-EVD walk-REFL-1 what-VRBZ-1.FUT-EVD
'Just **like** that I go about. What am I going to do?'

(5) *Huk rumi kayan warmi**hina**. Chaypish inkantara unay unay.* SP
huk rumi ka-ya-n warmi-hina chay-pi-sh inkanta-ra
one stone be-PROG-3 woman-COMP DEM.D-LOC-EVR enchant-PST
unay unay
before before
'There's a stone **like** [in the form of] a woman. A long, long time ago, it bewitched [people] there, they say.'

(6) *Tutakuna puriyan qarqarya**hina**.* AMV
tuta-kuna puri-ya-n qariya-hina
night-PL walk-PROG-3 zombie-COMP
'At night, he walks around like a zombie.'

(7) *Kay**hina**kunachatam (=kay**hina**chakunatam) ruwani.* AMV
kay-hina-kuna-cha-ta-m (=kay-hina-cha-kuna-ta-m) ruwa-ni
DEM.P-COMP-PL-DIM-ACC-EVD DEM.P-COMP-DIM-PL-ACC-EVD make-1
'I make all of them just **like** this.'

It can generally be translated 'like'. In Cacra and sometimes in Hongos, *-mish* is employed in place of *-hina* (8), (9).

(8) *Kilun paqwalun. Mikuyta atipanchu. Awila**mish**.* CH
kilu-n paqwa-lu-n   miku-y-ta atipa-n-chu
tooth-3 finish.off-URGT-3 eat-INF-ACC be.able-3-NEG
awila-mish
grandmother-COMP
'Her teeth finished off. He can't eat. **Like** an old lady.'

(9) *¿Ima**mish** wawipaq takin?* CH
ima-mish wawi-paq taki-n
what-COMP baby-GEN song-3
'What is a baby's song **like**?'

3.3 Substantive inflection

3.3.3.2 Limitative -*kama*

The limitative -*kama* – sometimes realized as *kaman* – generally indicates a limit in space (1), (2) or time (3–5).

(1) *Qatimushaq vakata kaykama.* AMV
    qati-mu-shaq   vaka-ta   kay-kama
    follow-CISL-1.FUT cow-ACC   DEM.P-LIM
    'I'm going to drive the cows **over** here.'

(2) *Chay wambraykita katrarunki mayurnikikama wawqikikamaqa.* LT
    chay   wambra-yki-ta   katra-ru-nki   mayur-ni-ki-kama
    DEM.D   child-2-ACC   release-URGT-2   eldest-EUPH-2-ALL
    wawqi-ki-kama-qa
    brother-2-ALL-TOP
    'You sent your children **over to** your older brother, **over to** your brother.'

(3) *Fibriru marsukamaraqtri paranqa.* AMV
    fibriru   marsu-kama-raq-tri   para-nqa
    February   March-LIM-CONT-EVC   rain-3.FUT
    'It will rain still until February or March.'

(4) *¿Imaykama kanki?* AMV
    imay-kama   ka-nki
    when-LIM   be-2
    '**Until** when are you going to be (here)?'

(5) *Kandawniypis warkurayan altupam. Manam kanankamapis trurachinichu.* LT
    kandaw-ni-y-pis   warku-raya-n   altu-pa-m   mana-m
    padlock-EUPH-1-ADD   hang-PASS-3   high-LOC-EVD   no-EVD
    kanan-kama-pis   trura-chi-ni-chu
    now-LIM-ADD   put-CAUS-1-NEG
    'My padlock, too, is hung up there. **Until** now I haven't had it put on.'

In case time is delimited by an event, the usual structure is STEM-NMLZ-POSS-*kama* (*puri-na-yki-kama* ('so you can walk') (6), (7).

3 Substantives

(6) *Traki paltanchikpis pushllunan**kama** purinchik. Trakipis ampulla hatarinan**kaman** rirqani.* AMV
traki palta-nchik-pis pushllu-na-n-kama puri-nchik traki-pis
foot sole-1PL-ADD blister-NMLZ-3-ALL walk-1PL foot-ADD
ampulla hatari-na-n-kaman ri-rqa-ni
blister get.up-NMLZ-3-ALL go-PST-1
'We walked **while** blisters formed on the souls of our feet. I went **while** blisters came up on my feet.'

(7) *Apuraw mikunan**kama** turuqa kayna tuksirikusa.* SP
apuraw miku-na-n-kama turu-qa kayna tuksi-ri-ku-sa
quickly eat-NMLZ-3-ALL bull-TOP thus prick-INCEP-REFL-NPST
'**Until** the bull ate quickly, she pricked him like this.'

-kama can appear simultaneously with *asta* (*Sp. hasta* 'up to', 'until') (8).

(8) *San Jerónimopaq **asta** kay**kama**.* AMV
San Jerónimo-paq asta kay-kama
San Jerónimo-ABL until DEM.P-ALL
'From San Jerónino **to** here.'

-kama can form distributive expressions: in this case, *-kama* attaches to the quality or characteristic that is distributed (9), (10). In case it indicates a limit, *-kama* can usually be translated as 'up to' or 'until'; in case it indicates distribution, it can usually be translated as 'each'.

(9) *Uñachayuq**kama** kayan.* AMV
uña-cha-yuq-kama ka-ya-n
calf-DIM-POSS-ALL be-PROG-3
'They **all [each]** have their little **young**.'

(10) *Trayaramun arman qipikusa**kama**. Manchaku:.* ACH
traya-ra-mu-n arma-n qipi-ku-sa-kama mancha-ku-:
arrive-URGT-CISL-3 weapon-3 carry-REFL-PRF-ALL scare-REFL-1
'They arrived **each** carrying weapons. I got scared.'

3.3 Substantive inflection

3.3.3.3 Allative, dative *-man*

The allative and dative (directional) *-man* generally indicates movement toward a point (1), (2) or the end-point of movement or action more generally (3), (4).

(1) *Qiñwal**man** trayarachiptiki wañukunman.* AMV
     qiñwal-man   traya-ra-chi-pti-ki   wañu-ku-n-man
     quingual.grove-ALL arrive-URGT-CAUS-SUBDS-2 die-REFL-3-COND
     'If you make her go **to** the quingual grove, she could die.'

(2) *Hinashpa chaypaq wichay**man** pasachisa chay Amador kaq**man**ñataq.* ACH
     hinashpa chay-paq   wichay-man   pasa-chi-sa   chay   Amador
     then   DEM.D-ABL   up.hill-ALL pass-CAUS-NPST DEM.D   Amador
     ka-q-man-ña-taq
     be-AG-ALL-DISC-SEQ
     'Then, from there they made them go up high **to** Don Amador's place.'

(3) *Wak wasikuna**man**shi yaykurun kundinawqa.* SP
     wak   wasi-kuna-man-shi   yayku-ru-n   kundinaw-qa
     DEM.D   house-PL-ALL-EVR   enter-URGT-3   zombie-TOP
     'The zombie entered those houses, they say.'

(4) *"¿Kabrata qaqa**man** imapaq qarquranki?" nishpa.* SP
     kabra-ta   qaqa-man   ima-paq   qarqu-ra-nki   ni-shpa
     goat-ACC   cliff-ALL   what-PURP   toss-PST-2   say-SUBIS
     '"Why did you let the goats loose **onto** the cliff?" he said.'

It may function as a dative, indicating a non-geographical goal (5), (6).

(5) *Pashñaqa quykurusa mushuqta watakurusa chumpita wiqawnin**man**.* AMV
     pashña-qa   qu-yku-ru-sa   mushuq-ta   wata-ku-ru-sa
     girl-TOP   give-EXCEP-URGT-NPST   new-ACC   tie-REFL-URGT-NPST
     chumpi-ta   wiqaw-ni-n-man
     sash-ACC   waist-EUPH-3-ALL
     'The girl gave [the young man] a sash, a new one, and she tied it **around** his waist.'

3 Substantives

(6) *Chay lliw lliw listamanshi trurara. Chay listaman trurasan rikura.* ACH
chay   lliw lliw lista-man-shi   trura-ra   chay   lista-man   trura-sa-n
DEM.D all all list-ALL-EVR   put-PST   DEM.D list-ALL   put-PRF-3
riku-ra
go-PST
'[The Shining Path] put everyone **on** the list. Those who were put **on** the list left.'

With verbs of giving, it marks the recipient (7), (8); with verbs of communication, the person receiving the communication (9), (10).

(7) *¿Imatataq qunki kay pubriman?* AMV
ima-ta-taq   qu-nki   kay   pubri-man
what-ACC-SEQ   give-2   DEM.P   poor.person-ALL
'What are you going to give **to** this poor man?'

(8) *¿Urquman qapishuptiki imatataq qaranki?* AMV
urqu-man   qapi-shu-pti-ki   ima-ta-taq   qara-nki?
hill-ALL   grab-3>1-SUBDS-3>1   what-ACC-SEQ   serve-2
'What are you going to serve **to** the hill when it grabs you?'

(9) *Chayshi mamanman willakun.* AMV
chay-shi   mama-n-man   willa-ku-n
DEM.D-EVR   mother-3-ALL   tell-REFL-3
'With that, she told her mother.'

(10) *Chayllapaq willakurusa tirruristaman hinaptin chayta wañurachin.* ACH
chay-lla-paq   willa-ku-ru-sa   tirrurista-man   hinaptin
DEM.D-RSTR-ABL   tell-REFL-URGT-NPST   terrorist-ALL   then
chay-ta   wañu-ra-chi-n
DEM.D-ACC   die-URGT-CAUS-3
'So they told it **to** the terrorists and then they killed him.'

It may indicate a very approximate time specification (11).

(11) *Trayanqa sabaduman.* AMV
traya-nqa   sabadu-man
arrive-3.FUT   Saturday-ALL
'She'll arrive **on** Saturday [**or around there**].'

3.3 Substantive inflection

With verbs indicating change of state, quantity or number, it may indicate the result or extent of change (12), (13).

(12) *Pasaypaq runapaq kunvirtirun kabra**man**.* LT
pasaypaq   runa-paq   kunvirti-ru-n   kabra-man
completely person-ABL convert-URGT-3 goat-ALL
'Completely, from people they **turned into** goats.'

(13) *Wiñarun hatun**man**.* AMV
wiña-ru-n   hatun-man
grow-URGT-3 big-ALL
'She grew tall.'

It may also indicate the goal in the sense of purpose of movement (14), (15). It can usually be translated as 'to', 'toward'.

(14) *Karu karum. ¿Imaynataq, ima**man**taq hamuranki?* AMV
karu   karu-m   imayna-taq   ima-man-taq   hamu-ra-nki
far   far-EVD   how-SEQ   what-ALL-SEQ   come-PST-2
'Very far. How, **for** what did you come?'

(15) *Chaypaq rishaq wak animalniy**man** wak infirmuykuna**man**.* LT
chay-paq   ri-shaq   wak   animal-ni-y-man   wak
DEM.D-ABL go-1.FUT DEM.D animal-EUPH-Y-ALL DEM.D
infirmu-y-kuna-man
sick.person-1-PL-LL
'I'm going to go **to** my animals and **to** my sick [husband] and all.'

3.3.3.4 Genitive, locative -*pa₁*, -*pa₂*

As a genitive, -*pa* indicates possession (1), (2); it is often paired with possessive inflection (3), (4).

(1) *Runa**pa** umallaña trakillaña kayashqa.* AMV
runa-pa   uma-lla-ña   traki-lla-ña   ka-ya-shqa
person-GEN head-RSTR-DISC leg-RSTR-DISC be-PROG-NPST
'There was only the head and the hand **of** the person.'

3 Substantives

(2) ¿Imaynataq qam**pa** trakikiqa kayan qillu qillucha? SP
imayna-taq qam-pa traki-ki-qa ka-ya-n qillu qillu-cha
how-SEQ you-GEN foot-2-TOP be-PROG-3 yellow yellow-DIM
'How are **your** feet nice and yellow?'

(3) Manañam mirañnachu ganawninqa pay**pa**qa. AMV
mana-ña-m mira-n-ña-chu ganaw-ni-n-qa pay-pa-qa
no-DISC-EVD reproduce-3-DISC-NEG cattle-EUPH-3-TOP he-GEN-TOP
'**His** animals no longer reproduce.'

(4) Puchkanchik. Vakata harkanchik vaka**pa** qipanpa millwinchik. AMV
puchka-nchik vaka-ta harka-nchik vaka-pa qipa-n-pa
spin-1PL cow-ACC herd-1PL cow-GEN behind-3-LOC
millwi-nchik
wool-1PL
'We spin. We herd the cows and **behind** the cows, we [twist] our yarn.'

As a locative, *-pa* indicates temporal (5) and spatial location (6–9).

(5) Manam biranu**pa**hinachu. AMV
mana-m biranu-pa-hina-chu
no-EVD summer-LOC-COMP-NEG
'Not like **in** summer.'

(6) Trabahu: may**pa**pis may**pa**pis. ACH
trabahu-: may-pa-pis may-pa-pis
work-1 where-LOC-ADD where-LOC-ADD
'I work **where**ever, **where**ever.'

(7) Fila**pa** trurakurun mana hukllachu. AMV
fila-pa trura-ku-ru-n mana huk-lla-chu
line-LOC put-REFL-URGT-3 no one-RSTR-NEG
'They put themselves **in** a line – not just one.'

3.3 Substantive inflection

(8) *Iskwila**pa**m niytu:kunaqa wawa:kunaqa rinmi. ñuqallam ka:
analfabitu.* SP
iskwila-pa-m   niytu-:-kuna-qa   wawa-:-kuna-qa   ri-n-mi
school-LOC-EVD nephew-1-PL-TOP   baby-1-PL-TOP   go-3-EVD
ñuqa-lla-m ka-: analfabitu
I-RSTR-EVD be-1 illiterate
'My grandchildren and my children are **in** school. Only I am illiterate.'

(9) *Takllawan haluyanchik chay**pa**qa. Uqa trakla. Yakuwan ichashpa
chay**pa**qa.* CH
taklla-wan   halu-ya-nchik   chay-pa-qa   uqa   trakla yaku-wan
plow-INSTR   plow-PROG-1PL   DEM.D-LOC-TOP   oca   field   water-INSTR
icha-shpa   chay-pa-qa
toss-SUBIS   DEM.D-LOC-TOP
'We're plowing with a [foot] plow **in** there. The oca fields. Adding water **in** there.'

In all dialects, *-paq* is often used in place of *-pa* and *-pi* as both a locative (10) and genitive (11); in the CH dialect, *-traw* is used in addition to *-pa* and *-pi* as a locative (12), (13). As a genitive, *-pa* can usually be translated 'of' or with a possessive pronoun; as a locative, it can usually translated 'in' or 'on'.

(10) *Dimunyum chayqa. Chay ... altu rumi**paq** ukun**paq** yatran.* ACH
Dimunyu-m   chay-qa   chay   altu rumi-paq   uku-n-paq
Devil-EVD   DEM.D-TOP   DEM.D   high stone-LOC   inside-3-LOC
yatra-n
live-3
'It was a devil. It ... lives **in** the stone up **inside** it.'

(11) *¿Ima pay**paq** huchan? Qaykuruptinqa hawkam sayakun uñankunata
fwiraman diharuptinchik.* AMV
ima   pay-paq   hucha-n   qayku-ru-pti-n-qa   hawka-m
what   she-GEN   fault-3   corral-URGT-SUBDS-3-TOP tranquil-EVD
saya-ku-n   uña-n-kuna-ta   fwira-man   diha-ru-pti-nchik
stand-REFL-3   calf-3-PL-ACC   outside-ALL   leave-URGT-SUBDS-1PL
'What fault is it **of her**s? When you toss her into the corral, she stands there calmly when we leave her babies outside.'

81

3 Substantives

(12) *Pusta**traw**shi chay mutu.* CH
pusta-traw-shi chay mutu
clinic-LOC-EVR DEM.D motorcycle
'That motorcycle **is in** the health clinic.'

(13) *Ñuqakunaqa fayna**traw**mi kaya:.* CH
ñuqa-kuna-qa fayna-traw-mi ka-ya-:
I-PL-TOP community.work.day-LOC-EVD be-PROG-1
'We're **in** the middle of community work days.'

(14) *Chaytam nin kichwa**pa**: "Wichayman qatishaq".* AMV
chay-ta-m ni-n kichwa-pa wichay-man qati-shaq
DEM.D-ACC-EVD say-3 Quechua-LOC up.hill-ALL follow-1.FUT
'They say that **in** Quechua: "I'll herd it up hill."'

3.3.3.5 Ablative, benefactive, purposive -*paq*

As an ablative, -*paq* indicates provenance in space (1–3) or time (4), (5); origin or cause (6), (7); or the material of which an item is made (8), (9).

(1) *¿Imaytaq llaqtayki**paq** lluqsimulanki?* CH
imay-taq llaqta-yki-paq lluqsi-mu-la-nki
when-SEQ town-2-ABL go.out-CISL-PST-2
'When did you go out **from** your country?'

(2) *Kusta**paq** altuta siqaptinchik umanchik nanan.* AMV
kusta-paq altu-ta siqa-pti-nchik uma-nchik nana-n
coast-ABL high-ACC go.up-SUBDS-1PL head-1PL hurt-3
'When we come up **from** the coast, our heads hurt.'

(3) *"¿May**paq**taqmi suwamuranki?" nishpa.* LT
may-paq-taq-mi suwa-mu-ra-nki ni-shpa
where-ABL-SEQ-EVD steal-CISL-PST-2 say-SUBIS
'"Where did you steal it **from**?" he said.'

3.3 Substantive inflection

(4) *Uchuklla kasa:**paq**.* ACH
    uchuk-lla   ka-sa-:-paq
    small-RSTR   be-PRF-1-ABL
    '**From** [the time when] I was little.'

(5) *Kanan**paq** riqsinakushun.* CH
    kanan-paq   riqsi-naku-shun
    now-ABL   know-RECIP-1PL.FUT
    '**From** now on, we're going to get to know each other.'

(6) *Chay huk walmitaqa talilushpaqa apalunñam uspitalman. Pasaypaq mikuy**paq** alalay**paq**, ¿aw?* CH
    chay   huk   walmi-ta-qa   tali-lu-shpa-qa
    DEM.D   one   woman-ACC-TOP   find-URGT-SUBIS-TOP
    apa-lu-n-ña-m   uspital-man   pasaypaq   miku-y-paq
    bring-URGT-3-DISC-EVD   hospital-ALL completely   eat-INF-ABL
    alala-y-paq   aw
    cold-INF-ABL   yes
    'When they found the other woman they brought her to the hospital – completely [sick] **from** hunger and cold, no?'

(7) *Wambray lichi**paq**, kisu**paq** waqaptin ñuqa rikurani urquta.* LT
    wambra-y   lichi-paq,   kisu-paq   waqa-pti-n   ñuqa   riku-ra-ni
    child-ACC   milk-ABL   cheese-ABL   cry-SUBDS-3   I   go-PST-1
    urqu-ta
    hill-ACC
    'When my children cried **for** [because they had no] milk or cheese, I went to the hill.'

(8) *Llikllakuna, punchukuna, puñunakuna, ruwa: lliw lliw imatapis ruwa: kay**paq**mi, kay millwa**paq**mi.* ACH
    lliklla-kuna, punchu-kuna,   puñu-na-kuna   ruwa-:   lliw   lliw
    shawl-PL   poncho-PL   sleep-NMLZ-PL   make-1   all   all
    ima-ta-pis   ruwa-:   kay-paq-mi   kay   millwa-paq-mi
    what-ACC-ADD   make-1   DEM.P-ABL-EVD   DEM.P   wool-ABL-EVD
    'Shawls, ponchos, blankets – everything, everything I make **from** this, **from** this yarn.'

3 Substantives

(9) *Ayvis ruwani wiqa**paq** uviha**paq**.* AMV
    ayvis   ruwa-ni   wiqa-paq   uviha-paq
    sometimes   make-1   twisted.wool-ABL   sheep-ABL
    'Sometimes I make them **out of** twisted wool, **out of** sheep's wool.'

As a benefactive, *-paq* indicates the individual who benefits from – or suffers as a result of – an event (10).

(10) *Chay allin chay qarikuna mana ishpayta atipaq**paq**.* AMV
     chay   allin   chay   qari-kuna   mana   ishpa-y-ta
     DEM.D   good   DEM.D   man-PL   no   urinate-INF-ACC
     atipa-q-paq
     be.able-AG-BEN
     'This is good **for** men who can't urinate.'

As a purposive, *-paq* indicates the purpose of an event (11), (12).

(11) *Quni quni plantam chayqa. Chiri**paq**mi allin.* AMV
     quni   quni   planta-m   chay-qa   chiri-paq-mi   allin
     warm   warm   plant-EVD   DEM.D-TOP   cold-PURP-EVD   good
     'This plant is really warm. It's good **for** (fighting) the cold.'

(12) *Qawanay**paq** imawan wañurun nishpa kitrani.* AMV
     qawa-na-y-paq   ima-wan   wañu-ru-n   ni-shpa   kitra-ni
     see-NMLZ-1-PURP   what-INSTR   die-URGT-3   say-SUBIS   open-1
     '"**To** see what he died from, I said, and I opened him up.'

-paq may also alternate with *-pa* and *-pi* to indicate the genitive (13) or locative (14), (15).

(13) *Manam kanchu ñuqa**paq** puchukarun.* AMV
     mana-m   ka-n-chu   ñuqa-paq   puchuka-ru-n
     no-EVD   be-3-NEG   I-GEN   finish-URGT-3
     'There aren't any – **mine** are all finished up.'

(14) *Asnu alla-allita atuq wataku kunka**paq** traki**paq** sugawan watarun.* SP
     asnu   alla-alli-ta   atuq   wata-ku-n   kunka-paq   traki-paq
     donkey   a.lot-a.lot-ACC   fox   tie-REFL-3   throat-ABL   foot-ABL
     suga-wan   wata-ru-n
     rope-INSTR   tie-URGT-3

84

3.3 Substantive inflection

'The fox tied the donkey up really well. He tied him up with a rope **on** his neck and **on** his foot.'

(15) *Kay llaqta**paq** kundinawmi lliw lliw runata puchukayan.* AMV
 kay llaqta-paq kundinaw-mi lliw lliw runa-ta puchuka-ya-n
 DEM.D town-LOC zombie-EVD all all person-ACC finish-PROG-3
 '**In** this town, a zombie is finishing off all the people.'

-paq also figures in a number of fixed expressions (16), (17).

(16) ***Pasaypaq** uyqaytapis puchukarun. ¿Imatataq mikushaq?* AMV
 pasaypaq uyqa-y-ta-pis puchuka-ru-n ima-ta-taq
 completely sheep-1-ACC-ADD finish-URGT-3 what-ACC-SEQ
 miku-shaq
 eat-1.FUT
 'My sheep are **completely** finished. What will I eat?'

(17) *Kuyaylla**paq** waqakuyan yutuqa, kuyakuylla**paq** chay waychawwan yutuqa.* SP
 kuya-y-lla-paq waqa-ku-ya-n yutu-qa kuya-ku-y-lla-paq
 love-INF-RSTR-ABL cry-REFL-PROG-3 partridge-TOP love-REFL-INF-ABL
 chay waychaw-wan yutu-qa
 DEM.D waychaw.bird-INSTR partridge-TOP
 'The partridge is singing beautiful**ly**. The *waychaw* and the partridge [sing] beautiful**ly**.'

Suffixed to the distal demonstrative *chay*, *-paq* indicates a close temporal or causal connection between two events, translating 'then' or 'so' (18).

(18) *Balinaku:. "¡Paqarin yanapamay!" u "Paqarin ñuqakta chay**paq** talpushun qampaktañataq", ninaku:mi.* CH
 bali-naku: paqarin yanapa-ma-y u paqarin
 request.a.service-RECIP-1 tomorrow help-1.OBJ-IMP or tomorrow
 ñuqa-kta chay-paq talpu-shun qam-pa-kta-ña-taq
 I-ACC DEM.D-ABL plant-1PL.FUT you-GEN-ACC-DISC-SEQ
 ni-naku-:-mi
 say-RECIP-1-EVD
 'We ask for each other's services. "Help me tomorrow!" or, "Tomorrow mine **then** we'll plant yours," we say to each other.'

3 Substantives

In comparative expressions, *-paq* attaches to the base of comparison (19), (20); it may be combined with the Spanish-origin comparatives *mihur* (*mejor* 'better') and *piyur* (*peor* 'worse') (21). It can generally be translated 'for'; in its capacity as a purposive, it can generally be translated 'in order to'.

(19) *Qayna puntraw**paq** masmi.* AMV
 qayna puntraw-paq mas-mi
 previous day-ABL more-EVD
 'It's more **than** yesterday.'

(20) *Celia**paq**pis masta chawan.* SP
 Celia-paq-pis mas-ta chawa-n
 Celia-ABL-ADD more-ACC milk-3
 'She milks more **than** Celia.'

(21) *Pular**paq**pis mas **mihur**tam chayqa allukun.* ACH
 pular-paq-pis mas mihur-ta-m chay-qa allu-ku-n
 fleece-ABL-ADD more better-ACC-EVD DEM.D-TOP wrap-REFL-3
 '**Better than** fleece – this bundles you up.'

3.3.3.6 Locative *-pi*

As a locative, *-pi* indicates temporal (1), (2) and spatial location (3–5).

(1) *Kanan puntraw**pi** rishaq.* AMV
 kanan puntraw-pi ri-shaq
 now day-LOC go-1.FUT
 'I'll go today.'

(2) *¿Uktubri paqway**pi**ñachu hamunki?* CH
 uktubri paqwa-y-pi-ña-chu hamu-nki
 October finish-INF-LOC-DISC-Q come-2
 'Are you coming **at** the end of October?'

(3) *Chay**pi** chakirusa walantin vistiduntinshi.* ACH
 chay-pi chaki-ru-sa wala-ntin vistidu-ntin-shi
 DEM.D-LOC dry-URGT-NPST skirt-INCL dress-INCL-EVR
 '**There** she dried out with her skirt and her dress.'

3.3 Substantive inflection

(4) *Chay laguna**pi** yatraqñataq nira, "¿Imaynam qam kayanki puka traki?"* SP
   chay   laguna-pi   yatra-q-ña-taq   ni-ra   imayna-m   qam
   DEM.D   lake-LOC   live-AG-DISC-SEQ   say-PST   how-EVD   you
   ka-ya-nki   puka   traki
   be-PROG-2   red   foot
   'The one that lives **in** the lake said, "How do you have red feet?"'

(5) *Kundurñataq atuqta apustirun, "¿Mayqinninchik lasta**pi** urqu**pi** wañurushun?"* SP
   kundur-ña-taq   atuq-ta   apusti-ru-n   mayqin-ni-nchik   lasta-pi
   condor-DISC-SEQ   fox-ACC   bet-URGT-3   which-EUPH-1PL   snow-LOC
   urqu-pi   wañu-ru-shun
   hill-LOC   die-URGT-1PL.FUT
   'The condor bet the fox, "Which of us will die **in** the snow, **in** the hills?"'

It is used in the expression to speak in a language (6).

(6) *Kastillanu**pi** rimaq chayllamanñam shimin riyan manayá kay kichwa.* AMV
   kastillanu-pi   rima-q   chay-lla-man-ña-m   shimi-n   ri-ya-n
   Spanish-LOC   talk-AG   DEM.D-RSTR-ALL-DISC-EVD   mouth-3   go-PROG-3
   mana-yá   kay   kichwa
   no-EMPH   DEM.P   Quechua
   'Those who speak **in** Spanish, their mouths are running just there. Not [those who speak in?] Quechua.'

It can be translated as 'in', 'on', or 'at'. *-pi* has a marginal use as a genitive indicating subordinative relations – including, prominently, relationships of possession – between nouns referring to different items (7). In this capacity it is translated as 'of' or with a possessive.

(7) *Chay planta**pi** yatan.* AMV
   chay   planta-pi   yata-n
   DEM.D   tree-GEN   side-3
   'The side **of** that tree.'

3 Substantives

3.3.3.7 Exclusive *-puRa*

-puRa – realized *-pula* in the CH dialect (1) and *-pura* in all others – indicates the inclusion of the marked individual among other individuals of the same kind. It can be translated as 'among' or 'between'. *-puRa* is not commonly employed; more commonly employed is the particle *intri* 'between', borrowed from Spanish (*entre* 'between') (2).

(1) *Walmi**pula** qutunakulanchik.* CH
 walmi-pula   qutu-naku-la-nchik
 woman-EXCL gather-RECIP-PST-1PL
 'We women gathered amongst ourselves.'

(2) ***Intri** warmiqa ¿Imatatr ruwanman hapinakushpa?* AMV
 intri   warmi-qa   ima-ta-tr   ruwa-n-man   hapi-naku-shpa
 between woman-TOP what-ACC-EVC make-3-COND grab-RECIP-SUBIS
 '**Between** women, what are they going to do when they grab each other?'

3.3.3.8 Reason *-rayku*

-rayku indicates motivation (1), (2) or reason (3), (4). It generally but not obligatorily follows possessive inflection (1–4).

(1) *Chawashiq lichillan**rayku** riymantri.* AMV
 chawa-shi-q   lichi-lla-n-rayku   ri-y-man-tri
 milk-ACMP-AG milk-RSTR-3-REASN go-1-COND-EVC
 'I could go help milk on account of her milk.'

(2) *Papallayki**rayku**pis awapakuruyman.* AMV
 papa-lla-yki-rayku-pis   awa-paku-ru-y-man
 potato-RSTR-2-REASN-ADD weave-MUTBEN-URGT-1-COND
 'Even **for** your potatoes, I'd weave.'

(3) *Waynayki shamunan**rayku**.* CH
 wayna-yki   shamu-na-n-rayku
 lover-2   come-NMLZ-3-REASN
 '**On account of** your lover's coming.'

3.3 Substantive inflection

(4) *Mikunallan**rayku**pis yanukunqatr.* AMV
    miku-na-lla-n-rayku-pis   yanu-ku-nqa-tr
    eat-NMLZ-RSTR-3-REASN-ADD cook-REFL-3.FUT-EVC
    '**On account of** her food, she'll probably cook.'

It can generally be translated 'because', 'because of' or 'on account of'. *-rayku* is not frequently employed: ablative *-paq* is more frequently employed to indicate motivation or reason (5), although this *-paq* does not, as an anonymous reviewer points out, mark the same relation. *-kawsu* (*Sp. causa* 'cause') may be employed in place of *-rayku* (6). Recognized but not attested spontaneously outside AMV and CH.

(5) *Qatra vakaqa wanuyan qutranman. Sikintin qaykusan**paq**.* AMV
    qatra vaka-qa wanu-ya-n   qutra-n-man siki-ntin
    dirty cow-TOP excrete-PROG-3 lake-3-ALL   calf-INCL
    qayku-sa-n-paq
    corral-PRF-3-ABL
    'That dirty cow is pissing in the reservoir! **For** having been let out with her calf.'

(6) *Manam lichi kanchu. Pastu **kawsu**.* AMV
    mana-m lichi ka-n-chu pastu-kawsu
    no-EVD milk-3 be-3-NEG pasture.grass-cause
    'There's no milk. **Because of** the grass.'

3.3.3.9 Accusative *-Kta* and *-ta*

In the CH dialect, the accusative is realized *-kta* after a short vowel and *-ta* after a long vowel or consonant (1), (2); in all other dialects it is realized as *-ta* in all environments. *-ta* indicates the object or goal of a transitive verb (3), (4).

(1) ***Tilivisyunta** likakuyan, piluta **pukllaqkunaktam**.* CH
    tilivisyun-ta   lika-ku-ya-n   piluta puklla-q-kuna-kta-m
    television-ACC   look-REFL-PROG-3 ball   play-AG-PL-ACC-EVD
    'They're watching **television**, ball **players**.'

3 Substantives

(2) **"Suti:tam apakunki",** ¡niy! **"Llapanta apakunki".** CH
    suti-:-ta-m   apa-ku-nki   ni-y   llapa-n-ta   apa-ku-nki
    name-1-ACC-EVD bring-REFL-2 say -IMP all-3-ACC   bring-REFL-2
    'Say, "You're going to take along my **name**. You're going to take along **them all**."'

(3) Asñuqa nin, "Ñuqa tarisisayki **sugaykitaqa**". SP
    asnu-qa   ni-n, ñuqa   tari-si-sayki   suga-yki-ta-qa
    donkey-TOP say-3   I   find-ACMP-1>2.FUT rope-2-ACC-TOP
    'The mule said, "I'm going to help you find **your rope**."'

(4) Wak Kashapatapiñam maqarura **César Mullidata**. LT
    wak   Kashapata-pi-ña-m   maqa-ru-ra   César Mullida-ta
    DEM.D   Kashapata-LOC-DISC-EVD beat-URGT-PST César Mullida-ACC
    'They beat **César Mullida** there in Kashapata.'

-ta may occur more than once in a clause, marking multiple objects (5), (6) or both object and goal. In case one noun modifies another, case-marking on the head N is obligatory (7); on the modifying N, optional (3).

(5) ¿**Maqtakunata** pushanki icha **pashñata**? AMV
    maqta-kuna-ta   pusha-nki   icha   pashña-ta
    young.man-PL-ACC   bring.along-2   or   girl-ACC
    'Are you going to take **the boys** or **the girl**?'

(6) ¡**Vakata lliwta** qaquruy! Rikurushaq hanaypim. AMV
    vaka-ta   lliw-ta   qaqu-ru-y   riku-ru-shaq   hanay-pi-m
    cow-ACC all-ACC   toss.out-URGT-IMP   go-URGT-1.FUT   up.hill-LOC-EVD
    'Toss out **the cows, all of them**! I'm going to go up hill.'

(7) **Sibadata trakrata** kwidanchik. AMV
    sibada-ta   trakra-ta   kwida-nchik
    barley-ACC field-ACC   care.for-1PL
    'We take care of the **barley field**.'

Complement clauses are suffixed with -ta (8–10).

3.3 Substantive inflection

(8) ***Qaqapaq lluqsiyta** atipanchu. Qayakun, "¿Imaynataq kanan lluqsishaq?"* SP
    qaqa-paq lluqsi-y-ta atipa-n-chu qaya-ku-n imayna-taq
    cliff-ABL go.out-INF-ACC be.able-3-NEG shout-REFL-3 how-SEQ
    kanan lluqsi-shaq
    now go.out-1.FUT
    'She couldn't **get off the cliff**. She shouted, "Now, how am I going to get down?"'

(9) *Chaypaq **kabrata mikuyta** qallakuykun.* SP
    chay-paq kabra-ta miku-y-ta qalla-ku-yku-n
    DEM.D-ABL goat-ACC eat-INF-ACC begin-REFL-EXCEP-3
    'So, the fox started **to eat the goat**.'

(10) *Wambra willasuptiki **imayna kutirimusanta**.* LT
    wambra willa-su-pti-ki imayna kuti-ri-mu-sa-n-ta
    child tell-3>2-SUBDS-3>2 how return-INCEP-URGT-PRF-3-ACC
    'When the children told you **how they had returned**.'

-ta always attaches to the last word in a multi-word phrase (11).

(11) *Chayshi yatrarun **kundur kashanta**.* AMV
    chay-shi yatra-ru-n kundur ka-sha-n-ta
    DEM.D-EVR know-URGT-3 condor be-PRF-3-ACC
    'That's how they found out **he was a condor**.'

With *-na* nominalizations, *-ta* may be omitted. In many instances, *-ta* does not indicate accusative case. *-ta* may indicate the goal of movement of a person, as in (12) and (13), *-n-ta* may indicate PATH (14) (see also §§3.3.3.1, ex.(7)).[6]

(12) *Siqashpaqa chuqaykaramun **ukuta** almataqa.* AMV
    siqa-shpa-qa chuqa-yka-ra-mu-n uku-ta alma-ta-qa
    ascend-SUBIS-TOP throw-EXCEP-URGT-CISL-3 inside-ACC soul-ACC-TOP
    'Going up, he threw the ghost **inside**.'

---

[6] Thanks to Willem Adelaar for pointing this out to me.

3 Substantives

(13) **Qiñwaltam** rirqani yanta qipikuq. AMV
qiñwal-ta-m　　　　　　ri-rqa-ni　yanta　　qipi-ku-q
quingual.grove-ACC-EVD　go-PST-1　firewood　carry-REFL-AG
'I went **to the quingual grove** to carry firewood.'

(14) **Ukunta** shamushpa. **Qaqunanta** shamushpapis. CH
uku-n-ta　　　shamu-shpa　Qaquna-n-ta　shamu-shpa-pis
inside-3-ACC　come-SUBIS　Qaquna-3-ACC　come-SUBIS-ADD
'Coming **via** the interior. Coming **via** Qaquna.'

-*ta* marks substantives – nouns, adjectives, numerals, derived nouns – when they function as adverbs (15–18).

(15) Kikinqa **allinta**raqtaq gusaq. SP
kiki-n-qa　allin-ta-raq-taq　　gusa-q
self-3-TOP　good-ACC-CONT-SEQ　enjoy-AG
'They themselves enjoyed them **well** still.'

(16) Rupanchikta trurakunchik **qilluta**. AMV
rupa-nchik-ta　　trura-ku-nchik　qillu-ta
clothes-1PL-ACC　put-REFL-1PL　yellow-ACC
'We dress ourselves **in yellow**.'

(17) **Ishkay ishkaytam** plantaramuni. AMV
ishkay　ishkay-ta-m　　planta-ra-mu-ni
two　　two-ACC-EVD　plant-URGT-CISL-1
'I planted them **two by two**.'

(18) "Kumpadri, ¿Imaynataq waqayanki qamqa? ¡**Kuyayllata** waqanki!" nin. SP
kumpadri,　imayna-taq　waqa-ya-nki　qam-qa　kuya-y-lla-ta
compadre　why-SEQ　　cry-PROG-2　you-TOP　love-INF-RSTR-ACC
waqa-nki　ni-n
cry-2　　say-3
'"*Compadre*, why are you crying? How **lovely** you sing!" he said.'

It may also mark an item directly affected by an event or time period culminating in an event (19).

3.3 Substantive inflection

(19) *Chay huk madrugaw **trinta i unu di abrilta** lluqsirun waway.* AMV
 chay huk madrugaw trinta i unu di abril-ta
 DEM.D one morning thirty and one of April-ACC
 lluqsi-ru-n wawa-y
 go.out-URGT-3 baby-1
 'On that morning, **the thirty-first of April**, my son left the house [and was kidnapped].'

With verbs referring to natural phenomena, *-ta* may mark a place affected by an event (20), (21).

(20) *Yakupis tukuy **pampata** rikullaq.* AMV
 yaku-pis tukuy pampa-ta ri-ku-lla-q
 water-ADD all ground-ACC go-REFL-RSTR-AG
 'The water, too, would go all over the ground.'

(21) *¿**Llaqtaykita** paranchu?* AMV
 llaqta-yki-ta para-n-chu?
 town-2-ACC rain-3-Q
 'Does it rain **on your town**?'

With verbs of communication, it may mark the person receiving the communication (22), (23).

(22) *"Kay swirupis allquypaqpis. Faltan", nikurunshi **subrinuntaqa**.* LT
 kay swiru-pis allqu-y-paq-pis falta-n ni-ku-ru-n-shi
 DEM.D whey-ADD dog-1-BEN-ADD lack-3 say-REFL-URGT-3-EVR
 subrinu-n-ta-qa
 nephew-3-ACC-TOP
 '"This whey of mine, too, is for my dog. There isn't enough," he said **to his nephew**.'

(23) *Tarpuriptinchikpis mikunchu wak **Shullita** wak **Erminiota** nini.* AMV
 tarpu-ri-pti-nchik-pis miku-n-chu wak Shulli-ta wak
 plant-INCEP-SUBDS-1PL-ADD eat-3-NEG DEM.D Shulli-ACC DEM.D
 Erminio-ta ni-ni
 Erminio-ACC say-1
 'If we plant it, they won't eat it, I said **to my younger brother, to Erminio**.'

3 Substantives

3.3.3.10 Instrumental, comitative -wan

-*wan* indicates means or company. -*wan* may mark an instrument or item which is essential to the event (1), (2).

(1) *Chaymi qalatuykushpa kuriyanwan alli-allita chikutita qura.* LT
    chay-mi   qalatu-yku-shpa   kuriya-n-wan   alli-alli-ta
    DEM.D-EVD strip.naked-EXCEP-SUBIS belt-3-INSTR   good-good-ACC
    chikuti-ta   qu-ra
    whip-ACC   give-PST
    'Then they stripped him naked and gave him a whipping **with** his belt.'

(2) *Qaliqa takllawanmi halun. Qipantañataq kulpakta maqanchik pikuwan.* CH
    qali-qa   taklla-wan-mi   halu-n   qipa-n-ta-ña-taq
    man-TOP plow-INSTR-EVD   turn.earth-3   behind-3-ACC-DISC-SEQ
    kulpa-kta   maqa-nchik   piku-wan
    clod-ACC   hit-1PL   pick-INSTR
    'Men turn the earth **with** a [foot] plow. Behind them, we break up the clods **with** a pick.'

-*wan* marks all means of transportation (3).

(3) *Karruwantri kapas trayamunña. Mutuwanshi hamula.* CH
    karru-wan-tri   kapas   traya-mu-n-ña   mutu-wan-shi
    car-INSTR-EVC   maybe   arrive-CISL-3-DISC   motorcycle-INSTR-EVR
    hamu-la
    come-PST
    'Maybe she came **on** the bus. She came **by** motorbike, she says.'

It may mark illnesses (4).

(4) *¿Prustatawantri kayanki?* CH
    prustata-wan-tri   ka-ya-nki
    prostate-INSTR-EVC   be-PROG-2
    'Would you have prostate [problems]?'

3.3 Substantive inflection

-*wan* may mark any animate individual who takes part in an event together with the performer (5), (6); it may also mark the actor in an event referred to by a causative verb (7).

(5) *Taytachalla:wan kawsakura: mamachalla:wan kawsakura:. Mama:qa huk kumprumisuwan rikun huk lawta.* ACH
tayta-cha-lla-:-wan   kawsa-ku-ra-:   mama-cha-lla-:-wan
father-DIM-RSTR-1-INSTR live-REFL-PST-1 mother-DIM-RSTR-1-INSTR
kawsa-ku-ra-:   mama-:-qa   huk kumprumisu-wan   ri-ku-n
live-REFL-PST-1 mother-1-TOP one commitment-INSTR go-REFL-3
huk law-ta
one side-ACC
'I lived **with** just my grandfather and my grandmother. My mother went to another place **with** another commitment.'

(6) *¿Imapaqmi wak kundinawwan puriyanki?* AMV
ima-paq-mi   wak   kundinaw-wan puri-ya-nki
what-PURP-EVD DEM.D zombie-INSTR zombie-PROG-2
'Why are you walking around **with** that zombie?'

(7) *Manaraqmi qari:pis kararaqchu. Sapalla: wak wasipa puñukura: vaka:wan.* ACH
mana-raq-mi   qari-:-pis   ka-ra-raq-chu   sapa-lla-:   wak
no-CONT-EVD man-1-ADD be-PST-CONT-NEG alone-RSTR-1 DEM.D
wasi-pa   puñu-ku-ra-:   vaka-:-wan
house-LOC sleepREFL-PST-1 cow-1-INSTR
'I still didn't have my husband. I slept alone in my house **with** my cows.'

wan may mark coordinate relations between nouns or nominal groups; case matching attaches to all items except the last in a coordinate series (8). It can usually be translated 'with'.

(8) *Milawan Aliciawan Hilda trayaramun.*† AMV
Mila-wan   Alicia-wan   Hilda traya-ra-mu-n
Mila-INSTR Alicia-INSTR Hilda arrive-URGT-CISL-3
'Hilda arrived **with** Mila and Alicia.'

3 Substantives

3.3.3.11 Possible combinations

Combinations of case suffixes are rare. They do occur, however, notably with *-pa*, *-wan*, and *-hina*. Where a noun phrase marked with genitive *-pa* or *-paq* functions as an anaphor, the phrase may be case marked as its referent would be (1), (2). Note that in (2) the accusative has no phonological reflex in the English gloss.

(1) *Paqarin yanapamay u paqarin **ñuqapakta** chaypaq talpashun **qampaktañataq**.* CH
paqarin   yanapa-ma-y   u   paqarin   ñuqa-pa-kta   chay-paq
tomorrow help-1.OBJ-IMP or tomorrow   I-GEN-ACC   DEM.D-ABL
talpu-shun   qam-pa-kta-ña-taq
plant-1PL.FUT   you-GEN-ACC-DISC-SEQ
'Help me tomorrow or tomorrow **mine** and then we'll plant **yours**.'

(2) *Piluntaqa yupayanshari chay chapu**paqta**. Ushachinchu yupayta.* AMV
pilu-n-ta-qa   yupa-ya-n-sh-ari   chay   chapu-paq-ta
hair-3-ACC-SEQ   count-PROG-3-EVR-ARI   DEM.D   dog-GEN-ACC
ushachi-n-chu   yupa-y-ta
be.able-3-NEG   count-INF-ACC
'He's counting the hairs of that small [hairless] dog, but he can't count them.'

In addition to functioning as a case marker, *-wan* also serves to conjoin noun phrases. In this capacity, *-wan* may follow other case markers (3), (4).

(3) *Mishkita yawarnintam mikurunchik muti**tawan** papan**tawan**.* AMV
mishki-ta   yawar-ni-n-ta-m   miku-ru-nchik
sweet-ACC   blood-EUPH-3-ACC-EVD   eat-URGT-1PL
muti-n-ta-wan   papa-n-ta-wan
hominy-3-ACC-INSTR   potato-3-ACC-INSTR
'We eat its delicious blood with hominy **and** with potatoes.'

(4) *Chay kabranpawan vakan**pawan**tri kisuchan.* AMV
chay   kabr-n-pa-wan   vaka-n-pa-wan   kisu-cha-n
DEM.D goat-3-GEN-INSTR   cow-3-GEN-INSTR   cheese-DIM-3
'Her cheese would be from her goats' [milk] **and** from her cows'[milk].'

3.3 Substantive inflection

Elicited examples (5), (6) follow Parker (1976).

(5) *Qari**purawan** kambyashun.* † AMV
    qari-pura-wan   kambya-shun
    man-EXCL-INSTR   change-1PL.FUT
    'Let's exchange husbands [**for one another**].'

(6) *Piliyarachin wambra**purata**.* † AMV
    piliya-ra-chi-n   wambra-pura-ta
    fight-URGT-CAUS-3   child-EXCL-ACC
    'He made the boys fight **among** themselves.'

Comparative *-hina* may also combine with other case markers (7), (8).

(7) *Karsil**pahinam** witrqamara. Wambra:kuna istudyaq pasan.* ACH
    karsil-pa-hina-m   witrqa-ma-ra   wambra-:-kuna   istudya-q
    prison-LOC-COMP-EVD   close.in-1.OBJ-PST child-1-PL   study-AG
    pasa-n
    pass-3
    'They closed me in **like in** a jail. My children leave to study.'

(8) *Kanan vakata pusillaman chawayanchik kabra**tahina**.* AMV
    kanan vaka-ta pusi-lla-man   chawa-ya-nchik   kabra-ta-hina
    now   cow-ACC cup-RSTR-ALL   milk-PROG-1PL   goat-ACC-COMP
    'Now we milk a cow into a cup **like** a goat.'

3.3.3.12 More specific noun–noun relations

Noun-noun relations more specific than the 'in' and 'of', for example, of *-pi* and *-pa* are expressed by noun phrases headed by nouns which name relative positions (see §3.2.1.4 on locative nouns) (1–4). Such nouns include, for example, *qipa* 'rear'; *hawa* 'top'; and *trawpi* 'center'. The head (relational) noun is inflected for person, agreeing with the noun to which it is related; this noun may be inflected with genitive *-pa* (*pantyun-**pa** qipa-n* 'behind the cemetery' lit. 'of the cemetery its behind').

3 Substantives

(1) *Wak urqu **qipa**npa karu karutam muyumunchik.* AMV
 wak urqu qipa-n-pa karu karu-ta-m muyu-mu-nchik
 DEM.D hill behind-3-LOC far far-ACC-EVD circle-CISL-1PL
 'We circle around very far **behind** that hill.'

(2) *Kundur tiya-ya-n rumi **hawa**-n-pa ima-tri-ki.* SP
 kundur tiya-ya-n rumi hawa-n-pa ima-tri-ki
 condor sit-PROG-3 rock top-3-LOC what-EVC-IKI
 'The condor must be sitting **on top** of a rock.'

(3) *Waka **uku**npatriki runa wañura unay.* ACH
 waka uku-n-pa-tri-ki runa wañu-ra unay
 ruins inside-3-LOC-EVC-IKI person die-PST before
 '**Inside** the ruins, people must have died before.'

(4) *Wak wambra qaqa **trawpin**tam pasayan manam manchakuyan.* AMV
 wak wambra qaqa trawpi-n-ta-m pasa-ya-n mana-m
 DEM.D child cliff center-3-ACC-EVD pass-PROG-3 no-EVD
 mancha-ku-ya-n
 scare-REFL-PROG-3
 'That boy passes **between** the cliffs. He's not afraid.'

3.4 Substantive derivation

In SYQ, as in other Quechuan languages, suffixes deriving substantives may be divided into two classes, governing and restrictive. Governing suffixes may be further divided into two subclasses: those which derive substantives from verbs (*-na, -q, -sHa, -y*) and those which derive substantives from other substantives (*-ntin, -sapa, -yuq, -masi*). SYQ has a single restrictive suffix deriving substantives, diminutive *-cha*. *-lla* also functions to restrict substantives, but it is treated here not as a derivational morpheme but as an enclitic. §§3.4.1 and 3.4.2 cover the the governing suffixes deriving substantives from verbs and those deriving substantives from other substantives, respectively.

3.4.1 Substantive derived from verbs

Four suffixes derive substantives from verbs in SYQ: *-na, -q, -sHa,* and *-y*. All four form both relative and complement clauses. *-na, -q, -sHa,* and *-y* form subjunc-

3.4 Substantive derivation

tive, agentive, indicative, and infinitive clauses, respectively. The nominalizing suffixes attach directly to the verb stem, with the exception that the first- and second-person object suffixes, *-wa/ma* and *-sHa*, may intervene. §3.4.1.1–3.4.1.4 cover *-na*, *-q*, *-sHa*, and *-y* in turn.

3.4.1.1 *-na*

-na derives nouns that refer to (a) the instrument with which the action named by the base is realized (*alla-na* 'harvesting tool') (1), (2); (b) the place in which the event referred to occurs (*michi-na* 'pasture') (3); and (c) the object in which the action named by the base is realized (*upya-na* 'drinking water', *milla-na* 'nausea') (4), (5).

(1) *Mulinchik makinapaq kamcharinchik **kallanapa**.* AMV
    muli-nchik makina-paq kamcha-ri-nchik kalla-na-pa
    grind-1PL machine-LOC toast-INCEP-1PL toast-NMLZ-LOC
    'We grind it in a machine and then we toast it in the **toasting pan**.'

(2) *Llikllakuna, punchukuna, **puñunakuna** ruwa:.* ACH
    lliklla-kuna, punchu-kuna, puñu-na-kuna, ruwa-:
    shawl-PL poncho-PL sleep-NMLZ-PL make-1
    'I make shawls, ponchos and **blankets**.'

(3) *Iskina hawanpa **michinayki**.* AMV
    iskina hawa-n-pa michi-na-yki
    corner above-3-LOC pasture-NMLZ-2
    'Above the corner **where you pasture**.'

(4) *Mamayqa wichayta **mikunayta** apashpa asnuchanwan kargachakusa hamuq.* AMV
    mama-y-qa wichay-ta miku-na-y-ta apa-shpa
    mother-1-TOP up.hill-ACC eat-NMLZ-1-ACC bring-SUBIS
    asnu-cha-n-wan karga-cha-ku-sa hamu-q
    donkey-DIM-3-INSTR carry-DIM-REFL-PRF come-AG
    'My mother would come up hill bringing my **food**, carrying it with her donkey.'

3 Substantives

(5) **Mikuna**ntapis lliw lliwshi sibadanta trigunta ima kaqtapis katriwan takurachisa. ACH
miku-na-n-ta-pis   lliw   lliw-shi sibada-n-ta trigu-n-ta   ima
eat-NMLZ-3-ACC-ADD   all   all-EVR   barley-3-ACC wheat-3-ADD what
ka-q-ta-pis   katri-wan   taku-ra-chi-sa
be-AG-ACC-ADD   salt-INSTR mix-URGT-CAUS-NPST
'Their **food**, too, everything, everything, their barley, their wheat, anything, they mixed it with salt.'

Followed by a possessive suffix plus the copula auxiliary inflected for third person (null just in case tense/aspect are not specified), -na indicates necessity (i.e., it forms a universal deontic/teleological modal) (taqsa-na-yki 'you have to wash') (6), (7).

(6) Sibadayta wayrachishaq abasniyta **pallanay** kayan. AMV
sibada-y-ta   wayra-chi-shaq   abas-ni-y-ta   palla-na-y
barley-1-ACC   wind-CAUS-1.FUT   broad.beans-EUPH-1-ACC pick-NMLZ-1
ka-ya-n
be-PROG-3
'I'm going to winnow my barley – **I have to pick** my broad beans.'

(7) Hinata risani **yanukunay** kakuyaptin. LT
hina-ta   risa-ni   yanu-ku-na-y   ka-ku-ya-pti-n
thus-ACC   pray-1   cook-REFL-NMLZ-1   be-REFL-PROG-SUBDS-3
'I pray like that – when he's there, **I have to cook**.'

The past tense of necessity is formed by adding ka-RQa, the third person simple past tense form of ka- 'be' (palla-na-y ka-ra 'I had to pick') (8), (9).

(8) Kutikamura qari wambra: **yaykunan** kara manaña atiparachu. ACH
kuti-ka-mu-ra   qari   wambra-:   yayku-na-n   ka-ra
return-PASSACC-CISL-PST   man   child-1   enter-NMLZ-3   be-PST
mana-ña   atipa-ra-chu
no-DISC   be.able-PST-NEG
'My son came back – he **was supposed to** enter [university] but he couldn't any more.'

3.4 Substantive derivation

(9) *Shinkakunaqa kasunan **kara** madriqa rabyasatr kutin.* AMV
shinka-kuna-qa kasu-na-n   ka-ra   madri-qa
drunk-PL-TOP   pay.attention-NMLZ-3 be-PST   nun-TOP
rabya-sa-tr   kuti-n
be.mad-PRF-EVC   return-3
'The drunks **had to** pay [**should have** paid] attention. The nun must have gotten mad.'

In combination with the purposive case suffix -*paq*, -*na* forms subordinate clauses that indicate the purpose of the action in the main clause (*qawa-na-y-paq* 'so I can see') (10–13).

(10) *Ganawkuna **michina:paq** chay chaytam trakra **trabahana:paq**.* SP
ganaw-kuna   michi-na-:-paq   chay   chay-ta-m   trakra
cattle-PL   pasture-NMLZ-1-PURP   DEM.D   DEM.D-ACC-EVD   field
trabaha-na-:-paq
work-NMLZ-1-PURP
'**So I can herd** the cows, **so I can work** in the fields.'

(11) *Tambopaq apamuq kani, "¡Mikuy! ¡**Hampishuna**ykipaq!" nini.* AMV
Tambo-paq   apa-mu-q   ka-ni, miku-y   hampi-shu-na-yki-paq
Tambo-ABL   bring-CISL-AG be-1   eat-IMP cure-3>2-NMLZ-3>2-PURP
ni-ni
say-1
'I used to bring it from Tambopata. "Eat it **so it can** cure you!" I said.'

(12) *Manaña yapa **maqashunaykipaq**.* AMV
mana-ña   yapa   maqa-shu-na-yki-paq
no-DISC   again hit-3>2-NMLZ-3>2-PURP
'**So she doesn't hit you** again.'

(13) *"¿Imay ura chay kunihuqa kutimunqa **yanapamananpaq**?" nin.* SP
imay   ura   chay   kunihu-qa   kuti-mu-nqa
when   hour   DEM.D   rabbit-TOP   return-CISL-3.FUT
yanapa-ma-na-n-paq   ni-n
help-1.OBJ-NMLZ-3-PURP   say-3
'"What time is that rabbit going to come back **so he can** help me?" said [the fox].'

3 Substantives

-na forms subjunctive complement clauses with the verb *muna-* 'want' (*tushu-na-n-ta muna-ni* 'I want her to dance') (14), (15).

(14) **Pagananta munayan, rantinanta** *gasolinata.* ACH
paga-na-n-ta muna-ya-n ranti-na-n-ta gasolina-ta
pay-NMLZ-3-ACC want-PROG-3 buy-NMLZ-3-ACC gasoline-ACC
'**He wants her to pay, to buy** gasoline.'

(15) *Hinaptinshi paytaqa mana* **tarpunanta munasachu.** ACH
hinaptin-shi pay-ta-qa mana tarpu-na-n-ta muna-sa-chu
then-EVR he-ACC-TOP no plant-NMLZ-3-ACC want-NPST-NEG
'Then, they say, they didn't **want him to plant**.'

-na nominalizations, relative to the event of the main clause, refer to actions still to be completed (16), (17).

(16) **Mansanapaq**ña *wak turun kayan.* AMV
mansa-na-paq-ña wak turu-n ka-ya-n
tame-NMLZ-PURP-DISC DEM.D bull-3 be-PROG-3
'That bull is **to be tamed**/for taming already.'

(17) *Ñuqa laqyarushaq sikipaq. Kiputaqa.* **Laqyapana**sh *kayan.* AMV
ñuqa laqya-ru-shaq siki-paq Kipu-ta-qa
I slap-URGT-1.FUT behind-LOC Kipu-ACC-TOP
laqya-pa-na-sh ka-ya-n
slap-REPET-NMLZ-EVR be-PROG-3
'I'm going to slap him on the behind. Kipu [a dog]. It's there to be hit.'

3.4.1.2 Agentive *-q*

-q is agentive, deriving nouns that refer to the agent of the verb to which it attaches (*michi-q* 'shepherd', *ara-q* 'plower') (1–4).

3.4 Substantive derivation

(1) *Qaripis kanmi **wawachikuq**. Wawachin hapishpa.* ACH
    qari-pis   ka-n-mi   wawa-chi-ku-q   wawa-chi-n
    man-ADD be-3-EVD give.birth-CAUS-REFL-AG give.birth-CAUS-3
    hapi-shpa
    grab-SUBIS
    'There are also men **midwives**. Holding on, they birth the baby.'

(2) ***Manam munaq**kunakta pushakuyan.* CH
    mana-m   muna-q-kuna-kta   pusha-ku-ya-n
    no-EVD   want-AG-PL-ACC   bring.along-REFL-PROG-3
    'They're bringing along **people who don't want to**.'

(3) *Wak bandiduqa munarqachu manash wawayuqta. **Wawapakuq**triki kidarqa.* ACH
    wak   bandidu-qa   muna-rqa-chu   mana-sh   wawa-yuq-ta
    DEM.D bastard-TOP want-PST-NEG want-EVR baby-POSS-ACC
    wawa-paku-q-tri-ki   kida-rqa
    baby-MUTBEN-AG-EVC-KI remain-PST
    'That bastard didn't want [a woman] with a baby, they say. She remained a **single mother**, for sure.'

(4) *¿Imaynataq wak **miyrdaq** ganayawan?* AMV
    imayna-taq   wak   miyrda-q   gana-ya-wa-n?
    how-SEQ   DEM.D shit-AG   win-PROG-1.OBJ-3
    'How is that **shithead** beating me?'

-q nominalizations may form adjectival and relative clauses (*chinka-ku-q pashña* 'the lost girl', 'the girl who was lost') (5–8).

(5) *Trabahapakuya: llapan **rigakuq** luna. Trabahaya:.* CH
    trabaha-paku-ya-:   llapa-n riga-ku-q   luna   trabaha-ya-:
    work-MUTBEN-PROG-1 all-3   irrigate-REFL-AG person work-PROG-1
    'All the **people who water** are working, we're working.'

(6) ***Istudyaq** wambrakunapaqshi mas mimuryanpaq.* AMV
    istudya-q   wambra-kuna-paq-shi   mas   mimurya-n-paq
    study-AG   child-PL-BEN-EVR   more memory-3-PURP
    'For the **children who study**, they say, so that they have more memory.'

3 Substantives

(7) ***maqtawan pashña chinkakuq**qa* ACH
    maqta-wan   pashña chinka-ku-q-qa
    young.man-INSTR girl   get.lost-REFL-AG-TOP
    '**the boy** and **the girl who were lost**'

(8) ***mana rikchaq runa**kuna* SP
    mana rikcha-q runa-kuna
    no   go-AG   person-pl
    'the **people who aren't going**'

With verbs of movement, -*q* forms complement clauses indicating the purpose of the displacement (*taki-q hamu-nqa* 'they will come to sing') (9–11).

(9) ***Maskakuq*** *wak vikuñachatam **wakchakuq** ritamunki.* LT
    maska-ku-q   wak   vikuña-cha-ta-m   wakcha-ku-q
    look.for-REFL-AG DEM.D   vicuña-DIM-ACC-EVD   raise-REFL-AG
    ri-tamu-nki
    go-IRREV-1
    'You **left to look** for that little vicuña to **domesticate**.'

(10) *Misa **lulaq** shamun.* CH
     misa lula-q   shamu-n
     mass make-AG   come-3
     'They **come to hold** mass.'

(11) *¡Haku michiq! Michimushun chay llamata.* LT
     haku   michi-q   michi-mu-shun   chay   llama-ta
     let's pasture-AG   pasture-CISL-1PL.FUT   DEM.D llama-ACC
     'Let's [go to] herd! We'll herd those llamas.'

With the verb *kay* 'be' -*q* forms the habitual past (*asi-ku-q ka-nki* 'you used to laugh') (12–14) (see §4.3.3.3.4).

(12) *Unayqa paykunaqa ... mantilta ruwaq, mantilta burdaq, unayqa.* AMV
     unay-qa   pay-kuna-qa   mantil-ta   ruwa-q   mantil-ta
     long.ago-TOP he-PL-TOP   table.cloth-ACC make-AG   table.cloth-ACC
     burda-q   unay-qa
     embroider-AG   long.ago-TOP

3.4 Substantive derivation

'Formerly, they **used to** make table cloths; they **used to** embroider table cloths, formerly.'

(13) *Huybisninpa dumingunpa kisuta **apaq ka:** ishkay.* ACH
huybis-ni-n-pa   dumingu-n-pa kisu-ta   apa-q   ka-:
Thursday-EUPH-3-LOC Sunday-3-LOC cheese-ACC bring-AG be-1
ishkay
two
'On Thursdays and Sundays, I **used to bring** two cheeses [to sell].'

(14) *Sirdallawan **chumakuq kanchik**, kaspichallawan **aychiq kanchik**.*
*Winku purucham **kaq**. Antis.* AMV
sirda-lla-wan   chuma-ku-q   ka-nchik, kaspi-cha-lla-wan
bristle-RSTR-INSTR strain-REFL-AG be-1PL   stick-DIM-RSTR-INSTR
aychi-q ka-nchik winku   puru-cha-m   ka-q   antis
stir-AG be-1PL   crooked pot-DIM-EVD be-AG   before
'**We used to strain** it with just bristles, **we used to stir** it with just a stick. **There used to be** a crooked little bottle. Before.'

3.4.1.3 Perfective -sHa

-*sHa* is perfective, deriving stative participles. It is realized as -*sa* in ACH, AMV, and SP and as -*sha* in LT and CH. -*sHa* nominalizations form adjectives (*chaki-sa* 'dried') (1–2) as well as relative (*apa-sa-y* 'that I bring') (3–7), and complement clauses (*atipa-sha-y-ta* 'what I can') (8–10).

(1) *Mandilllaykunaqa **chakisa** kayan.* AMV
mandil-lla-y-kuna-qa chaki-sa ka-ya-n
apron-RSTR-1-PL-TOP dry-PRF be-PROG-3
'My aprons and things with them are **dry**.'

(2) *Wak runapa trakinqa **punkisam** kayan tulluntri **kuyusa** kayan.* ACH
wak   runa-pa   traki-n-qa   punki-sa-m   ka-ya-n   tullu-n-tri
DEM.D   person-GEN foot-3-TOP   swell-PRF-EVD be-PROG-3   bone-3-EVC
kuyu-sa   ka-ya-n
move-PRF   be-PROG-3
'That person's foot is **swollen**, the bone must be **moved** [out of place].'

105

3 Substantives

(3) *Chay ganaw **dividisan**wan rikisiyantri.* SP
    chay   ganaw dividi-sa-n-wan   rikisi-ya-n-tri
    DEM.D cattle devide-PRF-3-INSTR   get.rich-PROG-3-EVC
    'They must be getting rich with the cattle **that they divided up** [among themselves].'

(4) *Pampakurun matraymanqa chay **wañusan** tardiqa.* AMV
    pampa-ku-ru-n   matray-man-qa chay   wañu-sa-n tardi-qa
    bury-REFL-URGT-3   cave-ALL-TOP   DEM.D die-PRF-3 afternoon
    'They buried him in a cave the afternoon **that he died**.'

(5) *Unay imas **pasamashanchik** ...* CH
    unay   ima-s   pasa-ma-sha-nchik
    before what-ADD   pass-1.OBJ-PRF-1PL
    'Before, anything **that happened** to us ...'

(6) *kalamina **rantishanchikkuna*** LT
    kalamina   ranti-sha-nchik-kuna
    corrugated.iron   buy-PRF-1PL-PL
    'the tin roofing **that we bought**'

(7) *Ratuskamanshi kisuta **ruwasayki**ta qawanqa.* AMV
    ratus-kaman-shi   kisu-ta   ruwa-sa-yki-ta   qawa-nqa
    moments-LIM-EVR   cheese-ACC make-PRF-2-ACC   see-3.FUT
    'A little later, she says, she'll see the cheese **that you made**.'

(8) *¿Imatataq kanan ñuqa Lutupa ubihawan **yatrasay**ta willakushaq?* AMV
    ima-ta-taq   kanan ñuqa Lutu-pa   ubiha-wan   yatra-sa-y-ta
    what-ACC-SEQ   now   I   Lutu-LOC sheep-INSTR   live-PRF-1-ACC
    willa-ku-shaq
    tell-REFL-1.FUT
    'Now what am I going to tell you about **what I lived** in Lutu with my sheep?'

(9) *Luchashaq. **Atipashay**tatrik ruwakushaq.* LT
    lucha-shaq   atipa-sha-y-ta-tri-k   ruwa-ku-shaq
    fight-1.FUT   be.able-PRF-1-ACC-EVC-IK   make-REFL-1.FUT
    'I'll fight. I'll do **what I can**.'

3.4 Substantive derivation

(10) Ñuqapataqa silinsyu kaptin **munashan**taña ruwayan. LT
 ñuqa-pa-ta-qa   silinsyu   ka-pti-n   muna-sha-n-ta-ña
 I-GEN-ACC-TOP   abandoned be-SUBDS-3   want-PRF-3-ACC-DISC
 ruwa-ya-n
 make-PROG-3
 'When it falls silent, they're doing **what they want** to my things.'

-sHa complement clauses are common with the verbs yatra- 'know', qunqa- 'forget', qawa 'see' and uyaRi- 'hear' (upya-sa-n-ta uyari-rqa-ni 'I heard that he drank') (11).

(11) Ñuqaqa wambran **qipikusan**ta qawarqanichu. AMV
 ñuqa-qa   wambra-n   qipi-ku-sa-n-ta   qawa-rqa-ni-chu
 I-TOP   child-3   carry-REFL-PRF-3-ACC   see-PST-1-NEG
 'I didn't see **that she carried** her baby.'

As substantives, they are inflected with possessive suffixes, not verbal suffixes (ranti-sa-**yki** *ranti-sa-**nki** 'that you sold'); these may be reinforced with possessive pronouns (**qam-pa** ranti-sa-yki 'that *you* sold') (12).

(12) Qam**pa rantikurasayki**yá chay shakash. AMV
 qam-pa   rantiku-ra-sayki-yá   chay   shakash
 you-GEN   sell-URGT-2>1-EMPH   DEM.D   guinea.pig
 'That guinea pig **that *you* sold me**.'

-sHa may also form nouns referring to the place where an event, E, occurs (dipurti ka-sha-n 'where there are sports') (13–15).

(13) Wambraqa **pukllayasan**pa tutaykarachin. SP
 wambra-qa   puklla-ya-sa-n-pa   tuta-yka-ra-chi-n
 child-TOP   play-PROG-PRF-3-LOC night-EXCEP-URGT-CAUS-3
 'Night fell **where the girls were playing**.'

(14) Tilivisyunta likakuyan piluta pukllaqkunaktam maytraw **dipurti kashan**kunakta. CH
 tilivisyun-ta   lika-ku-ya-n   piluta   puklla-q-kuna-kta-m
 television-ACC   look-REFL-PROG-3   ball   play-AG-PL-ACC-EVD
 may-traw   dipurti   ka-sha-n-kuna-kta
 where-LOC   sport   be-PRF-3-PL-ACC

3 Substantives

'They're watching television – the ball-players and **where there are sports**.'

(15) **Riyasan**piqa trayarun, pwintiman. AMV
ri-ya-sa-n-pi-qa   traya-ru-n,   pwinti-man
go-PROG-PRF-3-LOC-TOP arrive-URGT-3 bridge-ALL
'He arrived **where he was going**, at a bridge.'

-*sHa* nominalizations, relative to the E of the main clause, refer to actions already completed (16), (17).

(16) Yapa kutishqa **awakusanman**. AMV
yapa   kuti-shqa   awa-ku-sa-n-man
again return-SUBIS weave-REFL-PRF-3-ALL
'When she returned again to **what/where she had woven**.'

(17) ¿Pi yaykukuntri? Mana ya yatranichu pi **kashan**tapis. AMV
pi   yayku-ku-n-tri   mana ya   yatra-ni-chu pi
who enter-REFL-3-EVC mana EMPH know-1-NEG who
ka-sha-n-ta-pis
be-PRF-3-ACC-ADD
'Who would have entered? I don't know **who it was**, either.'

3.4.1.4 Infinitive -y

-*y* indicates the infinitive or what in English would be a gerund (*tushu-y* 'to dance, dancing') (1), (2).

(1) Ni **puñuy** ni **mikuy**. AMV
ni puñu-y   ni miku-y
nor sleep-INF nor eat-INF
'Neither sleep**ing** nor eat**ing**.'

(2) Paqwayanñam **talpukuy**. CH
paqwa-ya-n-ña-m   talpu-ku-y
finish-PROG-3-DISC-EVD plant-REFL-INF
'The plant**ing** is finishing up.'

3.4 Substantive derivation

-*y* nominalizations may refer to the object or event in which the verb stem is realized (*ishpa-* 'urinate' → *ishpa-y* 'urine'; *nana-* 'hurt' → *nana-y* 'pain'; *rupa-* 'burn' → *rupa-y* 'sunshine') (3–7).

(3) *Warminpa **ishpay**nintash tuman.* AMV
    warmi-n-pa   ishpa-y-ni-n-ta-sh   tuma-n
    woman-3-GEN urinate-INF-EUPH-3-ACC-EVR drink-3
    'He drinks his wife's **urine**, they say.'

(4) *Traki **nanay**wan karqani.* AMV
    traki nana-y-wan   ka-rqa-ni
    foot   hurt-INF-INSTR be-PST-1
    'I've had foot **pain**.'

(5) *Tutal **suday**llaña hamukuyan kwirpunchikpapis "¡Chaq! ¡Chaq! ¡Chaq!" sutukuyan **suday**niki.* ACH
    tutal   suda-y-lla-ña   hamu-ku-ya-n
    completely sweat-INF-RSTR-DISC come-REFL-PROG-3
    kwirpu-nchik-pa-pis chaq   chaq   chaq sutu-ku-ya-n
    body-1PL-LOC-ADD   tak   tak   tak   drip-REFL-PROG-3
    suda-y-ni-ki
    sweat-INF-EUPH-2
    'Just a whole lot of **sweat** is coming out on our bodies – "Chak! Chak! Chak!" – your **sweat** is dripping.'

(6) *¿Uktubri **paqway**piñachu hamunki?* CH
    uktubri paqwa-y-pi-ña-chu   hamu-nki
    October finish-INF-LOC-DISC-Q come-2
    'Are you coming at **the end** of October?'

(7) *Aligrakuyan suygran wañukusantatr. Manayá **pampakuy**ninpa karqachu, ¿aw?* AMV
    aligra-ku-ya-n   suygra-n   wañu-ku-sa-n-ta-tr
    happy-REFL-PROG-3 mother.in.law-3 die-REFL-PRF-3-ACC-EVC
    mana-yá pampa-ku-y-ni-n-pa   ka-rqa-chu aw
    no-EMPH bury-REFL-INF-EUPH-3-LOC be-PST-Q   yes
    'He must be very happy his mother-in-law died. He wasn't at her **burial**, was he?'

3 Substantives

-y nominalizations form adjectival and relative clauses (*ranti-y kahun* 'bought casket', *yanu-ku-y tardi* 'the afternoon that we cook') (8–10) and infinitive complement clauses (*waqa-y-ta qalla-ku-n* 'it started to wail') (11).

(8) **Rantiy** *kahun mana yaykunchu.* AMV
ranti-y   kahun   mana   yayku-n-chu
buy-INF   coffin no   enter-3-NEG
'**Bought** coffins won't fit it.'

(9) *Waqtakunata lluqsishpa runas* **puñuy.** ACH
waqta-kuna-ta   lluqsi-shpa   runa-s   puñu-y
hillside-PL-ACC   go.out-SUBIS   person-ADD   sleep-INF
'The people, too, **asleep**, they came out on the hillsides.'

(10) *Chay* **yanukuy** *tardish almaqa trayamun.* AMV
chay   yanu-ku-y   tardi-sh   alma-qa   traya-mu-n
DEM.D   cook-REFL-INF afternoon-EVR   soul-TOP   arrive-CISL-3
'The souls arrive on the afternoon **that we cook**, they say.'

(11) **Waqay**ta *qallakun, "¡Oooh oooohh oooohhhh ooh ooh!"* SP
waqa-y-ta   qalla-ku-n   oooh   oooohh   oooohhhh   ooh   ooh
cry-INF-ACC   start-REFL-3   oooh   oooohh   oooohhhh   ooh   ooh
'It started **to wail**, "Oooh oooohh oooohhhh ooh ooh!"'

The latter are particularly common with the auxiliary verbs *muna-* 'want,' *atipa-* 'be able,' and *yatra-* 'know' (*iskribi-y-ta muna-ni* 'I want to write') (12–16).

(12) *Manañam* **diskutiy**ta *ñuqa* **muna**nichu *kayna.* LT
mana-ña-m   diskuti-y-ta   ñuqa   muna-ni-chu   kayna
no-DISC-EVD   dispute-INF-ACC   I   want-1-NEG   thus
'I don't **want to fight** about it like this any more.'

(13) *¿Kukata* **akuykuyta muna**nkichu? AMV
kuka-ta   aku-yku-y-ta   muna-nki-chu
coca-ACC   chew-EXCEP-INF-ACC   want-2-Q
'Do you **want to chew** coca?'

3.4 Substantive derivation

(14) *Wak vakaypa atakanmi mal kayan **puriyta atipanchu**.* AMV
wak   vaka-y-pa   ataka-n-mi mal ka-ya-n   puri-y-ta
DEM.D COW-1-GEN leg-3-EVD   bal be-PROG-3 walk-INF-ACC
atipa-n-chu
be.able-3-NEG
'My cow's leg is hurt – she **can't walk**.'

(15) ***Iskribiy**tapis **usachi**nichu ni **firmay**tapis. Total analfabitu.* CH
iskribi-y-ta-pis   usachi-ni-chu ni   firma-y-ta-pis   total
write-INF-ACC-ADD be.able-1-NEG nor sign-INF-ACC-ADD totally
analfabitu
illiterate
'**I can't write or sign** [my name], either. Completely illiterate.'

(16) *Mana **risakuy**ta **yatra**rachu. Satanaswan yatrara.* SP
mana risa-ku-y-ta   yatra-ra-chu   Satanas-wan   yatra-ra
no   pray-REFL-INF-ACC know-PST-NEG Satan-INSTR   live-PST
'They didn't **know how to pray**. They lived with Satan.'

Infinitive complements are case-marked with accusative *-ta* (17).

(17) *Wakhina mana vininu **tumayta** munashpatri manam **yaykuyta**
munanchu ubihaqa.* AMV
wak-hina   mana vininu tuma-y-ta   muna-shpa-tri   mana-m
DEM.D-COMP no   poison take-INF-ACC want-SUBIS-EVC no-EVD
yayku-y-ta   muna-n-chu ubiha-qa
enter-INF-ACC want-3-NEG sheep-TOP
'Like that, not wanting to drink poison, the sheep don't want to go in.'

In the CH dialect, accusative marking in this structure is sometimes elided, (18).

(18) *Manam **lulay** munanchu.* CH
mana-m lula-y   muna-n-chu
no-EVD   make-INF want-3-NEG
'He doesn't want to do it.'

3 Substantives

3.4.2 Substantives derived from substantives

Four suffixes derive substantives from substantives in SYQ: *-kuna*, *-ntin*, *-sapa*, and *-yuq*. The first two of these – *-kuna* and *-ntin* – indicate accompaniment, adjacency, or completeness (*llama-n-kuna* 'with her llama', *amiga-ntin* 'with her friends'); *-yuq* and *-sapa* indicate possession (*llama-yuq* 'person with llamas', *llama-sapa* 'person with more llamas than usual'). §3.4.2.1–3.4.2.4 cover *-kuna*, *-ntin*, *-sapa*; and *-yuq*, in turn.

3.4.2.1 Non-exhaustivity *-kuna$_2$*

-kuna$_2$ indicates that the referent of its base is accompanied by another entity, generally of the same class (*qusa-yki-kuna* 'your husband and all') (1–4).

(1) *Ispusu:ta mama:kuna tayta:kunakta qayakushpa manam ... hiwyaku:chu.* CH
    ispusu-:-ta   mama-:-kuna   tayta-:-kuna-kta   qaya-ku-shpa
    husband-1-ACC mother-1-PL   father-1-PL-ACC   call-REFL-SUBIS
    mana-m   hiwya-ku-:-chu
    no-EVD   scare-REFL-1-NEG
    'Calling on my husbands and on my mothers and my fathers, I'm not scared.'

(2) *Chay kwirpuykikuna mal kanman umaykikuna nananman.* AMV
    chay   kwirpu-yki-kuna mal   ka-n-man   uma-yki-kuna nana-n-man
    DEM.D   body-2-PL   bad   be-3-COND head-2-PL   hurt-3-COND
    'Your body **among other things** could be sick; your head **among other things** could hurt.'

(3) *Wak rikisunninkunata narun warkurun.* AMV
    wak   rikisun-ni-n-kuna-ta   na-ru-n   warku-ru-n
    DEM.D   cheese.curd-EUPH-3-PL-ACC   DMY-URGT-3   hang-URGT-3
    'She did that, she hung up her cheese curd **along with other things**.'

(4) *"Pachamankakuna kayan alli allin mikushun kanan tardi", nishpa.* SP
    pachamanka-kuna   ka-ya-n   alli   allin   miku-shun   kanan
    barbecue-PL   be-PROG-3   good   good   eat-1PL.FUT now
    tardi   ni-shpa
    afternoon   say-SUBIS

112

3.4 Substantive derivation

'"There's a barbecue **and all** – we're going to eat really, really well this afternoon," said [the rabbit].'

3.4.2.2 Accompaniment, adjacency *-ntin*

-ntin indicates that the referent of the base accompanies or is adjacent to another entity (*allqu-**ntin*** 'with her dog') (1–4).

(1) *Vistigashpaqa pasakun vistigaq lliw gwardya**ntin** huysni**ntin**.* SP
vistiga-shpa-qa   pasa-ku-n   vistiga-q   lliw gwardya-ntin
investigate-SUBIS-TOP pass-REFL-3 investigate-AG all   police-ACMP
huys-ni-ntin
judge-EUPH-ACMP
'After they investigated, the investigators left **with** the policemen **and** judges.'

(2) *Hinashpash pwirtanta kandawni**ntin**ta kuchurusa, ¿aw?* AMV
hinashpa-sh   pwirta-n-ta   kandaw-ni-ntin-ta   kuchu-ru-sa   aw
then-EVR   door-3-ACC   lock-EUPH-3-ACC   cut-URGT-NPST   yes
'Then, they say, they cut the door **along with** its lock, no?'

(3) *Qullqi**ntin** riptin krusni**ntin**shi qullqi**ntin**shi.* AMV
qullqi-ntin   ri-pti-n   krus-ni-ntin-shi   qullqi-ntin-shi
money-ACMP   go-SUBDS-3   cross-EUPH-INCL-EVR   money-ACMP-EVR
'Leaving **with** her money – **with** her cross and **with** her money, they say.'

(4) *Trayamura punta**ntin** punta**ntin** payqa.* SP
*traya-mu-ra   punta-**ntin**   punta-**ntin**   pay-qa*
arrive-URGT-PST   point-ACMP   point-ACMP   he-TOP
'He arrived **peak by peak**, he did.'

3.4.2.3 Multiple possession *-sapa*

-sapa derives a nouns referring to the possessor of the referent of the base. It differs from *-yuq* in that what is possessed is possessed in greater proportion than is

3 Substantives

usual[7] (*uma* 'head' → *uma-sapa* 'person with a head bigger than usual', *yuya-y* 'memory' → *yuya-y-sapa* 'person with a memory better than usual'. In the literature on Quechua it is sometimes referred to as "super" possession (posession of more than usual).

(1) "*¡Ñam tukuchkaniña!*" *puk, puk, puk **sikisapa** sapu.* AMV
ña-m tuku-chka-ni-ña puk puk puk siki-sapa sapu
DISC-EVD finish-DUR-1-DISC puk puk puk behind-MULT.ALL frog
'"I'm already finishing up!" – *puk, puk, puk* – [said] the frog **with the rear bigger than usual**.'

(2) *Figura alli-allin **waqrasapa** ukunpa, iglisyapash.* AMV
figura alli-allin waqra-sapa uku-n-pa iglisya-pa-sh
figure good-good horn-MULT.ALL inside-3-loc church-GEN-EVR
'Inside the church, they say, a statue **with horns bigger than usual**.'

(3) *Qamqa **wawasapa** kayanki paypis **wawasapa**sh **churisapa**sh.* LT
qam-qa wawa-sapa ka-ya-nki pay-pis wawa-sapa-sh
you-TOP baby-MULT.ALL be-PROG-2 he-ADD baby-MULT.ALL-EVR
churi-sapa-sh
son-MULT.ALL-EVR
'You have **more children than usual**. He, too, has **more children than usual, more sons than usual**, they say.'

3.4.2.4 Possession *-yuq*

-yuq derives nouns referring to the possessor of the referent of the base (1–3).

(1) *Ayvis dimandakurun **tiyrayuqkunata**.* SP
ayvis dimanda-ku-ru-n tiyra-yuq-kuna-ta
sometimes denounce-REFL-URGT-3 land-POSS-PL-ACC
'Sometimes they denounced **the ones with land**.'

(2) *Kwirpu:mi **hutrayuq**.* CH
kwirpu-:-mi hutra-yuq
body-1-EVD fault-POSS
'My body is **the guilty one**.'

---
[7] Thanks to an anonymous reviewer for correcting my understanding of this structure.

3.4 Substantive derivation

(3) *Wiñan altupam puka **waytachayuq**mi.* AMV
    wiña-n altu-pa-m puka wayta-cha-yuq-mi
    grow-3 high-LOC-EVD red flower-DIM-POSS-EVD
    '**The one with a little red flower** grows in the hills.'

Ownership applies to substantives, including interrogative indefinites (4), numerals (5), pronouns (6), and so on.

(4) ***Imayuq**pis kankichu.* LT
    ima-yuq-pis ka-nki-chu
    what-POSS-ADD be-2-NEG
    '"You don't **have anything**.' (lit. 'you aren't one with something')'

(5) ***Kimsayuq** kayan.* AMV
    kimsa-yuq ka-ya-n
    three-POSS be-PROG-3
    'She **has three**.' (*lit.* 'she is one with three')'

(6) ***Chayyuq**triki chayqa.* CH
    chay-yuq-tri-ki chay-qa
    DEM.D-POSS-EVC-IKI DEM.D-TOP
    'It must **have that**.'

In case the base ends in a consonant, the semantically vacuous particle *-ni* precedes *-yuq* (7).

(7) *Kuknin kasa **kaqniqu** huknin mana **kaqniqu**.* AMV
    huk-ni-n ka-sa ka-q-ni-qu huk-ni-n mana
    one-EUPH-3 be-NPST be-AG-EUPH-POSS one-EUPH-3 no
    ka-q-ni-qu
    be-AG-EUPH-POSS
    'One was **wealthy**, one **had nothing**.'

[yuq] is in free variation with [qu] following [i] (8).

(8) *¿Ayka **watayuq** nishurankitaqqa?* AMV
    ayka wata-yuq ni-shu-ra-nki-taq-qa?
    how.many year-POSS say-3>2-PST-3>2-SEQ-TOP
    'How **old** did she tell you she was?'

3 Substantives

-yuq is used in the expression 'to be N years old' (9) as well as in the construction of compound numerals (10).

(9) *Chay **trunka pichqayuq** puntrawnintaqa ñam trakrantañam tapamun.* AMV
chay   trunka pichqa-yuq   puntraw-ni-n-ta-qa   ña-m
DEM.D   ten   five-POS   day-EUPH-3-ACC-TOP   DISC-EVD
trakra-n-ta-ña-m   tapa-mu-n
field-3-ACC-EVD   cover-CISL-3
'At **fifteen** days they cover the field.'

(10) *Ima**yuq**pis kankichu chay wambraykita katrarunki mayurnikikama.* LT
ima-yuq-pis   ka-nki-chu   chay   wambra-yki-ta   katra-ru-nki
what-POSS-ADD   be-2-NEG   DEM.D   child-2-ACC   release-URGT-2
mayur-ni-ki-kama
older-EUPH-2-LIM
'You don't have anything and you sent your son to your older brother.'

-yuq nouns may function adverbially without case-marking or other modification (11), (12).

(11) *Puntantam hamullarqani kuka kintu **quqawniyuq**llam.* SP
punta-n-ta-m   hamu-lla-rqa-ni   kuka   kintu
point-3-ACC-EVD   come-RSTR-PST-1   coca   leaf
quqaw-ni-yuq-lla-m
picnic-EUPH-POSS-RSTR-EVD
'I've come by the peak **with just a picnic** of coca leaves.'

(12) *Pallayara puka **pantalunniyuq** ginduntaqa nini.* LT
palla-ya-ra   puka   pantalun-ni-yuq   gindun-ta-qa   ni-ni
pick-PROG-PST   red   pants-EUPH-POSS   peach-ACC-TOP   say-1
'She was picking peaches **in red pants**, I said.'

3.4.2.5 Partnership -*masi*

-*masi* indicates partnership. It attaches to Ns to derive Ns generally translated 'N-mate' 'fellow N' (1), (2), or 'co-N' (*puñu-q* → *puñu-q-masi* 'bedmate'). -*masi* is not very widely employed.

3.4 Substantive derivation

(1) *¡Runa**masi**nchikta mikurunchik, wawqi!* AMV
    runa-masi-nchik-ta   miku-ru-nchik,   wawqi
    person-PART-1PL-ACC   eat-URGT-1PL   brother
    'We ate our **fellow** people, brother!'

(2) *Chaywan apakatrakushpam rikakayachin runa**masi**nchiktaqa.* LT
    chay-wan   apa-katra-ku-shpa-m   rika-ka-ya-chi-n
    DEM.D-INSTR   bring-FREQ-REFL-SUBIS-EVD   see-PASSACC-PROG-CAUS-3
    runa-masi-nchik-ta-qa
    person-PART-1PL-ACC-TOP
    'Carrying those [their arms], they made our **fellow** people look.'

(3) *Chay yatraq**masi**nqa ayqikuyan.* AMV
    chay   yatra-q-masi-n-qa   ayqi-ku-ya-n
    DEM.D   live-AG-PART-3-TOP   escape-REFL-PROG-3
    'Her **neighbor** is escaping.'

(4) *Qunqaytaqqa, chay ukucha**masi**n apamun trupataqa.* ACH
    qunqaytaq-qa, chay   ukucha-masi-n apa-mu-n   trupa-ta-qa
    suddenly-TOP   DEM.D   mouse-PART-3   bring-CISL-3 tail-ACC-TOP
    'Suddenly, the mouse's **companion** [arrived and] took away the tail.'

3.4.2.6 Restrictive suffix: *-cha*

-cha attaches to Ns to derive Ns with the meaning 'little N' (1–3).

(1) *Wambra, uchuchuk wambra. Kayna wambra**cha**kunalla.* LT
    wambra   uch-uchuk   wambra   kayna   wambra-cha-kuna-lla
    child   small-small   child   thus   child-DIM-PL-RSTR
    'Little, little children – like this – just **small** children.'

(2) *Santupa karqa kuruna**cha**nkuna.* AMV
    Santu-pa   ka-rqa   kuruna-cha-n-kuna
    Saint-GEN   be-PST   crown-DIM-3-PL
    'The saints had their **little** crowns.'

3 Substantives

(3) *Turnuchawan ñuqakunaqa trabaha:.* CH
    turnu-cha-wan   ñuqa-kuna-qa   trabaha-:
    turn-DIM-INSTR   I-PL-TOP   work-1
    'We work by **short** turns.'

It may also express an affectionate attitude toward the referent of N (4).

(4) *Katraramuy indikananpaq, Hildacha.* AMV
    katra-ra-mu-y   indika-na-n-paq   Hilda-cha
    send-URGT-CISL-IMP   indicate-NMLZ-3-PURP   Hilda-DIM
    'Send him so that he shows him, Hilda, **dear**.'

(5) is taken from a song in which a girl addresses her lover.

(5) *Pulvuchapaq tapaykullasa, wayrachapaq apaykullasa, kay sityuchaman trayaykamunki.* SP
    pulvu-cha-paq   tapa-yku-lla-sa   wayra-cha-paq
    dust-DIM-ABL   cover-EXCEP-RSTR-PRF   wind-DIM-ABL
    apa-yku-lla-sa   kay   sityu-cha-man   traya-yka-mu-nki
    bring-EXCEP-RSTR-PRF   DEM.P   place-DIM-ALL   arrive-EXCEP-CISL-2
    'Covered with dust, carried by the wind, you're going to come to this place.'

Applied to other substantives *-cha* may function as a limitative. In these cases, it is generally translated 'just' or 'only' (6).

(6) *Chaychapam kakullayan.* AMV
    chay-cha-pa-m   ka-ku-lla-ya-n
    DEM.D-DIM-LOC-EVD   be-REFL-RSTR-PROG-3
    'It's **just** right there.'

The forms *Mama-cha* (mother-DIM) and *tayta-cha* (father-DIM) are lexicalized, meaning 'grandmother' and 'grandfather' respectively (7).

(7) *Tiyu:pa sirvintin mamacha:pis sirvintin ñuqa kara:.* AMV
    tiyu-:-pa   sirvinti-n   mama-cha-:-pis   sirvinti-n   ñuqa   ka-ra-:
    uncle-1-GEN   servant-3   mother-DIM-1-ADD   servant-3   I   be-PST-1
    'I was my uncles's and my **grandmother's** servant.'

3.4 Substantive derivation

In addition to *-cha*, speakers sometimes employ the borrowed Spanish diminutive suffix, *-itu/a* (or its post-consonant form *-citu/a*) (8).

(8) *Chay urunguy**situ** lluqsiramushqa chay kahapaq.* AMV
 chay urunguy-situ lluqsi-ra-mu-shqa chay kaha-paq
 DEM.D fly-DIM go.out-URGT-CISL-SUBIS DEM.D coffin-ABL
 'That **little** fly came out of the coffin.'

4 Verbs

This chapter covers the verbal system of Southern Yauyos Quechua. Its four sections treat verb stems, verb types, verbal inflection and verbal derivation, in that order.

4.1 Verb stems

In Southern Yauyos Quechua, as in other Quechuan languages, verb stems always end in a vowel (*yanapa-* 'help'). Verb stems are bound forms: with the single exception of *haku* 'let's go!' they never appear in isolation. They are subject to both inflectional and derivational processes, both suffixing (*wañu-n*, die-3, 'they die'; *wañu-chi-n*, die-CAUS-3, 'they kill'). The order of inflectional suffixes is fixed; the order of derivational suffixes is highly regular but admits exception. Inflection for person is obligatory (**qawa-katra-ya* see-FREQ-PROG); derivational processes are optional (*qawa-n* see-3). The different person suffixes are mutually exclusive; different derivational suffixes may attach in series (*qipi-ra-chi-ku-sa* carry-URGT-CAUS-REFL-NPST 'she got herself carried').

4.2 Types of verbs

Quechua verb stems are usually classed as (di-)transitive (*qu-* 'give', *riku-* 'see'), intransitive (*puñu-* 'sleep'), or copulative (*ka-* 'be'). A fourth class can be set apart: onomatopoetic verbs (*chuqchuqya-* 'nurse, make the sound of a calf nursing'). Special cases include the deictic verb *hina-*, the dummy verb *na-*, and the combining verbs *-naya-* 'give desire' (§4.4.1.6) and *-na-* 'do what, matter, and happen' (§4.4.1.5). §4.2.1–4.2.4 cover transitive, intransitive, equational, and onomatopoetic verbs, in turn.

4.2.1 Transitive verbs

Transitive verbs are standardly defined for Quechuan languages as those that can take regular-noun direct objects case-marked accusative (*llama-ta maqa-rqa* 'They hit the llama') (1–4).

4 Verbs

(1) *Wak Kashapatapiñam maqarura **César Mullidata**.* LT
   wak   Kashapata-pi-ña-m   maqa-ru-ra   César Mullida-ta
   DEM.D Kashapata-LOC-DISC-EVD   beat-URGT-PST César Mullida-ACC
   'They beat **César Mullida** there in Kashapata.'

(2) *Asñuqa nin, "Ñuqa tarisisayki **sugaykitaqa"**.* SP
   asnu-qa   ni-n,   ñuqa tari-si-sayki   suga-yki-ta-qa
   donkey-TOP say-3   I   find-ACMP-1>2.FUT   rope-2-ACC-TOP
   'The mule said, "I'm going to help you find your **rope**."'

(3) *¿**Maqtakunata** pushanki icha **pashñata**?* AMV
   maqta-kuna-ta   pusha-nki   icha pashña-ta
   young.man-PL-ACC   bring.along-2   or   girl-ACC
   'Are you going to take **the boys** or **the girl**?'

(4) *¡**Vakata** lliwta qaquruy! Rikurushaq hanaypim.* AMV
   vaka-ta   lliw-ta   qaqu-ru-y   ri-ku-ru-shaq
   cow-ACC   all-ACC   toss.out-URGT-IMP   go-REFL-URGT-1.FUT
   hanay-pi-m
   up.hill-LOC-EVD
   'Toss out **the cows, all of them**! I'm going to go up hill.'

In addition to regular transitives, verbs of motion (*lluqsi-* 'leave') (5) and impersonal ("weather") verbs (*riti-* 'snow') (6), (7) may appear in clauses with regular nouns case-marked *-ta*. In these instances, however, *-ta* does not indicate accusative case.[1]

(5) *Yakupis tukuy **pampata** rikullaq.* AMV
   yaku-pis   tukuy pampa-ta   ri-ku-lla-q
   water-ADD   all   ground-ACC   go-REFL-RSTR-AG
   'The water used to run all **over** the ground.'

(6) *¿Llaqtaykita paranchu?* AMV
   llaqta-yki-ta   para-n-chu
   town-2-ACC   rain-3-Q
   'Does it rain **on** your town?'

---

[1] An anonymous reviewer points out that the verbs in (6) and (7) could be interpreted as transitive (telic) verbs with accusative arguments. *para-*, for example, is interpretable as 'rain on' and *pukuta-* as 'cloud over', in which case *-ta* in *llaqta-yki-ta* and *-kta* in *llaqta-kta* would have to be interpreted as genuine accusatives.

(7) *Tukuy puntraw pukutalunqa llaqta**kta**.* CH
    tukuy puntraw pukuta-lu-nqa   llaqta-kta
    all   day   cloud-URGT-3.FUT town-ACC
    'It's going to cloud over **on** the town all day.'

4.2.2 Intransitive verbs

Intransitive verbs are those, like *puñu-* 'sleep' (1) and *wiña-* 'grow' (2), that cannot occur in clauses including a regular noun case-marked accusative (**puñu-ni kama-ta* target meaning: 'I sleep the bed'). Also included among the intransitives are the impersonal weather verbs, like *qasa-* 'freeze', which do not take subjects (*qasa-ya-n* 'it's freezing').[2]

(1) *Kamapam ñuqa **puñu**kuya: ishkayni:.* ACH
    kama-pa-m   ñuqa   puñu-ku-ya-:   ishkay-ni-:
    bed-LOC-EVD I   sleepREFL-PROG-1 two-EUPH-1
    'We were both **sleep**ing in bed.'

(2) *Chaypaqa **wiña**raptinqa, ¿ayka puntrawnintataq riganchik?* AMV
    chay-pa-qa   wiña-ra-pti-n-qa   ayka
    DEM.D-LOC-TOP   grow-UNINT-SUBDS-3-TOP   how.many
    puntraw-ni-n-ta-taq   riga-nchik
    day-EUPH-3-ACC-SEQ   irrigate-1PL
    'When it **grow**s, at how many days do we water it?'

Verbs of motion (*hamu-* 'come', *lluqsi-* 'exit') form a subclass of intransitive verbs. These often have adverbial complements marked with the directional suffixes *-ta* (accusative), *-man* (allative, dative), *-paq* (ablative) and *-kama* (limitative) (3), (4), and they may occur in clauses that include a nominalization with the agentive suffix *-q* indicating the purpose of movement (5), (6).

(3) *Chay huk madrugaw **trinta i unu di abrilta lluqsi**run waway.* AMV
    chay   huk   madrugaw trinta i   unu di abril-ta
    DEM.D   one   morning   thirty and one of April-ACC
    lluqsi-ru-n   wawa-y
    go.out-URGT-3   baby-1
    'On that morning, **the thirty-first of April**, my son **left** the house [and was kidnapped].'

---

[2] The weather verbs admit only their corresponding weather nouns for subjects. *Para para-ya-n.* 'The rain is raining.'

4 Verbs

(4) *Hinashpa chaypaq wichayman pasachisa chay Amador kaqmanñataq.* ACH
 hinashpa chay-paq wichay-man pasa-chi-sa chay Amador
 then DEM.D-ABL up.hill-ALL pass-CAUS-NPST DEM.D Amador
 ka-q-man-ña-taq
 be-AG-ALL-DISC-SEQ
 'Then, **from** there they made them **march** [to] up high **to** Don Amador's place.'

(5) *Llaman **qutuq ri**sa, mayuta pawayashpash saqakarusa.* AMV
 llama-n qutu-q ri-sa mayu-ta pawa-ya-shpa-sh
 llama-3 gather-AG go-NPST river-ACC jump-PROG-SUBIS-EVR
 saqa-ka-ru-sa
 go.down-PASSACC-URGT-NPST
 'She **went to gather** her llamas and when she jumped the river, she fell.'

(6) *Kabraykiwan **qatishiq** hamusa ninkimiki.* AMV
 kabra-yki-wan qati-shi-q hamu-sa ni-nki-mi-ki
 goat-2-INSTR follow-ACMP-AG come-NPST say-2-EVD-IKI
 'He came **to help bring** your goats, you said.'

4.2.3 Copulative/equational verbs

SYQ counts a single copulative verb, *ka-*. Like the English verb *be*, *ka-* has both copulative ('I am a llama') (1), (2) and existential ('There are llamas') (3), (4) interpretations.

(1) *Ñuqa-nchik fwirti **kanchik**, patachita, matrkata, trakranchik lluqsiqta mikushpam.* AMV
 ñuqa-nchik fwirti ka-nchik patachi-ta matrka-ta
 I-1PL strong be-1PL wheat.soup-ACC ground.cereal.meal-ACC
 trakra-nchik lluqsi-q-ta miku-shpa-m
 field-1PL come.out-AG-ACC eat-SUBIS-EVD
 'We **are** strong because we eat what comes out of our fields – wheat soup and machka.'

4.2 *Types of verbs*

(2) *Qammi salvasyunniy **kanki**.* AMV
    qam-mi   salvasyun-ni-y   ka-nki
    you-EVD   salvation-EUPH-1 be-2
    'You **are** my salvation.'

(3) ***Kan**ña piña turu.* AMV
    ka-n-ña   piña turu
    be-3-DISC   mad bull
    '**There are** mean bulls.'

(4) *Rantiqpis **kan**taqmi.* AMV
    ranti-q-pis   ka-n-taq-mi
    buy-AG-ADD   be-3-SEQ-EVD
    '**There are** also buyers.'

Combined with the progressive, *ya-*, it may but need not have a stative interpretation as well (equivalent to the Spanish *estar*) (5), (6).

(5) *¿Cañete, maypahinañatr kayanchik? Karru, mutu, ¡Asu machu!* AMV
    Cañete,   may-pa-hina-ña-tr   ka-ya-nchik   karru mutu
    Cañete   where-LOC-COMP-DISC-EVC   be-PROG-1PL   bus   motorcycle
    'Cañete, like we **are** where already? Cars, motorcycles – My Lord!'

(6) *Qam sumaq sumaq warmim kayanki.* ACH
    qam sumaq   sumaq   warmi-m   ka-ya-nki
    you pretty pretty woman-EVD   be-PROG-2
    'You **are** a very pretty woman.'

ka- is irregular: the third person singular present tense form, *ka-n*, never appears in equational statements, but only in existential statements (7), (8).[3]

(7) *Wira wira**m** matraypi puñushpa, allin pastuta mikushpam.* AMV
    wira wira-m   matray-pi   puñu-shpa   allin pastu-ta
    fat   fat-EVD   cave-LOC   sleep-SUBIS good   pasture.grass-ACC
    miku-shpa-m
    eat-SUBIS-EVD
    'Sleeping in a cave and eating good pasture, my cow **is** really fat.'

---

[3] The verbal system includes just two irregularities, the second being that *haku* 'let's go' is never conjugated.

4 Verbs

(8) *Llutanshiki.* LT
     llutan-shi-ki
     deformed-EVR-IKI
     'They are deformed, they say.'

In these cases, *ka-ya-n* may be employed instead (9), (10).

(9) *Watunqa fiyu fiyu wiqam kayan.* AMV
     watu-n-qa   fiyu   fiyu   wiqa-m   ka-ya-n
     rope-3-TOP   ugly   ugly   twisted-EVD   be-PROG-3
     'Her rope is really horrid twisted wool.'

(10) *¿Alpakachu wak kayan?* AMV
     alpaka-chu   wak   ka-ya-n
     alpaca-Q   DEM.D   be-PROG-3
     'Is that alpaca [wool]?'

4.2.4 Onomatopoetic verbs

Onomatopoetic verbs can be distinguished from other verbs by the shape of their stem. The majority involve the repetition – two to four times – of a syllable or syllable group, most often with the suffixation of *-ya*. Four patterns dominate:

Pattern 1: $([C_1V_1(C_2)]_{S1})[C_1V_1(C_2)]_{S1}[C_1V_1(C_2)]_{S1}$ (*-ya*)(*-ku*)
Pattern 1 involves the repetition of a single syllable twice or three times, generally with *-ya* or, more rarely, *-ku* or *-ya-ku*, i.e., $(S_1)S_1S_1$ (*-ya*)(*-ku*).
qurqurya- 'snore' and *luqluqluqya-* 'boil' are two good examples. Further examples are given in Table 4.1.

Pattern 2: $[C_1V_1(C_2)]_{S1}[C_3V_1]_{S2}[C_3V_1]_{S2}[C_3V_1]_{S2}$(*-ya*)(*-ku*)
Pattern 2, like Pattern 1, involves the repetition of a single syllable generally with *-ya* or, more rarely, *-ku* or *-ya-ku*. Pattern 2 differs from Pattern 1, however, in that the repeated syllable is (1) always repeated three times; (2) never includes a coda; and (3) is preceded by a non-cognate syllable which generally if not always includes the same vowel as does the repeated syllable, i.e., $S_1S_2S_2S_2$(*-ya*)(*-ku*). *bunrururu-* 'thunder' is a good example of this pattern. Further examples are given in Table 4.2.

Pattern 3:
$([[C_1V_1(C_2)]_{S1}[C_1V_1(C_2)]_{S2}]_{U1})[[C_1V_1(C_2)]_{S1}[C_1V_1(C_2)]_{S2}]_{U1}[[C_1V_1(C_2)]_{S1}[C_1V_1(C_2)]_{S2}]_{U1}$(*-ya*)(*-ku*)

4.2 Types of verbs

Table 4.1: Onomatopoetic verbs Pattern 1 examples

(1)	*taqtaq-ya-*	knock, make the sound of knocking on wood
(2)	*qurqur-ya-*	snore, make the sound of snoring
(3)	*kurrkurr-ya-*	ribbit (make the sound of a frog)
(4)	*punpun-ya-*	flub-dub, beat (make the sound of the heart)
(5)	*qasqas-ya-*	make the sound of dry leaves
(6)	*katkat-ya-*	tremble, shake (intrans.)
(7)	*chuqchuq-ya-*	nurse, make the sound of an animal nursing
(8)	*pakpak-ya-ku-*	make the sound of a guinea pig
(9)	*qullqullqull-ya-*	gurgle, make the sound of a stomach
(10)	*luqluqluq-ya-*	boil, make the sound of water boiling
(11)	*quququ-ya-ku-*	croak (make the sound of a frog)

Table 4.2: Onomatopoetic verbs Pattern 2 examples

(1)	*taqlalala-*	clang, make the sound of a can knocking against something
(2)	*bunrururu-*	thunder, make the sound of thunder
(3)	*challallalla-*	drip, make the sound of water dripping
(4)	*lapapapa-ya-*	make the sound of a billy goat chasing a female goat

Table 4.3: Onomatopoetic verbs Pattern 3 examples

(1)	*chiplichipli-*	shine, sparkle
(2)	*piiiiichiwpiiiichiw-*	make the sound of a pichusa
(3)	*iraniraniran-ya-ku-*	moo (make the sound of a cow)
(4)	*wilwichwilwich-ya-ku-*	make the sound of a pheasant

Pattern 3 replaces the single syllable of Pattern 1 with a two-syllable unit, *i.e.*, $([S_1S_2]_{U1})[S_1S_2]_{U1}[S_1S_2]_{U1}$(-ya)(-ku).
One example is *chiplichipli-* 'sparkle'. Further examples are given in Table 4.3.

Pattern 4: Pattern 4, like Patterns 1 and 3, involves the repetition of a single syllable or two-syllable unit two or three times, generally with *-ya* or *-ku*. Pattern 4 differs from Patterns 1 and 3, however, in that the final consonant in the final iteration is eliminated or changed. Examples of this pattern include *waqwaqwaya-* 'guffaw' and *chalaqchalanya-* 'clang'. Table 4.4 supplies more.

There are further, less common variations. For example, *kurutukutu-* 'make the sound of a male guinea pig chasing a female guinea pig' involves the repe-

4 Verbs

Table 4.4: Onomatopoetic verbs Pattern 4 examples

(1)	*chalaqchalan/ya-*	clang, make the sound of metal things coming into contact with each other
(2)	*waqwaqwa-ya-*	laugh heartily, guffaw
(3)	*chiwachiwa-ya-ku-*	make the sound of a chivillo bird

tition of a three-syllable unit with the elimination of the second syllable in the final iteration.

(1) *Fwirapapis* **katkatyakuyanchik**. ACH
 fwira-pa-pis katkatyaku-ya-nchik
 outside-LOC-ADD tremble-PROG-1PL
 'Outside, too, we're **trembling**.'

(2) *Tutaña killapa sumaq sumaq kaballiriya hamukuyasa pampata* **chiplichiplishpa**. AMV
 tuta-ña killa-pa sumaq sumaq kaballiriya
 night-DISC moon-LOC pretty pretty horse
 hamu-ku-ya-sa pampa-ta chiplichipli-shpa
 come-REFL-PROG-NPST ground-ACC sparkle-SUBIS
 'At night, under the moon, a beautiful horse was coming across the ground, **sparkling**.'

(3) *Unayqa wamaq wamaq rayu kakullaq. "¡Qangran! ¡Qangran!"* **taqlaqyakuq**. AMV
 unay-qa wamaq wamaq rayu ka-ku-lla-q qangra-n
 before-TOP a.lot a.lot thunder be-REL-RSTR-AG growl-3
 qangra-n taqlaqyaku-q
 growl-3 rumble-AG
 'Before, there was a whole lot of thunder. "Bbrra-boom! Bbrra-boom!" it **rumbled**.'

(4) ***Chitchityaku**shpa rikullan kabrakunaqa*. LT
 chitchityaku-shpa ri-ku-lla-n kabra-kuna-qa
 say.chit.chit-SUBIS go-REFL-RSTR-3 goat-PL-TOP
 '**Chit-chitting**, the goats left.'

4.3 Verb inflection

4.3.1 Summary

Verbs in SYQ, as in other Quechuan languages, inflect for person, number, tense, conditionality, imperativity, aspect, and subordination.

In practice, SYQ counts three persons: first, second, and third (*ñuqa, qam,* and *pay*). SYQ verbs inflect for plurality in the first person (*-nchik*); singular and plural suffixes are identical in the second and third persons (*-nki, -n*). Although SYQ makes available a three-way distinction between dual, inclusive and exclusive in the first person plural (*ñuqanchik, ñuqanchikkuna, nuqakuna*), in practice, in all but the CH dialect, the dual form is employed in all three cases; inclusive and exclusive interpretations are supplied by context, both linguistic and extra-linguistic.

Transitive verbs with non-reflexive first or second person objects inflect for actor-object reference (*-wan, -yki,* etc.) Verbal inflection in SYQ marks three tenses, present, past (*-RQa*), and future (portmanteau); the perfect (*-sHa*); the progressive (*-ya*); the present and past conditional (*-man (karqa)*); and the second person and first person plural imperative (*-y, -shun*) and third person injunctive (*-chun*). In practice, SYQ counts two adverbial subordinating suffixes, one employed when the subjects of the main and subordinated clauses are different (*-pti*); the other when they are the identical (*-shpa*). A third subordinating suffix (*-shtin*), also employed when the subjects of the two clauses are identical, is recognized, if not frequently used. Inflectional suffixes (IA) follow derivational suffixes (DA), if any are present; derivational suffixes attach to the verb stem (VS). Thus, a SYQ verb is built: VS – (DA) – IA (see §7.1 and 7.12 on constituent order and sentences).

The dialects of SYQ differ in the suffixes they employ in the first person. One set – AMV and LT – follow the pattern of the QII languages, employing *-ni* to mark the first-person singular nominative and *-wa* to mark the accusative/dative; another set – ACH, SP, CH – follow the QI pattern, employing *-:* (vowel length) for the first-person singular nominative and *-ma* for the accusative dative. The person-number suffixes are: *-ni* or *-:* (1P), *-nki* (2P), *-n* (3P), and *-nchik* or *-ni/ -:* (1PL). SYQ verbs also inflect for actor-object reference. The subject-object suffixes are: *-yki* (1>2), *-wanki* or *-manki* (2>1), *-wan* or *-man* (3>1), *-shunki* (3>2), *-wanchik* or *-manchik* (3>1PL), and *-sHQayki* (1>2.FUT). Examples: *ni-nki* 'you say'; *qawa-yki* 'I see you' (see §4.3.2).

The simple present tense is unspecified for time. It generally indicates temporally unrestricted or habitual action. The simple present tense is indicated by the

4 Verbs

suffixation of person-number suffixes alone; these are unaccompanied by any other inflectional markers. Example: *yanu-ni* (*sapa puntraw*) 'I cook (every day)' (see §4.3.3.1).

Future suffixes simultaneously indicate person, number and tense. The future suffixes are: *-shaq* (1P), *-nki* (2P), *-nqa* (3P), and *-shun* (1PL). Note that the second person future suffix is identical to the second person simple present suffix. Examples: *chawa-shaq* 'I will milk'; *pawa-nki* 'you will jump'; *picha-nqa* 'they will sweep' (see §4.3.3.2).

The simple past tense alone generally does not receive a completive interpretation; indeed, speakers generally translate it into Spanish with the present perfect. The simple past tense is indicated by the suffix *-RQa*, realized as *-rqa* in AMV, *-ra* in ACH, LT, SP, and *-la* in CH. These are immediately followed by person-number suffixes which are identical to the present tense person-number suffixes with the single exception that the third person is realized not as *-n* but as *-ø*. Examples: *qawa-rqa-ni* 'I saw' or 'I have seen'; *patrya-la-ø* 'it/they exploded or 'it/they has/have exploded'; *hamu-ra-nki* 'you came' or 'you have come' (see §4.3.3.3.1).

The quotative simple past tense can be used in story-telling. The quotative simple past is indicated by the suffix *-sHQa*, realized as *-sa* in ACH, AMV and SP and *-sha* in CH and LT. It is sometimes realized in all dialects as *-shqa* in the first and sometimes last line of a story. Examples: *nasi-sa-:* 'I was born'; *ri-shqa* 'he went'; *hamu-sa-ø* 'they came' (see §4.3.3.3.2).

Within the morphological paradigm, *-sHa* – realized as *-sa* in ACH, AMV and SP and *-sha* in CH and LT – occupies a slot that seems to be reserved for the perfect. Its interpretation, however, is more subtle and it is most often employed as a completive past. *-sHa* is immediately followed by the same person-number suffixes as is simple past (i.e., the third person is realized as *-ø*). Example: *ri-sa-nki* 'you have gone' (see §4.3.3.3.3).

The iterative past is indicated by the combination – as independent words – of the agentive verb form (V-*q*) and – in the first and second persons – the corresponding present tense form of the verb *-ka* 'to be'. Examples: *ri-q* 'she used to go'; *ri-q ka-nchik* 'we used to go' (see §4.3.3.3.4).

The conditional (also called "potential" or "irrealis") covers more territory than does the conditional in English. It corresponds to the existential and universal ability, circumstantial, deontic, epistemic, and teleological modals of English. The regular conditional is indicated by the suffix *-man*. *-man* is immediately preceded by person-number suffixes. In the case of the first person singular, the suffixes of the nominal (possessive) paradigm are employed: *-y* in the AMV and LT dialects and *-:* in the ACH, CH, and SP dialects. Alternative conditional forms are attested in the second person both singular and plural in the AMV dialect and first person

4.3 Verb inflection

plural in all dialects. *-waq* indicates the second person conditional; *-chuwan*, the first person plural conditional. Both these morphemes simultaneously indicate person and conditionality and are in complementary distribution both with tense and inflectional morphemes. The past conditional is formed by the addition of *ka-RQa* – the third person simple past tense form of *ka-* 'be' to either the regular or alternative present tense conditional form. Examples: *ri-nki-man* 'you can go'; *ri-chuwan* 'we can go' (see §4.3.4).

Imperative suffixes simultaneously indicate person, number and imperativity. The imperative suffixes are: *-y* (2P) and *-shun* (1PL); the injunctive suffix is *-chun* (1PL). Examples: *¡Ri-y!* 'Go!', *¡Ruwa-shun!* 'Let's do it!', and *¡Lluqsi-chun!* 'Let him leave!' (see §4.3.5).

Progressive aspect is indicated by the derivational suffix *-ya*. *-ya* precedes[4] person-number suffixes and time suffixes, if any are present are present. Example: *ri-ya-n* 'she/he/they is/are going'; *ri-ya-ra-ø* 'she/he/they was/were going' (see §4.3.6).

Subordination is not entirely at home with verbal inflection. Subordinating suffixes are different from inflectional suffixes in that, first, they cannot combine with tense, imperativity, or conditionality suffixes, and, second, they are inflected with the person-number suffixes of the nominal paradigm and not those of the verbal paradigm. SYQ makes use of three subordinating suffixes: *-pti*, *-shpa* and *-shtin*: *-pti* is used when the subjects of the main and subordinate clauses are different; *-shpa* and *-shtin*, when the subjects are identical. Cacra, following the pattern of the QI languages, uses *-r* (realized [l]) in place of *-shpa*. *-pti* is generally translated 'when', but also occasionally receives the translations 'if', 'because', or 'although'. *-shpa* may receive any of these translations, but is most often translated with a gerund. *-shtin* is translated with a gerund exclusively. All three inherit tense, conditionality, and aspect specification from the main-clause verb. *-pti* always inflects for person-number; *-shpa* and *-shtin* never do. Person-number suffixes are those of the nominal paradigm: *-y* or *-:* (1P), *-Yki* (2P), *-n* (3P), and *-nchik* (1PL). Examples: *Hamu-**pti**-ki lluqsi-rqa-ø* 'when/because you came, she left'; *Kustumbra-ku-**shpa** hawka-m yatra-ku-nchik* 'When/if we adjust, we live peacefully' (see §4.3.7).

Table 4.5 summarizes this information. In this and the tables that follow, for reasons of space, unless otherwise specified, all dialects employ the same forms.

---

[4] The derivational affixes *-mu*, *-chi*, and *-ru* may intervene between *-ya* and the inflectional affixes.

4 Verbs

The following abbreviations and conventions are employed:

'you'	→ you.s/you.PL
'he'	→ he/she/it/they
'can …'	→ can/could/will/would/shall/should/may/might
'could …'	→ could/would/should/might
'when …'	→ when/if/because/although/not until or V-ing

A verb appearing inside angled brackets <like this> indicates a root without tense, conditionality or aspect specified.

Dialects differ from each other in four sets of cases. They diverge in terms of (1) their treatment of the first person singular and the first person plural exclusive; (2) their realization of the simple past tense morpheme -RQa; (3) their realization of the perfect morpheme -sHa and (4) their realization of */r/.

Table 4.5 displays the differences among the dialects that are relevant to verbal inflection.

Table 4.5: Verbal inflectional suffixes with different realizations in SYQ dialects

	First person singular	past tense suffix -RQa	Perfect -sHa	Second-person alternative conditional
AMV	-ni	-rqa	-sa	yes
ACH	-:	-ra	-sa	no
CH	-:	-la	-sha	no
SP	-:	-ra	-sa	no
LT	-ni	-ra	-sha	no

Tables 4.6 and 4.7 give the verbal inflection paradigm of SYQ. All processes are suffixing, i.e., a verb root precedes all inflectional morphemes. Translations are given as if for the verb *ni-* 'say.' Details of form and use as well as extensive examples follow in §4.3.2–4.3.7.

Table 4.6: Verbal inflection paradigm

Tense	1P	2P	3P	1PL
Present	-ni_{AMV,LT} / -:_{ACH,CH,SP} 'I say'	-nki 'you say'	-n 'he says'	-nchik 'we say'
Future	-shaq 'I will say'	-nki 'you will say'	-nqa 'he will say'	-shun 'we will say'
Past	-rqa-ni_{AMV} -ra-ni_{LT} -ra-:_{ACH,SP} -la-:_{CH} 'I (have) said'	-rqa-nki_{AMV} -ra-nki_{ACH,LT,SP} -la-nki_{CH} 'you (have) said'	-rqa-∅_{AMV} -ra-∅_{ACH,LT,SP} -la-∅_{CH} 'he (has) said'	-rqa-nchik_{AMV} -ra-nchik_{ACH,LT,SP} -la-nchik_{CH} 'we (have) said'
Narrative past	-sa-ni_{AMV} -sha-ni_{LT} -sa-:_{ACH,SP} -sha-:_{CH} 'I have said'	-sa-nki_{ACH,AMV,SP} -sha-nki_{CH,LT} 'you have said'	-sa-∅_{ACH,AMV,SP} -sha-∅_{CH,LT} 'he has said'	-sa-nchik_{ACH,AMV,SP} -sha-nchik_{CH,LT} 'we have said'
Habitual past	-q ka-ni_{AMV,LT} -q ka-:_{ACH,CH,SP} 'I used to say'	-q ka-nki 'you used to say'	-q 'he used to say'	-q ka-nchik 'we used to say'
Continuative	-ya-ni_{AMV,LT} -ya-:_{ACH,CH,SP} 'I am saying'	-ya-nki 'you are saying'	-ya-n 'he is saying'	-ya-nchik 'we are saying'

Continued on next page ...

4 Verbs

Table 4.6. Continued from previous page

Tense	1P	2P	3P	1PL
Conditional (potential)	-y-man$_{AMV,LT}$ -:-man$_{ACH,CH,SP}$ 'I can … say'	-nki-man 'you can … say'	-n-man 'he can … say'	-nchik-man 'we can … say'
Alternative conditional	X	-waq$_{AMV}$ 'you could … say'	X	-chuwan 'we could … say'
Past conditional	-y-man karqa$_{AMV}$ -y-man ka-ra$_{LT}$ -:-man ka-ra$_{ACH,SP}$ -:-man ka-la$_{CH}$ 'I could … have said'	-nki-man ka-rqa$_{AMV}$ -nki-man ka-ra$_{ACH,LT,SP}$ -nki-man ka-la$_{CH}$ 'you could … have said'	-n-man ka-rqa$_{AMV}$ -n-man ka-ra ACH, LT, SP -n-man ka-la$_{CH}$ 'he could … have said'	-nchik-man ka-rqa$_{AMV}$ -nchik-man ka-ra$_{ACH,LT,SP}$ - nchik-man ka-la$_{CH}$ 'we could … have said'
Alternative past conditional	X	-waq ka-rqa$_{AMV}$ -waq ka-ra$_{LT}$ 'you could … have said'	X	-chuwan ka-rqa$_{AMV}$ -chuwan ka-ra$_{ACH,SP,LT}$ -chuwan ka-la$_{CH}$ 'we could … have said'
Imperative	X	-y 'Say!'	-chun 'Let him say!'	-shun 'Let's say!'
Subordinator different subjects	-pti-y$_{AMV,LT}$ -pti-:$_{ACH,CH,SP}$ 'when … I <say>'	-pti-ki 'when … you <say>'	-pti-n 'when … he <say>'	-pti-nchik 'when … we <say>'
Subordinator identical subj. 1	-shpa 'when … I <say>'	-shpa 'when … you <say>'	-shpa 'when … he <say>'	-shpa 'when … we <say>'

Continued on next page …

134

4.3 Verb inflection

Table 4.6. Continued from previous page

Tense	1P	2P	3P	1PL
Subordinator identical subj. 2	-shtin 'saying'	-shtin 'saying'	-shtin 'saying'	-shtin 'saying'

Table 4.7: Verbal inflection paradigm, actor-object suffixes

Tense	2>1	3>1	3>1PL	1>2	3>2
Present	-wa-nki_{AMV,LT} -ma-nki_{ACH,CH,SP} 'you say to me'	-wa-n_{AMV,LT} -ma-n_{ACH,CH,SP} 'he says to me'	-wa-nchik_{AMV,LT} -man-chik_{ACH,CH,SP} 'he says to us'	-yki 'I say to you'	-shu-nki 'he says to you'
Future	-wa-nki_{AMV,LT} -ma-nki_{ACH,CH,SP} 'you will say to me'	-wa-nga_{AMV,LT} -ma-nga_{ACH,CH,SP} 'he will say to me'	-wa-shun_{AMV,LT} -ma-shun_{ACH,CH,SP} 'he will say to us'	-sHQayki 'I will say to you'	-shu-nki 'he will say to you'
Past	-wa-rqa-nki_{AMV} -wa-ra-nki_{LT} -ma-ra-nki_{ACH,SP} -ma-la-nki_{CH} 'you (have) said to me'	-wa-rqa-∅_{AMV} -wa-ra-∅_{LT} -ma-ra-∅_{ACH,SP} -ma-la-∅_{CH} 'he (has) said to me'	-wa-rqa-nchik_{AMV} -wa-ra-nchik_{LT} -ma-ra-nchik_{ACH,SP} -ma-la-nchik_{CH} 'he (has) said to us'	-rqa-yki_{AMV} -ra-yki_{LT, ACH, SP} -la-yki_{CH} 'I (have) said to you'	-shu-rqa-nki_{AMV} -shu-ra-nki_{LT, ACH, SP} -shu-la-nki_{CH} 'he (has) said to you'

Continued on next page …

135

Table 4.7. Continued from previous page

Tense	2>1	3>1	3>1PL	1>2	3>2
Narrative past	-wa-sa-nki$_{AMV}$ -wa-sha-nki$_{LT}$ -ma-sa-nki$_{ACH,SP}$ -ma-sha-nki$_{CH}$ 'you (have) said to me'	-wa-sa-ø$_{AMV}$ -wa-sha-ø$_{LT}$ -ma-sa-ø$_{ACH,SP}$ -ma-sha-ø$_{CH}$ 'he (has) said to me'	-wa-sa-nchik$_{AMV}$ -wa-sha-nchik$_{LT}$ -ma-sa-nchik$_{ACH,SP}$ -ma-sha-nchik$_{CH}$ 'he (has) said to us'	-sa-yki$_{AMV, ACH, SP}$ -sha-yki$_{LT, CH}$ 'I (have) said to you'	N/A N/A 'he (has) said to you'
Habitual past	-wa-q ka-nki$_{AMV,LT}$ -ma-q ka-nki$_{ACH,CH,SP}$	-wa-q$_{AMV,LT}$ -ma-q$_{ACH,CH,SP}$	N/A N/A	N/A N/A	N/A N/A
Continuous	-ya-wa-nki$_{AMV,LT}$ -ya-ma-nki$_{ACH,CH,SP}$ 'you are saying to me'	-ya-wa-n$_{AMV,LT}$ -ya-ma-n$_{ACH,CH,SP}$ 'he is saying to me'	-ya-wa-nchik$_{AMV,LT}$ -ya-ma-nchik$_{ACH,CH,SP}$ 'he is saying to us'	-ya-yki 'I am saying to you'	-ya-shu-nki 'he is saying to you'
Conditional	-wa-nki-man$_{AMV,LT}$ -ma-nki-man$_{ACH,CH,SP}$ 'you can ... say to me'	-wa-n-man$_{AMV,LT}$ -ma-n-man$_{ACH,CH,SP}$ 'he can ... say to me'	-wa-nchik-man$_{AMV,LT}$ -ma-nchik-man$_{ACH,CH,SP}$ 'he can ... say to us'	-yki-man 'I can ... say to you'	-shu-nki-man 'he can ... say to you'
Alternative conditional	× ×	× ×	-wa-chuwan$_{AMV,LT}$ -ma-chuwan$_{ACH,CH,SP}$ 'he ca ... say to us'	× ×	× ×

Continued on next page ...

4.3 Verb inflection

Table 4.7. Continued from previous page

Tense	2>1	3>1	3>1PL	1>2	3>2
Past conditional	-wa-nki-man ka-rqa$_{AMV}$ -wa-nki-man ka-ra$_{LT}$	-wa-n-man ka-rqa$_{AMV}$ -wa-n-man ka-ra$_{LT}$	-wa-nchik-man ka-rqa$_{AMV}$ -wa-nchik-man ka-ra$_{LT}$	-yki-man ka-rqa $_{AMV}$ -yki-man ka-ra $_{LT}$	-shu-nki-man ka-rqa$_{AMV}$ -shu-nki-man ka-ra$_{LT}$
	-ma-nki-man ka-ra$_{ACH,SP}$ -ma-nki-man ka-la$_{CH}$	-ma-n-man ka-ra$_{ACH,SP}$ -ma-n-man ka-la$_{CH}$	-ma-nchik-man ka-ra$_{ACH,SP}$ -ma-nchik-man ka-la$_{CH}$		
	'you could ... have said to me'	'he could ... have said to us'	'he could ... have said to us'	'I could ... have said to you'	'he could ... have said to you'
Alternative past conditional	×	×	-wa-chuwan ka-rqa$_{AMV}$	×	×
	×	×	-ma-chuwan ka-ra$_{LT,ACH,SP}$	×	×
	×	×	-ma-chuwan ka-la$_{CH}$	×	×
		'he could ... say to us'			
Subordinator different subjects	-wa-pti-ki$_{AMV,LT}$ -ma-pti-ki$_{ACH,CH,SP}$	-wa-pti-n$_{AMV,LT}$ -ma-pti-n$_{ACH,CH,SP}$	-wa-pti-nchik$_{AMV,LT}$ -ma-pti-nchik$_{ACH,CH,SP}$	-pti-ki	-shu-pti-ki
	'when ... you say to me'	'when ... he says to me'	'when ... he says to us'	'when ... I say to you'	'when ... he says to you'

4 Verbs

4.3.2 Person and number

SYQ non-subordinate verbs inflect for actor and object reference; substantives inflect for allocation.

4.3.2.1 Subject

The first person is indicated in both the verbal and substantive paradigms in ACH, CH, and SP by -:$_{ACH,CH,SP}$; in AMV, LT; these are indicated by -$ni_{AMV,LT}$, and -$y_{AMV,LT}$, respectively. -: and -*ni* attach to verb stems (plus derivational or inflectional suffixes, if any are present, with the single exception that -*ni* cannot precede the conditional suffix -*man*) (*puri-**ni***, *puri-:* 'I walk'). -: and -*y* attach to the subordinating suffix -*pti* (*qawa-pti-y*, *qawa-pti-:* 'when ... I see') and to the verb stem in the conditional (*lluqsi-y -man*, *lluqsi-:-man* 'I could leave').

In all dialects the second person is indicated in the verbal paradigm by -*nki* and in the substantive paradigm by -*yki*. -*nki* attaches to verb stems (plus derivational or inflectional suffixes, if any are present, except -*man*) (*puri-**nki*** 'you walk'); the -*yki* allomorph -*ki* attaches to the subordinator -*pti* (*qawa-pti-**ki*** 'when ... you see'. In Cacra, -*k* indicates that the second person is the object of an action by the first person in the present tense (*qu-k* 'I give you').

-*n* indicates the third person and -*nchik* refers to a group that includes the speaker and the addressee and, potentially, others in both the verbal and substantive paradigms. -*n* and -*nchik* attach to verb roots (plus derivational and inflectional suffixes, if any are present) (*puri-n* 'he/they walk/s'; *puri-**nchik*** 'we walk') and the the subordinating suffix -*pti* as well (*qawa-**pti-n*** 'when ... you see' *qawa-**pti-nchik*** 'when ... you see'). This information is summarized in Table 4.8.

4.3.2.2 Actor and object reference

-$wa_{AMV,LT}$ and -$ma_{ACH,CH,SP}$ indicate a first person object. Followed by the second person verbal suffix (-*nki*) -*wa* and -*ma* indicate that the speaker is the object of action by the addressee (*qu-**wa-nki***, *qu-**ma-nki*** 'you give me') (1), (2); followed by third person verbal suffix (-*n*), they indicate that the speaker is the object of action by a third person (*qu-**wa-n***, *qu-**ma-n*** 'he/she/they give/s me') (3), (4).

(1) ¡Dios Tayta! ¿Imata willakuyawanki? AMV
     Dios tayta   ima-ta   willa-ku-ya-wa-nki
     God   father what-ACC   tell-REFL-PROG-1.OBJ-2
     'My God! What are **you** telling **me**?'

4.3 Verb inflection

Table 4.8: Person suffixes by environment

Person	verb stem + suffixes	subordinator -shpa	subordinator -pti	substantive (short) i final	substantive (short) a, u final	substantive C. (or long V.) final	conditional V. stem + suffixes
1	-ni$_{AMV,LT}$	-y$_{AMV,LT}$	-y$_{AMV,LT}$	-y$_{AMV,LT}$	-y$_{AMV,LT}$	-ni-y$_{AMV,LT}$	-y$_{AMV,LT}$
	-:$_{ACH,CH,SP}$	-:$_{ACH,CH,SP}$	-:$_{ACH,CH,SP}$	-:$_{ACH,CH,SP}$	-:$_{ACH,CH,SP}$	-ni-:$_{ACH,CH,SP}$	-:$_{ACH,CH,SP}$
2	-nki	-yki	-ki	-ki	-yki	-ni-ki	-nki
3	-n	-n	-n	-n	-n	-ni-n	-n
1PL	-nchik	-nchik	-nchik	-nchik	-nchik	-ni-nchik	-nchik

(2) *Qam nima**ra**nki, "¿Kuyurayanchu?"* SP
    qam ni-**ma**-ra-nki,   kuyu-ra-ya-n-chu
    you say-1.OBJ-PST-2 move-PASS-ACC-PROG-3-Q
    'You asked **me**, "Was it moving?"'

(3) *Kaywan pampachi**wan**.* AMV
    kay-wan   pampa-chi-**wa**-n
    DEM.P-INSTR   bury-CAUS-1.OBJ-3
    'He'll bury **me** with this.'

(4) *Hapira**man**.* ACH
    hapi-ra-**ma**-n
    grab-URGT-1.OBJ-3
    'It took hold of **me**.'

-*nchik* pluralizes a first-person object (*qu-**wa**-nchik, qu-**ma**-nchik* 'he/she/they give/s us') (5–7).

(5) *Lliw lliw mushuq kambyachi**wanchik** rupanchiktam hinashpam kahunman wina**wanchik**.* AMV
    lliw lliw mushuq kambya-chi-**wa**-nchik   rupa-nchik-ta-m
    all all new   change-CAUS-1.OBJ-1PL   clothes-1PL-ACC-EVD
    hinashpa-m kahun-man   wina-**wa**-nchik
    then   coffin-ALL toss.in-1.OBJ-1PL
    'They change **us** into brand new clothes. Then they toss **us** into a coffin.'

4 Verbs

(6) *Mancharichi**manchik** tuta.* ACH
   mancha-ri-chi-man-chik   tuta
   scare-INCEP-CAUS-1.OBJ-1PL night
   'It scares **us** at night.'

(7) *Mitamik. Trura**manchik** kwadirnuman sutinchikta.* CH
   mita-mi-k   trura-ma-nchik   kwadirnu-man suti-nchik-ta
   quota-EVD-IK put-1.OBJ-1PL   notebook-ALL name-1PL-ACC
   'A water quota. They put **us**, our names, in a notebook.'

Followed by second person imperative suffix (*-y*), *-wa/-ma* indicates that the speaker is the object of action by the addressee (*¡Qu-**wa**-y!*, *¡Qu-**ma**-y!* 'Give me!') (8), (9).

(8) *¡Qawaykachi**way** chay kundinawpa wasinta!* AMV
   qawa-yka-chi-wa-y   chay   kundinaw-pa wasi-n-ta
   see-EXCEP-CAUS-1.OBJ-IMP DEM.D zombie-GEN   house-3-ACC
   'Show **me** the zombie's house!'

(9) *"¡Amayá dihara**may**chu!" nishpa lukuyakuyan.* ACH
   ama-yá   diha-ra-**ma**-y-chu   ni-shpa
   PROH-EMPH   leave-URGT-1.OBJ-IMP-NEG say-SUBIS
   luku-ya-ku-ya-n
   crazy-INCH-REFL-PROG-3
   'Saying, "Don't leave **me**!" he is going crazy.'

-shu, followed by a second person verbal suffix (*-nki*), indicates that the addressee is the object of action by a third person (*qu-shu-nki* 'he/she/they give/s you') (10).

(10) *Makinchikqa tusku kaptinqa vakapa nanachinqa chichinta saytarushpa diharu**shunki**.* AMV
   maki-nchik-qa tusku   ka-pti-n-qa   vaka-pa   nana-chi-nqa
   hand-1PL-TOP rough   be-SUBDS-3-TOP   cow-GEN   hurt-CAUS-3.FUT
   chichi-n-ta   sayta-ru-shpa   diha-ru-shunki
   teat-3-ACC   kick-URGT-SUBIS leave-URGT-3>2
   'When our hands are rough, they make the cow's teats hurt and **she** kicks and leaves **you**.'

-sHQayki indicates that the addressee is the object of future action by the speaker (*qu-**sa**-yki* 'I give you') (11–14).

4.3 Verb inflection

(11) *Wirayachisayki.* ACH
    wira-ya-chi-sayki
    fat-INCH-CAUS-1>2.FUT
    '**I'm going to** fatten **you** up.'

(12) *Kanallan shuyakaramusayki.* SP
    kanallan shuya-ka-ra-mu-sayki
    just.now wait-PASSACC-URGT-CISL-1>2.FUT
    'Right now, **I'm going to** wait for **you**.'

(13) *Kay qullqita qusqayki.* AMV
    kay qullqi-ta qu-sqayki
    DEM.P money-ACC give-1>2.FUT
    '**I'm going to** give **you** this money.'

(14) *Ñuqa qipirushqayki llaqtayta.* AMV
    ñuqa qipi-ru-shqayki llaqtayta
    I carry-URGT-1>2.FUT town-1-ACC
    '**I'm going to** carry **you** to my town.'

The object suffixes – -*wa*/-*ma*, -*shu* and -*sHQa* – succeed aspect suffixes (15–17) and precede tense (18–20) and subordinating suffixes (21–27), as well as the nominalizing suffix -*na* (28), (29) (*qu-ya--wa-nki* 'you are giving me'; *qu-wa-rqa-ø* 'you gave me'; *qu-su-pti-ki* 'when he/she/they gave you'; *qu-wa-na-n-paq* 'so he/she/they give/s me').

(15) *Munashantañam ruwan runaqa tantyayawantriki.* LT
    muna-sha-n-ta-ña-m ruwa-n runa-qa
    want-PRF-3-ACC-DISC-EVD make-3 person-TOP
    tantya-ya-wa-n-tri-ki
    size.up-PROG-1.OBJ-3-EVC-IKI
    'People do what they want already. They must be sizing me up, for sure.'

(16) *Kwirpum nanayan. Kaymi kay runam aysayamanña.* ACH
    kwirpu-m nana-ya-n kay-mi kay runa-m
    body-EVD hurt-PROG-3 DEM.P-EVD DEM.P person-EVD
    aysa-ya-ma-n-ña
    pull-PROG-1.OBJ-3-DISC

4 Verbs

'[My] body is hurting. These **people are** pull**ing me** over here like this.'

(17) *Huktriki apayashunki. ¿Kikillaykichu puriyanki mutuwan?* AMV
 huk-tri-ki apa-ya-shunki kiki-lla-yki-chu puri-ya-nki
 one-EVC-IKI bring-PROG-3>2 self-RSTR-2-Q walk-PROG-2
 mutu-wan
 motorcycle-INSTR
 '**Someone** else must **be** bring**ing you**. Or are you yourself wandering around with a motorbike?'

(18) *Chaynam kundur qipiwarqa matrayta.* AMV
 chayna-m kundur qipi-wa-rqa matray-ta
 thus-EVD condor carry-1.OBJ-PST cave-ACC
 'Like that, **the condor** carried **me** to his cave.'

(19) *"¿Imapaq aysapamaranki ñuqa hawka puñukupti:?" nishpash.* SP
 imapaq aysa-pa-ma-ra-nki ñuqa hawka puñu-ku-pti-:
 why pull-BEN-1.OBJ-PST-2 I tranquil sleep-REFL-SUBDS-1
 ni-shpa-sh
 say-SUBIS-EVR
 '"Why **did you** tug at **me** when I was sleeping peacefully?" said [the zombie].'

(20) *Nirayki.* SP
 ni-ra-yki
 say-PST-1>2
 'I said to **you**.'

(21) *Hamullarqani chikchik paralla **tapallawaptin** yana puyulla **ñitillawaptin**.* AMV
 hamu-lla-rqa-ni chikchik para-lla tapa-lla-wa-pti-n yana
 come-RSTR-PST-1 hail rain-RSTR cover-RSTR-1.OBJ-SUBDS-3 black
 puyu-lla ñiti-lla-wa-pti-n
 cloud-RSTR crush-RSTR-1.OBJ-SUBDS-3
 'I came **when** the freezing rain was **covering me, when** the black fog was **crushing me**.'

4.3 Verb inflection

(22) *¡Kay pampaman qatimuchun! Wakpa **ñitiruwaptin**qa.* AMV
 kay pampa-man qati-mu-chun wak-pa
 DEM.P plain-ALL follow-CISL-INJUNC DEM.D-LOC
 ñiti-ru-wa-pti-n-qa
 crush-URGT-1.OBJ-SUBDS-3-TOP
 'Let him bring it toward that plain – over there **he would crush me**.'

(23) *Mana yakukta **qumaptin**, ¿Imaynataq alfa:pis planta:pis kanqa?* CH
 mana yaku-kta qu-ma-pti-n, imayna-taq alfa-:-pis
 no water-ACC give-1.OBJ-SUBDS-3 how-SEQ alfalfa-ADD
 planta-:-pis ka-nqa
 plant-1-ADD be-3.FUT
 '**If they** don't **give me** water, how will I have alfalfa and plants?'

(24) *Wamra willa**suptiki**.* LT
 wamra willa-su-pti-ki
 child tell-2.OBJ-SUBDS-2
 '**When the** children told **you**.'

(25) *Sudarachi**shuptiki** kapasmi surqurunman.* AMV
 suda-ra-chi-shu-pti-ki kapas-mi surqu-ru-n-man
 sweat-URGT-CAUS-2.OBJ-SUBDS-2 perhaps-EVD take.out-URGT-3-COND
 '**When it** makes **you** sweat, it's possible he could remove it.'

(26) *Tantya**washpa** chayta ruwan.* LT
 tantya-wa-shpa chay-ta ruwa-n
 size.up-1.OBJ-SUBIS DEM.D-ACC make-3
 'Sizing **me** up, **they** do that.'

(27) *Wasari**mashpa**m nuchipis kwintakuq.* SP
 wasa-ri-ma-shpa-m nuchi-pis kwinta-ku-q
 wake-INCEP-1.OBJ-SUBIS-EVD night-ADD tell.story-REFL-AG
 'At night, **they** would wake **me** up and tell stories.'

(28) *Pipis fakultayku**wananpaq**.* LT
 pi-pis fakulta-yku-wa-na-n-paq
 who-ADD assist-EXCEP-1.OBJ-NMLZ-3-PURP
 '**So someone** can help **me** out.'

4 Verbs

(29) *Raki**shunaykipaq**.* AMV
raki-shu-na-yki-paq
separate-2.OBJ-NMLZ-2-PURP
'So he sets some aside **for you**.'

Both object and subject suffixes – -*wa*/-*ma*, -*shu* and -*sHQa*, as well as -*nki*, -*YkI*, and -*n* – precede the conditional suffix -*man* (*qu-**wa**-**nki**-**man*** 'you could give me') (30–32).

(30) *Sarurulla**wankiman**. Manam saruwanantaq munaniñachu.* AMV
saru-ru-lla-wa-nki-man   mana-m saru-wa-na-n-taq
trample-URGT-RSTR-1.OBJ-COND-2 no-EVD trample-1.OBJ-NMLZ-3-SEQ
muna-ni-ña-chu
want-1-DISC-NEG
'**You could** trample **me**. I don't want **him** to trample **me** any more.'

(31) *Mana chichiyuq kaptikiqa chayna lluqari**shunkiman**tri.* AMV
mana   chichi-yuq   ka-pti-ki-qa   chayna
no   breast-POSS   be-SUBDS-2-TOP   thus
lluqa-ri-shu-nki-man-tri
top-INCEP-2.OBJ-2-COND-EVC
'When you don't have breasts **they can** top **you**.'

(32) *¡Kwidadu! Chaypitaq qalqali mikulu**shunkiman**.* CH
kwidadu chay-pi-taq   qalqali   miku-lu-shunki-man
careful DEM.D-LOC-SEQ   zombie   eat-URGT-2.OBJ-2-COND
'Be careful! **A demon could** eat **you** there.'

Exceptions to these rules arise when object is 1PL. First, the first-person object pluralizer, -*nchik*, does not precede aspect, tense, subordinating, nominalizing and conditional suffixes, but, rather, succeeds them (*ñiti-ru-wa-n-**man**-**chik*** 'it could crush us') (33–35).

(33) *Mana kanan tumaytam munanchu qaninpaq*
    ***shinkarachiwarqanchik**.* AMV
mana kanan tuma-y-ta-m   muna-n-chu   qanin-paq
no   now   drink-INF-ACC-EVD   want-3-NEG   previous-ABL
shinka-ra-chi-wa-rqa-nchik
get.drunk-URGT-CAUS-1.OBJ-PST-1PL
'She doesn't want to drink now. Earlier, **they had got us drunk**.'

4.3 Verb inflection

(34) *Chiri **pasawaptinchikpis**, wiksa nanaykunapaq.* AMV
chiri pasa-wa-pti-nchik-pis wiksa nana-y-kuna-paq
cold pass-3l.OBJ-SUBDS-1PL-ADD stomach hurt-INF-PL-ABL
'**When we get chills** or for stomach pain [this plant is good].'

(35) *Ñitiruwanmanchik.* AMV
ñiti-ru-wan-ma-nchik
crush-URGT-1.OBJ-1PL-COND-3>1PL
'It could crush **us**.'

Second, 3>1PL future is not indicated by *-wa/ma-**nqa-nchik**, as it would were it regular, but rather by *-wa/mashun* (36), (37).

(36) *Mundum **ñitiramashun**. Kaytam sustininkiqa.* SP
mundu-m ñiti-ra-ma-shun kay-ta-m sustini-nki-qa
world-EVD crush-URGT-1.OBJ-1PL.FUT DEM.P-ACC-EVD sustain-2-TOP
'**The world is going to crush us**. Hold this one up.'

(37) *Watyarunshi. Chaynatr **watyaramashun** ñuqanchiktapis.* ACH
watya-ru-n-shi chayna-tr watya-ra-ma-shun
bake-URGT-3-EVR thus-EVC bake-URGT-1.OBJ-1PL.FUT
ñuqa-nchik-ta-pis
I-1PL-ACC-ADD
'They got baked, they say. Like that, **we're going to get baked**, us, too.'

Finally, third, just as the 1PL conditional may be indicated by either of two forms, one regular (*-nchik-man*) one alternative/portmanteau (*-chuwan*), the 3>1PL conditional, too, may be indicated by both regular (*-wa/ma-n-man-chik*) and portmanteau forms (*-wa/ma-chuwan*) (*chuka-ru-**wa-chuwan*** 'it can make us sick'):

(38) *Kayanmi uniku qullqiyuqpaq. ¿Maypam rigala**wachuwan** runaqa?* AMV
ka-ya-n-mi uniku qullqi-yuq-paq may-pa-m
be-PROG-3-EVD only money-POSS-BEN where-LOC-EVD
rigala-wa-chuwan runa-qa
gift-1.OBJ-1PL.COND person-TOP
'There are only for rich people. Where **can people give us** things for free?'

4 Verbs

(39) *Miku**machuwan**tri.* ACH
 miku-ma-chuwan-tri
 eat-1.OBJ-1PL.COND-EVC
 'He could eat **us**.'

In all other cases, subject-object suffixes combine with standard morphology (40–42).

(40) *Qampis kuntistamu**wanki**má.* AMV
 qam-pis kuntista-mu-wa-nki-m-á
 you-ADD answer-CISL-1.OBJ-2-EVD-EMPH
 '**You**, too, are going to answer **me**.'

(41) *¿**Allichawanqa**chu manachu? Yatrarunqaña kukantaqa qawaykushpa.* AMV
 alli-cha-wa-nqa-chu mana-chu yatra-ru-nqa-ña
 good-FACT-1.OBJ-3.FUT-Q no-Q know-URGT-3.FUT-DISC
 kuka-n-ta-qa qawa-yku-shpa
 coca-3-ACC-TOP see-EXCEP-SUBIS
 'Is **he going to heal me** or not? He'll find out by looking at his coca.'

(42) *Tirruristam hamuyan. Wak turutatr pagaykushaqqa manam **wañuchimanqa**chu.* ACH
 tirrurista-m hamu-ya-n wak turu-ta-tr
 terrorist-EVD come-PROG-3 DEM.D bull-ACC-EVC
 paga-yku-shaq-qa mana-m wañu-chi-ma-nqa-chu
 pay-EXCEP-1.FUT-TOP no-EVD die-CAUS-1.OBJ-3.FUT-NEG
 'The terrorists are coming. I'll pay them a bull and **they won't kill me**.'

A typological note: number is expressed in spontaneously-occurring examples only in those cases in which there is a first-person plural object (43). In these cases all SYQ dialects follow the Southern QII pattern ordering suffixes: OBJ-TNS-SBJ-NUM. Note, though, that while in the Southern QII languages *-chik* pluralizes the subject, in SYQ *-chik* pluralizes the object. There are no spontaneous examples following the Central QII pattern NUM-OBJ-TNS-SBJ.

4.3 Verb inflection

(43) *Mana ri**k**una, ¿Imatam rima**sayki**? Yatra**nchik**chu.* AMV
   mana ri-q-kuna ima-ta-m rima-sayki yatra-nchik-chu
   no   go-AG-PL what-ACC-EVD talk-1>2 know-1PL-NEG
   '**People** who haven't gone, what am **I going to say to you**? **We** don't know.'

There are no special forms for third-person objects. A third-person object is indicated by the case-marking of the third-person pronoun *pay* with either accusative *-ta* or allative/dative *-man* (***pay-ta** qawa-nchik* 'we see him/her,' ***pay-kuna-man** qu-nki* 'you give them') (44).

(44) *Kay swirupis allquypaqpis ... nikurunshi **subrinuntaqa**.* LT
   kay swiru-pis allqu-y-paq-pis ni-ku-ru-n-shi
   DEDM.P whey-ADD dog-1-BEN-ADD say-REFL-URGT-3-EVR
   subrinu-n-ta-qa
   nephew-3-ACC-TOP
   'This whey also for my dog also ... he said, they say, **to his nephew**.'

First-and second-person object suffixes may be reinforced with similarly case-marked pronouns (45).

(45) ***Ñuqata uywamara** mamacha: tiyu: tiya:.* SP
   ñuqa-ta uywa-ma-ra mama-cha-: tiyu-: tiya-:
   I-ACC   raise-1.OBJ-PST mother-DIM-1 uncle -1 aunt-1
   'My grandmother and my uncle and aunt **raised me**.'

There are no special forms for actors acting on themselves or any group that includes them: reflexive action is indicated with the derivational suffix *-ku*. 'I see myself' is *ñuqa qawa-**ku**-ni/-:* and 'I see us' is '*ñuqa ñuqanchik-ta qawa-ni/-:*.

Actor-object suffixes are employed both with transitive and ditransitive verbs (*Miku-ru-**shunki*** 'He's going to eat you'; *Kay qullqi-ta qu-**sqayki*** 'I'm going to give you this money'). Actor-object suffixes may be reinforced – but not replaced – by accusative- and dative-marked personal pronouns (*Ñuqa--ta-s harqu-ru-**wa**-ra-ø* 'He tossed **me** out, too').

Except in the two cases 2>1PL and 3>1PL, where *-chik* indicates a plural object, when either the actor or the object is plural, the verb optionally takes the joint action suffix *-pakU* (3PL>2 *Pay-kuna qu-**paku**-shunki tanta-ta qam-man.* 'They give you.s bread'; 1>2PL *Ñuqa qu-**paku**-yki tanta-ta qam-kuna-man* 'I give you.PL bread'). In practice, the plural forms, although recognized, are not spontaneously invoked.

4 Verbs

This information is summarized in Table 4.9. Naturally-occurring examples of the five principal subject-object reference processes (1>2, 2>1, 3>1, 3>2, 3>1PL) are presented in (1–45).

Table 4.9: Actor-object inflectional suffixes

	1OBJ	2OBJ	1PL OBJ
1 SBJ	×	Present: -YkI$_{\text{ACH,AMV,LT,SP}}$ Future: -sHQa-yki	×
2 SBJ	-wa-nki$_{\text{AMV,LT}}$ -ma-nki$_{\text{ACH,CH,SP}}$	×	
3 SBJ	-wa-N$_{\text{AMV,LT}}$ -ma-N$_{\text{ACH,CH,SP}}$	-shu-nki	-wa-nchik$_{\text{AMV,LT}}$ -ma-nchik$_{\text{ACH,CH,SP}}$

4.3.3 Tense

SYQ counts three tenses: present, past, and future (*maska-nchik* 'we look for', *maska-rqa-nchik* 'we looked for', *maska-shun* 'we will look for'). With the exception of the first person plural, person suffixes in SYQ are unmarked for number. *-nki* corresponds to the second person singular and plural (*yanapa-nki* 'you.S/PL help; *maylla-nki* 'you.S/PL wash'). *-N* corresponds to the third person singular and plural (*taki-n* 'she/he/it/they sing(s)'). §4.3.3.1–4.3.3.3 cover the simple present, future and past tenses, in turn.

4.3.3.1 Simple present

The present tense subject suffixes in SYQ are *-ni* and *-:* (1P), *-nki* (2P), *-n* (3P), and *-nchik* (1PL). Examples include: (*atrqay-tuku-ni/-:* 'I pretend to be an eagle', *kundur-tuku-nki* 'you pretend to be a condor', *rutu-tuku-n* 'he pretends to be a *rutu*' (small mountain bird), *qari-tuku-nchik* 'we pretend to be men'). Table 4.10 displays the present tense inflectional paradigm; Table 4.11 displays the paradigm for present tense inflection with actor-object reference (see Subsection 4.3.2.2 for discussion). 1–8 supply examples.

(1) Wasiyta **ñuqaqa pichakuni tallawanmi.** AMV
    wasi-y-ta   ñuqa-qa picha-ku-ni   talla-wan-mi
    house-1-ACC   I-TOP   sweep-REFL-1   straw-INSTR-EVD
    'I sweep my house with straw.'

4.3 Verb inflection

Table 4.10: Present tense inflection

Person	Singular	Plural	
1		-nchik	(dual, incl.)
	-ni$_{AMV,LT}$	-ni$_{AMV,LT}$	(excl.)
	-:$_{ACH,CH,SP}$	-:$_{ACH,CH,SP}$	(excl.)
2	-nki	-nki	
3	-n	-n	

Table 4.11: Present tense inflection – actor-object suffixes

2>1	3>1	3>1pl	1>2	3>2
-wa-nki$_{AMV,LT}$	-wa-n$_{AMV,LT}$	-wa-nchik$_{AMV,LT}$	-yki	-shunki
-ma-nki$_{ACH,CH,SP}$	-ma-n$_{ACH,CH,SP}$	-ma-nchik$_{ACH,CH,SP}$		

(2) *Manam **ñuqa** yatra:chu.* ACH
mana-m ñuqa yatra-:-chu
no-EVD I know-1-NEG
'**I** don't know (how).'

(3) *Qamqa ritamunki urquta.* LT
qam-qa ri-tamu-nki urqu-ta
you-TOP go-IRREV-2 hill-ACC
'**You** left for the hill for good.'

(4) *Allqu mikukun wakchuchataqa.* AMV
allqu miku-ku-n wakchu-cha-ta-qa
dog eat-REFL-3 lamb-DIM-ACC-TOP
'**The dog** ate up the lamb.'

(5) *Viyhunchikta ruwa**nchik** hinashpaqa kaña**nchik**mi.* AMV
viyhu-nchik-ta ruwa-nchik hinashpa-qa kaña-nchik-mi
effigy-1PL-ACC make-1PL then-TOP burn-1PL-EVD
'**We** make our effigy then burn it.'

4 Verbs

(6) *Familyallan **ñuqakuna** suya:.* CH
    familya-lla-n ñuqa-kuna suya-:
    family-RSTR-3 I-PL wait-1
    'Just their relatives – **we** waited.'

(7) *Kanan **qamkuna**tr hamuyanki.* SP
    kanan qam-kuna-tr hamu-ya-nki
    now you-PL-EVC come-PROG-2
    'Now **you**.PL are coming.'

(8) ***Suqta wanka** vakata tumban.* AMV
    suqta wanka vaka-ta tumba-n
    six hired.hand cow-ACC tackle-3
    '**Six hired hands** tackle the cow.'

Although it generally indicates temporally unrestricted or habitual action, the simple present is in fact unmarked for time. Present tense forms may also receive past tense or future tense interpretations in different contexts (*qawa-chi-n* 'he showed/shows/will show') (9).

(9) *Chaytaqa qawaykushpa valurta hapi**ni**.* AMV
    chay-ta-qa qawa-yku-shpa valur-ta hapi-ni
    DEM.D-ACC-TOP see-EXCEP-SUBIS courage-ACC grab-1
    'Looking at that, I gather**ed** courage.'

SYQ makes available a three-way distinction in the first person plural, between *ñuqanchik* (dual), *ñuqanchikkuna* (inclusive), and *ñuqakuna* (exclusive). In practice, *ñuqanchik* is employed with dual, inclusive and exclusive interpretations to the virtual complete exclusion of the other two forms, except in the CH dialect. Verbs and substantives appearing with the inclusive *ñuqanchikkuna* inflect following the same rules as do verbs and substantives appearing with the dual/default *ñuqanchik* (10); verbs and substantives appearing with the exclusive *ñuqakuna* inflect following the same rules as do verbs and substantives appearing with the singular *ñuqa* (11).

(10) *Kaypi **ñuqanchikkuna**qa kustumbrawmi kaya**nchik**.* AMV
     kay-pi nuqa-nchik-kuna-qa kustumbraw-mi ka-ya-nchik
     DEM.P-LOC I-1PL-PL-TOP accustomed-EVD be-PROG-1PL
     'Here, **we**'re accustomed to it.'

4.3 Verb inflection

(11) *Wañuq taytachaymi chaytaqa **ñuqakuna**man willawarqa.* AMV
wañu-q tayta-cha-y-mi chay-ta-qa ñuqa-kuna-man
die-AG father-DIM-1-EVD DEM.D-ACC-TOP I-PL-ALL
willa-wa-rqa
tell-1.OBJ-PST
'Our late grandfather told that to **us**.'

Although *ñuqa* is generally interpreted as singular – likely an implicature attributable to the availability of plural forms in the first person – it is, in fact, unspecified for number and may receive plural interpretations (12).

(12) *Kamapam **ñuqa** puñukuya: ishkayni:.* ACH
kama-pa-m ñuqa puñu-ku-ya-: ishkay-ni-:
bed-LOC-EVD I sleep-REFL-PROG-1 two-EUPH-1
'**We** were **both** sleeping in bed.'

(13) *Dispidichin churinkunata hinashpaqa kañan.* AMV
dispidi-chi-n churi-n-kuna-ta hinashpa-qa kaña-n
bid.farewell-CAUS-3 child-3-PL-ACC then-TOP burn-3
'One has their children say good bye and then burns it [the effigy].'

4.3.3.2 Future

The future tense suffixes in SYQ are *-shaq* (1PL), *-nki* (2), *-nqa* (3), and *-shun* (1S) (1–6). Table 4.12 displays this paradim; Table 4.13 displays the paradidm of future tense inflection with actor-object reference (see Subsection 4.3.2.2 for discussion).

Table 4.12: Future tense inflection

Person	Singular	Plural
1	-shaq	-shun
2	-nki	-nki
3	-nqa	-nqa

4 Verbs

Table 4.13: Future tense inflection – actor-object suffixes

2>1	3>1	3>1pl	1>2	3>2
-wa-nki$_{\text{AMV,LT}}$	-wa-nqa-ø$_{\text{AMV,LT}}$	-wa-shun$_{\text{AMV,LT}}$	-sHQayki	-shunki
-ma-nki$_{\text{ACH,CH,SP}}$	-ma-nqa-ø$_{\text{ACH,CH,SP}}$	-ma-shun$_{\text{ACH,CH,SP}}$		

(1) *Manam iskapanqachu. Wañurachi**shaq**mi.* AMV
    mana-m   iskapa-nqa-chu   wañu-ra-chi-shaq-mi
    no-EVD   escape-3.FUT-NEG die-URGT-CAUS-1.FUT-EVD
    'She's not **going to** escape. **I'll** kill her.'

(2) *Ubiha:ta michimu**shaq** vaka:ta chawaru**shaq** kisuta ruwaru**shaq**.* SP
    ubiha-:-ta   michi-mu-shaq   vaka-:-ta   chawa-ru-shaq
    sheep-1-ACC   pasture-CISL-1.FUT cow-1-ACC   milk-URGT-1.FUT
    kisu-ta   ruwa-ru-shaq
    cheese-ACC   make-URGT-1.FUT
    '**I'm going to** herd my sheep; **I'm going to** milk my cows; **I'm going to** make cheese.'

(3) *Vakatash harka**nki** vakata chawa**nki**.* AMV
    vaka-ta-sh   harka-nki   vaka-ta   chawa-nki
    cow-ACC-EVR   herd-2   cow-ACC   milk-2
    '**You'll** herd the cows; **you'll** milk the cows.'

(4) *Rupari**nqa**tr.* AMV
    rupa-ri-nqa-tr
    burn-INCEP-3.FUT-EVC
    '**It will** be warm [tomorrow].'

(5) *Shimikita siraru**shun**.* SP
    shimi-ki-ta   sira-ru-shun
    mouth-2-ACC   sew-URGT-1PL.FUT
    '**We're going to** sew your mouth shut.'

(6) *Kaytatr paqarikushun.* AMV
 kay-ta-tr   paqa-ri-ku-shun
 DEM.P-ACC-EVC wash-INCEP-REFL-1PL.FUT
 '**We'll** wash this.'

The second person suffix is ambiguous between present and future tense. Second person and third person plural suffixes are the same as those for the second and third persons singular (7–9).

(7) *Qamkunallam parlanki.* CH
 qam-kuna-lla-m   parla-nki
 you-PL-RSTR-EVD talk-2
 'Just **you.PL are going to** talk.'

(8) *Qampa mamaykis taytaykis wañukunqa turikipis ñañaykipis.* ACH
 qam-pa   mama-yki-s   tayta-yki-s   wañu-ku-nqa   turi-ki-pis
 you-GEN mother-2-ADD father-2-ADD die-REFL-3.FUT brother-2-ADD
 ñaña-yki-pis
 sister-2-ADD
 '**Your mother and father will** die, your brother and your sister, too.'

(9) *Manalaq yakukta qumanqachu.* CH
 mana-laq yaku-kta   qu-ma-nqa-chu
 no-CONT water-ACC give-1.OBJ-3.FUT-NEG
 '**They** still **aren't going to** give me water.'

4.3.3.3 Past

SYQ distinguishes between the simple past, the perfect, and the iterative past. The simple past is indicated by the past tense morpheme -*RQa* (*rima-rqa/ra-nchik* 'we spoke'). In practice -*RQa* is assigned both simple past and present perfect (non-completive) interpretations. The quotative simple past (-*sHQa*) is used in story-telling (*apa-mu-sa-ø* 'she brought it'). The past tense (completive) is indicated by the suffix -*sHa* (*uyari-sa-ni* 'I heard'). The habitual past is indicated by the agentive noun – formed by the suffixation of -*q* to the verb stem – in combination with the relevant present tense form of *ka-* 'be' (*taki-q ka-nki* 'you used to sing'). §4.3.3.3.1–4.3.3.3.4 cover the simple past, the narrative past, the perfect, and the iterative past, in turn. The past conditional is covered in §4.3.4.3.

4 Verbs

4.3.3.3.1 Simple past -*RQa* -*RQa* indicates the past tense.[5] The morpheme is realized -*rqa* in AMV (1), (2); -*ra* in ACH (3), LT (4), (5), and SP (6); and -*la* in CH (7), (8). Table 4.14 displays the simple past tense inflectional paradigm; Table 4.15 displays the paradigm for simple past tense inflection with actor-object reference (see Subsection 4.3.2.2 for discussion).

Table 4.14: past tense inflection

Person	Singular	Plural
1	-rqa-ni$_{AMV}$	-rqa-nchik$_{AMV}$
	-ra-ni$_{LT}$	-ra-nchik$_{ACH,SP,LT}$
	-ra-:$_{ACH,SP}$	-la-nchik$_{CH}$
	-la-:$_{CH}$	
2	-rqa-nki$_{AMV}$	-rqa-nki$_{AMV}$
	-ra-nki$_{ACH,SP,LT}$	-ra-nki$_{ACH,SP,LT}$
	-la-nki$_{CH}$	-la-nki$_{CH}$
3	-rqa-ø$_{AMV}$	-rqa-ø$_{AMV}$
	-ra-ø$_{ACH,SP,LT}$	-ra-ø$_{ACH,SP,LT}$
	-la-ø$_{CH}$	-la-ø$_{CH}$

Table 4.15: past tense inflection – actor-object suffixes

2>1	3>1	3>1pl	1>2	3>2
-wa-rqa-nki$_{AMV}$	-wa-rqa-ø$_{AMV}$	-wa-rqa-nchik$_{AMV}$	-rqa-yki$_{AMV}$	-shu-rqa-nki$_{AMV}$
-wa-ra-nki$_{LT}$	-wa-ra-ø$_{LT}$	-wa-ra-nchik$_{LT}$	-ra-yki$_{LT,ACH,SP}$	-shu-ra-nki$_{LT,ACH,SP}$
-ma-ra-nki$_{ACH,SP}$	-ma-ra-ø$_{ACH,SP}$	-ma-ra-nchik$_{ACH,SP}$		
-ma-la-nki$_{CH}$	-ma-la-ø$_{CH}$	-ma-la-nchik$_{CH}$	-la-yki$_{CH}$	-shu-la-nki$_{CH}$

---

[5] -*RQa* signals the preterite in all Quechuan languages; -*RU*, according to Cerrón-Palomino (1987), is a later evolution in some Quechuan languages from the modal suffix -*RQu* (outward direction). In Tarma Q and Pacaraos Q -*rQu* is now a perfective aspect marker Adelaar (1988: 18–29). An anonymous reviewer points out that in Southern Conchucos Quechua, -*ru* in Southern Conchucos Q originally indicated outward direction. It became a derivational perfective then an inflectional past (see Hintz 2011: 192–197).

4.3 Verb inflection

(1) *Iskwilanta lliwta ya wamrayta puchukachirqani.* AMV
    iskwila-n-ta   lliw-ta   ya   wamra-y-ta puchuka-chi-rqa-ni
    school-3-ACC all-ACC EMPH child-1-ACC finish-CAUS-PST-1
    '**I made** all my children finish their schooling.'

(2) *¿Imapaqtaq niwarqanki? ¡Pagarullawanmantri karqa!* AMV
    ima-paq-taq   ni-wa-rqa-nki   paga-ru-lla-wa-n-man-tri
    what-PURP-SEQ say-1.OBJ-PST-2 pay-URGT-RSTR-1.OBJ-3-COND-EVC
    ka-rqa
    be-PST
    'Why **did you say** that to me? He would have sacrificed me!'

(3) *Kutikamura: lliw ganawnintin wamra: lliw listu hishpiruptinña.* ACH
    kuti-ka-mu-ra-:   lliw ganaw-ni-ntin   wamra-: lliw listu
    return-REFL-CISL-PST-1 all   cattle-EUPH-INCL child-1 all   ready
    hishpi-ru-pti-n-ña
    educate-URGT-SUBDS-3-DISC
    '**I came** back with all my cattle when my children had been educated.'

(4) *Kanan Primitivoqa ñuqa istankamurani.* LT
    kanan Primitivo-qa   ñuqa istanka-mu-ra-ni
    now   Primitovo-TOP   I   fill.reservoir-CISL-PST-1
    'Now Primitivo [says] **I filled** the reservoir.'

(5) *Qam pasaypaqtriki riranki Diosninchikta tariq.* LT
    qam pasaypaq-tri-ki   ri-ra-nki   Dios-ni-nchik-ta   tari-q
    you completely-EVC-IKI go-PST-2 God-EUPH-1PL-ACC find-AG
    '**You** surely **went** to look for our God.'

(6) *Antaylumata tarirushpaqa pallakullara hinaptinshi.* SP
    antayluma-ta   tari-ru-shpa-qa   palla-ku-lla-ra
    antayluma.berry-ACC find-URGT-SUBIS-TOP pick-REFL-RSTR-PST
    hinaptin-shi
    then-EVR
    'When she found the antayluma berries, **she picked** them then, they say.'

4 Verbs

(7) *Suwanakushpatr lluqsila.* CH
  suwa-naku-shpa-tr   lluqsi-la
  steal-RECIP-SUBIS-EVC go.out-PST
  'They **left** eloping.'

(8) *¿Manachu rimidyukta apakamulanki?* CH
  mana-chu rimidyu-kta apa-ka-mu-la-nki
  no-Q   remedy-ACC   bring-PASSACC-CISL-PST-2
  '**You didn't bring** any medicine?'

In all five dialects, person-number inflection in the past tense is as in the present tense, with the exception that in the third person, -*n* is replaced by -ø (9), (10).

(9) *¿Llaqtaykipa pasarqachu?* AMV
  llaqta-yki-pa pasa-rqa-chu
  town-2-LOC   pass-PST-Q
  '**Did** [the earthquake] **go** through your town?'

(10) *Unaymi chayna pulilaø chay tirruku. Awturidadkunakta ashushpa wañuchiyta munala.* CH
  unay-mi   chayna puli-la   chay   tirruku
  before-EVD thus   walk-PST DEM.D Shining.Path
  awturidad-kuna-kta ashu-shpa   wañu-chi-y-ta   muna-la
  authority-PL-ACC   approach-SUBIS die-CAUS-INF-ACC want-PST
  'The Shining Path **walked** about like that. They **approached** the officials. They **wanted** to kill them.'

In all five dialects, -*RQa* indicates tense but not aspect and is thus consistent with both perfective (11) and imperfective aspect (12–15).

(11) *Alliallitayari lucharanchik wak hurquruptinqa.* LT
  alli-alli-ta-ya-ri   lucha-ra-nchik wak
  good-good-ACC-EMPH-ARI fight-PST-1PL   DEM.D
  hurqu-ru-pti-n-qa
  remove-URGT-SUBDS-3-TOP
  'We **fought** really well when they took that out.'

(12) *Manam ñuqakunaqa talpula:chu.* CH
  mana-m ñuqa-kuna-qa talpu-la-:-chu
  no-EVD I-PL-TOP   plant-PST-1-NEG
  'We **haven't** planted.'

4.3 Verb inflection

(13) *Chayllatam tumachirqani. Manam iksistirqachu chay rantiypaq kay Viñacpaqa wak Gloria.* AMV
chay-lla-ta-m   tuma-chi-rqa-ni   mana-m   iksisti-rqa-chu
DEM.D-RSTR-ACC-EVD   drink-CAUS-PST-1   no-EVD   exist-PST-NEG
chay   ranti-y-paq   kay   Viñac-pa-qa   wak   Gloria
DEM.D   sell-INF-ABL   DEM.P   Viñac-LOC-TOP   DEM.D   Gloria
'I **fed** them only goat milk and cheese. Gloria, milk for sale, **didn't exist** here in Viñac.'

(14) *Chay limpu limpu chunyakulanchik ayvis.* CH
chay   limpu   limpu   chunya-ku-la-nchik   ayvis
DEM.D   all   all   silent-REFL-PST-1PL   sometimes
'But we **were** completely **silent** here sometimes.'

(15) *Ripukuytam munarqanchik.* AMV
ripu-ku-y-ta-m   muna-rqa-nchik
go-REFL-INF-ACC-EVD   want-PST-1PL
'We **wanted** to run away.'

Perfective aspect is, rather, indicated by the derivational suffix *-RU* (16–22).

(16) *Uyqa, chayta kasarashpa puchukarunchik.* AMV
uyqa   chay-ta   kasara-shpa   puchuka-ru-nchik
sheep   DEM.D-ACC   marry-SUBIS   finish-URGT-1PL
'When we got married, we **finished** with those, the sheep.'

(17) *Wak runaqa wawanta pamparun qipichaykushpam.* AMV
wak   runa-qa   wawa-n-ta   pampa-ru-n
DEM.D   person-TOP   baby-3-ACC   bury-URGT-3
qipi-cha-yku-shpa-m
carry-DIM-REFL-SUBIS-EVD
'The people **buried** their son, carrying him.'

(18) *Yaqam wañurun.* ACH
yaqa-m   wañu-ru-n
almost-EVD   die-URGT-3
'He almost **died**.'

4 Verbs

(19) *Pusuman hiqaykuruni. kaypaq urayman.* LT
pusu-man   hiqa-yku-ru-ni   kay-paq   uray-man
reservoir-ALL go.down-EXCEP-URGT-1 DEM.P-ABL down.hill-ALL
'I **fell** towards the reservoir. From here down hill.'

(20) *Mana ganaw uywaqkunaman chayman partikurun.* SP
mana ganaw uywa-q-kuna-man   chay-man   parti-ku-ru-n
no   cattle raise-AG-PL-ALL   DEM.D-ALL   divide-REFL-URGT-3
'They **distributed** it to those who don't raise cattle.'

(21) *Disparisirunñam. Manam uyari:chu.* SP
disparisi-ru-n-ña-m   mana-m   uyari-:-chu
disappear-URGT-3-DISC-EVD   no-EVD   hear-1-NEG
'They **disappeared** already. I don't hear them [anymore].'

(22) *Chay walmita talilushpaqa apalunñam uspitalman.* CH
chay   walmi-ta   tali-lu-shpa-qa   apa-lu-n-ña-m
DEM.D   woman-ACC   find-URGT-SUBIS-TOP   bring-URGT-3-DISC-EVD
uspital-man
hospital-ALL
'**When they found** the woman they took her to the hospital.'

-rQa and *-Ru* are thus not in paradigmatic opposition and differ in their distribution. *-RQa*, but not *-Ru*, is used in the construction of the habitual past (23), (24) and the past conditional (2), (25); while *-Ru*, but not *-RQa*, may be used in combination with *-sHa* (26), (27) as well as with *-shpa* (6), (22) and *-pti* (3), (28), (29), in which case it indicates the precedence of the subordinated event to the main-clause event.

(23) *Dumingunpa kisuta apaq kara: (*karu:) ishkay.* ACH
dumingu-n-pa   kisu-ta   apa-q   ka-ra-:   ishkay
Sunday-3-LOC   cheese-ACC bring-AG be-PST-1   two
'On Sundays, **I would bring** two cheeses.'

(24) *Trayamushpa manchachikuq kala.* CH
traya-mu-shpa   mancha-chi-ku-q   ka-la
arrive-CISL-SUBIS   scare-CAUS-REFL-AG   be-PST
'When she came, **she would scare** them.'

(25) *Kundinakurunmantri kara (*karun) qullqi chay kasa.* SP
kundina-ku-ru-n-man-tri   ka-ra   qullqi chay   ka-sa
condemn-REFL-URGT-3-COND-EVC be-PST money DEM.D be-NPST
'She **would have condemned** herself – that was money.'

(26) *Cañeteta ayarikura:. Ispusu:ta listaman trurarusa (*trurarqasa, *trurasarqa).* ACH
Cañete-ta   ayari-ku-ra-:   ispusu-:-ta   lista-man
Cañete-ACC escape-REFL-PST-1 husband-1-ACC list-ALL
trura-ru-sa
put-URGT-NPST
'I escaped to Cañete. They **had put** my husband on the list.'

(27) *Chayllapaq willakarusa. (*willakarqasa).* ACH
chay-lla-paq   willa-ka-ru-sa
DEM.D-RSTR-ABL tell-PASSACC-URGT-NPST
'That's why **they had told** on him.'

(28) *Chay hawlaruptinshi, atuq trayarun (*hawlaraptin).* SP
chay   hawla-ru-pti-n-shi   atuq   traya-ru-n
DEM.D cage-URGT-SUBDS-3-EVR fox   arrive-URGT-3
'**When he had caged** [the rabbit], the fox arrived.'

(29) *Chay mulapaq siqaykuruptin puñukuratrik shinkaqqa.* ACH
chay   mula-paq   siqa-yku-ru-pti-n
DEM.D   mule-ABL   go.down-EXCEP-URGT-SUBDS-3
puñu-ku-ra-tri-k   shinka-q-qa
sleep-REFL-PST-EVC-IK   get.drunk-AG-TOP
'**When he fell** off that mule, the drunk must have been asleep.'

4.3.3.3.2 Quotative simple past tense -sHQa In SYQ, as in other Quechuan languages, when speakers have only second-hand knowledge of the events they report, they may recur to a another past tense form, -sHQa, often referred to as the "narrative past" because it is used systematically in story-telling. In SYQ, -sHQa – realized as -sa in ACH, AMV and SP and as -sha in CH and LT – is used predominantly in story-telling (1), (2), historical narrative (3–5), and, generally, in relating information one has received from others (6–10).

4 Verbs

(1) *Huklla atuqshi kasa.* SP
    huk-lla   atuq-shi   ka-sa
    one-RSTR   fox-EVR   be-NPST
    '[Once upon a time] there **was** a fox, they say.'

(2) *Chay ukucha kasa maqtatukushpa.* AMV
    chay   ukucha   ka-sa   maqta-tuku-shpa
    DEM.D   mouse   be-NPST   young.man-SIMUL-SUBIS
    '**It was** a rat pretending to be a man.'

(3) *Hinashpa qalay qalay Chavin miniruwanshi partisa.* ACH
    hinashpa   qalay   qalay   Chavin   miniru-wan-shi   parti-sa
    then   all   all   Chavin   miner-INSTR-EVR   divide-NPST
    'Then they divid**ed** everything up with the Chavin miners.'

(4) *Chay intanadanqa ayqikusa.* ACH
    chay   intanada-n-qa   ayqi-ku-sa
    DEM.D   step.daughter-3-TOP   escape-REFL-NPST
    'His step-daughter escap**ed**.'

(5) *Tariramusha armata.* LT
    tari-ra-mu-sha   arma-ta
    find-URGT-CISL-NPST   weapon-ACC
    'They **found** firearms.'

(6) *"¡Mátalo!" nishashiki.* CH
    mátalo   ni-sha-shi-ki
    [Spanish]   say-NPST-EVR-IKI
    '"Kill him!" she **said**, they say.'

(7) *Wañukachishpash qipirusa karuta mana disiyananpaq.* AMV
    wañu-ka-chi-shpa-sh   qipi-ru-sa   karu-ta   mana
    die-PASSACC-CAUS-SUBIS-EVR   carry-URGT-NPST   far-ACC   no
    disya-na-n-paq
    suspect-NMLZ-3-PURP
    'When she kill**ed** him, they say, she carri**ed** him far, so they wouldn't suspect.'

4.3 Verb inflection

(8) *Wak warmiqa llaman qutuq risa. Mayuta pawayashpash siqaykuru**sa**;
karu karutash aparu**sa**.* AMV
wak   warmi-qa   llama-n   qutu-q   ri-sa   mayu-ta
DEM.D woman-TOP   llama-3   gather-AG go-PST   river-ACC
pawa-ya-shpa-sh   siqa-yku-ru-sa   karu karu-ta-sh
jump-PROG-SUBIS-EVR   go.down-EXCEP-URGT-NPST   far   far-ACC-EVR
apa-ru-sa
bring-URGT-NPST
'That woman **went** to gather up her llamas. Jumping the river, she **fell** and [the river] **took** her far, they say.'

(9) *Fiystaman hamushpa siqaykuru**sha**.* ACH
fiysta-man   hamu-shpa   siqa-yku-ru-sha
festival-ALL come-SUBIS go.down-EXCEP-URGT-NPST
'When they were coming to the festival they **fell** [into the canyon].'

(10) *Wak runaqa achka aychata aparamu**sa** llama aychash sibadawan
kambyakunanpaq.* AMV
wak   runa-qa   achka   aycha-ta   apa-ra-mu-sa   llama
DEM.D   person-TOP a.lot   meat-ACC bring-URGT-CISL-NPST llama
aycha-sh   sibada-wan   kambya-ku-na-n-paq
meat-EVR   barley-INSTR   exchange-REFL-NMLZ-3-PURP
'Those people **brought** a lot of meat – llama meat, they say, to exchange for barley.'

It may also be used in dream reports (11).

(11) *Lliw lliw kuchihinam mituman yayku**ru**sa.* SP
lliw   lliw   kuchi-hina-m   mitu-man   yayku-ru-sa
all   all   pig-COMP-EVD mud-ALL   enter-URGT-NPST
'All, like pigs, **entered** the mud.'

The morpheme is realized as *-shqa*, it seems, only in the first or culminating line of a story, and rarely even there (12).

(12) *Ishkay Wanka samaku**shqa** huk matraypi, tarukapa kasanpi. Wama
wamaq karka kasa.* AMV
ishkay   Wanka   sama-ku-shqa   huk   matray-pi,   taruka-pa
two   Wanka   rest-REFL-NPST   one   cave-LOC   taruka-GEN
ka-sa-n-pi   wama   wamaq   karka   ka-sa
be-PRF-3-LOC   a.lot   a.lot   manure be-NPST

161

4 Verbs

'Two Huancayoans were resting in a cave, in some tarucas' place. There was a whole lot of manure.'

-RQa and *-Ru*, may also be employed in the same contexts as is *-sHQa*, even in combination with the reportative evidential, *-shI* (13), (14).

(13) *Rutupis ingañarqash maqtatukushpa pashñata.* AMV
 rutu-pis ingaña-rqa-sh maqta-tuku-shpa pashña-ta
 rutu.bird-ADD trick-PST-EVR young.man-SIMUL-SUBIS girl-ACC
 'A rutu-bird, too, **deceived** a girl by making himself out to be a young man, **they say**.'

(14) *Millisunqa wañururqash huknin.* AMV
 millisu-n-qa wañu-ru-rqa-sh huk-ni-n
 twin-3-TOP die-URGT-PST-EVR one-EUPH-3
 'His twin, the other one, **died, they say**.'

Inside quotations in story-telling, *RQa* and *-Ru* are generally employed (15), (16).

(15) *Trayarunshari, '¿Maymi chay warmiy?'* AMV
 traya-**ru**-n-sh-ari, may-mi chay warmi-y
 arrive-URGT-EVR-ARI where-EVD DEM.D woman-1
 'The condor **arrived**, they say, [and said], "Where is my wife?"'

(16) *Chaynam kundur qipiwarqa matrayta chaypi wawakuruni.* AMV
 chayna-m kundur qipi-wa-rqa matray-ta chaypi
 thus-EVD condor carry-1.OBJ-PST cave-ACC DEM.D-LOC
 wawa-ku-ru-ni
 give.birth-REFL-URGT-1
 'That condor **carried** me like that to a cave and I **gave birth** there.'

4.3.3.3.3 Perfect *-sHa* – realized as *-sa* in ACH, AMV and SP and as *-sha* in CH and LT – may be argued sometimes to admit interpretations cognate with the English perfect, indicating events beginning in the past and either continuing into the present or with effects continuing into the present (1–3). Table 4.16 displays the paradigm for perfect inflection with *-sHa*; Table 4.17 displays the paradigm for the inflection of *-sHa* for actor-object reference (see Subsection 4.3.2.2 for discussion).

4.3 Verb inflection

Table 4.16: Inflection of -sHa

Person	Singular	Plural
1	-sa-ni$_{AMV}$ -sha-ni$_{LT}$ -sha-:$_{CH}$ -sa-:$_{AMV,SP}$	-sa-nchik$_{AMV,ACH,SP}$ -sha-nchik$_{CH,LT}$
2	-sa-nki$_{AMV,ACH,SP}$ -sha-nki$_{CH,LT}$	-sa-nki$_{AMV,ACH,SP}$ -sha-nki$_{CH,LT}$
3	-sa-ø$_{AMV,ACH,SP}$ -sha-ø$_{CH,LT}$	-sa-ø$_{AMV,ACH,SP}$ -sha-ø$_{CH,LT}$

Table 4.17: Inflection of sHa – actor-object suffixes

2>1	3>1	3>1pl	1>2	3>2
-wa-sa-nki$_{AMV}$	-wa-sa-ø$_{AMV}$	-wa-sa-nchik$_{AMV}$	-sa-yki$_{AMV,ACH,SP}$	N/A
-wa-sha-nki$_{LT}$	-wa-sha-ø$_{LT}$	-wa-sha-nchik$_{LT}$	-sha-yki$_{LT,CH}$	N/A
-ma-sa-nki$_{ACH,SP}$	-ma-sa-ø$_{ACH,SP}$	-ma-sa-nchik$_{ACH,SP}$		
-ma-sha-nki$_{CH}$	-ma-sha-ø$_{CH}$	-ma-sha-nchik$_{CH}$		

(1) *Chay alkulta mana tapasanichu.* AMV
 chay alkul-ta mana tapa-sa-ni-chu
 DEM.D alcohol-ACC no cover-SA-1-NEG
 '**I haven't** capped that alcohol.'

(2) *Grasyusu kasanki.* AMV
 grasyusu ka-sa-nki
 funny be-SA-2
 '**You've been** funny.'

(3) *Mikushayari. Mikushayari.* LT
 miku-sha-y-ari miku-sha-y-ari
 miku-SHA-EMPH-ARI eat-SHA-EMPH-ARI
 '**They've eaten** them, all right. **They've eaten** them.'

4 Verbs

That said, the non-nominalizing instances of -*sHa* in the corpus, almost without exception, have more readily-available interpretations as narrative pasts (see §4.3.3.3.2) (4).[6]

(4) *Mulankunawan kargarikushpa pasan wañurichishpa wak Chavin lawpash. Hinashpa qalay qalay Chavin miniruwanshi partisa.* ACH
mula-n-kuna-wan   karga-ri-ku-shpa   pasa-n
mule-3-PL-INSTR   carry-INCEP-REFL-SUBIS   pass-3
wañu-ri-chi-shpa   wak   Chavin law-pa-sh   hinashpa qalay
die-INCEP-CAUS-SUBIS   DEM.D   Chavin side-LOC-EVR then   all
qalay Chavin miniru-wan-shi   parti-sa
all   Chavin miner-INSTR-EVR   divide-SA
'Carrying everything with their mules, they left, killing people over by Chavin, they say. Then they **divided** up absolutely everything with the miners.'

Indeed, speakers offer only simple past translations for verbs suffixed with -*sHa*; perfect translations may be offered, rather, for -*Rqa*, -*RU* (very rarely), or the present[7] (5–7) (see §4.3.3.3.1).[8]

(5) '*¿Maypaqtaq **suwamuranki**?*' *nishpa.* LT
may-paq-taq   suwa-mu-ra-nki   ni-shpa
where-ABL-SEQ   steal-CISL-PST-2   say-SUBIS
'"Where **have you stolen** these from?" he said.'

(6) *Kananqa shimi:lla **qacharun** hat-hatun.* SP
kanan-qa   shimi-:-lla   qacha-ru-n   hat-hatun
now-TOP   mouth-1-RSTR   rip-URGT-3   big-big
'Now my mouth **has ripped** open wide.'

---

[6] The corpus counts 1157 instances of -*sHa*; a sample of 50 turned up no translation to the Spanish perfect.

[7] In elicitation sessions, speakers of SYQ do interpret -*ri* as indicating the present perfect; in a sample of 50 of the 353 instances of -*Ri* in the corpus, however, only once did the speakers assign it a perfect interpretation (*Spkr 1: Yapa-mi-k kuti-nqa, ¿aw? Spkr 2: Puchuka-ri -n-chu.* 'She's going to go back again, no?' 'She hasn't finished yet.')

[8] The the translations in (1–3) were proposed only to suggest possible perfect interpretations of sentences that, I argued, are better interpreted as narrative pasts.

4.3 Verb inflection

(7) *Ni pi **qawan**chu ni pi **tarin**chu.* ACH
ni pi qawa-n-chu ni pi tari-n-chu
nor who see-3-NEG nor who find-3-NEG
'No one **has seen** her and no one **has found** her.'

Speakers do consistently translate the combination of *-RU* and *-sHa* with the Spanish past perfect (8–10); in Andean Spanish, however, this construction does not share the semantics of the Standard Spanish.[9]

(8) *¡Wak suwa liyunqa ubihayta tumbarusa!* AMV
wak suwa liyun-qa ubiha-y-ta tumba-ru-sa
DEM.D thief lion-TOP sheep-1-ACC knock.down-URGT-SA
'That thieving puma **had knocked off** my sheep!'

(9) *Trakraymi tuñirun. Yakutam **katraykurusa**.* AMV
trakra-y-mi tuñi-ru-n yaku-ta-m katra-yku-ru-sa
field-1-EVD crumble-URGT-3 water-ACC-EVD release -EXCEP-URGT-SA
'My field washed away. They **had released** water.'

(10) *Payllatam wañurachira runa ... **hapirusa** karrupi.* ACH
pay-lla-ta-m wañu-ra-chi-ra runa hapi-ru-sa karrupi
he-RSTR-ACC-EVD die-URGT-CAUS-PST person grab-URGT-SA car-LOC
'The people killed just him ... They **had grabbed** him on the bus.'

Given, however, the restrictions on the distribution of *-RU-sHa* – it inflects only for third person[10] and it is not contentful either with stative verbs or with the copulative, *ka-* – it is improbable that it that would constitute the language's principal strategy for rendering the past perfect. Rather, to indicate the sequence of two completed events, speakers of SYQ generally employ ether the subordinator *-pti* (11), (12) or a connective like *hinashpa* or *hinaptin* (13).[11]

---

[9] This construction generally can only awkwardly be translated as a past perfect in English, however.

[10] The corpus counts 330 instances of *-RU* (*-ø/-chi/-mu*) *-sHa*; in only two cases is it not inflected for third person.

[11] It has been suggested to me that an additional function of *-sHa* might be to indicate 'sudden discovery' (Adelaar 1977) or surprise. That is, *-sHa* might indicate the mirative, as do the perfect marker *-shka* in Ecuadorian Q (Muysken 1977) and 'non-experienced' past tense marker *-sqa* in Cuzco Q (Faller 2003) (as cited in Peterson 2014: 223–33). This is a hypothesis I am currently investigating.

4 Verbs

(11) *Liluptinqa, li:.* CH
li-lu-pti-n-qa   li-:
go-URGT-SUBDS-3-TOP go-1
'When (**after**) he went, I went.'

(12) *Hinaptinshi iskinapa kayaptin baliyarun.* ACH
*hinaptin-shi iskina-pa ka-ya-**pti**-n   baliya-ru-n*
then-EVR   corner-LOC be-PROG-SUBDS-3 shoot-URGT-3
'Then, they say, **when** he was in the corner, they shot him.'

(13) *Suyarusa **hinashpa** maqarusa. Chayshi nirqamik tumarun.* AMV
*suya-ru-sa   **hinashpa** maqa-ru-sa   chay-shi   ni-rqa-mi-k*
wait-URGT-SA   then   beat-URGT-SA   DEM.D-EVR   say-PST-EVD-IK
tuma-ru-n
take-URGT-3
'She had waited for her **then** she had hit her. That's why he took [the poison], they say.'

4.3.3.3.4 Habitual past -*q ka*- The habitual past is indicated by the combination of the agentive noun – formed by the addition of -*q* to the verb stem – and the relevant present tense form of *ka*- 'be' (zero in the third person) (1–4). Table 4.18 displays this paradim; Table 4.19 displays the paradidm of habitual past inflection with actor-object reference (see Subsection 4.3.2.2 for discussion).

Table 4.18: Habitual past inflection

Person	Singular	Plural
1	-q ka-ni$_{AMV,LT}$ -q ka-:$_{ACH,CH,SP}$	-q ka-nchik
2	-q ka-nki	-q ka-nki
3	-q	-q

(1) *Wak Marcopukyopa, triguta hurqupakamuq kani.* AMV
wak   Marcopukyo-pa, trigu-ta   hurqu-paka-mu-q   ka-ni
DEM.D   Marcopukyo-LOC   wheat-ACC   remove-MUTBEN-CISL-AG   be-1
'There in Marcopukyo, I **used to** harvest wheat.'

4.3 Verb inflection

Table 4.19: Habitual past inflection – actor-object suffixes

2>1	3>1	3>1pl	1>2	3>2
-wa-q ka-nki$_{AMV,LT}$ -ma-q ka-nki$_{ACH,CH,SP}$	-wa-q$_{AMV,LT}$ -ma-q$_{ACH,CH,SP}$	N/A	N/A	N/A

(2) *Chayhina puriq **kanchik** ayvis fusfuru puchukaruq.* AMV
    chay-hina   puri-q   ka-nchik   ayvis   fusfuru   puchuka-ru-q
    DEM.D-COMP walk-AG   be-1PL   sometimes   match   finish-URGT-AG
    'We **would** walk around like that; sometimes the matches **would** run out.'

(3) *Awturidadkunaqa pakakuq huk law likuq.* CH
    awturidad-kuna-qa   paka-ku-q   huk   law   li-ku-q
    authority-PL-TOP   hide-REFL-AG one   side   go-REFL-AG
    'The officials **would** hide, they **would** go other places.'

(4) *Chay tirruristawan kay Azángaropaq rikuyaq. Wama wamaq piliyakuyaq.* ACH
    chay   tirrurista-wan   kay   Azángaro-paq   riku-ya-q   wama
    DEM.D   terrorist-INSTR   DEM.P   Azángaro-ABL   go-PROG-AG   a.lot
    wamaq   piliya-ku-ya-q
    a.lot   fight-REFL-PROG-AG
    'They **would** be going from Azángaro with the terrorists. They **would** be fighting a lot.'

Generally translated in Spanish with the imperfect, the structure can be translated in English as 'used to V' or 'would V'. Object suffixes precede -*q* (5), (6).

(5) *Wasiyta hamuruptiy uquchiwaq. Huk vidatam wakwanqa pukllarirqani.* AMV
    wasi-y-ta   hamu-ru-pti-y   uqu-chi-wa-q   huk
    house-1-ACC   come-URGT-SUBDS-1   wet-CAUS-1.OBJ-AG   one
    vida-ta-m   wak-wan-qa   puklla-ri-rqa-ni
    life-ACC-EVD   DEM.D-INSTR-TOP   play-INCEP-PST-1
    'When I **would** come home, they **would** get me wet. I played around with them a lot.'

4 Verbs

(6) *Taytacha: willamaq chayhinam antigwu viyhukuna purira nishpa.* SP
 tayta-cha-: willa-ma-q chay-hina-m antigwu viyhu-kuna
 father-DIM-1 tell-1.OBJ-AG DEM.D-COMP-EVD ancient old-PL
 puri-ra ni-shpa
 walk-PST say- SUBIS
 'My grandfather **used to** tell **me** [stories]. The ancients walked about like that, he said.'

4.3.4 Conditional

SYQ verbs inflect for conditionality, present and past. Two different forms indicate the conditional in SYQ. The first, the regular conditional, is attested in all persons, singular and plural, in all dialects. Alternative conditional forms are attested in the first person plural in all dialects and in the second person both singular and plural in the AMV dialect. Both the regular and alternative conditional may be interpreted as ability, circumstantial, deontological, epistemological, and teleological modals, both existential and universal, at least. For more extensive discussion of the interpretation of the conditional under the scope of the various evidential enclitics and their modifiers, see §6.2.11.

4.3.4.1 Regular conditional (potential) -*man*

All SYQ dialects indicate the conditional with the suffix -*man*. In the first person, it is the person-number suffixes of the nominal (possessive) paradigm that are used in combination with -*man* (i.e., -*y* and not -*ni* is used for the first-person singular in the QII-aligned dialects) (28). -*man* follows all other inflectional suffixes (*ri-**nki**-man* **ri-**man**-ni-nki*) (34); -*man* is in complementary distribution with tense morphemes (**ri-**rqa**-nki-**man***) (the examples cited are given in §4.3.4.2). Table 4.20 displays this paradigm; Table 4.21 displays the paradigm of regular conditional inflection with actor-object reference (see Subsection 4.3.2.2 for discussion).

4.3.4.2 Modality

The SYQ conditional covers far more territory than does the conditional in Spanish or English, receiving ability (1–5), circumstantial (6), (7), (8), deontic (9), (10), (11), (12), teleological (13), (14), and epistemological (15), (16), (17) modal readings, both existential and universal. Table 4.22 displys the modal system of SYQ.

4.3 Verb inflection

Table 4.20: Regular conditional inflection

Person	Singular	Plural
1	-y-man$_{AMV,LT}$ -:-man$_{ACH,CH,SP}$	-nchik-man
2	-nki-man	-nki-man
3	-n-man	-n-man

Table 4.21: Regular conditional inflection – actor-object suffixes

2>1	3>1	3>1pl	1>2	3>2
-wa-nki-man$_{AMV,LT}$ -ma-nki-man$_{ACH,CH,SP}$	-wa-n-man$_{AMV,LT}$ -ma-n-man$_{ACH,CH,SP}$	-wa-nchik-man$_{AMV,LT}$ -ma-nchik-man$_{ACH,CH,SP}$	-yki-man	-shu-nki-man

Table 4.22: Modal system

	Existential	Universal*
Ability	V-COND-EVD *qawa-n-man-mi* manam V-INF-ACC atipa-INFL-chu *EV *manam qawa-y-ta atipa-n-chu*	x
Circumstantial	V-COND-EVD *wiña-n-man-mi*	x
Deontic	V-COND-EVD *qawa-n-man-mi* Hawka V-FUT-EVD *hawka qawa-nqa-m*	V-COND-EVD *qawa-n-man-mi* V-NMLZ-POSS-EVD (be-PST) *qawa-na-n-mi*
Epistemic	V-COND-EVC *qawa-n-man-tri*	V-COND-EVC (be-PST) *qawa-n-man-tri*
Teleological	V-COND-EVD *qawa-n-man-mi* V-PRES-EVD *qawa-n-mi*	V-COND-EVD *qawa-n-man-mi* V-PRES-EVD *qawa-n-m*

*The verbs *usHachi-* 'be able', *puydi-* 'be able', and *yatra-* 'know' can replace *atipa-*.

4 Verbs

(1) *Kanan chayta rinman.* LT
kanan chay-ta ri-n-man
now DEM.D-ACC go-3-COND
'Now, he **could** go there.'

(2) *¿Manachu kuska linman?* CH
mana-chu kuska li-n-man
no-Q together go-3-COND
'**Can**'t they go together?'

(3) *Ulvidaru:, manayá yuyari:manchu.* SP
ulvida-ru-: mana-yá yuyari-:-man-chu
forget-URGT-1 no-EMPH remember-1-COND-NEG
'I've forgotten. I **can**'t remember.'

(4) *¿Imatataq ruwankiman? ¿Imatataq ruwanman?* ACH
ima-ta-taq ruwa-nki-man ima-ta-taq ruwa-n-man
what-ACC-SEQ make-2-COND what-ACC-SEQ make-3-COND
'What **can** you do? What **can** they do?'

(5) *Manañam kawsa:manchu.* CH
mana-ña-m kawsa-:-man-chu
no-DISC-EVD live-1-COND-NEG
'I **can't** live any more.'

(6) *Manatr wak lawpa pastu kanmanchu.* AMV
mana-tr wak law-pa pastu ka-n-man-chu
no-EVC DEM.D side-LOC pasture.grass be-3-COND-NEG
'There **can**'t be any pasture on that side.'

(7) *Sarurullawanman.* AMV
saru-ru-lla-wa-n-man
trample-URGT-RSTR-1.OBJ-3-COND
'She **could** trample me.'

4.3 Verb inflection

(8) *Suwapis rikarunman chaypa.* ACH
    suwa-pis   rika-ru-n-man   chay-pa
    thief-ADD   see-URGT-3-COND   DEM.D-LOC
    'Thieves also **can** pop up around there.'

(9) *Wawakunkimanmi hukllatas.* ACH
    wawa-ku-nki-man-mi   huk-lla-ta-s
    give.birth-REFL-2-COND-EVD   one-RSTR-ACC-ADD
    'You **should** give birth to at least one [child].'

(10) *Yatarunkimantaq.* AMV
     yata-ru-nki-man-taq
     catch-URGT-2-COND-SEQ
     '**Be careful** not to catch it.'

(11) *Chayshi manash invidyusu kaytaq **atipanchikman**chu.* LT
     chay-shi   mana-sh   invidyusu   kay-taq   atipa-nchik-man-chu
     DEM.D-EVR   no-EVR   jealous   DEM.P-SEQ   be.able-1PL-COND-NEG
     'That's why we **shouldn't** be jealous.'

(12) *Ishchallataña shutuykachiyman, ¿aw?* AMV
     ishcha-lla-ta-ña   shutu-yka-chi-y-man   aw
     little-RSTR-ACC-DISC   drip-EXCEP-CAUS-1-COND   yes
     '**I should** make it drip just a little, right?'

(13) *Allin nutata surqunaykipaq istudyankimanmiki.* † AMV
     allin   nuta-ta   surqu-na-yki-paq   istudya-nki-man-mi-ki
     good   grade-ACC   take.out-NMLZ-2-PURP   study-2-COND-EVD-IKI
     '**If you want** to get good grades, **you have to** study.'

(14) *Agua floridata u krisutapis apamunkimanmi.* ACH
     agua   florida-ta   u   krisu-ta-pis   apa-mu-nki-man-mi
     water   florida-ACC   or   Croesus-ACC-ADD   bring-CISL-2-COND-EVD
     'You **can** bring florida water or croesus [so as not to get sick].'

4 Verbs

(15) *Wasikunapis saqaykun**man**tri fwirti kaptinqa.* AMV
 wasi-kuna-pis saqa-yku-n-man-tri   fwirti ka-pti-n-qa
 house-PL-ADD go.down-EXCEP-3-COND-EVC strong be-SUBDS-3-TOP
 'The houses, also, **could** fall if there were a strong one [earthquake].'

(16) *Chayqa waqayan. ¿Imataq **kanman**?* SP
 chay-qa   waqa-ya-n   ima-taq   ka-n-man
 DEM.D-TOP cry-PROG-3 what-SEQ be-3-COND
 'It's crying. What **could** that be?'

(17) *Wañukun**man**triki.¿Imayna mana kutikamunmanchu?* ACH
 wañu-ku-n-man-tri-ki   imayna mana
 die-REFL-3-COND-EVC-IKI   how   no
 kuti-ka-mu-n-man-chu
 return-REFL-CISL-3-COND-NEG
 'He **might** have died. Why can't he come back?'

As detailed in §6.2.11, SYQ modals are themselves unspecified for force: modal force is determined by context and is generally specified by the evidential modifiers. Weak modal readings result when the modal is under the scope either of no evidential or of an evidential modified by the evidential modifier ø; strong universal readings result when the evidential is modified by the evidential modifier *-iki* (*siqa-yku-n-man-tri-ø* 'it **might** fall', *siqa-yku-n-man-tri-ki* 'it **will most likely** fall'; *istudya-nki-man-mi-ø* 'you **should** study', *istudya-nki-man-mi-ki* 'you **must** study'); moderately strong modal readings result when the modifier *-ik* takes scope over the modal. Ability modals also result from the combination of the infinitive and the verb *atipa-* 'be able' (18–19).

(18) *Manaña riyta **atipa**nchu pishipakuyan.* AMV
 mana-ña   ri-y-ta   atipa-n-chu   pishipa-ku-ya-n
 no-DISC go-INF-ACC be.able-3-NEG tire-REFL-PROG-3
 'They **can't** go – they're getting tired.'

(19) *Wawan kaptinqa, manaña uywayta **atipa**nchu.* ACH
 wawa-n ka-pti-n-qa,   mana-ña   uywa-y-ta   atipa-n-chu
 baby-3 be-SUBDS-3-TOP no-DISC raise-INF-ACC be.able-3-NEG
 'When they have babies, **they can't** raise [cattle] any more.'

The verbs *usHachi-* and *puydi-*, both translated 'be able,' as well as *yatra-* 'know' may also be employed in this construction (20–22).

4.3 Verb inflection

(20) *Chay ninaman pawayta hawanta munayan mana **usachi**nchu.* AMV
 chay nina-man pawa-y-ta hawa-n-ta muna-ya-n mana
 DEM.D fire-ALL jump-INF-ACC above-3-ACC want-PROG-3 no
 usachi-n-chu
 be.able-3-NEG
 'They want to jump over the fire, but they **can't**.'

(21) *Piluntaqa yupayanshari chay chapupaqta. **Ushachi**nchu yupayta.* AMV
 pilu-n-ta-qa yupa-ya-n-sh-ari chay chapu-paq-ta
 hair-3-ACC-TOP count-PROG-3-EVR-ARI DEM.D little.dog-GEN-ACC
 ushachi-n-chu yupa-y-ta
 be.able-3-NEG count-INF-ACC
 '[The zombie] is counting the hairless dog's hairs. He **can't** count them.'

(22) *Puriyta **yatra**nñam.* AMV
 puri-y-ta yatra-n-ña-m
 walk-INF-ACC know-3-DISC-EVD
 'She **can** already walk.'

atipa-, *usHachi-*, and *puydi-* appear in verbal constructions only when negated; they appear non-negated only in nominalizations (23), (24).

(23) *Hinashpa trayarushpaqa ... waqtakuyanchikña **atipa**sanchikkama.* CH
 hinashpa traya-ru-shpa-qa waqta-ku-ya-nchik-ña
 then arrive-URGT-SUBIS-TOP hit-REFL-PROG-1PL-DISC
 atipa-sa-nchik-kama
 be.able-PRF-1PL-LIM
 'Then, when you get there, when there is any, you're already hitting it as much as you **can**.'

(24) *Burrunchikwan rinchik Cañetekama maykamapis
 atipasanchikkama.* AMV
 burru-nchik-wan ri-nchik Cañete-kama may-kama-pis
 donkey-1PL-INSTR go-1PL Cañete-LIM where-LIM-ADD
 atipa-sa-nchik-kama
 be.able-PRF-1PL-LIM
 'With our donkeys we went to Cañete, to wherever, wherever we **could**.'

4 Verbs

Universal deontic readings additionally follow from the combination of the nominalizer, *-na* with nominal (possessive) person inflection (25); they are available, too, with the simple present tense.

(25) *Chaymi vaka harkaq ri**kunayki**miki.* AMV
 chay-mi vaka harka-q riku-na-yki-mi-ki
 DEM.D-EVD cow herd-AG go-NMLZ-2-EVD-IKI
 'That's why **you have to** go pasture the cows.'

In (26), the adverb *hawka* 'tranquil' modifying a future tense verb receives an existential deontic modal reading. As detailed in §6.2.11.3, under the scope of the conjectural evidential, *-trI*, conditionals are generally restricted to epistemic interpretations; under the scope of the direct evidential *-mI*, they receive all but conjectural interpretations.

(26) ***Hawkañam** tushunqa.* AMV
 hawka-ña-m tushu-nqa
 tranquil-DISC-EVD dance-3.FUT
 'She **can** go dancing.'

Attaching to verbs inflected with second-person *-iki*, *-man*, may be interpreted as a caution (27).

(27) *Viñacta rishpa kichkata **manam** saruramunkiman.* AMV
 Viñac-ta ri-shpa kichka-ta mana-m saru-ra-mu-nki-man
 Viñac-ACC go-SUBIS thorn-ACC no-EVD trample-URGT-CISL-2-COND
 'Be careful not to step on thorns when you go to Viñac.'

And finally, it appears that *-man* never attaches to either of the alternative-conditional morphemes, *-waq* or *-chuman*.[12] This information is summarized in Table 4.22 (examples are given for the third person with the verb *qawa-* 'see').

(28) *Ruwa**yman** lliw lliw.* AMV
 ruwa-y-man lliw lliw
 make-1-COND all all
 '**I can** do everything.'

---

[12] I have not yet tested these for grammaticality in elicitation sessions. I can only say that in a corpus with 85 instances of *-iki-man* and 24 instances of *-nchick-man*, *-waq-man* and *-chuwan-man* remain unattested.

4.3 Verb inflection

(29) *Suwakun**mantriki**.* LT
    suwa-ku-n-man-tri-ki
    rob-REFL-3-COND-EVC-IKI
    '[Where it's abandoned] **it's very likely** they will rob [you].'

(30) *Turantin siqaykurusa. Chay ukupaqa puchukarun**mantriki**.* AMV
    tura-ntin siqa-yku-ru-sa   chay   uku-pa-qa
    bull-INCL go.down-EXCEP-URGT-NPST DEM.D inside-LOC-TOP
    puchuka-ru-n-man-tri-ki
    finish-URGT-3-COND-EVC-IKI
    'He fell [from the roof] with the bull. He **really might** [have] been finished off inside.'

(31) *Qutrash. Manash pawayta **atipanchu** chaypaq.* AMV
    qutra-sh   mana-sh pawa-y-ta   atipa-n-chu   chaypaq
    reservoir-EVR no-EVR jump-INF-ACC be.able-3-NEG DEM.D-ABL
    'It's a lake, they say. They **can't** jump out of there, they say.'

(32) *¡Kwidadu! Chaypitaq qalqali miku lu**shunkiman**.* CH
    kwidadu   chay-pi-taq   qalqali miku-lu-shunki-man
    be.careful DEM.D-LOC-SEQ zombie eat-URGT-3>2-COND
    'Be careful! A zombie **could** eat you there.'

(33) *Manam wañu:**man**chu.* SP
    mana-m   wañu-:-man-chu
    no-EVD die-1-COND-NEG
    'I **can't** die.'

(34) *Mana chichiyuq kaptikiqa chayna lluqari**shunkiman**tri.* AMV
    mana chichi-yuq ka-pti-ki-qa   chayna
    no   breast-POSS be-SUBDS-2-TOP thus
    lluqa-ri-shu-nki-man-tri
    walk.grabbing-INCEP-2.OBJ-2-COND-EVC
    'If you don't have breasts **they might lean on you**.'

175

4 Verbs

(35) *Sarurullawanman manam saruwanantaq munanichu.* AMV
   saru-ru-lla-wa-n-man   mana-m saru-wa-na-n-taq
   trample-URGT-RSTR-1.OBJ-3-COND no-EVD trample-1.OBJ-NMLZ-3-SEQ
   muna-ni-chu
   want-1-NEG
   'She might trample me. I don't want her to trample me.'

4.3.4.3 Alternative conditional -*waq* and -*chuwan*

Alternative conditional forms are attested in the second person both singular and plural in the AMV dialect and first person plural in all dialects. -*waq* indicates the second person conditional (1–3); -*chuwan* indicates the first person plural conditional (4–7); -*waq* may be explicitly pluralized with -*pa(:)ku* (8).

(1) *¿Imallatapis mikuchaykuwaqchu mamay?* AMV
   ima-lla-ta-pis   miku-cha-yku-waq-chu   mama-y?
   what-RSTR-ACC-ADD eat-DIM-EXCEP-2.COND-Q mother-1
   '**Can you** eat any little thing, Miss?'

(2) *Wak tinapa alchawaq.* AMV
   wak   tina-pa   alcha-waq
   DEM.D tub-LOC fix-2.COND
   '**You can** fix it in that tub.'

(3) *¡Ama! Huk lawman hitraykurullawaq.* AMV
   ama   huk law-man   hitra-yku-ru-lla-waq
   PROH one side-ALL spill-EXCEP-URGT-RSTR-2.COND
   'Don't! **Be careful you don't** spill it on the other side.'

(4) *Ratu ratum chaywanqa shinkaruchuwan.* ACH
   ratu   ratu-m   chay-wan-qa   shinka-ru-chuwan
   moment moment-EVD DEM.D-INSTR-TOP get.drunk-URGT-1PL.COND
   '**We can** get drunk really quickly with that.'

(5) *Huk quptinqa mikuruchuwanmi.* ACH
   huk qu-pti-n-qa   miku-ru-chuwan-mi
   one give-SUBDS-3-TOP eat-URGT-1PL.COND-EVD
   'When another gives, **we can** eat.'

176

4.3 Verb inflection

(6) *Manañam kwintaku**chuwan**ñachu.* LT
    mana-ña-m   kwinta-ku-chuwan-ña-chu
    no-DISC-EVD account-REFL-1PL.COND-DISC-NEG
    '**We can** no longer become aware of it.'

(7) *Tutayaqpaq, manam imatapis ruwa**chuwan**.* AMV
    tuta-ya-q-paq   mana-m   ima-ta-pis   ruwa-chuwan
    night-INCH-AG-LOC no-EVD   what-ACC-ADD   make-1PL.COND
    'In the darkness, **we could**n't do anything.'

(8) *Yanapa**pakuwaq**.* AMV
    yanapa-paku-waq
    help-JTACC-2.COND
    '**You.PL should** help.'

Both morphemes simultaneously indicate person and conditionality and both are in complementary distribution with both tense and inflectional morphemes. -*w/ma-chuwan* is used with a first-person plural object (9–12).

(9) *Vinina**machuwan**tri.* ACH
    vinina-ma-chuwan-tri
    poison-1.OBJ-1PL.COND-EVC
    'It **can** poison **us**.'

(10) *Sapallanchiktaqa mikuru**machuwan**tri.* ACH
     sapa-lla-nchik-ta-qa   miku-ru-ma-chuwan-tri
     alone-REST-1PL-ACC-TOP   eat-URGT-1.OBJ-1PL.COND
     '[When we're] alone, [the Devil] **can** eat **us**.'

(11) *Dibil kaptinchik chukaru**wachuwan**yá.* AMV
     dibil   ka-pti-nchik   chuka-ru-wa-chuwan-yá
     weak be-SUBDS-1PL crash-URGT-1.OBJ-1PL.COND-EMPH
     'When we're weak, it **can** make **us** sick.'

(12) *Midiku hudiru**wachuwan**mi.* AMV
     midiku   hudi-ru-wa-chuwan-mi
     doctor   screw-URGT-1.OBJ-1PL.COND-EVD
     'Doctors **can** screw **us** up.'

4 Verbs

Ability (13), (14), circumstantial (15), deontic (16), (19) epistemic (17) and teleological (18) readings are all available. If a word ends with *-chuwan*, stress is shifted to the antepenultimate syllable (19).

(13) *¿Vakata chuqamuwaqchu?* AMV
vaka-ta   chuqa-mu-waq-chu
cow-ACC   throw.stones-CISL-2.COND-Q
'**Can you** throw stones at [herd] cows?'

(14) *Yaku usun chaymi llaqtata rishaq. Manam rigachuwanchu.* LT
yaku   usu-n   chay-mi   llaqta-ta   ri-shaq
water   waste.on.the.ground-3 DEM.D-EVD town-ACC   go-1.FUT
mana-m   riga-chuwan-chu
no-EVD   irrigate-1PL.COND-NEG
'Water is spilling. So I'm going to go to town. **We can't** irrigate.'

(15) *Kayanmi uniku qullqiyuqpaqyá ¿Maypam rigalawachuwan runaqa?* AMV
ka-ya-n-mi   uniku qullqi-yuq-paq-yá   may-pa-m
be-PROG-3-EVD   only   money-POSS-BEN-EVD   where-LOC-EVD
rigala-wa-chuwan   runa-qa?
give.as.a.gift-1.OBJ-1PL.COND person-TOP
'There are some just for people with money. Where **can** people give **us** things as gifts?'

(16) *Chikitu llamachata apakuwaq.* AMV
chikitu llama-cha-ta   apa-ku-waq
small   llama-DIM-ACC   bring-REFL-2.COND
'**You could** bring a small little llama.'

(17) *Wañuypaqpis kayachuwantri.* AMV
wañu-y-paq-pis   ka-ya-chuwan-tri
die-INF-PURP-ADD   be-PROG-1PL.COND-EVC
'**We could be** also about to die.'

(18) *Trabahawaqmi mikuyta munashpaqa.* AMV
trabaha-waq-mi   miku-y-ta   muna-shpa-qa
work-2.COND-EVD   eat-INF-ACC want-SUBIS-TOP
'**You have to** work if you want to eat.'

4.3 Verb inflection

(19) *Pulíchuwan kuskanchik.* CH
 puli-chuwan   kuska-nchik
 walk-1PL.COND together-1PL
 '**We should** walk together.'

4.3.4.4 Past conditional (irrealis)

The past conditional is indicated by the combination – as distinct words – of the conditional with *ka-RQa*, the third person past tense form of *ka-* 'be' (1–4). Table 4.23 displays this paradigm; Table 4.24 displays the paradigm for past conditional inflection with actor-object reference.

Table 4.23: Past conditional inflection

Person	Singular	Plural
1	-y-man karqa-ø$_{AMV}$	-nchik-man karqa-ø$_{AMV}$
	-y-man kara-ø$_{LT}$	-nchik-man kara-ø$_{ACH,LT,SP}$
	-:-man kara-ø$_{ACH,SP}$	-nchik-man kala-ø$_{CH}$
	-:-man kala-ø$_{CH}$	-chuwan karqa-ø$_{AMV}$
		-chuwan kara-ø$_{ACH,LT}$
2	-nki-man karqa-ø$_{AMV}$	-nki-man karqa-ø$_{AMV}$
	-nki-man kara-ø$_{ACH,LT,SP}$	-nki-man kara-ø$_{ACH,LT,SP}$
	-nki-man kala-ø$_{CH}$	-nki-man kala-ø$_{CH}$
	-waq karqa-ø$_{AMV}$	-waq karqa-ø$_{AMV}$
3	-n-man karqa-ø$_{AMV}$	-n-man karqa-ø$_{AMV}$
	-n-man kara-ø$_{ACH,SP,LT}$	-n-man kara-ø$_{ACH,SP,LT}$
	-n-man kala-ø$_{CH}$	-n-man kala-ø$_{CH}$

(1) *Riruyman karqa ñuqapis yanga hanaypaq.* AMV
 ri-ru-y-man   ka-rqa ñuqa-pis yanga hanay-paq
 go-URGT-1-COND be-PST I-ADD lie up.hill-ABL
 'I, too, **would have gone** in vain from up hill.'

(2) *Chay pachalla ... ruwashinkiman karqa.* AMV
 chay   pacha-lla ruwa-shi-nki-man   ka-rqa
 DEM.D date-RSTR make-ACMP-2-COND be-PST
 'That time, **you could have** helped make it.'

4 Verbs

Table 4.24: Past conditional inflection – actor-object suffixes

2>1	3>1	3>1pl
-wa-nki-man ka-rqa_{AMV}	-wa-n-man ka-rqa_{AMV}	-wa-nchik-man ka-rqa_{AMV}
-wa-nki-man ka-ra_{LT}	-wa-n-man ka-ra_{LT}	-wa-nchik-man ka-ra_{LT}
-ma-nki-man ka-ra_{ACH,SP}	-ma-n-man ka-ra_{ACH,SP}	-ma-nchik-man ka-ra_{ACH,SP}
-ma-nki-man ka-la_{CH}	-ma-n-man ka-la_{CH}	-ma-nchik-man ka-la_{CH}
1>2	3>2	
-yki-man ka-rqa _{AMV}	-shu-nki-man ka-rqa_{AMV}	
-yki-man ka-ra _{LT}	-shu-nki-man ka-ra_{LT}	

(3) *Mastam katray**kurunman karqa**.* AMV
    mas-ta-m   katra-yku-ru-n-man   ka-rqa
    more-ACC-EVD release-EXCEP-URGT-3-COND be-PAST
    'She **should have let** more out.'

(4) *¿Imapis mas piyurtri **kanchikman karqa**?* AMV
    ima-pis   mas   piyur-tri   ka-nchik-man   ka-rqa
    what-ADD more worse-EVC be-1PL-COND   be-PST
    'What worse thing **could we have** been?'

The regular conditional form may be used in all dialects (5–8); the alternative conditional forms may be used in those dialects in which they are available in the present tense (9–10).

(5) *Dimunyu chayqa kara. Mikura**manmantri** kara icha apara**manmantri** kara.* ACH
    Dimunyu chay-qa   ka-ra   miku-ra-ma-n-man-tri   ka-ra   icha
    Devil   DEM.D-TOP be-PST eat-URGT-1.OBJ-3-COND-EVC be-PST   or
    apa-ra-ma-n-man-tri   ka-ra
    bring-URGT-1.OBJ-3-COND-EVC   be-PST
    'That was the devil. He **could have** eaten me or he **could have** taken me away.'

(6) *Kundinakuru**nmantri** kara. Qullqi chay kasa.* SP
    kundina-ku-ru-n-man-tri   ka-ra   qullqi chay   ka-sa
    condemn-REFL-URGT-3-COND-EVC   be-PST   money   DEM.D   be-NPST

'She **would have** condemned herself [to being a zombie]. That was money.'

(7) *"Lusta paga**nki**mantri **karqa** lusninta,"* niniyá. AMV
lus-ta paga-nki-man-tri ka-rqa lus-ni-n-ta ni-ni-yá
light-ACC pay-2-COND-EVC be-PST light-EUPH-3-ACC say-1-EMPH
'"**You should have** paid the electric bill, his electric bill," I said then.'

(8) *Chayta pushakarunki**man** **kara**.* LT
chay-ta pusha-ka-ru-nki-man ka-ra
chay-ACC bring.along-PASSACC-URGT-2-COND be-PST
'You **should have** taken her.'

(9) *Mastam chawaruwaq **karqa**.* AMV
mas-ta-m chawa-ru-waq ka-rqa
more-ACC-EVD milk-URGT-2.COND be-PST
'You **could have** milked more.'

(10) *¿Chay rikisun kayarachu? Rikushpatr miku**chuwan** **kara**.* AMV
chay rikisun ka-ya-ra-chu riku-shpa-tr miku-chuwan
DEM.D cheese.curd be-PROG-PST-Q go-SUBIS-EVC eat-1PL.COND
ka-ra
be-PST
'Was there the cheese curd? We **could have** gone and eaten it.'

4.3.5 Imperative and injunctive

4.3.5.1 Imperative -y

-*y* indicates the second-person singular imperative (1).

(1) *¡Chay kullarnikitaqa surquruy!* AMV
chay kullar-ni-ki-ta-qa surqu-ru-y
DEM.D necklace-EUPH-2-ACC-TOP take.out-URGT-IMP
'That necklace of yours, **take** it out!'

-*y* is suffixed to the verb stem, plus derivational suffixes, if any are present (2).

4 Verbs

(2) *¡Wañurachiy wakta!* ACH
    wañu-ra-chi-y   wak-ta
    die-URGT-CAUS-IMP DEM.D-ACC
    '**Kill** that one!'

When verb has a first-person singular direct or indirect object, -*y* attaches to the 2>1 actor-object suffix -*ma/wa* (3), (4).

(3) *¡Ñuqamanpis qachamay!* SP
    ñuqa-man-pis   qacha-ma-y
    I-ALL-ADD   rip-1.OBJ-IMP
    '**Rip** it for **me**, too!'

(4) *¡Samaykachillaway, awilita!* AMV
    sama-yka-chi-lla-wa-y   awilita
    rest-EXCEP-CAUS-RSTR-1.OBJ-IMP   grandmother
    'Just **make (have/let)** me rest, grandmother!'

The second-person plural imperative may be indicated by the joint action derivational suffix, -*pa(:)kU* in combination with -*y*, and -*ma/wa* (5), (6).

(5) *¡Lluqsipakuy (llapayki)!*[†] AMV
    lluqsi-paku-y   (llapa-yki)
    go.out-JTACC-IMP   all-2
    'Leave.PL!'

(6) *¡Takipakuy!*[†] ACH
    taki-paku-y
    sing-JTACC-IMP
    'Sing PL!'

The first-person plural imperative is identical to the first person plural future: it is indicated by the suffix -*shun* (7), (8).

(7) *¡Tushushun!* AMV
    tushu-shun
    dance-1PL.FUT
    '**Let's** dance!'

4.3 Verb inflection

(8) *¡Kuskallam wañukushun!* LT
 kuska-lla-m wañu-ku-shun
 together-RSTR-EVD die-REFL-1PL.FUT
 '**Let's** die together!'

Prohibitions are formed by suffixing the imperative with *-chu* and preceding it with *ama* (9–12).

(9) *"¡Amayá diharamaychu!" nishpa lukuyakuyan.* ACH
 ama-yá diha-ra-ma-y-chu ni-shpa
 PROH-EMPH leave-URGT-1.OBJ-IMP-NEG say-SUBIS
 luku-ya-ku-ya-n
 crazy-INCH-REFL-PROG-3
 '"**Don't** leave me!" he said, going crazy.'

(10) *¡Ama ñuqaktaqa imanamaypischu!* CH
 ama ñuqa-kta-qa ima-na-ma-y-pis-chu
 PROH I-ADD-TOP what-VRBZ-1.OBJ-IMP-ADD-NEG
 '**Don't** do anything to me!'

(11) *¡Ama manchariychu! ¡Ama qawaychu!* AMV
 ama mancha-ri-y-chu ama qawa-y-chu
 PROH scare-INCEP-IMP-NEG PROH look-IMP-NEG
 '**Don't** be scared! Don't look!'

(12) *¡Amam nunka katraykanakushunchu!* LT
 ama-m nunka katra-yka-naku-shun-chu
 PROH-EVD never release-EXCEP-RECP-1PL.FUT-NEG
 '**Let's never** leave each other!'

¡Haku! 'Let's go!' is irregular: it cannot be negated or inflected (13), (14), except, optionally, with the first-person plural *-nchik*.

(13) *¡Hakuña, taytay, pakananpaq chay aychata!* AMV
 haku-ña, tayta-y paka-na-n-paq chay aycha-ta
 let's.go-DISC father-1 hide-NMLZ-3-PURP DEM.D meat-ACC
 '**Let's go**, mate, so he can hide this meat!'

183

4 Verbs

(14) *¡Ama rishunchu (*haku)!* AMV
 ama ri-shun-chu
 PROH go-1PL.FUT-NEG
 'Let's not go!' 'We shouldn't go.'

The second-person future tense, too, is often interpreted as an imperative (15), and prohibitions can be formed by preceding this with *ama* (16).

(15) *Diosninchikqa nin, "¡Iha, apanki pukatrakita, wamanripata!"* LT
 Dios-ni-nchik-qa ni-n iha apa-nki pukatraki-ta
 God-EUPH-1PL-TOP say-3 daughter bring-2 pukatraki.flower-ACC
 wamanripa-ta
 wamanripa.flower-ACC
 'Our God said, "Daughter, **bring** pukatraki plants and wamanripa plants!"'

(16) *¡Ama kutimunkichu! Qamqa isturbum kayanki.* CH
 ama kuti-mu-nki-chu qam-qa isturbu-m ka-ya-nki
 PROH return-CISL-2-NEG you-TOP nuisance-EVD be-PROG-2
 '**Don't come** back! You're being a nuisance.'

4.3.5.2 Injunctive *-chun*

-chun indicates the third person injunctive (1–3), the suggestion on the part of the speaker as to the advisability of action by a third party.

(1) *¡Kukantaraq akuykuchun!* AMV
 kuka-n-ta-raq aku-yku-chun
 coca-3-ACC-CONT chew-EXCEP-INJUNC
 '**Let her** take her coca still!'

(2) *¡Uqusakuna hinalla kachun!* AMV
 uqu-sa-kuna hina-lla ka-chun
 wet-PRF-PL thus-RSTR be-INJUNC
 '**Let the** wet ones be like that!'

(3) *¡Witrqachun piliyaqkunata kalabusupi!* AMV
 witrqa-chun piliya-q-kuna-ta kalabusu-pi
 close.in-INJUNC fight-AG-PL-ACC prison-LOC
 'Let them shut the brawlers up in the prison!'

4.3 Verb inflection

There are no first or second person injunctive suffixes. *-chun* attaches to the verb stem, plus derivational suffixes, if any are present (4–6).

(4) ¡Kuti**muchun**! Wañuchina:paq. ACH
kuti-mu-chun wañu-chi-na-:-paq
return-CISL-INJUNC die-CAUS-NMLZ-1-PURP
'**Have him** come back – so I can kill him!'

(5) Papaniy wañu**kuchun**pis wamran kawsa**kuchun** ninshi. Chaykunata upyachiwaptinshi kawsakurqani. AMV
papa-ni-y wañu-ku-chun-pis wamra-n kawsa-ku-chun
father-EUPH-1 die-REFL-INJUNC-ADD child-3 live-REFL-INJUNC
ni-n-shi chay-kuna-ta upya-chi-wa-pti-n-shi
say-3-EVR DEM.D-PL-ACC drink-CAUS-1.OBJ-SUBDS-3-EVR
kawsa-ku-rqa-ni
live-REFL-PST-1
'**Let** him die; **let** his child live, my father said, they say. When they made me take those [cures], I lived.'

(6) ¡Hinallaña ka**yachun**! LT
hina-lla-ña ka-ya-chun
thus-RSTR-DISC be-PROG-INJUNC
'**Let it** be just like that!'

It simultaneously indicates injunctivity and person, and is in complementary distribution with other inflectional suffixes. The negative injunctive is formed by suffixing *-chu* to the injunctive and preceding it with *ama* (7), (8).

(7) ¡**Ama** lluqsi**chunchu** tukuy puntraw! CH
ama lluqsi-chun-chu tukuy puntraw
PROH go.out-INJUNC-NEG all day
'**Don't let him** leave all day!'

(8) Ishkay palumaqa nin, "¡**Ama** yantataqa apaya**chunchu**!" ACH
ishkay paluma-qa ni-n ama yanta-ta-qa
two dove-TOP say-3 PROH firewood-ACC-TOP
apa-ya-chun-chu
bring-PROG-INJUNC-NEG
'The two doves said, "**Don't let them** bring the firewood!"'

4 Verbs

The third-person future tense can sometimes be interpreted as an injunctive (9).

(9) *Wañuchiptin, '¡Amam pampankichu! ¡Hinam ismunqa!' ninshi.* ACH
wañu-chi-pti-n   ama-m   pampa-nki-chu hina-m ismu-nqa
die-CAUS-SUBDS-3 PROH-EVD bury-2-NEG   thus-EVD rot-3.FUT
ninshi
say-3-EVR
'When they killed him, "**Don't bury** him! **Let him rot** like that!" he said.'

4.3.6 Aspect

In SYQ, continuous aspect is indicated by *-ya*. *-ya* belongs to the set of derivational affixes. Unlike inflectional morphemes, *-ya* can appear in subordinate clauses and nominalizations (*puñu-ya-pti-n* 'when he is sleeping'; *ruwa-ya-q* 'one who is making') and can – and, indeed, sometimes must – precede some derivational suffixes (*miku-ya-chi-n* 'he is making him eat'). Perfective aspect, generally indicated by *-Ru*, may, in some cases, also be indicated by reflexive *-kU*. §4.3.6.1–4.3.6.3 cover *-ya* and *-kU*, respectively.

4.3.6.1 Continuous *-ya*

All dialects of SYQ indicate continuous aspect with *-ya*. *-ya* marks both the progressive (1–6) and durative components (7), (8) of the continuous, indicating both actions and states continuing in time.

(1) *Lliwmantriki invitayan payqa.* AMV
lliw-man-tri-ki   invita-ya-n   pay-qa
all-ALL-EVC-IKI   invite-PROG-3   she-TOP
'She must **be inviting** everyone, for sure, her.'

(2) *Kumunidadllañam napa:kuya: trabahapa:kuya:.* CH
kumunidad-lla-ña-m   na-pa:ku-ya-:   trabaha-pa:ku-ya-:.
community-RSTR-DISC-EVD DMY-JTACC-PROG-1 work-JTACC-PROG-1
'Just the community, **we're doing** it, **we're working**.'

4.3 Verb inflection

(3) *Walmikunaqa talpuya: allichaya: kulpakta maqaya:.* CH
walmi-kuna-qa talpu-ya-: alli-cha-ya-: kulpa-kta
woman-PL-TOP plant-PROG-1 good-FACT-PROG-1 clod-ACC
maqa-ya-:
hit-PROG-1
'The women **are planting, improving, hitting** big clumps of earth.'

(4) *¿Imatatrik ruwayan? Trabahayantriki.* ACH
ima-ta-tri-k ruwa-ya-n trabaha-ya-n-tri-ki
what-ACC-EVC-K make-PROG-3 work-PROG-3-EVC-IKI
'What **is** he doing? He must **be** working.'

(5) *Chayshi Diosninchik, "¿Imatam ashiyanki?" nin.* LT
chay-shi Dios-ni-nchik ima-ta-m ashi-ya-nki ni-n
DEM.D-EVR God-EUPH-1PL what-ACC-EVD look.for-PROG-2 say-3
'Then Our God said, "What **are** you **searching** for?"'

(6) *Uchuypis pasapasaypaqmi chakirun, uchuypis chakisham kayan.* LT
uchu-y-pis pasa-pasaypaq-mi chaki-ru-n, uchu-y-pis
chili-1-ADD complete-completely-EVD dry-URGT-3 chili-1-ADD
chaki-sha-m ka-ya-n
dry-PRF-EVD be-PROG-3
'The chilies completely dried out; the chilies **are** dried out.'

(7) *Pipis. Ñuqa ukupaw kakuyani.* AMV
pi-pis ñuqa ukupaw ka-ku-ya-ni
who-ADD I busy be-REFL-PROG-1
'No one. **I'm busy.**'

(8) *Hitakaruyta munayani.* AMV
hita-ka-ru-y-ta muna-ya-ni
fall-PASSACC-URGT-INF-ACC wany-PROG-1
'I **want** to fall.'

-ya may be used with or in place of *-q* to mark habitual action (9–11) when such action is customary.[13]

---

[13] An anonymous reviewer points out that *-ya* in Yauyos seems to resemble the cognate suf-

4 Verbs

(9) *Mana suliyasa kaptinqa wakta suliyachiyanchik.* AMV
mana   suliya-sa   ka-pti-n-qa   wak-ta   suliya-chi-ya-nchik
no   sun-PRF   be-SUBDS-3-TOP   DEM.D-ACC   sun-CAUS-PROG-1PL
'When [the oca] hasn't been sunned, we **sun** it.'

(10) *Uyqapa millwantam kaypaq puchkayanchik.* AMV
uyqa-pa   millwa-n-ta-m   kay-paq   puchka-ya-nchik
sheep-GEN   wool-3-ACC-EVD   DEM.P-ABL   spin-PROG-1PL
'We **spin** sheep's wool here.'

(11) *Fwirsawan wawakuyanchik.* ACH
fwirsa-wan   wawa-ku-ya-nchik
force-INSTR   give.birth-REFL-PROG-1PL
'With effort, we **give birth**.'

-*ya* can appear in subordinate clauses (12), (13).

(12) *Hinaptinshi iskinapa kayaptin baliyarun.* ACH
Hinaptin-shi   iskina-pa   ka-ya-pti-n   baliya-ru-n
then-EVR   corner-LOC   be-PROG-SUBDS-3   shoot-URGT-3
'Then when he **was** in the corner, they shot him.'

(13) *Wak runaqa warminta wañurachin maqayashpalla.* AMV
wak   runa-qa   warmi-n-ta   wañu-ra-chi-n
DEM.D   person-TOP   woman-3-ACC   die-URGT-CAUS-3
maqa-ya-shpa-lla
beat-PROG-SUBIS-RSTR
'That man, turning jealous, killed his wife, when he **was beating** her.'

-*ya* precedes -*mu* and -*chi* (14), (15) and precedes all inflectional suffixes.

(14) *Limpu limpu runata firmakayachin.* LT
limpu   limpu   runa-ta   firma-ka-ya-chi-n
all   all   person-ACC   sign-PASSACC-PROG-CAUS-3
'They're **making** all the people sign.'

---

fix -*yka:* in Huallaga Q, which Weber (1989) calls a general imperfective. The cognate suffix in South Conchucos Q, -*yka*, in contrast, does not appear in habitual contexts. Hintz (2011) observes that while it is not a general imperfective, it is still much broader than a simple progressive; Hintz concludes that -*yka:* in South Conchucos is continuous aspect.

(15) *Ladirankunapaq rumipis hinku**ya**muntriki.* ACH
ladira-n-kuna-paq rumi-pis hinku-ya-mu-n-tri-ki
hillside-3-PL-ABL stone-ADD roll-PROG-CISL-EVC-IKI
'Stones, too, would **be rolling** down the sides [of the mountain].'

It forms the present (16), past (17), (18) and future (19) progressive.

(16) *¡Suyaykamay! ¡Qarqaryam qipa:ta shamuku**ya**n!* CH
suya-yka-ma-y qarqarya-m qipa-:-ta shamu-ku-ya-n
wait-EXCEP-1.OBJ-IMP zombie-EVD behind-1-ACC come-REFL-PROG-3
'Wait for me! A zombie **is coming** behind me!'

(17) *¿Maypa saqaykurqa? Paypis wishtu ka**ya**rqa.* AMV
may-pa saqa-yku-rqa pay-pis wishtu ka-ya-rqa
where-LOC go.down-EXCEP-PST she-ADD lame be-PROG-PST
'Where did she fall? She, too, **was limping**.'

(18) *Antaylumata tarirushpaqa pallaku**ya**ra hinaptinshi ...* SP
antayluma-ta tari-ru-shpa-qa palla-ku-ya-ra
antayluma.berries-ACC find-URGT-SUBIS-TOP pick-REFL-PROG-PST
hina-pti-n-shi
then-EVR
'After finding some antayluma berries, she **was** gathering them up. Then ...'

(19) *Vakamik mandaku**ya**nqa.* AMV
vaka-mi-k manda-ku-ya-nqa
cow-EVD-IK be.in.charge-REFL-PROG-3.FUT
'The cows are **going to be giving** orders.'

4.3.6.2 Durative *-chka*

-chka is very rarely employed, occuring spontaneously in a non-quotative context only seven times in the corpus. Indeed, it is probably best qualified as non-productive in all but SP. *-chka* is in complementary distribution with continuative *-ya*, but it is more semantically restricted than *-ya*. A *-chka* action or state is necessarily simultaneous with some other action or state, either expilicit in the dialogue (1), (2) or supplied by context (3), (4).

4 Verbs

(1) *Kayllapam kwida**chka**nki ñuqaqa aparamu:.* ACH
kay-lla-pa-m kwida-chka-nki ñuqa-qa apa-ra-mu-:
DEM.P-RSTR-LOC-EVD care.for -DUR-2 I-TOP bring-URGT-CISL-1
'**You'll go on taking** care of this here [**while**] I bring it.'

(2) *Mundum ñitiramashun kaytam sustininkiqa. Kayta sustini**chka**nki ñuqañataqmi huk waklawpis siqaykayamun.* SP
mundu-m ñiti-ra-ma-shun kay-ta-m sustini-nki-qa
world-EVD crush-URGT-1.OBJ-1PL.FUT DEM.P-ACC-EVD sustain-2-TOP
kay-ta sustini-**chka**-nki ñuqa-ña-taq-mi huk wak law-pis
DEM.P-ACC sustain-DUR-2 I-DISC-SEQ-EVD one DEM.D side-ADD
siqa-yka-ya-mu-n
go.down-EXCEP-PROG-CISL-3
'The world is going to crush us. Hold this! **You go on holding** this one. **I, too** – another is falling over there.'

(3) *Aviva, tiya**chka**nki chayllapa.* AMV
Aviva tiya-chka-nki chay-lla-pa
Aviva sit-DUR-2 DEM.D-RSTR-LOC
'Aviva, **you're going to be sitting** just right there [**while the others** go looking].'

(4) *¡Taqsachkay!*[†] CH
taqsa-chka-y
wash-DUR-IMP
'**You go on washing** [while I play].'

4.3.6.3 Perfective -*ku*

-*ku* may indicate completion of change of position with *ri-* 'go' and other verbs of motion (1–3); it also commonly occurs with *wañu-* 'die' (4), (5). Adelaar (2006: 135) writes of Tarma Quechua: "This -*ku*-, probably the result of a functional split of the 'reflexive' marker -*ku*-, has acquired a marginal aspectual function and indicates the completion of a change of position."

(1) *Pashñalla kidalun. ¿Qaliqa li**ku**n maytataq?* CH
pashña-lla kida-lu-n qali-qa li-ku-n may-ta-taq
girl-RSTR stay-URGT-3 man-TOP go-REFL-3 where-ACC-SEQ
'Just the girl stayed. The man **went** where?'

(2) *Qullqita quykuptin ... **pasakun**.* AMV
    qullqi-ta   qu-yku-pti-n   pasa-ku-n
    money-ACC give-EXCEP-SUBDS-3   pass-REFL-3
    'When he gave him the money, he **went away**.'

(3) ***Ripukun** paqwash llapa wawan tudu **ripukun**.* LT
    ripu-ku-n   paqwash   llapa   wawa-n   tudu   ripu-ku-n
    go-REFL-3 completely all   child-3   everything go-REFL-3
    'Then, he **left** for good – all his children – all **left**.'

(4) *Baliyaptinqa **wañukun**.* ACH
    baliya-pti-n-qa   wañu-ku-n
    shoot-SUBDS-3-TOP   die-REFL-3
    'When they shot him, he **died**.'

(5) *¿Imanarunqatr? **Wañukuntri**.* ACH
    ima-na-ru-nqa-tr   wañu-ku-n-tri
    what-VRBZ-URGT-3.FUT-EVC   die-REFL-3-EVC
    'What will happen? He must have **died**.'

4.3.7 Subordination

SYQ counts three subordinating suffixes – -*pti*, -*shpa*, and -*shtin* – and one subordinating structure – -*na*-POSS-*kama*. In addition, the nominalizing suffixes, -*na*, -*q*, -*sa*, and -*y* form subordinate relative and complement clauses (see §3.4.1).

-*pti* is employed when the subjects of the main and su1432bordinate clauses are different (*Huk qawa-**pti-n-qa**, ñuqa-nchik qawa-nchik-chu* 'Although **others** see, we don't see'); *shpa* and -*shtin* are employed when the subjects of the two clauses are identical (*tushu-**shpa**/-**shtin** wasi-ta kuti-mu-n* 'Dancing they return home'). Cacra, but not Hongos, employs -*r* (realized [l]) in place of -*shpa* (*traqna-l pusha-la-mu-n* 'binding his hands and feet, they took him along'). -*pti* generally indicates that the event of the subordinated clause began prior to that of the main clause but may also be employed in the case the events of the two clauses are simultaneous (*urkista-qa traya-mu-**pti**-n tushu-rqa-nchik* 'When the band arrived, we danced'). -*shpa* generally indicates that the event of the subordinated clause is simultaneous with that of the main clause (*Sapu-qa kurrkurrya-**shpa** kurri-ya-n* 'The frog is running going *kurr-kurr!*') but may also be employed when event of the subordinated event precedes that of the main clause. -*shtin* is employed

191

4 Verbs

only when the main and subordinate clause events are simultaneous (*awa-**shtin** miku-chi-ni wamra-y-ta* '(By) weaving, I feed my children'). -*pti* subordinates are suffixed with allocation suffixes (*tarpu-**pti**-nchik* 'when we plant'); in contrast, -*shpa* and -*shtin* subordinates do not inflect for person or number (*tarpu-shpa-nchik; *tarpu-shtin-yki). -*shpa* appears 1432 times in the corpus; in three instances it is inflected for person. In elicitation, speakers adamantly reject the use of personal suffixes after -*shpa*. Subordinate verbs are never suffixed with any other inflectional morphemes, with the exception of -*ya* (*tarpu-rqa-shpa; *tarpu-shaq-shpa). The evidentials, -*mI*, *shI*, and -*trI* cannot appear on the interior of subordinate clauses, and the negative particle -*chu* can neither appear on the interior nor suffix to subordinate clauses (*mana-m rima-pti-ki* (*chu) 'if you don't talk'). Subordinate verbs inherit tense, aspect and conditionality specification from the main clause verb (*ri-shpa qawa-y-**man karqa** 'If I **would have** gone, I **would have** seen'). Depending on the context, -*pti* and -*shpa* can be translated by 'when', 'if', 'because', 'although', or with a gerund; -*shtin* can be translated by a gerund only. This information is summarized in Table 4.25.

Table 4.25: Subordinating suffixes

	Subordinate-clause event begins *before* main-clause event	Subordinate-clause event *simultaneous* with main-clause event
Identical Subjects	-*shpa*	-*shpa*, -*shtin*
Different Subjects	-*pti*	-*pti*

-*na*-POSS-*kama* is limitative. It forms subordinate clauses indicating that the event referred to either (1) is simultaneous with or (2) limits the event referred to in the main clause (*puñu-**na**-y-**kama*** 'while I was sleeping'; *wañu-na-n-kama* 'until she died').

4.3.7.1 Different subjects -*pti*

-*pti* is employed when the subjects in the main and subordinated clauses are different (1), (2) and the event of the subordinated clause begins before (3) or is simultaneous with (4) the event of the main clause. Table 4.26 displays the pattern of -*pti* inflection; Table 4.27 gives this pattern with actor-object reference.

4.3 Verb inflection

Table 4.26: -*pti* inflection

Person	Singular	Plural
1	-pti-y_{AMV,LT} -pti-:_{ACH,CH,SP}	-pti-nchik
2	-pti-ki	-pti-ki
3	-pti-n	-pti-n

Table 4.27: -*pti* inflection – actor-object suffixes

2>1	3>1	3>1pl	1>2	3>2
-wa-pti-ki_{AMV,LT} -ma-pti-ki_{ACH,CH,SP}	-wa-pti-n_{AMV,LT} -ma-pti-n_{ACH,CH,SP}	-wa-pti-nchik_{AMV,LT} -ma-pti-nchik_{ACH,CH,SP}	-pti-ki	-shu-pti-ki

(1) ¿Aruschata kumbida**pti**nchik mikunmanchu? AMV
arus-cha-ta kumbida-pti-nchik miku-n-man-chu
rice-DIM-ACC share-SUBDS-1PL eat-3-COND-Q
'**If we** share the rice, will **she** eat it?'

(2) **Qusa:** tiniynti alkaldi ka**ptin**, "Kumpañira, ¿maypim qusayki?"
ni**ma**n. CH
qusa-: tiniynti alkaldi ka-pti-n kumpañira
husband-1 lieutenant mayor be-SUBDS-3 compañera
may-pi-m qusa-yki ni-ma-n
where-LOC-EVD husband-2 say-1.OBJ-3
'**When my husband** was vice-mayor **they** asked me, "Compañera, where is your husband?"'

(3) Chay kundurqa qipi**ptin** huk turuta pagaykun. SP
chay kundur-qa qipi-pti-n huk turu-ta paga-yku-n
DEM.D condor-TOP carry-SUBDS-3 one bull-ACC pay-EXCEP-3
'**After** the condor carried her, she payed him a bull.'

4 Verbs

(4) *Huk mumintu puriyaptiki imapis prisintakurushunki.* AMV
huk mumintu puri-ya-pti-ki ima-pis
one moment walk-PROG-SUBDS-2 what-ADD
prisinta-ku-ru-shu-nki
present-REFL-URGT-2.OBJ-2
'One moment you're walking **and** something presents itself to you.'

-pti subordinates always inflect for person with allocation suffixes (5), (6).

(5) *Kalurniyuq ka**pti**kiqa **yawarnin** yanash.* AMV
kalur-ni-yuq ka-pti-ki-qa yawar-ni-n yana-sh
fever-EUPH-POSS be-SUBDS-2-TOP blood-EUPH-3 black-EVR
'**When you** have a fever, its blood is black, they say.'

(6) *Chay plantaman siqaru**pti**:pis chay turuqa … siqaramun qipa:paq plantaman.* ACH
chay planta-man siqa-ru-pti-:-pis chay turu-qa
DEM.D tree-ALL go.up-URGT-SUBDS-1-ADD DEM.D bull-TOP
siqa-ra-mu-n qipa-:-paq planta-man
go.up-URGT-CISL-3 behing-1-ABL tree-ALL
'**When I** climbed up the tree, the bull … climbed up the tree from behind me.'

The structure is usually translated in English by 'when' (7), (8) or, less often, 'if' (9), (10), 'because' (11–13), or 'although' (14).

(7) *Kundinawqa, witrqakuru**pti**nqa, wasi utrkunta altukunapash [yaykurun].* SP
kundinaw-qa, witrqa-ku-ru-pti-n-qa wasi utrku-n-ta
zombie-TOP close-REFL-URGT-SUBDS-3-TOP house hole-3-ACC
altu-kuna-pa-sh yayku-ru-n
high-PL-LOC-EVR enter-URGT-3
'**When** they shut themselves in, the zombie [entered] through a hole in the attic.'

(8) *Hinaptinshi "Wak turuta pagaykusayki," ni**ptin** asiptan.* ACH
hinaptin-shi wak turu-ta paga-yku-sayki ni-pti-n
then-EVR DEM.D bull-ACC pay-EXCEP-1>2.FUT say-SUBDS-3
asipta-n
accept-3
'Then, they say, **when** he said, "I'll pay you that bull," they accepted.'

(9) *Manam pagawaptikiqa manam wamraykiqa alliyanqachu.* LT
    mana-m   paga-wa-pti-ki-qa   mana-m   wamra-yki-qa
    no-EVD   pay-1.OBJ-2-TOP   no-EVD   child-2-TOP
    alli-ya-nqa-chu
    good-INCH-3.FUT-NEG
    '**If** you don't pay me, your son isn't going to get better.'

(10) *Wañuymantri karqa. Mana hampiptinqa.* AMV
     wañu-y-man-tri   ka-rqa   mana   hampi-pti-n-qa
     die-1-COND-EVC   be-PST   no   cure-SUBDS-3-TOP
     'I might have died. **If** they hadn't cured her.'

(11) *Payqa rikunñash warmin saqiruptin.* AMV
     pay-qa   ri-ku-n-ña-sh   warmi-n   saqi-ru-pti-n
     he-TOP   go-REFL-3-DISC-EVR   woman-3   abandon-URGT-SUBDS-3
     'He left **because** his wife abandoned him, they say.'

(12) *Priykupaw puriyan siyrtumpatr warmin mal kaptin nin.* AMV
     priykupaw   puri-ya-n   siyrtumpa-tr   warmi-n   mal   ka-pti-n
     worried   walk-PROG-3   certainly-EVC   woman-3   bad   be-SUBDS-3
     n-in
     say-3
     'Certainly, he'd be wandering around worried **because** his wife is sick.'

(13) *Mana qusa: kaptin. Mana qali: kaptin trabahaya:.* CH
     mana   qusa-:   ka-pti-n   mana   qali-:   ka-pti-n   trabaha-ya-:
     no   husband-1   be-SUBDS-3   no   man-1   be-SUBDS-3   work-PROG-1
     '**Because** I don't have a husband. I'm working **because** I don't have a husband.'

(14) *Huk qawaptinqa, ñuqa-nchik qawanchikchu.* AMV
     huk   qawa-pti-n-qa   ñuqa-nchik   qawa-nchik-chu
     one   see-SUBDS-3-TOP   I-1PL   see-1PL-NEG
     '**Although** others see it, we don't see it.'

Topic marking with *-qa* does not generally disambiguate these readings. With *-raq*, *-pti* subordinates generally receive a 'not until' interpretation (15), (16).

4 Verbs

(15) *Hamuptiyraq ñuqaqa manam lluqsirqachu.* † AMV
hamu-pti-y-raq   ñuqa-qa mana-m   lluqsi-rqa-chu
come-SUBDS-1-CONT I-TOP   no-EVD   go.out-PST-NEG
'**Not until** I came did she leave. (='Until I came, she didn't leave.')'

(16) *Manañam puntrawyaruptin vakay chawachikunqachu.* AMV
mana-ña-m   puntraw-ya-ru-pti-n   vaka-y
no-DISC-EVD   day-INCH-URGT-SUBDS-3   cow-1
chawa-chi-ku-nqa-chu
milk-CAUS-REFL-3.FUT-NEG
'**Until** it's day time, my cow won't let herself be milked.'

The first-person and second-person object suffixes, *-wa/ma* and *-sHu* precede *-pti* (17).

(17) *Chay pasarushpa sudarachishuptiki kapasmi surqurunman.* AMV
chay   pasa-ru-shpa   suda-ra-chi-shu-pti-ki
DEM.D   pass-URGT-SUBIS   sweat-URGT-CAUS-2.OBJ-SUBDS-2
kapas-mi   surqu-ru-n-man
perhaps-EVD   remove-URGT-3-COND
'When you have it passed over you, when **it makes you** sweat, it's possible it could remove it.'

4.3.7.2 Same-subjects *-shpa*

-shpa is employed when the subjects in the main and subordinated clauses are identical and the event of the subordinated clause is simultaneous with the event of the main clause (1); the event of the subordinated clause may, however, precede that of the main clause (2).

(1) *Chitchityakushpa rikullan kabrakunaqa.* LT
chitchitya-ku-shpa   riku-lla-n   kabra-kuna-qa
say.chit.chit-REFL-SUBIS   go-RSTR-3   goat-PL-TOP
'Chit-chit**ing**, the goats just left.'

(2) *Familyanchikta wañurichishpaqa lliw partiyan.* SP
familya-nchik-ta   wañu-ri-chi-shpa-qa   lliw   parti-ya-n
family-1PL-ACC   die-INCEP-CAUS-SUBIS-TOP   all   divide-PROG-3
'**After** they killed our relatives, they distributed everything.'

4.3 Verb inflection

-shpa subordinates do not inflect for person. *-shpa* can generally be translated with a gerund (3), as 'when' (4) or, less often, 'if' (5).

(3) *Traguwan, kukawan tushuchi**shpa**llam kusichakuni.* AMV
     tragu-wan   kuka-wan   tushu-chi-shpa-lla-m   kusicha-ku-ni
     liquor-INSTR coca-INSTR dance-CAUS-SUBIS-RSTR-EVD harvest-REFL-1
     'With liquor and coca, mak**ing** them dance, I harvest.'

(4) *Kustumbrawku**shpa** hawkam yatrakunchik kaypahina.* AMV
     kustumbraw-ku-shpa   hawka-m   yatra-ku-nchik   kay-pa-hina
     accustom-REFL-SUBIS tranquil-EVD live-REFL-1PL   DEM.P-LOC-COMP
     '**When** we adjust, we live peacefully, like here.'

(5) *Kuti**shpa**qa kutimushaq kimsa tawa watata.* AMV
     kuti-shpa-qa   kuti-mu-shaq   kimsa tawa wata-ta
     return-SUBIS-TOP   return-CISL-1.FUT   three four year-ACC
     '**If** I come back, I'll come back in three or four years.'

Negated, V *-shpa* can be translated 'without' (6), 'although' (7) or 'despite'.

(6) ***Mana** yanushpallam likwarunchik.* AMV
     mana   yanu-shpa-lla-m   likwa-ru-nchik
     no   cook-SUBIS-RSTR-EVD   liquify-URGT-1PL
     '**Without** boiling it, we liquify it.'

(7) *Qullqita gana**shpa**s bankuman ima trurakunki.* ACH
     qullqi-ta   gana-shpa-s   banku-man   ima   trura-ku-nki
     money-ACC   win-SUBIS-ADD   bank-ALL   what put-REFL-2
     '**Although** you earn money and save it in the bank.'

-shpa may attach to coordinated verbs (8), (9).

(8) *Kulurchakunata kayna trura**shpa** qawa**shpa** ñakarini.* AMV
     kulur-cha-kuna-ta   kayna trura-shpa qawa-shpa   ñaka-ri-ni
     color-DIM-PL-ACC   thus   put-SUBIS   look-SUBIS suffer-INCEP-1
     'Look**ing**, putt**ing** the colors like this, I suffer.'

4 Verbs

(9) *Kukachakunata aku**shpa** sigaruchakunata fuma**shpa** richkan tutakama.* AMV
kuka-cha-kuna-ta aku-shpa sigaru-cha-kuna-ta fuma-shpa
coca-DIM-PL-ACC chew-SUBIS cigarette-DIM-PL-ACC smoke-SUBIS
ri-chka-n tuta-kama
go-DUR-3 night-LIM
'Chew**ing** coca, smok**ing** cigarettes, they go on until the night.'

Only Cacra uses the QI *-r* in place of the QII *-shpa* (compare (10–14) with (15)).

(10) *Vakata harkanchik puchkashpa millwata **puchkapuchkashpa**.* AMV
vaka-ta harka-nchik puchka-shpa millwa-ta puchka-puchka-shpa
cow-ACC herd-1PL spin-SUBIS wool-ACC spin-spin-SUBIS
'We herd the cows spinning – spinning and spinning wool.'

(11) *Kutimu**shpa**qa kayna baldillawan apakushaq niwan.* LT
kuti-mu-shpa-qa kayna baldi-lla-wan apa-ku-shaq
return-CISL-SUBIS-TOP thus bucket-RSTR-INSTR bring-REFL-1.FUT
ni-wa-n
say-1.OBJ-3
'"**When** I come back, I'll bring them like this, with just a bucket," he said to me.'

(12) *Hina**shpa** maska**shpa** puriya:.* ACH
hinashpa maska-shpa puri-ya-:
then look.for-SUBIS walk-PROG-1
'Then I'm walk**ing** around looking for them.'

(13) *Wirtaman yaykuru**shpa** klavilta lliw usharusa.* SP
wirta-man yayku-ru-shpa klavil-ta lliw
garden-ALL enter-URGT-SUBIS carnation-ACC all
usha-ru-sa
waste.on.the.ground-URGT-NPST
'Enter**ing** the garden, he left all the carnations discarded on the ground.'

(14) *Wiqawninchikman kayna katawan simillakta watakurushpa talpu:.* CH
 wiqaw-ni-nchik-man kayna kata-wan similla-kta
 waist-EUPH-1PL-ALL thus shawl-INSTR seed-ACC
 wata-ku-ru-shpa talpu-:
 tie-REFL-URGT-SUBID plant-1
 'Like this, **tying** it to our waists with a shawl we plant seeds.'

(15) *Waqal likun atuq kampukta.* CH
 waqa-l li-ku-n atuq kampu-kta
 cry-SUBIS go-REFL-3 fox countryside-ACC
 '**Crying**, the fox went to the countryside.'

4.3.7.3 Adverbial *-shtin*

-shtin is employed when the subjects of the main and subordinated clauses are identical (1), (2) and the events of the two clauses are simultaneous (3).

(1) *Yatrakunchik imaynapis ... waqakushtinpis ... asikushtinpis ... imaynapis.* ACH
 yatra-ku-nchik imayna-pis maski waqa-ku-shtin-pis
 live-REFL-1PL how-ADD maski cry-REFL-SUBADV-ADD
 asi-ku-shtin-pis imayna-pis
 laugh-REFL-SUBADV-ADD how-ADD
 'We live however we can, although **we're crying** ... **laughing** ... however we can.'

(2) *Yantakunata qutushtin lliptakunata kañakushtin, ... yatrana karqa.* AMV
 yanta-kuna-ta qutu-shtin llipta-kuna-ta kaña-ku-shtin
 firewood-PL-ACC gather-SUBADV ash-PL-ACC burn-REFL-SUBADV
 yatra-na ka-rqa
 live-NMLZ be-PST
 '**Gathering** wood, **burning** ash, we had to live [in the mountains].'

(3) *Wak pubri ubiha watrashtin riyan.* AMV
 wak pubri ubiha watra-shtin ri-ya-n
 DEM.D poor sheep give.birth-SUBADV go-PROG-3
 'Those poor sheep are **giving birth** even as they walk.'

4 Verbs

-shtin subordinates do not inflect for person or number. *-shtin* subordinates are adverbial and can generally be translated by 'while' or with a gerund (4–7). While attested in spontaneous speech, *-shtin* is rare. Speakers overwhelmingly employ *-shpa* in place of *-shtin*.

(4) *Pushaykushtinqa wamrataqa makin yatapasha yantaman katran.* ACH
pusha-yku-shtin-qa wamra-ta-qa maki-n
bring.along-EXCEP-SUBADV-TOP child-ACC-TOP hand-ACC
yata-pa-sha yanta-man katra-n
feel-REPET-PRF firewood-ALL release-3
'**Bringing** the boys [home], their hands held, she sent them for firewood.'

(5) *Chay iskwilapaq wamran mikushtin.* LT
chay iskwila-paq wamra-n miku-shtin
DEM.D school-ABL child-3 eat-SUBADV
'His child [came out] of school **eating**.'

(6) *"¡Qarqaryam qipa:ta!" waqashtin shamukuyan.* CH
qarqarya-m qipa-:-ta waqa-shtin shamu-ku-ya-n
zombie-EVD behind-1-ACC cry-SUBADV come-REFL-PROG-3
'"A zombie is behind me!" he was coming **crying**.'

(7) *Waqakushtin kayqa apayan waytakunakta.* CH
waqa-ku-shtin kay-qa apa-ya-n wayta-kuna-kta
cry-REFL-SUBADV DEM.P-TOP bring-PROG-3 flower-PL-ACC
'**Crying**, they are bringing flowers.'

(8) *Waqakushtin tristim ñuqanchikqa kidaranchik ñuqa mama:.* SP
waqa-ku-shtin tristi-m ñuqa-nchik-qa kida-ra-nchik ñuqa
cry-REFL-SUBADV sad-EVD I-1PL-TOP stay-PST-1PL I
mama-:-
mother-1
'**Crying**, sad, we stayed, my mother and I.'

4.3.7.4 Limitative -*kama*

In combination with the nominalizer -*na* and possessive inflection, *kama* forms subordinate clauses indicating that the event referred to is either simultaneous with (1) or limits (2–5) the event referred to in the main clause.

(1) *Mana vilakuranichu puñunaykamam.* AMV
 mana vila-ku-ra-ni-chu puñu-na-y-kama-m
 no keep.watch-REFL-PST-1-NEG sleep-NMLZ-1-LIM-EVD
 'I didn't keep watch **while I was sleeping**.'

(2) *Taksalla taksallapitaqa tarpukuni, mana hat-hatunpichu. Yaku kanankamalla.* AMV
 taksa-lla taksa-lla-pi-ta-qa tarpu-ku-ni mana
 small-RSTR small-RSTR-LOC-ACC-TOP plant-REFL-1 no
 hat-hatun-pi-chu yaku ka-na-n-kama-lla
 big-big-LOC-NEG water be-NMLZ-3-LIM-RSTR
 'I plant in just small, small [fields], not in really big ones. **While/as long as** there's water.'

(3) *Chaytri wañuq qarin wañunankamam maqarqa.* AMV
 chay-tri wañu-q qari-n wañu-na-n-kama-m maqa-rqa
 DEM.D-EVR die-AG man-3 die-NMLZ-3-LIM-EVD beat-PST
 'That's why her₁ late husband beat her₂ **until she₂ died**.'

(4) *Almaqa wañunankama pampaman saqarun.* AMV
 alma-qa wañu-na-n-kama pampa-man saqa-ru-n
 soul-TOP die-NMLZ-3-LIM ground-ALL go.down-URGT-3
 'The ghost fell to the floor, **to his death**.'

(5) *Trayanaykama ya hinalla kakun.* LT
 traya-na-y-kama ya hina-lla ka-ku-n
 arrive-NMLZ-1-LIM EMPH thus-RSTR be-REFL-3
 'He's like that **until I arrive**.'

4.4 Verb derivation

Five suffixes derive verbs from substantives: factive *-cha*, reflexive *-ku*, simulative *-tuku*, inchoative *-ya*. Additionally, two verbs can suffix to nouns to derive verbs: *na-* 'do, act' and *naya-* 'give desire'.

A set of eighteen suffixes derives verbs from verbs. These are: *-cha* (diminutive); *-chi* (causative); *-ka* (passive, accidental); *-katra* (iterative); *-kU* (reflexive, middle, medio-passive, passive, completive); *-lla* (restrictive, limitative); *-mu* (cislocative, translocative);[14] *-nakU* (reciprocal); *-naya* (desiderative); *-pa* (repetitive); *-pa(:)kU* (joint action); *-pU* (benefactive); *-ra* (uninterrupted action); *-Ri* (inceptive); *-RU* (action with urgency or personal interest, completive); *-shi* (accompaniment); *-ya* (intensifying); and *-YkU* (exceptional performance). §4.4.1 and 4.4.2 cover suffixes deriving verbs from substantives and from other verbs, respectively.

4.4.1 Suffixes deriving verbs from substantives

The suffixes deriving verbs from substantives are: factive *-cha*, reflexive *-ku*, simulative *-tuku*, and inchoative *-ya*, as displayed in Table 4.28. §4.4.1.1–4.4.1.4 cover each of these in turn.

Table 4.28: Suffixes deriving verbs from substantives, with examples

-cha	factive	*Mama-n kanan qatra-**cha**-ru-nqa.*	'Now his mother is going to dirty it.'
-ku	reflexive	*Qishta-**ku**-ru-n.*	'They **made a nest**.'
-tuku	simulative	*Atrqray-shi huvin-**tuku**-sa.*	'The eagle **disguised himself** as a young man.'
-ya	inchoative	*Puntraw-**ya**-ru-n.*	'It dawned.'
na-	'do'	*¿I**ma-na**-ku-shaq-taq mana kay pacha muna-wa-na-n-paq?*	'**What am I going to do** so that this earth won't want me?'
naya-	'give desire'	*Pashña-**naya**-shunki.*	'You **want** a girl.'

---

[14] W. Adelaar (p.c.) points out that *-mu* might also be treated as an inflectional suffix. An anonymous reviewer agrees: "the suffixes *-ya*, *-ru* and *-ri* are all more derivational than *-mu*, [which] never co-occurs with *-ma* in QI," they write. "Rather, *-mu* and and *-ma* seem to be in paradigmatic contrast, where *-ma* essentially means 'to ego,' and *-mu* means more generally 'to any deictic center."

4.4 Verb derivation

4.4.1.1 Factive *-cha*

-cha suffixes to adjectives and nouns to derive verbs with the meanings 'to make A' (*qatra-cha-* 'to make dirty') (1–3), 'to make N' or 'to make into N' (*siru-cha-* 'form a hill') (4, (5), 'to locate something in N' (*kustal-cha-* 'to put into sacks') (6), 'to locate N in/on something' (7), 'to remove N' (*usa-cha* 'to remove lice', *qiwa-cha* 'to remove weeds').

(1) *Maman kanan qatracharunqa pawakatrashpa.* AMV
    mama-n   kanan   qatra-cha-ru-nqa   pawa-katra-shpa
    mother-3 now   dirty-FACT-URGT-3.FUT   jump-FREQ-SUBIS
    'Now his mother is going to **make it dirty** jumping.'

(2) *Hatunchanqatri kay.* AMV
    hatun-cha-nqa-tri   kay
    big-FACT-3.FUT   DEM.P
    'This one is going to **make it big**.'

(3) *Cañeteman allicharachimunki kaypitr siguranaykipaqqa.* LT
    Cañete-man   alli-cha-ra-chi-mu-nki   kay-pi-tr
    Cañete-ALL   good-FACT-URGT-CAUS-CISL-2   DEM.P-LOC-EVC
    sigura-na-yki-paq-qa
    insure-NMLZ-2-PURP-TOP
    'You're going to have that **fixed** in Cañete to be able to insure yourself here.'

(4) *Chayna siruchakurun.* AMV
    chayna   siru-cha-ku-ru-n
    thus   hill-FACT-REFL-URGT-3
    'It **formed** a hill like that.'

(5) *Partichaykuptinqa chaki, chaki.* AMV
    parti-cha-yku-pti-n-qa   chaki chaki
    parts-FACT-EXCEP-SUBDS-3-TOP   dry   dry
    'When she **breaks it into parts** – dry, dry!'

(6) *Kustalchayan papatam.* AMV
    kustal-cha-ya-n   papa-ta-m
    sack-FACT-PROG-3   potato-ACC-EVD
    'She's **bagging** potatoes.'

4 *Verbs*

(7) *Chay turutaqa llampuchaykun chay yubuchanman.* AMV
chay   turu-ta-qa   llampu-cha-yku-n   chay   yubu-cha-n-man
DEM.D   bull-ACC-TOP llampu-FACT-EXCEP-3 DEM.D   yoke-DIM-3-ALL
'They **put llampu** on his little yoke.'

4.4.1.2 Reflexive *-ku*

Suffixing to nouns referring to objects, *-ku* may derive verbs with the meaning 'to make/prepare N' (*qisha-ku-* 'to make a nest') (1), (2); suffixing specifically to nouns referring to clothing and other items that can be placed on a person's body, *-ku* derives verbs with the meaning 'to put on N' (*kata-ku* 'put on a shawl') (3), (4); suffixing to adjectives referring to human states – angry, guilty, envious – A-*ku* has the meaning 'to become A' (*piña-ku-* 'to become angry') (5), (6).

(1) *Misakun. Manam kasunchu misata.* AMV
misa-ku-n   mana-m   kasu-n-chu   misa-ta
mass-REFL-3 no-EVD   pay.attention-3-NEG mass-ACC
'She's **making [holding] mass**. They don't pay attention to mass.'

(2) *Hirakurun.* ACH
hira-ku-ru-n
herranza-REFL-URGT-3
'They **made [held] an herranza**.'

(3) *Walakuykurushaq.* AMV
wala-ku-yku-ru-shaq
skirt-REFL-EXCEP-URGT-1.FUT
'I'm going to **put on** my skirt.'

(4) *Manash waytakunchikchu.* AMV
mana-sh   wayta-ku-nchik-chu
no-EVR   flower-REFL-1PL-NEG
'We don't **put flowers on** our hats [on All Saints' Day], they say.'

(5) *Kumudakurun.* AMV
kumuda-ku-ru-n
comfortable-REFL-URGT-3
'He's **made himself comfortable**.'

(6) ¡Kurriy! **Qillaku**yankitrari. LT
     kurri-y   qilla-ku-ya-nki-tr-ari
     run-IMP   lazy-REFL-PROG-2-EVC-ARI
     'Run! You must be **getting lazy**.'

-*ku* derivation is very productive and can be idiosyncratic (*llulla-ku* 'tell a lie', *midida-ku* 'measure') (7), (8).

(7) Manam mansuchu yatran waqra**ku**yta. AMV
     mana-m   mansu-chu   yatra-n   waqra-ku-y-ta
     no-EVD   tame-NEG   know-3   horn-REFL-INF-ACC
     'He's not tame – he can **horn** [gore] people.'

(8) Karruwan … **sillaku**ykushpam riyanchik. SP
     karru-wan   silla-ku-yku-shpa-m   ri-ya-nchik
     bus-INSTR   seat-REFL-EXCEP-EVD   go-PROG-1PL
     'In a car … [it's like] we're **riding horseback in a saddle**.'

4.4.1.3 Simulative -*tuku*

Suffixing to nouns, -*tuku* derives verbs with the meaning 'to pretend to be N' or 'to become N' (*maqta-tuku-* 'pretend to be a young man') (1–3).

(1) Chay ukucha kasa maqta**tuku**shpa. AMV
     chay   ukucha   ka-sa   maqta-tuku-shpa
     DEM.D   mouse   be-PST   young.man-SIMUL-SUBIS
     'It was a mouse **pretending to be** a man.'

(2) ¡Sinvirgwinsa! ¡Qam ingañamalanki qali**tuku**shpa! CH
     sinvirgwinsa   qam   ingaña-ma-la-nki   qali-tuku-shpa
     shameless   you   trick-1.OBJ-PST-2   man-SIMUL-SUBIS
     'Shameless bastard! You fooled me **pretending to be a man**!'

(3) Wak wañuq wañurun … asnuqa wañuq**tuku**run. AMV
     wak   wañu-q   wañu-ru-n   asnu-qa   wañu-q-tuku-ru-n
     DEM.D   die-AG   die-URGT-3   donkey-TOP   die-AG-SIMUL-URGT-3
     'That "dead" one died … the donkey had **pretended to be dead**.'

The structure appears primarily – indeed, almost exclusively – in the corpus in the context of a very popular genre of stories in which an animal dresses up, pretending to be a man, to trick a girl.

4 Verbs

4.4.1.4 Inchoative -ya

-ya suffixes to nouns and adjectives to derive verbs with the meanings 'to become N' (*rumi-ya* 'petrify') (1), (2), 'to become A' (*alli-ya* 'get well') (3–6), and 'to perform a characteristic action with N' (*kwahu-ya* 'add curdling agent').

(1) **Puntrawyaruptinqa.** LT
puntraw-ya-ru-pti-n-qa
day-INCH-URGT-SUBDS-3-TOP
'When it **becomes day** [dawns].'

(2) **Hukyaruni.** LT
huk-ya-ru-ni
one-INCH-URGT-1
'I **join**ed them.'

(3) *Siyrtumpimik chay rumikunamik **yanaya**sa kayan.* AMV
siyrtumpi-mi-k   chay   rumi-kuna-mi-k   yana-ya-sa   ka-ya-n
certainly-EVD-IK DEM.D stone-PL-EVD-IK back-PROG-PRF be-PROG-3
'It's true – even the stones **turn black** there.'

(4) *"Manam wamraykiqa **alliyanqachu**", nini.* LT
mana-m   wamra-yki-qa   alli-ya-nqa-chu   ni-ni
no-EVD child-2-TOP good-INCH-3.FUT-NEG say-1
'"Your son isn't going to **get better**," I said.'

(5) **Duruyarunña. Duruyaruptin** *hurqunchik wankuman.* AMV
duru-ya-ru-n-ña   duru-ya-ru-pti-n   hurqu-nchik
hard-INCH-URGT-3-DISC hard-INCH-URGT-SUBDS-3 remove-1PL
wanku-man
mold-ALL
'It's already **hard**. When it **gets hard**, take it out [and put it] in the mold.'

(6) *Chay wañuruptikiqa, ¿pima qawashunki? ¿**Yasqayaruptikiqa**?* ACH
chay   wañu-ru-pti-ki-qa   pi-m-a   qawa-shunki
DEM.D die-URGT-SUBDS-2-TOP who-EVD-EMPH see-3>2
yasqa-ya-ru-pti-ki-qa
old-INCH-URGT-SUBDS-2-TOP
'When you die, who's going to see to you? Or when you **get old**?'

4.4.1.5 'To do' *na-*

na-, following a demonstrative pronoun, yields a transitive verb meaning 'to be thus' (1), (2) or 'to do thus' (3).

(1) *Mana hampichiptikiqa **chaynanqam**.* AMV
    mana hampi-chi-pti-ki-qa   chay-na-nqa-m
    no   cure-CAUS-SUBDS-2-TOP   DEM.D-VRBZ-3.FUT-EVD
    'If you don't have her cured, it's going to **be like that**.'

(2) *Qayna puntraw **chayna**n pararun tardi usyarirun.* AMV
    qayna   puntraw chay-na-n   para-ru-n   tardi
    previous   day   DEM.D-VRBZ-3   rain-URGT-3 afternoon
    usya-ri-ru-n
    clear-INCEP-URGT-3
    'Yesterday **it was like that** – it rained and in the afternoon and it cleared up.'

(3) *Mana apuraw alliyananchikpaqmi, qatra shakash **chaynan**.* AMV
    mana apuraw   alli-ya-na-nchik-paq-mi   qatra shakash
    no   quickly good-INCH-NMLZ-1PL-PURP-EVD   dirty guinea.pig
    chay-na-n
    DEM.D-VRBZ-3
    'So that we don't get better quickly, the filthy guinea pig **goes like that**.'

Following the interrogative indefinite *ima* 'what', *na-* derives the transitive verb *imana-*, meaning 'to do something' (4), (5), 'to happen to' (6).

(4) *Chay mamakuqa yataykun. ¿**Imana**nqataq? Yataykachin.* ACH
    chay   mamaku-qa   yata-yku-n   ima-na-nqa-taq
    DEM.D   grandmother-TOP   touch-EXCEP-3   what-VRBZ-3.FUT-SEQ
    yata-yka-chi-n
    touch-EXCEP-CAUS-3
    'The old woman touched [their arms]. **What are they going to do**? They let her touch their arms.'

4 Verbs

(5) **Manam** ñuqaqa **imanashaykipischu**. Kwirpu:mi hutrayuq. CH
mana-m   ñuqa-qa   ima-na-shayki-pis-chu   kwirpu-:-mi
no-EVD   I-TOP   what-VRBZ-1>2.FUT-ADD-NEG   body-1-EVD
hutra-yuq
fault-POSS
'I'm **not going to do anything to you**. My body is guilty.'

(6) ¿Wawayta **imanaruntri**? ACH
wawa-y-ta   ima-na-ru-n-tri
baby-1-ACC   what-VRBZ-3-EVC
'What would have **happened** to my son?'

4.4.1.6 Sensual and psychological necessity *naya-*

naya- – 'to give desire' – suffixing to a noun derives a verb meaning 'to give the desire for N' (1–3).

(1) *Pashña**naya**shunki.* † AMV
pashña-naya-shu-nki
girl-DESR-2.OBJ-2
'You want a girl.'

(2) *Mishki**naya**ruwan.* AMV
mishki-naya-ru-wa-n
fruit-DESR-URGT-1.OBJ-3
'I want to eat fruit.'

(3) "*Yaku**naya**wanmi*", nin runaqa. Chayshi wamranta nin, "¡Yakuta apamuy!" LT
yaku-naya-wa-n-mi   ni-n   runa-qa   chayshi   wamra-n-ta
water-DESR-1.OBJ-3-EVD   say-n   person-TOP DEM.D-EVR child-3-ACC
ni-n   yaku-ta   apa-mu-y
say-3   water-ACC bring-CISL-IMP
'The person said, "I'm thirsty." So he said to his child, "Bring water!"'

208

4.4.2 Verbs derived from verbs

A set of eighteen suffixes derives verbs from verbs. They are: *-cha, -chi, -ka, -katra, -kU, -lla, -mu, -nakU, -naya, -pa, -pa(:)kU, -pU, -Ra, -Ri, -RU, -shi, -tamu,* and *-YkU*.

-chi (causative) derives verbs with the meaning 'cause V' or 'permit V' (*wañu-chi-* 'kill' (lit. 'make die')). Compounded with reflexive *-ku, -chi* derives verbs with the meaning 'cause oneself to V' or 'cause oneself to be V-ed' (*yanapa-chi-ku-* 'get oneself helped').

-ka (passive/accidental) indicates that the event referred to is not under the control either of a participant in that event or of the speaker (*puñu-ka-* 'fall asleep').

-katra (iterative) indicates extended or repetitive action (*kurri-katra-* 'to run around and around').

-kU (reflexive, middle, medio-passive, passive) derives verbs with the meanings 'V oneself' (*mancha-ku-* 'scare oneself', 'get scared'), 'V for oneself/one's own benefit (*suwa-ku* 'steal') 'be V-ed' (*pampa-ku-* 'be buried').

-lla (restrictive, limitative) indicates that the event referred to remains limited to itself and is not accompanied by other events (*lluqsi-lla-* 'just leave').

-mu (cislocative, translocative) indicates – in the case of verbs involving motion – motion toward the speaker or toward a place which is indicated by the speaker (*apa-mu-* 'bring here').

-nakU (reciprocal) derives verbs with the meaning 'V each other' (*willa-naku-* 'tell each other'); compounded with causative *-chi, -nakU* derives verbs with the meaning and 'cause each other to V' (*willa-chi-naku-* 'cause each other to tell').

-naya (desiderative) derives a compound verb meaning 'to give the desire to V' (*miku-naya-* 'be hungry' (lit. 'gives the desire to eat')).

-pa (repetitive) indicates renewed or repetitive action (*tarpu-pa-* 're-seed', 'repeatedly seed'); compounded with *-ya* (intensive) *-paya* derives verbs meaning 'continue to V' (*trabaha-paya-* 'continue to work').

-pa(:)kU (joint action) indicates joint action by a plurality of individuals (*trabaha-pa:ku-* 'work (together with others)').

-pU (benefactive) indicates that an action is performed on behalf – or to the detriment – of someone other than the subject (*pripara-pu-* 'prepare (for s.o. else)'); compounded with *-kU, -pU* indicates that indicates the action is performed as a means or preparation for something else more important (including all remunerated labor) (*awa-paku-* 'weave (for others, to make money)').

-Ra (persistence) derives verbs with the meaning 'continue to V' (*qawa-ra-* 'look at persistently'); compounded with *-ya* (intensive) *-raya* derives passive

4 Verbs

from transitive verbs; that is, *-raya* derives verbs meaning 'be V-ed' (*wata-raya-* 'be tied').

-Ri (inceptive) derives verbs meaning 'begin to V' (*shinka-ri-* 'begin to get drunk').

-RU (various) indicates action with urgency or personal interest (*chaki-ru-* 'dry out (dangerously)'); it is very frequently used with a completive interpretation (*kani-ru-n* 'bit').

-shi (accompaniment) derives verbs meaning 'accompany in V-ing' or 'help V' (*harka-shi-* 'help herd').

-tamu (irreversible) indicates a change of state that is irreversible (*wañu-tamu-* 'die').

-YkU (exceptional) is perhaps the derivative suffix for which is it hardest to identify any kind of central interpretation; with regard to cognates in other Quechuan languages, it is sometimes said that it indicates action performed in some way different from usual.

Table 4.29 lists the VV derivational suffixes; associated examples are fully glossed in the corresponding sections.

Of the eighteen, arguably only four – causative *-chi*, reflexive *-ku*, reciprocal *-nakU*, and desierative *-naya* – actually change the root's theta structure and derive new lexical items. The rest specify mode and/or aspect and/or otherwise function adverbally.

The analyses of §4.4.2.1 identify some of the more common possible interpretations of these suffixes. That said, the interpretations given are hardly exhaustive or definitive, not least because each generally includes multiple vectors. §4.4.2.3 looks at each of these suffixes in turn. *-ya* (continuative), also VV derivative suffix, was treated above in §4.3.6.1.

4.4.2.1 Distribution of VV derivational suffixes

The default order of VV derivational suffixes is given in Table 4.30.
Although this order is generally rigid, some suffixes show optional order when appearing consecutively. Causative *-chi* is likely the most mobile; change in its placement results in a change in verb meaning (*wañu-chi-naya-wa-n* 'it makes me want to kill' *wañu-naya-chi-wa-n* 'it makes me feel like I want to die' (example from Albó (1964), as cited in Cerrón-Palomino 1987: 284). *-chi* and continuative *-ya* regularly commute (1), (2), as do exceptional *-ykU* and reflexive *-kU* (3), (4).

4.4 Verb derivation

Table 4.29: Verb-verb derivational suffixes, with examples

Suffix	Meaning	Example	Translation
-cha	diminutive	Wilka-y-ta puklla-**cha**-ya-n.	'My grandson is playing'.
-chi	causative	Ishpa-y-cha-ta tuma-ra-**chi**-rqa-ni.	'I **made him** drink urine.'
-ka	passive/accidental	Puñu-**ka**-ru-n-mi.	'She has fallen asleep'.
-katra	iterative	Pawa-**katra**-shpa	'jumping and jumping'
-kU	reflexive, passive	Kikinpis Campiona**kurun**.	'They **themselves** poisoned **themselves** with Campión.'
-lla	restrictive	Wak runa-qa ... piliya-ku-**lla**-n.	'Those people ... **just** fight.'
-mu	cislocative	Qati-**mu**-shaq kay-man.	'I'm going to bring it over here.'
-nakU	reciprocal	Kay visinu-kuna-qa dinunsiya-**naku**-n maqa-**naku**-n.	'The neighbors denounce **each other**, they hit **each other**.'
-naya	desiderative	Ishpa-**naya**-wa-n.	'I **want to** urinate.'
-pa	repetitive	Qawa-**pa**-yku-pti-n-ña-taq-shi.	'If he's looking **every second**.'
-pa(:)kU	joint action	Tari-pa:ku-n-man-pis ka-rqa.	'They might have found him.'
-pU	benefactive	Chay-lla-pa pripara-**pu**-nki.	'Just there prepare it **for me**.'
-Ra	uninterrupted	¿Ima-ta-m qawa-ra-ya-nki?	'What are you looking at (**persistently**)?'
-Ri	inceptive	Warmi-kuna-qa shinka-**ri**-shpa ... waqa-n.	'When the women [start to] get drunk ... they cry.'
-RU	urgency, completive	Miku-**ru**-shunki wak kundinaw-qa.	'(**Careful!**) that zombie will eat you.'
-shi	accompaniment	"Harka-**shi**-sa-yki-m", ni-n.	'"I'm going to **help** you pasture," he said.'
-tamu	irreversible	Wañu-**tamu**-sha qari-qa.	'The man **died**.'
-YkU	exceptional	Kay-lla-pi, Señor, tiya-**yku**-y.	'Right here, Sir, **please** have a seat.'

Table 4.30: Default order of modal suffixes

ka	pa	Ra	katra	cha	Ri	ykU	RU	chi	shi	pU	na	kU	mu	lla

4 Verbs

(1) *Llamputa mikuykayachin shakashta.* AMV
llampu-ta   miku-yka-ya-chi-n   shakash-ta
llampu-ACC eat-EXCEP-PROG-CAUS-3 guinea.pig-ACC
'He's making the guinea pig eat the *llampu*.'

(2) *Mana suliyasa kaptinqa wakta suliyachiyanchik.* AMV
mana   suliya-sa   ka-pti-n-qa   wak-ta   suliya-chi-ya-nchik
no   sun-PRF   subds-3-TOP   DEM.D-ACC   sun-CAUS-PROG-1PL
'When it hasn't been sunned, we **sun** it.'

(3) *Ima kuchilluwanpis imawanpis apuntaykukushpa kayhina kurriyamun.* ACH
ima   kuchillu-wan-pis ima-wan-pis   apunta-yku-ku-shpa
what   knife-INSTR-ADD   what-INSTR-ADD   point-EXCEP-REFL-SUBIS
kay-hina   kurri-ya-mu-n
DEM.P-COMP   run-PROG-CISL-3
'With a knife or whatever, **taking aim** [at us] they're running like this.'

(4) *Ñuqanchikqa paraptin uvihanchik yatanpi puñunchik muntita mashtakuykushpam, ukunchikta yaku riptin.* AMV
ñuqa-nchik-qa   para-pti-n   uviha-nchik   yata-n-pi   puñu-nchik
I-1PL-TOP   rain-SUBDS   sheep-1PL   side-3-LOC   sleep-1PL
munti-ta   mashta-ku-yku-shpa-m   uku-nchik-ta   yaku
brush-ACC   spread-REFL-EXCEP-SUBIS-EVD   below-1PL-ACC   water
ri-pti-n
go-SUBDS-3
'When it rains, we spread out brush and sleep next to our sheep – when the water goes below us.'

Some combinations are not possible. Although some combinations are, arguably, precluded for pragmatic reasons (i.e., they would denote highly unlikely or even impossible states or events), the exclusion of others begs other accounts (5).

(5) **kumudashikuyan *kumudakushiyan* AMV
*kumuda-shi-ku-ya-n   *kumuda-ku-shi-ya-n
comfortable-ACMP-REFL-PROG-3   comfortable-REFL-ACMP-PROG-3
'They **accompanied getting** comfortable.'

4.4.2.2 Morphophonemics

In SYQ, as in other Quechuan languages, the first-person-object suffix -ma (1) and the cislocative suffix -mu (2) trigger the lowering of a preceding vowel -U- to -a-; causative suffix -chi does so as well when it precedes -kU, -RU, or -ykU (3). Table 4.31 displays the pattern of morphophonemic alterations in SYQ.

Table 4.31: VV derivational suffixes – morphophonemics

U represents an alternation between [u] and [a].

Morpheme	Realized as	Before					Elsewhere as
-kU	-ka	-ma₁.ₒʙJ	-mu			-chi	-ku
-pU	-pa	-ma₁.ₒʙJ	-mu	-kU			-pu
-RU	-Ra	-ma₁.ₒʙJ	-mu	-kU	-pU	-chi	-Ru
-ykU	-yka	-ma₁.ₒʙJ	-mu		-pU	-chi	-yku

(1) *Chay gwardya paqarinnintaq kaypaq traya**ramun**.* SP
   chay gwardya paqarin-ni-n-taq   kay-paq
   DEM.D police   tomorrow-EUPH-3-SEQ   DEM.P-LOC
   traya-ra-mu-n
   arrive-URGT-CISL-3
   'The next day the police arrived here.'

(2) *Makiyta ñuqaqa paqa**karamu**niñam.* AMV
   maki-y-ta   ñuqa-qa paqa-ka-ra-mu-ni-ña-m
   hand-1-ACC I-TOP   wash-REFL-URGT-CISL-1-DISC-EVD
   'I've already washed my hands.'

(3) *Wiraya**ykachi**shpam qamtaqa mikushunki.* ACH
   wira-ya-yka-chi-shpa-m   qam-ta-qa   miku-shunki
   fat-INCH-EXCEP-CAUS-SUBIS-EVD   you-ACC-TOP eat-3>2
   'After she's fattened you up, she's going to eat you.'

Additionally, in SYQ, both -pU and -kU trigger vowel lowering, the first with -RU (4) and -ykU (5), and the second with -RU (6) and -pU.

4 Verbs

(4) *Tapumuptin traskirapamuway hinashpa allicharapuway.* AMV
   tapu-mu-pti-n   traski-ra-pa-mu-wa-y   hinashpa
   ask-CISL-SUBDS-3   accept-UNINT-BEN-CISL-1.OBJ-IMP   then
   alli-cha-ra-pu-wa-y
   good-FACT-UNINT-BEN-1.OBJ-IMP
   'When he asks, receive it for me then put it in order it **for me**.'

(5) *Chaytatrik indikaykapuwanki.* AMV
   chay-ta-tri-k   indika-yka-pu-wa-nki
   DEM.D-ACC-EVC-IK   indicate-EXCEP-BEN-1.OBJ-2
   'You're going to point that out **to me**.'

(6) *Wak warmiqa wawapakurusam.* AMV
   wak   warmi-qa   wawa-pa-ku-ru-sa-m
   DEM.D   woman-TOP   give.birth-MUTBEN-URGT-NPST-EVD
   'That woman gave birth to an illegitimate child.'

W. Adelaar (p.c.) points out that that "the morphophomemic vowel lowering presented [here] is not locally restricted." In *miku-yka-ya-chi-n*, for example, he writes, *-ykU-* is apparently modified to *-yka-* under the influence of a non-adjacent suffix *-chi-*, and in *ushtichi-ka-la-mu-y*, *-kU* is apparently modified to *-ka* under the influence of the non-adjacent *-mu*. In these and similar cases, SYQ patterns with the Central Peruvian QI, he writes. He suggests that this non-local vowel lowering may be an archaic feature since Southern Peruvian Quechua does not have it.

4.4.2.3 Individual derivational and complementary suffixes

4.4.2.3.1 -*cha* Diminutive. *-cha* indicates action performed by a child or in the manner of a child (1) or action of little importance.

(1) *Chay willkayta uchuklla pukllachayan qawaykuni.* AMV
   chay   willka-y-ta   uchuk-lla   puklla-cha-ya-n   qawa-yku-ni
   DEM.D   grandson-1-ACC   small-RSTR   play-DIM-PROG-3   look-EXCEP-1
   'I look. My little grandson is playing.'

It may also indicate an affectionate attitude on the part of the speaker (2), (3). Not attested in the CH dialect.

4.4 Verb derivation

(2) *¿Imatataq ruwayan pay? Graba**cha**yan.* AMV
    ima-ta-taq   ruwa-ya-n   pay graba-cha-ya-n
    what-ACC-SEQ make-PROG-3 she record-DIM-PROG-3
    'What is she doing? Recording.'

(3) *Kanan nasi**cha**ramunña.* AMV
    kanan   nasi-cha-ra-mu-n-ña
    now   be.born-DIM-URGT-CISL-DISC-DISC
    'She's already born now.'

4.4.2.3.2 Causative *-chi*, *-chi-ku* *-chi* indicates that the subject causes or permits an action on the part of another participant; that is, *-chi* derives verbs with the meaning 'cause to V' (1–4).

(1) *Ishpaychata tumara**chi**rqani.* AMV
    ishpay-cha-ta   tuma-ra-chi-rqa-ni
    urine-DIM-ACC drink-URGT-CAUS-PST-1
    'I **made/had** him drink urine.'

(2) *¿Imash waqa**chi**shunki? ¿Ayvis waqankichu?* ACH
    ima-sh   waqa-chi-shu-nki ayvis   waqa-nki-chu
    what-EVR cry-CAUS-2.OBJ-2 sometimes cry-2-Q
    'What **makes** you cry, she asks? Do you cry sometimes?'

(3) *Ishchallataña shutuyka**chi**yman, ¿aw?* AMV
    ishcha-lla-ta-ña   shutu-yka-chi-y-man   aw
    a.little-RSTR-ACC-DISC drip-EXCEP-CAUS-1-COND yes
    'I have to **make** it drip just a little, right?'

(4) *Ñakaya**chi**wanmi.* AMV
    ñaka-ya-chi-wa-n-mi
    suffer-PROG-CAUS-1.OBJ-3-EVD
    'He's **making** me suffer.'

Compounded with reflexive *-ku*, *-chi* indicates that the actor causes him/herself to act or causes or permits another to act on him/her (5), (6).

4 Verbs

(5) *Chirirushpaqa manañam llushti**chiku**nchu.* AMV
    chiri-ru-shpa-qa   mana-ña-m   llushti-chi-ku-n-chu
    cold-URGT-SUBIS-QA no-DISC-EVD skin-CAUS-REFL-3-NEG
    'When it's cold, it doesn't **let itself** be [=can't be] skinned any more.'

(6) *Yanapa**chiku**nki.* AMV
    yanapa-chi-ku-nki
    help-CAUS-REFL-2
    'You're going to **get yourself** helped.'

4.4.2.3.3 Passive/accidental -*ka*   -*ka* indicates that the event referred to is not under the control either of a participant in that event or of the speaker (1–5).

(1) *Puñu**ka**runmi.* AMV
    puñu-ka-ru-n-mi
    sleep-PASSACC-URGT-3-EVD
    'She **fell** asleep.'

(2) *Pasaypaq punkisa purirqa. Qapari**ka**shtin rin ninmi.* AMV
    pasaypaq   punki-sa   puri-rqa   qapari-ka-shtin   ri-n
    completely swell-PRF walk-PST shout-PASSACC-SUBADV go-3
    ni-n-mi
    say-3-EVD
    'He was walking totally swollen. He was shouting [**despite himself**].'

(3) *Suyñu**ka**yanchik runallata fiyullataña.* ACH
    suyñu-ka-ya-nchik   runa-lla-ta   fiyu-lla-ta-ña
    dream-PASSACC-PROG-1PL person-RSTR-ACC ugly-RSTR-ACC-DISC
    'We're **having** terrible **dreams** [nightmares] about the people.'

(4) *Wakhina lliw lliw tumba**ka**rushpa ...* AMV
    wak-hina   lliw lliw tumba-ka-ru-shpa
    DEM.D-COMP all   all   fall-PASSACC-URGT-SUBIS
    'All of them, **falling** down like that ...'

4.4 Verb derivation

(5) *Achka luna huntalamusha. Taytalla:qa kallipa pulikusha ashikayan tayta:taq.* CH
achka luna hunta-la-mu-sha tayta-lla-:-qa kalli-pa
a.lot person gather-URGT-CISL-TK father-RSTR-1-TOP street-LOC
puli-ku-sha ashi-ka-ya-n tayta-:-ta-qa
walk-REFL-NPST laugh-PASSACC-PROG-3 father-1-ACC-TOP
'A lot of people had gathered. My father was walking in the street and they **made fun** of him.'

4.4.2.3.4 Iterative -*katra* -*katra* indicates extended (1–2), or repetitive (3–6) action.

(1) *Qawakatrayan.* AMV
qawa-katra-ya-n
look-FREQ-PROG-3
'She's **staring**', 'She's **looking around**.'

(2) *Mana wayrakunaykipaq kaynacham apakatrakunki.* AMV
mana wayra-ku-na-yki-paq kayna-cha-m apa-katra-ku-nki
no wind-REFL-NMLZ-2-PURP thus-DIM-EVD bring-FREQ-REFL-2
'So that you don't get bad air [sick], you'll **carry along** some just like this.'

(3) *Killantin killantin maskani tapukatrashpa.* AMV
killa-ntin killa-ntin maska-ni tapu-katra-shpa
month-INCL month-INCL search.for-1 ask-FREQ-SUBIS
'I looked for him for months and months, **asking and asking**.'

(4) *Wak maqtaqa pukllayta atipanchu, qay. Yangam saytakatrayan.* AMV
wak maqta-qa puklla-y-ta atipa-n-chu qay yanga-m
DEM.D young.man-TOP play-INF-ACC be.able-3-NEG hey in.vain-EVD
sayta-katra-ya-n
kick-FREQ-PROG-3
'That boy can't play [ball], eh. In vain, he's **kicking and kicking**.'

217

4 Verbs

(5) *Qunirichirqatriki. Qapari**katra**rqa. Arruhaytash qallakuykun.* AMV
quni-ri-chi-rqa-tri-ki   qapari-**katra**-rqa   arruha-y-ta-sh
warm-INCEP-CAUS-PST-EVC-IKI shout-FREQ-PST   vomit-INF-ACC-EVR
qalla-ku-yku-n
begin-REFL-EXCEP-3
'It must have heated him up. He **shouted and shouted**. [Then] he starts to throw up, they say.'

(6) *Hinaptinqa qaya**katra**kun, "¡Abuelo Prudencio! ¡Suyaykamay! Qarqaryam qipa:ta shamukuyan."* CH
hinaptin-qa   qaya-**katra**-ku-n   abuelo   Prudencio
then-TOP   shout-FREQ-REFL-3   grandfather Prudencio
suya-yka-ma-y   qarqarya-m   qipa-:-ta   shamu-ku-ya-n
wait-EXCEP-1.OBJ-IMP zombie-EVD behind-1-ACC come-REFL-PROG-3
'Then he called **several times**, "Grandfather Prudencio! Wait for me! A zombie is coming behind me!"'

4.4.2.3.5 Reflexive, middle, medio-passive, passive -kU -kU indicates that the subject acts on him/herself or that the subject of the verb is the object of the event referred to; that is, -kU derives verbs with the meanings 'V oneself' (1–2), and 'be V-ed' (3).

(1) *Kikinpis Campiona**ku**run.* AMV
kiki-n-pis   Campiona-ku-ru-n
self-3-ADD poison.with.Campion-REFL-URGT-3
'They themselves **poisoned themselves with Campión**.'

(2) *Kundina**ku**rushpa chay pashña kaqta trayaramun.* AMV
kundina-ku-ru-shpa   chay   pashña   ka-q-ta
condemn-REFL-URGT-SUBIS DEMD   girl   be-AG-ACC
traya-ra-mu-n
arrive-URGT-CISL-3
'**Condemning himself** [becoming a zombie], he arrived at the girl's place at night.'

4.4 Verb derivation

(3) *Manam huya**ku**:chu. Manam imapis manchachimanchu.* CH
    mana-m huya-ku-:-chu   mana-m ima-pis
    no-EVD scare-REFL-1-NEG no=EVD what-ADD
    mancha-chi-ma-n-chu
    scare-CAUS-1.OBJ-3-NEG
    'I'm not **scared**. Nothing scares me.'

-kU often functions as a dative of interest, indicating that the subject has some particular interest in the event referred to (4), (5).

(4) *Kay inbidyusu wawqin, "¡Suwa**ka**muranki tuta!" nishpa.* LT
    kay   inbidyusu wawqi-n   suwa-ka-mu-ra-nki   tuta   ni-shpa
    DEM.P   jealous   brother-3 steal-REFL-CISL-PST-2 night say-SUBIS
    'His jealous brother said, "You stole those at night!"'

(5) *Mashwakuna ullu**ku**kunaktam ayvis talpu**ku**nchik.* CH
    mashwa-kuna ulluku-kuna-kta-m   ayvis   talpu-ku-nchik
    mashwa-PL   ulluco-REFL-ACC-EVD   sometimes plant-REFL-1PL
    'Sometimes we plant mashua and olluco and all.'

-kU is used with impersonal weather verbs (6); it can indicate completed action (a completed or more or less irreversible change of state) (7) (see §4.3.6.3 on perfective *-ku*), and excess of action (8), (9).

(6) *Wayra**ku**yanmari. Wayra**ku**yan, qasa**ku**yan, rupa**ku**yan.* AMV
    wayra-ku-ya-n-m-ari   wayra-ku-ya-n   qasa-ku-ya-n
    wind-REFL-PROG-3-EVD-ARI wind-REFL-PROG-3 ice-REFL-PROG-3
    rupa-ku-ya-n
    burn-REFL-PROG-3
    'It's windy. It's windy, it's freezing, it's hot.'

(7) *Traputaqa aparikushpa pasa**ku**n.* SP
    trapu-ta-qa   apa-ri-ku-shpa   pasa-ku-n
    rag-ACC-TOP   bring-INCEP-REFL-SUBIS   pass-REFL-3
    'Taking along the rag, she **left**.'

(8) *Kashtu**ku**yan.* AMV
    kashtu-ku-ya-n
    chew-REFL-PROG-3
    'He's chewing **a lot**.'

4 Verbs

(9) *Tilivisyunta lika**ku**yan. Manam ñuqakunaqa gustamanchu chayqa tantu.* CH
    tilivisyun-ta   lika-ku-ya-n   mana-m   ñuqa-kuna-qa
    television-ACC look.at-REFL-PROG-3 no-EVD   I-PL-TOP
    gusta-ma-n-chu   chay-qa   tantu
    be.pleasing-1.OBJ-3-NEG DEM.D   a.lot
    'They're watching television [**a lot**]. We don't like that too much.'

-ku appears in reflexive verbs borrowed from Spanish, translating the Spanish pronouns *me, te, se,* and *nos* (10), (11).

(10) *Manañam kwinta**ku**chuwanchu.* LT
    mana-ña-m   kwinta-ku-chuwan-chu
    no-DISC-EVD   realize-REFL-1PL.COND-NEG
    'We can no longer realize it.' *Sp.* '*Ya no podemos darnos cuenta*'.

(11) *Iskapa**ku**shaq maymanpis.* CH
    iskapa-ku-shaq   may-man-pis
    escape-REFL-1.FUT where-ALL-ADD
    'I'm going escape to wherever.' *Sp.* '**Me** *voy a escapar*'.

When it precedes either of the derivational suffixes *-mu* or *-chi* or the inflectional suffix *-ma*, *-kU* is realized as *-ka* (4).

4.4.2.3.6 Restrictive, limitative *-lla*

-lla indicates that the event referred to remains limited to itself and is not accompanied by other events (1), (2).

(1) *Wak runaqa wama wamaqtam piliyaku**lla**n.* AMV
    wak   runa-qa   wama wamaq-ta-m   piliya-ku-lla-n
    DEM.D   person-TOP   a.lot   a.lot-ACC-EVD   fight-REFL-RSTR-3
    'Those people fight too much, **do nothing but** fight.'

(2) *Alkansaptin, "¡Suyayku**lla**way!" nishpa.* AMV
    alkansa-pti-n,   suya-yku-lla-wa-y   ni-shpa
    reach-SUBDS-3 wait-EXCEP-RESTR-IMP say-SUBIS
    'When he reached her, he said, "**Just** wait for me!"'

It may also express (a) an affectionate or familiar attitude toward the event (3), (4), (b) regret with regard to the event (5), (6), or (c) pity for event participants (7).

4.4 Verb derivation

(3) *Fiystapa tushukunki. Kanan irransa kakullanqatriki.* AMV
 fiysta-pa tushu-ku-nki kanan irransa
 festival-LOC dance-REFL-2 now herranza
 ka-ku-lla-nqa-tri-ki
 be-REFL-RSTR-3.FUT-EVC-IKI
 'You'll dance at the festival. Now there's going to be an herranza, for sure.'

(4) *Aspirinakunata qayna puntraw apamu**lla**wan qaquwan trakiyta.* AMV
 aspirina-kuna-ta qayna puntraw apa-mu-lla-wa-n
 aspirin-PL-ACC previous day bring-CISL-RSTR-1.OBJ-3
 qaqu-wa-n traki-y-ta
 massage-1.OBJ-3 foot-1-ACC
 'She brought me aspirin and everything yesterday and she rubbed my foot.'

(5) *Shunquy hunta llakiyuqtam saqi**lla**sqayki; ñawiy hunta wiqiyuqtam diha**lla**sqayki.* AMV
 shunqu-y hunta llaki-yuq-ta-m saqi-lla-sqayki ñawi-y
 heart-1 full sorrow-POSS-ACC-EVD leave-RSTR-1>2.FUT eye-1
 hunta wiqi-yuq-ta-m diha-lla-sqayki
 full tear-POSS-ACC-EVD leave-RSTR-1>2.FUT
 'My heart full of sadness I'm going to abandon you, my eyes full of tears, I'm going to leave you.'

(6) *Chay pubrikunaqa mana imatas yatranchu. Qullqitapis falsutapis traskillan.* ACH
 chay pubri-kuna-qa mana ima-ta-s yatra-n-chu
 DEM.D poor-PL-TOP no what-ACC-ADD know-3-NEG
 qullqi-ta-pis falsu-ta-pis traski-lla-n
 money-ACC-ADD false-ACC-ADD accept-RSTR-3
 'Those poor people don't know anything. They accept counterfeit money [**poor things**].'

4 Verbs

(7) *Chay wawakuna kidan hukvida tristi sapan. Runapam makinpaña yatrakullan.* ACH
chay   wawa-kuna   kida-n   hukvida tristi sapa-n   runa-pa-m
DEM.D   baby-PL   stay-3   a.lot   sad   alone-3   person-GEN-EVD
maki-n-pa-ña   yatra-ku-**lla**-n
hand-3-LOC-DISC   live-REFL-RSTR-3
'Those children remain really sad, alone. They live out of other people's hands.'

Other interpretations are also available (8).

(8) *Qariqarillaraqchu qariqarillaraqmi niytaq niyallan hinashpa wañukun.* SP
qari-qari-lla-raq-chu   qari-qari-lla-raq-mi   ni-y-taq
man-man-RSTR-CONT-Q   man-man-RSTR-CONT-EVD   say-IMP-SEQ
ni-ya-**lla**-n   hinashpa   wañu-ku-n
say-PROG-RSTR-3   then   die-REFL-3
'"Still brave and strong?" "Yes, still brave and strong!" he said for the sake of saying and died.'

4.4.2.3.7 -*mu* In the case of verbs involving motion, -*mu* indicates motion toward the speaker (1), (2) or toward a place which is indicated by the speaker (3–5).

(1) *Ishkay killanta papaniy kartata pachimuwan wañukusanña.* AMV
ishkay   killa-n-ta   papa-ni-y   karta-ta   pachi-**mu**-wa-n
two   month-3-ACC   father-EUPH-1 letter-ACC send-CISL-1.OBJ-3
wañu-ku-sa-n-ña
die-REFL-PRF-3-DISC
'Two months later, my father sent me a letter that [the vicuña] had died.'

(2) *Navidadninchik traya**mu**ptinqa tushukunchik.* CH
navidad-ni-nchik   traya-**mu**-pti-n-qa   tushu-ku-nchik
Christmas-EUPH-1PL   arrive-CISL-SUBDS-3-TOP   dance-REFL-1PL
'When our Christmas **comes**, we dance.'

(3) *Yuraq kaballuqa yuraq vakata arrastra**mu**sa.* AMV
yuraq   kaballu-qa   yuraq   vaka-ta   arrastra-**mu**-sa
white   horse-TOP   white   cow-ACC   drag-CISL-NPST
'A white horse was dragging along a white cow.'

4.4 *Verb derivation*

(4) *Ladirankunapaq rumipis hinku**ya**muntriki.* ACH
ladira-n-kuna-paq rumi-pis hinku-ya-mu-n-tri-ki
hillside-3-PL-ABL stone-ADD roll-PROG-CISL-3-EVC-IKI
'Stones, too, must be **roll**ing down from the hillsides.'

(5) *Kanan wichayta riya: uvihaman. Uviha:ta michi**mu**shaq.* SP
kanan wichay-ta ri-ya-: uviha-man uviha-:-ta
now up.hill-ACC go-PROG-1 sheep-ALL sheep-1-ACC
michi-mu-shaq
herd-CISL-1.FUT
'Now I'm going up hill to my sheep. I'm going to **herd** my sheep.'

In the case of verbs that do not involve motion, *-mu* may have various senses. These may have in common that they all add a vector of movement to the action named by the V and, further, that such movement is away from ego, as an anonymous reviewer suggests (6), (7).

(6) *Lichita mañakara**mu**y tiyuykipa.* LT
lichi-ta maña-ka-ra-mu-y tiyu-yki-pa
milk-ACC ask-REFL-URGT-CISL-IMP uncle-2-LOC
'**Go ask** your uncle for milk.'

(7) *¡Llushtichikala**mu**y hakuykikta!* CH
llushti-chi-ka-la-mu-y haku-yki-kta
skin-CAUS-REFL-URGT-CISL-IMP jacket-2-ACC
'**Go take off** your jacket!'

4.4.2.3.8 Reciprocal *-nakU* *-nakU* indicates that two or more actors act reciprocally on each other; that is, *-nakU* derives verbs with the meaning 'V each other' (1–3).

(1) *¿Wakpaq pantyunpa pampa**naku**nman?* AMV
wak-paq pantyun-pa pampa-naku-n-man
DEM.D-ABL cemetery-LOC bury-RECP-3-COND
'Can people there bury **each other** in the cemetery?'

223

4 Verbs

(2) *Kaypaqmá kay visinukuna piliyakullan hukvidata dinunsiyanakun maqanakun.* ACH
kay-paq-m-á   kay   visinu-kuna piliya-ku-lla-n
DEM.P-ABL-EVD-EMPH DEM.P neighbor-PL fight-REFL-RSTR-3
hukvida-ta dinunsiya-naku-n maqa-naku-n
a.lot-ACC denounce-RECP-3 hit-RECP-3
'Around here, my neighbors fight a lot. They denounce **each other**; they hit **each other**.'

(3) *Kikinkunatrik ruwanakun wak pastuta kitanakushpa.* LT
kiki-n-kuna-tri-k ruwa-naku-n wak   pastu-ta
self-3-PL-EVC-IK make-RECP-3 DEM.D pasture.grass-ACC
kita-naku-shpa
take.away-RECP-SUBIS
'They themselves do that to **each other**, taking that pasture grass from **each other**.'

-na never appears independently of *-kU*. *-chinakU* derives verbs with the meaning 'cause each other to V' (4–6). When it precedes either of the derivational suffixes *-mu* or *-chi* or the inflectional suffix *-ma*, *-(chi)nakU* is realized as *-(chi)naka*.

(4) *Yuyarichinakuyan.* AMV
yuya-ri-chi-naku-ya-n
remember-INCEP-CAUS-RECP-PROG-3
'They're making **each other** remember.'

(5) *Kikinkamatr wañuchinakura. Gwardyakunatr wañuchira.* ACH
kiki-n-kama-tr wañu-chi-naku-ra gwardya-kuna-tr wañu-chi-ra
self-3-LIM-EVC die-CAUS-RECP-PST police-PL-EVC   die-CAUS-PST
'They must have killed **each other** themselves.' (*lit.* 'caused e.o. to die')

(6) *Ishkay kimsam. Yatrachinakuykushpa misita watarun kunkanman.* ACH
ishkay kimsa-m   yatra-chi-naku-yku-shpa   misi-ta   wata-ru-n
two   three-EVD know-CAUS-RECP-EXCEP-SUBIS cat-ACC   tie-URGT-3
kunka-n-man
throat-3-ALL
'Two or three. Teaching each other, they tied cats to their necks.'
(*lit.* 'cause e.o. to know')

4.4 Verb derivation

4.4.2.3.9 -naya In combination with a verb stem, V, it yields a compound verb meaning 'to give the desire to V' (1–4).

(1) *Tutakuykunña mikunayan lliwña.* SP
 tuta-ku-yku-n-ña miku-naya-n lliw-ña
 night-REFL-EXCEP-3-DISC eat-DESR-3 all-DISC
 'Night falls already and he **is hungry** and everything already.'

(2) *Mashwata mikuptinchik ishpanayawanchik. Chay riñunninchikta limpiyanshi.* AMV
 mashwa-ta miku-pti-nchik ishpa-naya-wa-nchik chay
 mashwa-ACC eat-SUBDS-1PL urinate-DESR-1.OBJ-1PL DEM.D
 riñun-ni-nchik-ta limpiya-n-shi
 kidney-EUPH-1PL-ACC wash-3-EVR
 'When we eat mashua, it makes us **want to** urinate. It cleans our kidneys, they say.'

(3) *Chayta siguruta watanki Hilda icha tiranayashpa iskaparunman.* AMV
 chay-ta siguru-ta wata-nki Hilda icha tira-naya-shpa
 DEM.D-ACC secure-ACC tie-2 Hilda or pull-DESR-SUBIS
 iskapa-ru-n-man
 escape-URGT-3-COND
 'Tie it up tight, Hilda, or else, **wanting to** pull, it could escape.'

(4) *Hildapa turin maqta kay hanaypaq uraypaqa aritita ushtunayarachin.* AMV
 Hilda-pa turi-n maqta kay hanay-paq
 Hilda-GEN brother-3 young.man DEM.P up.hill-ABL
 uray-pa-qa ariti-ta ushtu-naya-ra-chi-n
 down.hill-LOC-TOP earring-ACC dress-DESR-URGT-CAUS-3
 'Hilda's brother from up here, down [on the coast] **wanted to** have an earring put on.'

Particularly with weather verbs, *-naya* may indicate that the E named by the root V is imminent (5), (6).

(5) *Paranayamun.* ACH
 para-naya-mu-n.
 rain-DESR-CISL-3
 'It's **about to** rain.'

4 Verbs

(6) *Shakashqa wañu**naya**nña.* AMV
shakash-qa   wañu-**naya**-n-ña
giunea.pig-TOP die-DESR-3-DISC
'The guinea pig is **about to** die already.'

4.4.2.3.10 Repetitive *-pa* *-pa* indicates repetitive action, deriving verbs with the meaning 're-V' or 'V again' or 'repeatedly V' (1–6) (*yata* 'touch' → *yata-pa* 'fondle'). It is unattested in the CH dialect.

(1) *Liyun mikusa. Tuqa**pa**ykun. '¿Wañusachu kayan?' nishpa.* AMV
liyun miku-sa tuqa-**pa**-yku-n   wañu-sa-chu ka-ya-n
puma   eat-NPST spit-REPET-EXCEP-3   dead-PRF-Q   be-PROG-3
ni-shpa
say-SUBIS
'The puma [began to] eat it. He spit **repeatedly**. "Is it dead?" he said.'

(2) *Huk puntraw huk tuta nana**pa**shunki.* ACH
huk puntraw huk tuta   nana-**pa**-shu-nki
one day   one night   hurt-REPET-2.OBJ-2
'One day and one night it's **hurting and hurting** you [to give birth].'

(3) *'¿Imapaqtaq wak yawar yawar kayan?' diciendo dice qawa**pa**ykun.* AMV
ima-paq-taq   wak   yawar ka-ya-n   qawa-**pa**-yku-n
what-PURP-SEQ   DEM.D   blood be-PROG-3 look-REPET-EXCEP-3
'[They said,] "Why is there this blood, all this blood?" and stared at him.'

(4) *Qawa**pa**ykaramushpam.* LT
qawa-**pa**-yka-ra-mu-shpa-m
look-REPET-EXCEP-URGT-CISL-SUBIS-EVD
'Going to go **check** it.'

(5) *Warmi ka-pti-n-qa yata-**pa**-shpa-tr qaqu-ya-n.* AMV
warmi   ka-pti-n-qa   yata-**pa**-shpa-tr   qaqu-ya-n
woman   be-SUBDS-3-TOP   touch-REPET-SUBIS-EVC   rub-PROG-3
'If it's a woman he'll be **fondling** her while he massages.'

(6) *¿Imapaq aysapamaranki ñuqa hawka puñukupti:? ¡Manchachiman!* SP
 imapaq   aysa-pa-ma-ra-nki   ñuqa   hawka   puñu-ku-pti-:
 what-PRUP pull-BEN-1.OBJ-PST-2 I   peaceful sleep-REFL-SUBDS-1
 mancha-chi-ma-n
 scare-CAUS-1.OBJ-3
 'Why did you **tug/yank** at me when I was sleeping peacefully? It scares me.'

When it is compounded with intensive *-ya*, *-pa* indicates uninterrupted action; that is, *-paya* derives verbs meaning 'continue to V' (7).

(7) *¿Pukllapayanchu? ¿Kaniruytachu munayan?* AMV
 puklla-pa-ya-n-chu   *kani-ru-y-ta-chu*   *muna-ya-n*
 play-REPET-INTENS-3-Q   bite-URGT-INF-ACC-Q   want-PROG-3
 'Is it **still** playing? Or does it want to bite?'

4.4.2.3.11 *-pU*

-pU indicates that an action is performed on behalf (1), (2) – or to the detriment – of someone other than the subject.

(1) *Chayllapa priparapunki.* AMV
 chay-lla-pa   *pripara-pu-nki*
 DEM.D-RESTR-LOC   prepare-BEN-2
 'Just there prepare it [**for her**].'

(2) *"¡Hinata risarapuway! Pagashaykim," niwan.* LT
 hina-ta   risa-ra-pu-wa-y   *paga-shayki-m*   *ni-wa-n*
 thus-ACC pray-UNINT-BEN-1.OBJ-IMP   pay-1>2.FUT-EVD   say-1.OBJ-3
 'He said to me, "Pray **for me** like that! I'll pay you."'

When it precedes either of the derivational suffixes *-mu* or *-chi* or the inflectional suffix *-ma*, *-pU* is realized as *-pa* (3), (4).

(3) *Sigaru rantipamuwanki, Hilda, fumakushtin kutikamunanpaq.* AMV
 sigaru   ranti-pa-mu-wa-nki   Hilda   fuma-ku-shtin
 cigarette buy-BEN-CISL-1.OBJ-2   Hilda   smoke-REFL-SUBIS
 kuti-ka-mu-na-n-paq
 return-REFL-CISL-NMLZ-3-PURP
 'Hilda, go and buy **me** a cigarette so he can smoke while he's coming back.'

4 Verbs

(4) *"¡Gwarda**pama**nki! ¡Gwarda**pama**nki!" niman.* CH
gwarda-pa-ma-nki gwarda-pa-ma-nki ni-ma-n
save-BEN-1.OBJ-2 save-BEN-1.OBJ-2 say-1.OBJ-3
'He said to me, "Save it **for me**! Save it **for me**!"'

4.4.2.3.12 Joint action *-pa(:)kU* -pa:kU indicates action performed jointly by two or more (groups of) actors, i.e., it indicates a plurality of actors (1–7). The long vowel may be dropped in those dialects where the first person is not indicated by vowel lengthening.

(1) *Kutiramushpaqa kapastri tari**pa:ku**nman karqa.* AMV
kuti-ra-mu-shpa-qa kapas-tri tari-pa:ku-n-man
return-URGT-CISL-SUBIS-TOP perhaps-EVC find-JTACT-URGT-COND
ka-rqa
be-PST
'If **they** had returned maybe **they** would have found him.'

(2) *Kayna hapi**paku**nchik.* ACH
kayna hapi-paku-nchik
thus grab-JTACC-1PL
'Like this. We hold on [to the woman to help her give birth].'

(3) *Pasan. Lliw lliw ri**pa:ku**yan. Sapalla: kashaq.* SP
pasa-n lliw lliw ri-pa:ku-ya-n sapa-lla-: ka-shaq
pass-3 all all go-JTACC-PROG-3 alone-RSTR-1 be-BE-1.FUT
'They're leaving. **All [of them] are** going. I'm going to be all alone.'

(4) *Chayshik chay susiyukuna ruwa**paku**rqa chay nichutanta.* AMV
chay-shi-k chay susiyu-kuna ruwa-paku-rqa chay
DEM.D-EVR-K DEM.D associate-REFL MAKE-MUTBEN-PST DEM.D
nichu-ta-n-ta
CRYPT-ACC-3-ACC
'That's why, they say, before, the members made the crypts **together**.'

(5) *Kukakunata aku**paku**nchik. Kustumbrinchikmi.* AMV
kuka-kuna-ta aku-paku-nchik kustumbri-nchik-mi
coca-PL-ACC chew-MUTBEN-1PL custom-1PL-EVD
'We chew coca [**together**]. It's our custom.'

4.4 Verb derivation

(6) *Uqaktam talpupa:kuya:.* CH
    uqa-kta-m   talpu-pa:ku-ya-:
    oca-ACC-EVD   plant-JTACC-PROG-1
    '**We**'re planting oca.'

(7) *Kañapa:kurqani rupanta. Comp. Kañapakurqanchik.* AMV
    kaña-pa:ku-rqa-ni   rupa-n-ta   kaña-paku-rqa-nchik
    burn-JTACC-PST-1   clothes--3-ACC burn-JTACC-PST-1PL
    '**We**'ve been burning her clothes.' 'We have burned [for someone else].'

4.4.2.3.13 Mutual benefit *-pakU* *-pakU* indicates actions performed outside the scope of original planning (1–3) as well as actions performed as a means or preparation for something else more important (including all remunerated labor) (4–6).

(1) *Sakristantam wañuchipakuruni.* AMV
    sakristan-ta-m   wañu-chi-paku-ru-ni
    sacristan-ACC-EVD   die-CAUS-MUTBEN-URGT-1
    'I killed the deacon [**by accident**].'

(2) *Urqupaqa puchukapakunchikmiki.* AMV
    urqu-pa-qa   puchuka-paku-nchik-mi-ki
    hill-LOC-TOP   finish-MUTBEN-1PL-EVD-IKI
    'In the hills, we finish them [our matches] off [they run out **on us**].'

(3) *Wak warmiqa wawapakurusam. Wawapakuqtriki kidarqa.* AMV
    wak   warmi-qa   wawa-paku-ru-sa-m
    DEM.D   woman-TOP   give.birth-MUTBEN-URGT-NPST-EVD
    wawa-paku-q-tri-ki   kida-rqa
    give.birth-MUTBEN-AG-EVC-IKI   remain-PST
    'That woman gave birth to an **illegitimate child**. She must have stayed a **single mother**.'

(4) *Tihipakushpalla wamran uywan.* AMV
    tihi-paku-shpa-lla   wamra-n   uywa-n
    weave-MUTBEN-SUBIS-RSTR   child-3   raise-3
    'Just weaving [**for pay**], she's raising her son.'

229

4 Verbs

(5) *Kay siyrapaqa pasiya**paku**: michi**paku**:.* SP
kay siyra-pa-qa pasiya-paku-: michi-paku-:
DEM.P mountain-LOC-TOP walk-MUTBEN-1 herd-MUTBEN-1
'In these mountains, I pasture, I herd [**for others**].'

(6) *Karruwanñatr kanan imatapis ranti**paku**yan chay llamayuqkuna alpakayuqkuna.* ACH
karru-wan-ña-tr kanan ima-ta-pis ranti-paku-ya-n
car-INSTR-DISC-EVC now what-ACC-ADD buy-MUTBEN-PROG-3
chay llama-yuq-kuna alpaka-yuq-kuna
DEM.D llama-POSS-PL alpaca-POSS-PL
'Now the people with llamas and the people with alpacas must be buying everything [**in order to sell it**] with a car.'

When it precedes either of the derivational suffixes *-mu* or *-chi* or the inflectional suffix *-ma*, *-pakU* is realized as *-paka* (7).

(7) *Sibadata taka**paka**ramushaq waway machka mikunanpaq.* AMV
sibada-ta taka-paka-ra-mu-shaq wawa-y machka
barley-ACC beat-MUTBEN-CISL-1.FUT baby-1 cereal.meal
miku-na-n-paq
eat-NMLZ-3-PURP
'I'm going to thresh barley [**for someone else**] so my children can eat toasted barley.'

4.4.2.3.14 Uninterrupted action -Ra
-Ra – realized as *-la* in the CH dialect and as *-ra* in all others – indicates that the event referred to persists in time; that is, it derives verbs with the meaning 'continue to V' (1–3).

(1) *Rinki qaqaman tiya**ra**chishunki.* SP
ri-nki qaqa-man tiya-ra-chi-shu-nki
go-2 cliff-ALL sit-UNINT-CAUS-2.OBJ-2
'You'll go to the cliff and he'll make you sit and sit [**stay**] there.'

(2) *Durasnu ... llullu mashta**ra**kuyan.* LT
durasnu llullu mashta-ra-ku-ya-n
peach unripe spread.out-UNINT-REFL-PROG-3
'Peaches ... They're **spread out** unripe.'

4.4 Verb derivation

(3) *Qawarayamun pashñaqa urata.* LT
qawa-ra-ya-mu-n   pashñaqa ura-ta
look-UNINT-INTENS-CISL-3 girl-TOP hour-ACC
'The girl **kept checking** the time.'

In combination with intensive *-ya*, *-Ra* derives passive verbs from active verbs (4–7).

(4) *Qaqapa ismu kundurlla warkurayan.* AMV
qaqa-pa ismu   kundur-lla warku-ra-ya-n
cliff-LOC rotted condor-RSTR hang-UNINT-INTENS-3
'A rotten condor is **hanging** from a cliff, they say.'

(5) *Pwintikama trayaruptin huk mamakucha traqnarayasa pwintipa.* AMV
pwinti-kama traya-ru-pti-n   huk mamakucha
bridge-ALL   arrive-URGT-SUBDS-3   one grandmother
traqna-ra-ya-sa   pwinti-pa
bind.limbs-UNINT-INTENS-NPST   bridge-LOC
'When he arrived at the bridge, an old woman **was tied up** to the bridge.'

(6) "*Qala tullatam aparun.*" "*¿Maypaqtaq chay aparusa?*" "*Ukllupam trurarayasa.*" SP
qala tulla-ta-m   apa-ru-n   may-paq-taq   chay
dog bone-ACC-EVD   bring-URGT-3 where-ABL-SEQ DEM.D
apa-ru-sa   ukllu-pa-m   trura-ra-ya-sa
bring-URGT-NSPT   store.house-LOC-EVD   put-UNINT-INTENS-NPST
'"The dog took a bone." "Where was it taken from?" "It **was stored** in the store-house."'

(7) *Kamallapaña sapalla: hitarayapti: runa trayaramun.* ACH
kama-lla-pa-ña   sapa-lla-:   hita-ra-ya-pti-:
bed-RSTR-LOC-DISC   alone-RSTR-1 throw.out-UNINT-INTENS-SUBDS-1
runa   traya-ra-mu-n
person arrive-URGT-CISL-3
'When I **was layed out** in bed all alone, a person came.'

4 Verbs

4.4.2.3.15 Inceptive -Ri   -Ri, realized -li in Cacra (1), indicates that the event referred to is in its initial stage, that it has not yet concluded (2–4).

(1) *Nina:qa manalaq lupaliyanchu. Manalaq shansha: kanchu.* CH
 nina-:-qa   mana-laq   lupa-li-ya-n-chu   mana-laq   shansha-:
 fire-1-TOP   no-CONT   burn-INCEP-PROG-3-NEG   no-CONT   ember-1
 ka-n-chu
 be-3-NEG
 'My fire still isn't starting to burn. I still don't have any embers.'

(2) *Pararirunqañam.* AMV
 para-ri-ru-nqa-ña-m
 rain-INCEP-URGT-3.FUT-DISC-EVD
 'It's starting to rain already.'

(3) *Warmikunaqa shinkarishpa takishpam waqan.* AMV
 warmi-kuna-qa   shinka-ri-shpa   taki-shpa-m   waqa-n
 woman-PL-TOP   get.drunk-INCEP-SUBIS sing-SUBIS-EVD cry-3
 'When the women start to get drunk and sing, they cry.'

(4) *Chaypa kalabasuy chinkariyannam.* LT
 chay-pa   kalabasu-y   chinka-ri-ya-n-ña-m
 DEM.D-LOC   squash-1   lose-INCEP-PROG-3-DISC-EVD
 'My squash there are getting lost.'

-ri is common in apologetic statements and supplicatory commands (5), (6). -li is attested in Carcra but not in Hongos.

(5) *¡Pasakamuy! ¡Tiyarikuy!* AMV
 pasa-ka-mu-y   tiya-ri-ku-y
 pass-REFL-CISL-IMP   sit-INCEP-REFL-IMP
 'Come in! **Please** sit down.'

(6) *Kaytatr paqarikushun.* AMV
 kay-ta-tr   paqa-ri-ku-shun
 DEM.D-ACC-EVC   pay-INCEP-REFL-1PL.FUT
 '**Let's** wash this.'

4.4.2.3.16 Urgency, personal interest -RU

-RU is realized as -lU in the CH dialect (4) and as -rU in all others. It has a variety of interpretations, all subsumed, in some grammars of other Quechuan languages, as "action with urgency or personal interest" (1–3).

(1) *"Mana virdita mikushpaqa lukiyarushaq", nin.* AMV
mana virdi-ta miku-shpa-qa luki-ya-ru-shaq ni-n
no green-ACC eat-SUBIS-TOP crazy-INCH-URGT-1.FUT say-3
'They say, "If I don't eat green [pasture grass], I'm going to go crazy."'

(2) *Chay mana rantikuptinqa ... chakirunqa.* AMV
chay mana ranti-ku-pti-n-qa chaki-ru-nqa
DEM.D no buy-REFL-SUBDS-3-TOP dry-URGT-3.FUT
'If she doesn't sell it [right away], it's going to dry out [and be worthless].'

(3) *"¡Sinvirgwinsa! ¡Ñuqaqa willakurushaqmi gwardyanman tirruku kasaykita!"* AMV
sinvirgwinsa ñuqa-qa willa-ku-ru-shaq-mi gwardyan-man
shameless I-TOP tell-REFL-URGT-1.FUT-EVD police-ALL
tirruku ka-sa-yki-ta
terrorist be-PRF-2-ACC
'"Shameless bastard! I'm going to tell the police that you were a terrorist!"'

It very often marks perfective aspect (4–6) (see §4.3.3.3.1 on past tense marker -RQa).[15]

(4) *Qali paqwalun allichalu:.* CH
qali paqwa-lu-n alli-cha-lu-:.
man finish-URGT-3 good-FACT-URGT-1
'The men finished and we fixed it up.'

---

[15] An anonymous reviewer suggests that Yauyos -ru is a "budding completive/perfective aspect marker, very similar to -rQu in Cuzco and in Huallaga, but less well developed than perfective -ru in Tarma. And far less developed than past tense/perfective -ru in South Conchucos, where it has moved to the inflectional tense slot and is in paradigmatic relation with -rQa, -shQa, futures, conditional, etc." The reviewer cites Bybee, Perkins & Pagliuca (1994): the inference of recent past is not uncommon for derivational completive aspect markers.

4 Verbs

(5) *Chinkarun. Ni may risan yatrakunchu.* ACH
chinka-ru-n ni may ri-sa-n yatra-ku-n-chu
lose-URGT-3 nor where go-PRF-3 know-REFL-3-NEG
'They **got lost**. We don't know where they went.'

(6) *Mana chichinanpaq tardi watarun mamanta wawanta kapacharun.* AMV
mana chichi-na-n-paq tardi wata-ru-n mama-n-ta
no nurse-NMLZ-3-PURP late tie-URGT-3 mother-3-ACC
wawa-n-ta kapacha-ru-n
baby-3-ACC muzzle-URGT-3
'So that he wouldn't nurse, she ti**ed** up his mother and **put** a muzzle on her baby.'

When it precedes any of the derivational suffixes *-mu, -pU, -kU, -chi* or the inflectional suffix *-ma*, *-RU* is realized as *-Ra* (7), (8).

(7) *Campionchata winarun aytrikurun qarinta mikurachin.* AMV
Campion-cha-ta wina-ru-n aytri-ku-ru-n
Campion.rat.poison-DIM-ACC add.in-URGT-3 stir-REFL-URGT-3
qari-n-ta miku-ra-chi-n
man-3-ACC eat-URGT-CAUS-3
'She threw in the rat poison, stirred it, and made her husband eat it.'

(8) *Chaymi, "¡Kaypaq hurqaramanki kay hawlapaq."* SP
chay-mi kay-paq hurqa-ra-ma-nki kay hawla-paq
DEM.D-EVD DEM.P-ABL remove-URGT-1.OBJ-2 DEM.P cage-ABL
'So, [he said,] "Take me out of this! [Let me out] of this cage here!"'

4.4.2.3.17 Accompaniment *-sHi*

-sHi is realized as *-si* in the SP dialect (1) and as *-shi* in all others.

(1) *Asnuqa nin, "Ñuqa tarisisayki sugaykitaqa".* SP
asnu-qa ni-n, ñuqa tari-si-sayki suga-yki-ta-qa
donkey-TOP say-3 I find-ACMP-1>2.FUT rope-2-ACC-TOP
'The donkey said, "I'm going to **help** you find your rope."'

-sHi indicates accompaniment for the purpose of aiding or protecting; that is, *-sHi* derives verbs meaning 'accompany in V-ing' (2) or 'help V' (3–5).

4.4 Verb derivation

(2) *Manam hamurqachu tiyashiq.* AMV
mana-m hamu-rqa-chu tiya-shi-q
no-EVD come-PST-3-NEG sit-ACMP-AG
'She didn't come to **help** sit.'

(3) *Harkashisaykim nin huvin.* AMV
harka-shi-sayki-m ni-n huvin
herd-ACMP-1>2.FUT-EVD say-3 young.man
'"I'm going to **help** you pasture," the young man said.'

(4) *Hampishirqatrik. ¿Imataq kutichirqa?* AMV
hampi-shi-rqa-tri-k ima-taq kuti-chi-rqa
heal-ACMP-PST-EVC-IK what-SEQ return-CAUS-PST
'She must have **helped** cure. What did she offer?'

(5) *Kwidashimanchu. Hapalla: kwidaku: hapalla:.* CH
kwida-shi-ma-n-chu hapa-lla-: kwida-ku-: hapa-lla-:
care.for-ACMP-1.OBJ-3-NEG alone-RSTR-1 take.care-REFL-1 alone-RSTR-1
'He didn't **help** take care [of the animals]. Alone, I took care of them. Alone.'

4.4.2.3.18 Irreversible change *-tamu* *-tamu* indicates change that is irreversible (1–4). It is very frequently used in the CH dialect but not often spontaneously attested in other dialects.

(1) *Kaman mastakuyashpa kamanpa tiyakuykushpaqa wañutamusha.* CH
kama-n masta-ku-ya-shpa kama-n-pa
bed-3 spread.out-REFL-PROG-SUBIS bed-3-LOC
tiya-ku-yku-shpa-qa wañu-tamu-sha
sit-REFL-EXCEP-SUBIS-TOP die-IRREV-NPST
'When she was making the bed, when she sat on the bed, she **died**.'

(2) *Wañutamusha qariqa; warmiqa kidarusha.* LT
wañu-tamu-sha qari-qa warmi-qa kida-ru-sha
die-IRREV-NPST man-TOP woman-TOP remain-URGT-NPST
'The man **died**; the woman remained.'

4 Verbs

(3) *Puchuka**tamu**n*. AMV
    puchuka-tamu-n
    finish-IRREV-3
    'It **finished off**.'

(4) *Atuqtaqa ñiti**tamu**n umapaq*. AMV
    atuq-ta-qa   ñiti-tamu-n   uma-paq
    fox-ACC-TOP   crush-IRREV-3 head-ABL
    'They **crushed** the fox from the head.'

4.4.2.3.19 Intensive -ya, -raya, -paya -ya is dependent; it never occurs independent of -ra or -pa. (see §4.4.2.3.9 and 4.4.2.3.12).
-raya is a detransitivizer, deriving passive from transitive verbs; that is, -raya derives verbs meaning 'be V-ed' (1–3).

(1) *Pwintikama trayaruptin huk mamakucha traqna**ra**yasa pwintipa*. AMV
    pwinti-kama   traya-ru-pti-n   huk   mamakucha
    bridge-ALL   arrive-URGT-SUBDS-3 one   grandmother
    traqna-**ra**-**ya**-sa   pwinti-pa
    bind.limbs-UNINT-INTENS-NPST bridge-LOC
    'When he arrived at the bridge, an old woman **was tied up** to the bridge.'

(2) *"Qala tullatam aparun." "¿Maypaqtaq chay aparusa?" "Ukllupam trura**ra**yasa."* SP
    qala tulla-ta-m   apa-ru-n   may-paq-taq   chay
    dog   bone-ACC-EVD   bring-URGT-3   where-ABL-SEQ   DEM.D
    apa-ru-sa   ukllu-pa-m   trura-**ra**-**ya**-sa
    bring-URGT-NSPT   store.house-LOC-EVD   put-UNINT-INTENS-NPST
    '"The dog took a bone." "Where was it taken from?" "It **was stored** in the store-house."'

(3) *Kamallapaña sapalla: hita**ra**yapti: runa trayaramun*. ACH
    kama-lla-pa-ña   sapa-lla-:   hita-ra-ya-pti-:
    bed-RSTR-LOC-DISC   alone-RSTR-1   throw.out-UNINT-INTENS-SUBDS-1
    runa   traya-ra-mu-n
    person   arrive-URGT-CISL-3
    'When I **was layed out** in bed all alone, a person came.'

4.4 Verb derivation

-*raya* may also indicate persistent or repetitive action (4). (see §4.4.2.3.12 for further examples).

(4) Qawa***raya****mun pashñaqa urata.* LT
     qawa-ra-ya-mu-n   pashñaqa ura-ta
     look-UNINT-INTENS-CISL-3 girl-TOP hour-ACC
     'The girl **kept checking** the time.'

-*paya* indicates uninterrupted action; that is, -*paya* derives verbs meaning 'continue to V' (5) (see §4.4.2.3.9 for further examples).

(5) ¿*Puklla****paya****nchu? ¿Kaniruytachu munayan?* AMV
     puklla-pa-ya-n-chu   kani-ru-y-ta-chu   muna-ya-n
     play-REPET-INTENS-3-Q   bite-URGT-INF-ACC-Q   want-PROG-3
     'Does it **keep on** playing? Or does it want to bite?'

4.4.2.3.20 Exceptional -*YkU* -*YkU* has a broad range of meanings; in early grammars of other Quechuan languages -*YkU* is said to indicate 'action performed in some way different from usual' (1–6).

(1) *Pilata****yka****chishpash baliyasa. Baliyayta munasa.* ACH
     pilata-yka-chi-shpa-sh   baliya-sa   baliya-y-ta
     lie.face.down-EXCEP-CAUS-SUBIS-EVR   shoot-NPST shoot-INF-ACC
     muna-sa
     want-NPST
     'They **made them lie face-down** on the ground and shot them. They wanted to shoot.'

(2) *Chaypash alma trayan hinashpash kurasunninta tapaku****yku****n.* AMV
     chay-pa-sh   alma traya-n   hinashpa-sh kurasun-ni-n-ta
     DEM.D-LOC-EVR   soul arrive-3 then-EVR   heart-EUPH-3-ACC
     tapa-ku-yku-n
     knock-REFL-EXCEP-3
     'The souls arrive there, they say, then they **knock** their hearts.'

(3) *Hinashpa chaypa lliw lliw qutunaku****yku****shpa almata dispachashun.* AMV
     hinashpa chay-pa   lliw lliw qutu-naku-yku-shpa   alma-ta
     then   DEM.D-LOC   all   all   gather-RECP-EXCEP-SUBIS   soul-ACC
     dispacha-shun
     dispatch-1PL.FUT

4 Verbs

'Then, when we are all **grouped** together, we'll bid farewell to the souls.'

(4) *Kay karruwan trayamuptinqa sillakuykushpam riyanchik.* SP
 kay   karru-wan traya-mu-pti-n-qa   silla-ku-yku-shpa-m
 DEM.P car-INSTR arrive-CISL-SUBDS-3-TOP seat-REFL-EXCEP-SUBIS-EVD
 ri-ya-nchik
 go-PROG-1PL
 'When they arrive with the car, we're going **galloping** in a saddle.'

(5) *Chay tirrimutukunapimik kahun saqaykaramun chaykunawan.* AMV
 chay   tirrimutu-kuna-pi-mi-k   kahun saqa-yka-ra-mu-n
 DEM.D earthquake-PL-LOC-EVD-IK box go.down-EXCEP-URGT-CISL-3
 chay-kuna-wan
 DEM.D-PL-INSTR
 'In that earthquake the coffins **fell down** with those.'

(6) *Piluyta yupaykushpaqa wak duñuytaqa mikukurunkitriki.* AMV
 pilu-y-ta   yupa-yku-shpa-qa   wak   duñu-y-ta-qa
 hair-1-ACC count-EXCEP-SUBIS-TOP DEM.D owner-1-ACC-TOP
 miku-ku-ru-nki-tri-ki
 eat-REFL-URGT-2-EVC-IKI
 '"If you **count** my hairs," [said the hairless dog to the zombie] "you can eat my mistress."'

It merits further analysis. -*YkU* is common in polite imperatives (7), (8).

(7) *Sumbriruyta kumadricha quykamuway.* AMV
 sumbriru-y-ta kumadri-cha   qu-yka-mu-wa-y
 hat-1-ACC   comadre-DIM give-EXCEP-CISL-1.OBJ-IMP
 'Comadre, do me a favor and hand me my hat.'

(8) *Kayllapi, Señor. ¡Tiyaykuy!* AMV
 kay-lla-pi,   señor tiya-yku-y
 DEM.P-RSTR-LOC sir   sit-EXCEP-IMP
 'Right here, Sir, **please** have a seat.'

-*YkU* also occurs with nouns referring to a time of day (9).

4.4 Verb derivation

(9) *Chaypaq tutaykurun. Tutaykuruptin vilata prindirun.* AMV
 chay-paq   tuta-yku-ru-n   tuta-yku-ru-pti-n
 DEM.D-ABL night-EXCEP-URGT-3 night-EXCEP-URGT-SUBDS-3
 vila-ta   prindi-ru-n
 candle-ACC light-URGT-3
 'Later, **night fell**. When it **got dark**, he lit a candle.'

When it precedes any of the derivational suffixes *-mu*, *-pU*, *-chi*, *-RU* or the inflectional suffix *-ma*, *-ykU* is realized as *-yka* (1), (5).

5 Particles

This chapter covers particles in Southern Yauyos Quechua. In SYQ, as in most other Quechuan languages, the class of particles can be sorted into seven subclasses: interjections (*¡Alaláw!* 'How cold!'); assenters and greetings (*aw* 'yes'); prepositions (*asta* 'until'); adverbs (*ayvis* 'sometimes'); coordinators (*icha* 'or'); negators (*mana* 'no, not'); and prenumerals (*la*, *las*, occurring with expressions of time). Interjections, assenters and greetings, prepositions, and adverbs are covered in §5.1–5.4, respectively. Coordinators are discussed in §7.3 on coordination; negators in §7.5 on negation; and prenumerals in Sub §3.2.5.3 on time numerals and prenumerals.

5.1 Interjections

All spontaneously attested indigenous exclamations share a common pattern: they begin with *a* and end in *w* or, less commonly, in *k* or *y*, as in (a-h); with the exception of the final *w*, they feature almost exclusively the alveolar and palatal consonants *ch*, *ll*, *l*, *n*, *ñ*, *t*, and *y* (which accounts for the entire catalogue of SYQ alveolars and palatals with the exception of voiceless fricatives *s*, *sh*, and retroflex *tr*); they include no vowels except for *a*; they consist, with few exceptions, of three or four syllables; and they bear stress on the final syllable. Syllable repetition is not uncommon. Non-exclamatory interjections do not follow this pattern, like in (i) and (j). Curse words are freely borrowed from Spanish (k–m). Table 5.1 lists some of the more commonly-heard interjections. (1–7) give a few examples in context.

(1) *Primay Amaciatapis chayhinashiki intrigaykururqa. ¡**Achachalláw**!* AMV
    prima-y   Amacia-ta-pis   chay-hina-shi-ki
    cousin-1 Amacia-ACC-ADD   DEM.D-COMP-EVR-IKI
    intriga-yku-ru-rqa   achachalláw
    deliver-EXCEP-URGT-PST how.awful
    'They delivered my cousin Amacia, too [to the Devil], they say. **How awful!**'

5 Particles

Table 5.1: Interjections

(a)	¡Atratráw!	'Yikes!' 'What a fright!'
(b)	¡Achachalláw!	'How awful!' 'How ugly!'
(c)	¡Achalláw!'	'How beautiful!'
(d)	¡Alaláw!'	'How cold!'
(e)	¡Atatacháw!	'How beautiful!'
(f)	¡Ananáw!	'Ouch!'
(g)	¡Añalláw!	'How delicious!'
(h)	¡Atratrák!	'Yikes!' 'What a fright!'
(i)	¡Hinata!	'So be it!'
(j)	¡Pay!	'Enough!' 'Thanks!'
(k)	¡Karay!	'Darn!'
(l)	¡Karahu!	'Damn!'
(m)	¡Miyrda!	'Shit!'

(2) *Fiyu fiyu qatram warmi kasa chay warmi. ¡**Atatayáw**!* AMV
 fiyu fiyu qatra-m warmi ka-sa chay warmi
 ugly ugly dirty-EVD woman be-NPST DEM.D woman
 atatayáw
 how.disgusting
 'That woman was a horrible, filthy woman. **How disgusting!**'

(3) *¡**Ayayáw**! Yo me asusté.* AMV
 ayayáw [Spanish]
 yikes
 '**Yikes!** I got scared.'

(4) *Hinaptinshi chay katataqa tiyaykun ukuman "¡**Achachá**!" qayakun.* AMV
 hinaptin-shi chay kata-ta-qa tiya-yku-n uku-man achachá
 then-EVR DEM.D shawl-ACC-TOP sit-EXCEP-3 inside-ALL how.hot
 qaya-ku-n
 shout-REFL-3
 'Then he sat on the shawl and [fell] in [the boiling water]. "**It's burning!**" he shouted.'

(5) *¿Sapallaykitr hamuyankiyá? ¡**Atratrák**!* ACH
 sapa-lla-yki-tr hamu-ya-nki-yá atratrák
 alone-RSTR-2-EVC come-PROG-2-EMPH how.frightening
 'You're coming all alone, then? **Yikes!**'

(6) *¡Dios Tayta! ¿Imapaq kimawanchikman? **¡Achachalláw!*** AMV
    Dios tayta ima-paq   kima-wa-nchik-man   achachalláw
    God father what-PURP burn-1.OBJ-1PL-COND how.awful
    'Good God! Why would they burn [cremate] us? **How awful!**'

(7) *¡**Acháchaw**! Apuríman lapcharun kichkata.* AMV
    acháchaw Apurí-man lapcha-ru-n   kichka-ta
    ouch   Apurí-ALL grab-URGT-3   thorn-ACC
    '**Ouch**! She grabbed onto a thorn bush [going to] Apurí.'

5.2 Assenters and greetings

The list of assenters includes three members: *arí*, *aw*, and *alal*, exemplified in (1) and (2).

(1) *Pukapis kasa vakahina. **Arí**, wak sintakusa kayan.* AMV
    puka-pis ka-sa   vaka-hina arí wak   sinta-ku-sa   ka-ya-n
    red-ADD   be-NPST   cow-COMP   yes DEM.D   ribbon-REFL-PRF   be-PROG-3
    '*Spkr* 1: "The colored one was like a cow." *Spkr* 2: "**Yes**, it has [its ears pierced with] ribbons."'

(2) ***Aw**, lavashuntriki, kaypis qatra qatra kayan.* AMV
    aw   lava-shun-tri-ki   kay-pis   qatra qatra ka-ya-n
    yes wash-1PL.FUT-EVC-IKI   DEM.P-ADD dirty dirty be-PROG-3
    '**Yes**, we'll wash it. It's really dirty.'

The first and second are used in all dialects, while the the third is used only in CH. *arí* often carries the emphatic enclitic *-yá* (3).

(3) *"Kutimushaq," nishpash chay pindihuqa manam warminman trayachinchu. **¡Ariyá** warmiyuq!* AMV
    kuti-mu-shaq   ni-shpa-sh   chay   pindihu-qa   mana-m
    return-CISL-1.FUT say-SUBIS-EVR   DEM.D   bastard-TOP   no-EVD
    warmi-n-man   traya-chi-n-chu   ari-yá   warmi-yuq
    woman-3-ALL   arrive-CAUS-3-NEG yes-EMPH   woman-POSS
    'Although the bastard [had] said, "I'm going to return," he never made it back to his wife. **Yes**! He had a wife!'

5 Particles

aw is used to check for agreement from interlocutors and to form tag questions (4), (5).

(4) *Chay chaqla kinraytatr pasarurqa, ¿aw?* AMV
 chay chaqla kinray-ta-tr pasa-ru-rqa aw
 DEM.D stone.outcropping across-ACC-EVC pass-URGT-PST yes
 'He must have come by around that stone outcropping, **no**?'

(5) *Yapamik kutinqa, ¿aw?* AMV
 yapa-mi-k kuti-nqa aw
 again-EVD-IK return-3.FUT yes
 'She's going to come back, **isn't she**?'

The Spanish greetings, *buynus diyas* 'good day', *buynas tardis* 'good afternoon' and *buynas nuchis* 'good evening', 'good night' (6) have been borrowed into SYQ and are employed with greater frequency than are greeting indigenous to the language. *¡Rimallasayki!* 'I greet you!' is the most common of the greetings indigenous to SYQ. *¡Saludallasayki!* is also used.

(6) *Mana ganawniki kanchu ni "**Buynus diyas**" ni "**Buynus diyas, primacha**", nada nishunkichu.* AMV
 mana ganaw-ni-ki ka-n-chu ni buynus diyas ni buynus diyas
 no cattle-EUPH-2 be-3-NEG nor good day nor good day
 prima-cha nada ni-shunki-chu
 cousin-DIM nothing say-2.OBJ-2-NEG
 'When you don't have cattle, they don't even say "**Good morning**," "**Good morning**, cousin," to you – nothing.'

5.3 Prepositions

SYQ makes use of some prepositions borrowed from Spanish. The preposition most frequently employed is *asta* ('up to', 'until', 'even', *Sp.* 'hasta' 'up to', 'until') (1). *asta* is usually employed redundantly, in combination with the indigenous case suffix *-kama*, apparently with the same semantics (*asta aka-kama* 'until here').

(1) *Asta wañukunay puntraw**kama**triki chayna purishaq.* LT
    asta wañu-ku-na-y   puntraw-kama-tri-ki chayna puri-shaq
    until die-REFL-NMLZ-1   day-LIM-EVC-IKI   thus   walk-1.FUT
    '**Until** the day I die, I'm going to walk around like that.'

(2) *Tinkuyani ubihaywan ñuqa **disdi** uchuychallay**paq** kani.* AMV
    tinku-ya-ni   ubiha-y-wan   ñuqa disdi   uchuy-cha-lla-y-paq   kani
    find-PROG-1   sheep-1-INSTR   I   since   small-DIM-RSTR-1-ABL   be-1
    'I've found myself with my sheep **since** I was very small.'

5.4 Adverbs

The class of adverbs native to SYQ is rather small (1–3).

(1) *Chafliwan pikarun, **yapa** hapin, **yapa** pikarun, **yapa** hapin, **yapa** pikarun.* AMV
    chafli-wan   pika-ru-n   yapa   hapi-n yapa   pika-ru-n   yapa
    pick-INSTR   pick-URGT-3 again grab-3 again pick-URGT-3 again
    hapi-n yapa   pika-ru-n
    grab-3 again pick-URGT-3
    'He struck with a pick. **Again**, [the zombie] grabs him. **Again** he struck with the pick. **Again** he grabs. **Again** he struck.'

(2) ***Yaqa** wañurqani chayshi tiyay.* AMV
    yaqa   wañu-rqa-ni   chay-shi   tiya-y
    almost   die-PST-1   DEM.D-EVR   aunt-1
    'I **almost** died, then, [says] my aunt.'

(3) *Hinallatañam **qaninpa** apakaramun wak yantata.* LT
    hina-lla-ta-ña-m   qaninpa apa-ka-ra-mu-n   wak
    thus-RSTR-ACC-DISC-EVD   before   bring-PASS-ACC-URGT-CISL-3   DEM.D
    yanta-ta
    firewood-ACC
    'Just like before already, they brought that firewood.'

Verbal modification in SYQ, as in other Quechuan languages, is accomplished primarily by derivatives and enclitics (*-pa* 'repeatedly', *-ña* 'already'). SYQ makes

5 Particles

heavy use of the adoped/adapted Spanish adverbs *apuraw* 'quick', *pasaypaq* 'completely,' *siympri* 'always' and *ayvis* 'sometimes' (4–7).

(4) *Mana **apuraw** hurquptinqa chayqa wañuchin.* ACH
    mana   apuraw   hurqu-pti-n-qa   chay-qa   wañu-chi-n
    no   quick   remove-SUBDS-3-TOP DEM.D-TOP   die-CAUS-3
    'If [the placenta] is not taken out **quickly**, it kills.'

(5) *Uchuypis **pasa-pasaypaq**mi chakirun, uchuypis chakisham kayan.* LT
    uchu-y-pis   pasa-pasaypaq-mi   chaki-ru-n   uchu-y-pis
    chile-1-ADD   comp-completely-EVD   dry-URGT-3   chile-1-ADD
    chaki-sha-m   ka-ya-n
    dry-PRF-EVD   be-PROG-3
    'My chiles, too, **completely** dried out. My chiles, too, are dried out.'

(6) *Waqayaniyá **siympri** yuyariyaniyá.* AMV
    waqa-ya-ni-yá   siympri   yuya-ri-ya-ni-yá
    cry-PROG-1-EMPH   always   remember-INCEP-PROG-1-EMPH
    'I'm crying. I'm **always** remembering.'

(7) ***Ayvis** lliw chinkarun **ayvis** huklla ishkayllata tariru:.* ACH
    ayvis   lliw   chinka-ru-n   ayvis   huk-lla   ishkay-lla-ta
    sometimes   all   lose-URGT-3   sometimes   one-RSTR   two-RSTR-ACC
    tari-ru-:
    find-URGT-1
    '**Sometimes** all get lost; **sometimes** I find just one or two.'

Additionally, adverbs can sometimes be derived from adjectives with the suffixation of *-lla* (8), (9); and adjectives may sometimes occur adverbally, in which case they are usually inflected with *-ta*, as in (10–12).

(8) *Ni pitapis kritika:chu dañukuruptinpis **sumaqllam** nikulla:.* ACH
    ni   pi-ta-pis   kritika-:-chu   dañu-ku-ru-pti-n-pis
    nor   who-ACC-ADD   criticize-1-NEG   damage-REFL-URGT-SUBDS-3-ADD
    sumaq-lla-m   ni-ku-lla-:
    pretty-REST-EVD   say-REFL-RSTR-1
    'I don't criticize anyone. When they do harm, I talk to them **nicely**.'

5.4 Adverbs

(9) ¡Kayta pasarachiy! Kargarayanñamiki. ¡**Sumaqlla** winaruy! AMV
kay-ta   pasa-ra-chi-y   karga-ra-ya-n-ña-mi-ki
DEM.P   pass-PASSACC-CAUS-IMP   carry-UNINT-INTENS-3-DISC-3-EVD-IKI
sumaq-lla   wina-ru-y
pretty-RSTR   add.in-URGT-IMP
'Have him come here! It's being carried already. Add it in **nicely**!'

(10) Kanan tutaqa suyñukuruni **fiyutam**. ¿Ima pasaruwanqa? AMV
kanan tuta-qa   suyñu-ku-ru-ni   fiyu-ta-m   ima
now   night-TOP dream-REFL-URGT-1 ugly-ACC-EVD   what
pasa-ru-wa-nqa
pass-URGT-1.OBJ-3.FUT
'Last night I dreamed **horribly**. What's going to happen to me?'

(11) ¿Manachu chay Aliciawan risachiwaq? Aliciam **sumaq sumaqta**
risan. AMV
mana-chu chay   Alicia-wan   risa-chi-waq   Alicia-m   sumaq
no-Q   DEM.D   Alicia-INSTR   pray-CAUS-2.COND   Alicia-EVD pretty
sumaq-ta   risa-n
pretty-ACC   pray-3
'Can't you have Alicia pray for her? Alicia prays **really nicely**.'

(12) Tushuptiypis **alli-allita** pigakuq. AMV
tushu-pti-y-pis   alli-alli-ta   piga-ku-q
dance-SUBDS-1-ADD   good-good-ACC   stick-REFL-AG
'When I would dance, he would stick himself [to me] **really well**.'

Some nouns referring to time may occur adverbally without inflection, as in (13) and (14), others are inflected with -ta, as (see §3.2.1.2) (15) shows.

(13) "¡**Kanallan** intrigaway!" nishpash chay kundur trayarun. AMV
kanallan   intriga-wa-y   ni-shpa-sh   chay   kundur
right.now   deliver-1.OBJ-IMP   say-SUBIS-EVR   DEM.D condor
traya-ru-n
arrive-URGT-3
'"Hand her over to me **right now**!" said the condor [when] he arrived.'

5 Particles

(14) *Rinrilla:pis uparura **qayna wata**qa.* ACH
  rinri-lla-:-pis upa-ru-ra   qayna   wata-qa
  ear-RSTR-1-ADD deaf-URGT-PST previous year-TOP
  'My ears went deaf **last year**.'

(15) *Chaymi shamula: **qaspalpuqta**. Chaymi karkarya qipa:ta shamusha.* CH
  chay-mi   shamu-la-: qaspalpuq-ta chay-mi   karkarya
  DEM.D-EVD   come-PST-1 nightfall-ACC DEM.D-EVD zombie
  qipa-:-ta   shamu-sha
  behind-1-ACC   come-NPST
  'Then I came **at nightfall**. Then a zombie came behind me.'

5.5 Particles covered elsewhere

Coordinators are discussed in §7.3 on coordination, negators in §7.5 on negation, and prenumerals in Sub §3.2.5.3 on time numerals and prenumerals.

6 Enclitics

This chapter covers the enclitic suffixes of Southern Yauyos Quechua. In SYQ, as in other Quechuan languages, enclitics attach to both nouns and verbs as well as to adverbs and negators. Enclitics always follow all inflectional suffixes, verbal and nominal; and, with the exception of restrictive *-lla*, all follow all case suffixes, as well. SYQ counts sixteen enclitics. *-Yá* (emphatic) indicates emphasis. Consistently translated in Spanish by *pues*.[1] *-chu* (interrogation, negation, disjunction) indicates absolute and disjunctive questions, negation, and disjunction. *-lla* (restrictive) generally indicates exclusivity or limitation in number; it is generally translated as 'just' or 'only'. *-lla* may express an affective or familiar attitude. *-ña* (discontinuitive) indicates transition, change of state or quality. In affirmative statements, it is generally translated as 'already'; in negative statements, as 'no more' or 'no longer'; in questions, as 'yet'. *-pis* (inclusion) indicates the inclusion of an item or event into a series of similar items or events; it is generally translated as 'too' or 'also' or, when negated, 'neither'. *-puni* (certainty, precision); it is generally translated 'necessarily', 'definitely', 'precisely'. This last is attested only in the QII dialects, where it is infrequently employed. *-qa* (topic marker) indicates the topic of the clause; it is generally left untranslated.[2]
-raq (continuative) indicates continuity of action, state or quality. Translated 'still' or, negated, 'yet'. *-taq* (sequential) indicates the sequence of events. In this capacity, translated 'then' or 'so'. *-taq* also marks content questions. *-mI* (evidential – direct experience) indicates that the speaker has personal-experience evidence for the proposition under the scope of the evidential. Usually left untranslated.
-shI (evidential – reportative/quotative) indicates that the speaker has non-personal-experience evidence for the proposition under the scope of the evidential. *-shI* appears systematically in stories. Often translated as 'they say.' *-trI* (ev-

---

[1] An anonymous reviewer points out that *pues* is used in Andean Spanish "to negotiate common ground, shared knowledge. As such, it is possible that *-ya* is also an interactional or stance marker," a way a participant in a conversation may negotiate what other participants know or should know.

[2] *-qa* may nevertheless be indicated in Spanish translations by intonation, gesture, and various circumlocutions of speech, as an anonymous reviewer points out.

idential – conjectural) indicates that the speaker is making a conjecture to the proposition under the scope of the evidential from a set of propositions for which she has either direct or not-direct evidence. Generally translated in Spanish as *seguro* 'for sure', indicating possibility or probability. *-ari* (assertive force) indicates conviction on the part of the speaker. Translated as 'certainly' or 'of course'.[3] *-ik* and *-iki* (evidential modifiers) indicate increasing evidence strength (and increased assertive force or conjectural certainty, in the case of the direct and conjectural modifiers, *-mI* and *-trI*, respectively). Generally translated in Spanish as *pues* and *seguro*, respectively. Examples in Table 6.1 are fully glossed in the corresponding sections.

6.1 Sequence

Combinations of individual enclitics generally occur in the following order.

-lla	-puni	-pis	-ña	-taq	-chu	-qa -mI -shI -trI	-Yá	-ikI -aRi
						-Raq		

In complementary distribution are: *-raq* with *-ña*; the evidentials with each other as well as with *-qa*; *-ari* with *-ikI*; and *-Yá* with *-ikI*.

6.2 Individual enclitics

In SYQ, as in other Quechuan languages, the enclitics can be divided into two classes: (a) those which position the utterance with regard to others salient in the discourse (restrictive/limitative *-lla*, discontinuative *-ña*, additive *-pis*, topic marking *-qa*, continuative *-Raq*, sequential *-taq*, and interrogative/negative/disjunctive *-chu*); and (b) those that position the speaker with regard to the utterance (emphatic *-YÁ*, certainty marker *-puni*, and the evidentials *-mi*, *-shi*, and *-tri* along with their modifiers *-ik*, *-iki*, and *-aRi*.). §6.2.1–6.2.10 cover all enclitics except the evidentials and their modifiers, in alphabetical order. The evidentials and their modifiers are the subject of §6.2.11.

---

[3] An anonymous reviewer writes that in other varieties of Quechuan, "*-ari* is interpersonal. It expresses solidarity, affirming what someone else says, thinks or believes to be true."

6.2 Individual enclitics

Table 6.1: Enclitic suffixes, with examples

-yá	emphasis	¡Mana-**yá** rupa-chi-nchik-chu! ¡Ari-**yá**!	'We do **not** set on fire!' 'Yes, indeed!'
-chu$_1$	interrogation	¿Iskwila-man trura-shu-rqa-nki-**chu** mama-yki?	'**Did** your mother put you in school?'
-chu$_2$	negation	Chay-tri mana suya-wa-rqa-**chu**.	'That must be why she wouldn't have waited for me.'
-chu$_3$	disjunction	¿Qari-**chu** ka-nki warmi-**chu** ka-nki?	'Are you a man **or** a woman?'
-lla	restriction	Uma-**lla**-ña traki-**lla**-ña ka-ya-sa.	'There was **only** the head **only** the hand.'
-ña	discontuity	Chay-shi ni-n kundinadaw-**ña**-m wak-qa ka-ya-n.	'That one, they say, is **already** condemned.'
-pis	inclusion	Tukuy tuta tusha-n qaynintin-ta-**pis**.	'They dance all night and the next day, **too**.'
-puni	certainty	Mana-**puni**-m.	'By no means', 'Not on your life'
-qa	topic	Mana yatra-q-ni-n-**qa**.	'Those of them who didn't know'
-raq	continuity	Kama-n-pi puñu-ku-ya-pti-n-**raq** tari-ru-n.	'He found him **still** sleeping in his bed.'
-taq	sequence	hinaptin-ña-**taq**-shi	'then' 'so'
-mI	evidential-direct	Yanga-ña-**m** qipi-ku-sa puri-ni.	'In vain, I walk around carrying it.'
-shI	evidential-reportative	Qari-n-ta-**sh** wañu-ra-chi-n.	'She killed her husband, **they say**.'
-trI	evidential-conjecture	Awa-ya-n-**tr-iki** kama-ta.	'He **must** be weaving a blanket.'
-ari	assertive force	Chay-**sh-ari** kanan avansa-ru-nqa.	'That one **definitely** will advance now, **they say**.'
-ikI	evidential modification	Kay-na-lla-**m-iki** kay urqu-pa-qa yatra-nchik.	'Just like this we live on this mountain.'

6 Enclitics

6.2.1 Emphatic -*Yá*

Realized as -*yá* in all environments (1–5) except following an evidential, in which case both the *I* of the evidential and the *Y* of the emphatic are elided and *Yá* is realized as *á* (6–8).

(1) ¡*Ariyá!* AMV
 ari-yá
 yes-EMPH
 'Yes **indeed**.'

(2) ¡*Mana-yá rupa-chi-nchik-chu!* AMV
 mana-yá rupa-chi-nchik-chu
 no-EMPH burn-CAUS-1PL-NEG
 'We do ***not*** set on fire!'

(3) *Pantyunpayá. ¡Ima wasiypitr pampamushaq!* AMV
 pantyun-pa-yá ima wasi-y-pi-tr pampa-mu-shaq
 cemetery-LOC-EMPH what house-1-LOC-EVC bury-CISL-1.FUT
 'In the cemetery! I doubt I'm going to bury someone in my house.'

(4) ¿*Imaynayá piru paykuna yatran warmi u qari?* AMV
 imayna-yá piru pay-kuna yatra-n warmi u qari
 how-EMPH but they-PL know-3 woman or man
 'How **ever** can they know if it will be a woman or a man?'

(5) *Sirbisatatr mas mastaqa rantikurun. Sirbisatayá.* AMV
 sirbisa-ta-tr mas mas-ta-qa ranti-ku-ru-n sirbisa-ta-yá
 beer-ACC-EVC more more-ACC-TOP buy-REFL-URGT-3 beer-ACC-EMPH
 '*Spkr* 1: "They must have sold a lot more beer." *Spkr* 2: "Beer, **all right**!"'

(6) *Balikushatr kara. Paytamá rikarani.* LT
 baliku-sha-tr ka-ra pay-ta-m-á rika-ra-ni
 request.a.service-PRF-EVC be-PST he-ACC-EVD-EMPH see-PST-1
 'He must have been requested. I saw him.'

252

6.2 Individual enclitics

(7) Trabahayta kanan kumunalta trulalamá. CH
 trabaha-y-ta   kanan kumunal-ta   trula-la-m-á
 work-INF-ACC now   community-ACC put-PST-EVD-EMPH
 'Now he's put the community to work.'

(8) Unayqa Awkichanka inkantakurashá wak altupa yantaman riptiki. SP
 unay-qa   Awkichanka   inkanta-ku-ra-sh-á   wak
 before-TOP Awkichanka enchant-REFL-PST-EVR-EMPH DEM.D
 altu-pa   yanta-man   ri-pti-ki
 high-LOC   firewood-ALL go-SUBDS-2
 'In olden times, Awkichanka, too, bewitched, **they say**, up hill if you went for firewood.'

6.2.2 Interrogation, negation, disjunction -*chu*

-*chu* indicates absolute (1) and disjunctive questions (2), (3), negation (4), and disjunction (5).[4]

(1) ¿Iskwilaman trurashurqanki**chu** mamayki? AMV
 iskwila-man   trura-shu-rqa-nki-chu   mama-yki
 school-ALL   put-2.OBJ-PST-2-Q   mother-3
 '**Did** your mother put you in school?'

(2) ¿Qari**chu** kanki warmi**chu** kanki? AMV
 ¿qari-chu ka-nki warmi-chu ka-nki
 man-Q   be-2   woman-Q   be-2
 'Are you a man **or** a woman?'

(3) ¿Don Juan**chu** icha alman**chu** hamuyan? AMV
 Don Juan-chu   icha alma-n-chu   hamu-ya-n
 Don Juan-Q   or   soul-3-Q   come-PROG-3
 'Is it Don Juan, **or** is his spirit coming?'

(4) Chaytri **mana** suyawarqa**chu**. AMV
 chay-tri   mana   suya-wa-rqa-chu
 DEM.D-EVC   no   wait-1.OBJ-PST-NEG
 'That's why she would**n't** have waited for me.'

---

[4] An anonymous reviewer points out that in Huaylas Q, negative -*tsu* is distinguished from polar question -*ku*. Huaylas is not unique among Quechuan languages in making this distinction.

6 Enclitics

(5) *Kandilaryapa**chu** bintisinkupa**chu**.* AMV
    kandilarya-pa-chu   binti-sinku-pa-chu
    Candelaria-LOC-DISJ twenty-five-LOC-DISJ
    '**Either** on Candelaria **or** on the twenty-fifth.'

Where it functions to indicate interrogation or negation, *-chu* attaches to the sentence fragment that is the focus of the interrogation or negation (6).

(6) *¿Chaypa**chu** tumarqanki?* AMV
    chay-pa-chu   tuma-rqa-nki
    DEM.D-LOC-Q   take-PST-2
    'Did you take [pictures] **there**?'

Where it functions to indicate disjunction – in either disjunctive questions or disjunctive statements – *-chu* generally attaches to each of the disjuncts (7).

(7) *Mario**chu** karqa Julián**chu** karqa.* AMV
    Mario-chu   ka-rqa   Julián-chu   ka-rqa
    Mario-DISJ   be-PST   Julián-DISJ   be-PST
    'It was **either** Mario **or** Julián.'

Questions that anticipate a negative answer are indicated by *mana-chu* (8).

(8) *¿**Manachu** kuska linman?* CH
    mana-chu   kuska   li-n-man
    no-Q   together   go-3-COND
    '**Couldn't** they go together?'

mana-chu may also "soften" questions (9).

(9) *Paysanu, ¿**manachu** vakata rantiyta munanki?* AMV
    paysanu   mana-chu   vaka-ta   ranti-y-ta   muna-nki
    countryman   no-Q   cow-ACC   buy-INF-ACC   want-2
    'My countryman, **do you not** want to buy a cow?'

It may also be used, like *aw* 'yes', in the formation of tag questions (10).

(10) *Lliw lliwtriki wañukushun, puchukashun entonces, ¿**manachu**?* ACH
     lliw lliw-tr-iki   wañu-ku-shun   puchuka-shun   intunsis
     all all-EVC-IKI   die-REFL-1PL.FUT finish.off-1PL.FUT therefore
     mana-chu
     no-Q
     'We'll all have to die, to finish off then, **isn't that so**?'

6.2 Individual enclitics

In negative sentences, -*chu* generally co-occurs with *mana* 'not' (11); -*chu* is also licensed by additive enclitic -*pis* (12), (13) and *ni* 'nor' (14), (15).

(11) *Aa, **manayá** kan**chu**. **Manayá** bula kan**chu**.* LT
 aa mana-yá ka-n-chu mana-yá bula ka-n-chu
 ah no-EMPH be-3-NEG no-EMPH ball be-3-NEG
 'Ah, there aren't any. There aren't any balls.'

(12) *Kaspin**pis** kan**chu**.* AMV
 kaspi-n-pis ka-n-chu
 stick-3-ADD be-3-NEG
 'She doesn't have a stick.'

(13) *Manchakushpa tutas puñu:**chu**.* ACH
 mancha-ku-shpa tuta-s puñu-:-chu
 scare-REFL-SUBIS night-ADD sleep-1-NEG
 'Being scared, I **don't** sleep at night.'

(14) *Apuraw wañururqariki. **Ni** apanña**chu**.* AMV
 apuraw wañu-ru-rqa-r-iki ni apa-n-ña-chu
 quick die-URGT-PST-R-IKI nor bring-3-DISC-NEG
 'He died quickly. They **didn't even** bring him [to the hospital].'

(15) ***Manam** wayta**chu** **ni** pishqu**chu**.* AMV
 mana-m wayta-chu ni pishqu-chu
 no-EVD flower-NEG nor bird-NEG
 '**Neither** a flower **nor** a bird.'

In prohibitions, -*chu* co-occurs with *ama* 'don't' (16).

(16) *"¡**Ama** wawqi:taqa wañuchiy**chu**!" niptinshi wañurachin paywantapis.* ACH
 ama wawqi-:-ta-qa wañu-chi-y-chu ni-pti-n-shi
 PROH brother-1-ACC-TOP die-CAUS-IMP-NEG say-SUBDS-3-EVR
 wañu-ra-chi-n pay-wan-ta-pis
 die-URGT-CAUS-3 he-INSTR-ACC-ADD
 'When he said, "**Don't** kill my brother!" they killed him with him, too.'

6 Enclitics

-chu does not appear in subordinate clauses, where negation is indicated with a negative particle alone (17), (18).[5]

(17) **Mana** *qali kaptinqa ñuqanchikpis taqllakta hapishpa qaluwanchik.* CH
    mana qali ka-pti-n-qa   ñuqanchik-pis taqlla-kta hapi-shpa
    no   man be-SUBDS-3-TOP we-ADD   plow-ACC grab-SUBIS
    qaluwa-nchik
    turn.earth-1PL
    'When there are **no men**, we grab the plow and turn the earth.'

(18) **Mana** *qatrachakunanpaq mandilchanta watachakun.* AMV
    mana qatra-cha-ku-na-n-paq   mandil-cha-n-ta wata-cha-ku-n
    no   dirty-FACT-REFL-NMLZ-3-PURP apron-DIM-3-ACC tie-DIM-REFL-3
    'She's tying on an apron **so she doesn't** get dirty.'

(19) *Manam lluqsiptiyki(qa *chu), waqashaqmi.* AMV
    mana-m lluqsi-pti-yki-qa   chu waqa-shaq-mi
    no-EVD go.out-SUBDS-2-TOP neg cry-1.FUT-EVD
    '**If** you **don't** go, I'll cry.'

In negative sentences, *-chu* never occurs on the same segment as does an evidential enclitic (20).

(20) *Mana lluqsirqanki(*mi)chu.* AMV
    mana lluqsi-rqa-nki-mi-chu
    no   go.out-PST-2-EVD-NEG
    'You **didn't** leave.'

Finally, interrogative *-chu* is further restricted in that it does not appear in questions using interrogative pronouns (21).[6]

(21) **¿Pi hamurqachu?* AMV
    pi   hamu-rqa-chu
    who come-PST-NEG
    '**Who** came?'

---

[5] An anonymous reviewer points out that elsewhere in Quechua, the correlates of negative *-chu* typically can appear in subordinate clauses. There are no naturally-occurring examples of this in the Yauyos corpus.

[6] *¿*Pi-taq hamu-n-chu? ¿*Pi-taq-chu hamu-n?* 'Who is coming?'

6.2 Individual enclitics

6.2.3 Restrictive, limitative -*lla*

-*lla* indicates exclusivity or limitation in number: the individual (1–3) or event/event type (4), (5) remains limited to itself and is accompanied by no other.

(1) *Iskwilapam niytu:kunaqa wawa:kunaqa rinmi ñuqallam ka: analfabitu.* SP
    iskwila-pa-m   niytu-:-kuna-qa   wawa-:-kuna-qa   ri-n-mi
    school-LOC-EVD nephew-1-PL-TOP   baby-1-PL-TOP   go-3-EVD
    ñuqa-lla-m   ka-:   analfabitu
    I-RSTR-EVD   be-1   illiterate
    'My grandchildren are in school. My children went. I'm the **only** illiterate one.'

(2) *Runapi umallaña trakillaña kayasa.* AMV
    runa-pi   uma-lla-ña   traki-lla-ña   ka-ya-sa
    person-GEN head-RSTR-DISC foot-RSTR-DISC be-PROG-NPST
    '**Just** the head and the hand remained of the person.'

(3) *Kichwallaktam limakuya: kaytrawlaq manam kastillanukta lima:chu.* CH
    kichwa-lla-kta-m   lima-ku-ya-:   kay-traw-laq   mana-m
    Quechua-RSTR-ACC-EVD speak-REFL-PROG-1 DEM.P-LOC-CONT no-EVD
    kastillanu-kta   lima-:-chu
    Spanish-ACC   speak-1-NEG
    'I'm talking **just** Quechua. Here, still, we don't speak Spanish.'

(4) *Fwirti kashpallamá linchik pustaman.* CH
    fwirti   ka-shpa-lla-m-á   li-nchik   pusta-man
    strong   be-SUBIS-RSTR-EVD-EMPH   go-1PL   clinic-ALL
    '**Only** if it's bad will we go to the health clinic.'

(5) *Lliw lliwtam rantishpallañam kanan kamatapis chay polarkunatapis.* ACH
    lliw lliw-ta-m   ranti-shpa-lla-ña-m   kanan   kama-ta-pis
    all all-ACC-EVD buy-SUBIS-RSTR-DISC-EVD now   blanket-ACC-ADD
    chay   polar-kuna-ta-pis
    DEM.D   fleece-PL-ACC-ADD
    'Now **just** buying everything – blankets, [polyester] fleece.'

257

6 Enclitics

-lla can generally be translated as 'just' (6), (7) or 'only' (8); it sometimes has an 'exactly' interpretation (9).

(6) *Chaynallam mikuchin ... pachachin.* AMV
 chayna-lla-m miku-chi-n pacha-chi-n
 thus-RSTR-EVD eat-CAUS-3 dress-CAUS-3
 '**Just** like that, she feeds him, she clothes him.'

(7) *Sirkallatam riya: manam karutachu.* SP
 sirka-lla-ta-m ri-ya-: mana-m karu-ta-chu
 close-RSTR-ACC-EVD go-PROG-1 no-EVD far-ACC-NEG
 'I **just** go close; I don't go far.'

(8) *Chayllatam yatrani. Masta yatranichu.* AMV
 chay-lla-ta-m yatra-ni mas-ta yatra-ni-chu
 DEM.D-LIM-ACC-EVD know-1 more-ACC know-1-NEG
 'I **only** know that. I don't know more.'

(9) *Iskinanpi sikya tunallanpi wallpay watrakunraq.* LT
 iskina-n-pi sikya tuna-lla-n-pi wallpa-y
 corner-3-LOC aqueduct corner-RSTR-3-LOC chicken-1
 watra-ku-n-raq
 give.birth-REFL-3-CONT
 'My hen lays eggs in the corner, **right** in the corner of the canal.'

It is very, very widely employed (10–12).

(10) *Lliwta abaskuna albirhakuna ayvislla rantikuni apani llaqtatam.* AMV
 lliw-ta abas-kuna albirha-kuna ayvis-lla ranti-ku-ni
 all-ACC broad.beans-PL peas-PL sometimes-RSTR buy-REFL-1
 apa-ni llaqta-ta-m
 bring-1 town-ACC-EVD
 'Everything – broad beans, peas – **once in while** I sell stuff – I bring it into town.'

(11) *Chaynallam. Chayllam kwintuqa. Mas kanchu manam.* SP
 chayna-lla-m chay-lla-m kwintu-qa mas ka-n-chu mana-m
 thus-RSTR-EVD DEM.D-RSTR-EVD story-TOP more be-3-NEG no-EVD
 'That's the way it goes. That's **all** there is to the story. There's no more.'

6.2 Individual enclitics

(12) *Chaytam aysashpalla pasachiwaq.* AMV
 chay-ta-m aysa-shpa-lla pasa-chi-wa-q
 DEM.D-ACC-EVD pull-SUBIS-RSTR pass-CAUS-1.OBJ-AG
 'They had me cross the river pulling [me by the hand].'

6.2.4 Discontinuative *-ña*

Discontinuitive. *-ña* indicates transition – change of state or quality. In affirmative statements, it can generally be translated as 'already' (1–3); in negative statements, as 'no more' or 'no longer' (4), (5); and in questions, as 'yet' (6), (7).

(1) *Kundinadawñam wakqa kayan.* AMV
 kundinadaw-ña-m wak-qa ka-ya-n
 condemned-DISC-EVD DEM.D-TOP be-PROG-3
 'That one is **already** condemned.'

(2) *Ñuqaqa kukaywanñam qawaruni.* AMV
 ñuqa-qa kuka-y-wan-ña-m qawa-ru-ni
 I-TOP coca-1-INSTR-DISC-EVD see-URGT-1
 'I saw it with my coca **already**.'

(3) *Paqwayanchikñam talpuyta, ¿aw? Papaktapis talpulalu:ñam, kanan halakta, ¿aw?* CH
 paqwa-ya-nchik-ña-m talpu-y-ta aw papa-kta-pis
 finish-PROG-1PL-DISC-EVD plant-INF-ACC yes potato-ACC-ADD
 talpu-la-lu-:-ña-m kanan hala-kta aw
 plant-UNINT-URGT-1-DISC-EVD now corn-ACC yes
 'We're finishing the planting **already**, no? We've **already** planted the potatoes, now the corn, no?'

(4) *Unaytrik. Kananqa kanñachu imapis.* SP
 unay-tri-k kanan-qa ka-n-ña-chu ima-pis
 before-EVC-IK now-TOP be-3-DISC-NEG what-ADD
 'That would be a long time ago. Now there isn't anything **any more**.'

(5) ***Manaña*** *ni santu ni imapis.* AMV
 mana-ña ni santu ni ima-pis
 no-DISC nor saint nor what-ADD
 'There are **no longer** saints or anything.'

259

6 Enclitics

(6) *¿Pasarunñachu? Tapushun.* AMV
 pasa-ru-n-ña-chu tapu-shun
 pass-URGT-3-DISC-Q ask-1PL.FUT
 'Did she go by **yet**? Let's ask.'

(7) *¿Rimayanñachu kanan wakpi?* LT
 rima-ya-n-ña-chu kanan wak-pi
 talk-PROG-3-DISC-Q now DEM.D-LOC
 'Are they talking **yet** there now?'

It can appear freely but never unaccompanied, redundantly, by *ña* (8), (9).

(8) *"¡Ñam tukuchkaniña!" ¡Puk! ¡Puk! ¡Puk! sikisapa sapu.* AMV
 ña-m tuku-chka-ni-ña puk puk puk siki-sapa sapu
 DISC-EVD finish-DUR-1-DISC puk puk puk behind-MULT.POSS frog
 '"I'm **already** finishing up!" Puk! Puk! Puk! said the frog with the behind bigger than usual.'

(9) *Ñam riqsiyanña hukya yaykun.* LT
 ña-m riqsi-ya-n-ña huk-ya yayku-n
 DISC-EVD know-PROG-3-DISC one-EMPH enter-3
 'They're getting to know it **already** and another comes in.'

6.2.5 Inclusion *-pis*

-pis indicates the inclusion of an item or event into a series of similar items or events. Translated as 'and', 'too', 'also', and 'even' (1–5) or, when negated, 'neither' or 'not even' (6–8).

(1) *Turnuchawan ñuqakunaqa trabaha: walmipis qalipis.* CH
 turnu-cha-wan ñuqa-kuna-qa trabaha-: walmi-pis qali-pis
 turn-DIM-INSTR I-PL-TOP work-1 woman-ADD man-ADD
 'We work in turns, the women **and** the men.'

(2) *Tukuy tuta tushun qaynintintapis.* AMV
 tukuy tuta tushu-n qaynintin-ta-pis
 all night dance-3 next.day-ACC-ADD
 'They dance all night and the next day, **too**.'

6.2 Individual enclitics

(3) *Pay**pis** chay subrinu wañukuptinñamik payqa tumarun.* AMV
    pay-pis   chay   subrinu wañu-ku-pti-n-ña-mi-k   pay-qa
    he-ADD DEM.D nephew die-REFL-SUBDS-3-DISC-EVD-IK he-TOP
    tuma-ru-n
    take-URGT-3
    'He, **too**, when his nephew died, took it [poison].'

(4) *Salchipullu rantikuqta**pis** tumarun.* AMV
    salchipullu   ranti-ku-q-ta-pis   tuma-ru-n
    fried.chicken buy-REFL-AG-ACC-ADD take-URGT-3
    'She took [pictures] of the people selling fried chicken **also**.'

(5) *Maman wañukuptin**pis** manam waqanchu.* AMV
    mama-n   wañu-ku-pti-n-pis   mana-m waqa-n-chu
    mother-3 die-REFL-SUBDS-3-ADD no-EVD   cry-3-NEG
    '**Even** when his mother died, he didn't cry.'

(6) *"¿Imapaqtaq ñuqa waqashaq?" nin. "Warmiypaq**pis** waqarqani**chu**."* AMV
    ima-paq-taq   ñuqa waqa-shaq   nin   warmi-y-paq-pis
    what-PURP-SEQ I   cry-1.FUT   say-3   woman-1-BEN-ADD
    waqa-rqa-ni-chu
    cry-PST-1-NEG
    '"Why am I going to cry?" he said. "I did**n't** cry for my wife, **either**."'

(7) *Paykunaqa **manam** qawarqapis**chu**.* AMV
    pay-kuna-qa mana-m qawa-rqa-pis-chu
    he-PL-TOP   no-EVD   see-PST-ADD-NEG
    '**Neither** did they see us.'

(8) *Pata saqayta**pis** atipan**chu**.* AMV
    pata   saqa-y-ta-pis   atipa-n-chu
    terrace go.up-INF-ACC-ADD be.able-3-NEG
    'They can't **even** go up one terrace.'

-*pis* may – or, even, may generally – imply contrast with some preceding element. Where it scopes over subordinate clauses, it can often be translated 'although' or 'even' (9), (10).

6 Enclitics

(9) *Uratam muna**shpapis**.* AMV
    ura-ta-m   muna-shpa-pis
    hour-ACC-EVD   want-SUBIS-ADD
    '**Although** I want to know the time.'

(10) *Hinaptin wasipiña rumiwan takaptin**pis** uyanchu.* SP
     hinaptin   wasi-pi-ña   rumi-wan   taka-pti-n-pis   uya-n-chu
     then   house-LOC-DISC stone-INSTR   hit-SUBDS-3-ADD   be.able-3-NEG
     'Later, at home, **even when** they hit it with a rock, it couldn't.'

Attaching to interrogative-indefinite stems, it forms indefinites and, with *mana*, negative indefinites (11–13).

(11) *Chaynam **imallatapis** wasiman apamun.* AMV
     chayna-m   ima-lla-ta-pis   wasi-man   apa-mu-n
     thus-EVD   what-RSTR-ACC-ADD   house-ALL   bring-CISL-3
     'That way he brings a little **something** to his house.'

(12) *Llapa tiyndaman yaykushpaqa lliw lliwshi **imantapis** apakun.* ACH
     llapa   tiynda-man   yayku-shpa-qa   lliw   lliw-shi   ima-n-ta-pis
     all   store-ALL   enter-SUBIS-TOP   all   all-EVR   what-3-ACC-ADD
     apa-ku-n
     bring-REFL-3
     'They entered all the stores and took everything and **anything** they had.'

(13) *Alli chambyakuqpaq **manam imapis** faltanmanchu.* AMV
     alli   chambya-ku-q-paq   mana   ima-pis   falta-n-man-chu
     good   work-REFL-AG-BEN   no   what-ADD   be.missing-3-COND-NEG
     '**Nothing** can be lacking for a good worker.'

It is in free variation with *-pas*, and, after a vowel, with *-s* (14–16), the latter particularly common in the ACH dialect.

(14) *"¡Diskansakamuy wasikipa!" niwan kikin**pas** diskansuman ripun.* LT
     diskansa-ka-mu-y   wasi-ki-pa   ni-wa-n   kiki-n-pas   diskansu-man
     rest-REFL-CISL-IMP   house-2-LOC   say-1.OBJ-3   self-3-ADD   rest-ALL
     ripu-n
     go-3
     '"Go rest in your house," he said to me and he, himself, **too**, went to rest.'

262

(15) *Hinaptinqa yutu pawaptinqa chay, "¡Aaaapship ship ship!" Yutu**pas**
"¡Wwaaaayyy!"* SP
hinaptin-qa   yutu   pawa-pti-n-qa   chay   aaaapship ship   ship
then-TOP   partridge fly-SUBDS-3-TOP   DEM.D   aaaapship ship   ship
yutu-pas   wwaaaayyy
partridge-ADD   wwaaaayyy
'Then, when the partridge jumped, he [cried],
"Aaaap-ship-ship-ship!" The partridge, **too**, [cried] "Wwaaaayyy!"'

(16) *Ñuqatas harquruwara Kashapataman riranim.* LT
ñuqa-ta-s   harqu-ru-wa-ra   Kashapata-man   ri-ra-ni-m
I-ACC-ADD   toss.out-URGT-1.OBJ-PST   Kashapata-ALL   go-PST-1-EVD
'They threw me out, **too**, and I went to Kashapata.'

6.2.6 Precision, certainty *-puni*

-puni indicates certainty or precision. It can be translated as 'necessarily', 'definitely', 'precisely'. It is attested only in the AMV dialect, where, still, it is not widely employed.

(1) *Paqarin**puni**m rishaq.* † AMV
paqarin-puni-m   ri-shaq
tomorrow-CERT-EVD   go-1.FUT
'I'm going to go **precisely** tomorrow.'

(2) *Mana**puni**m.* † AMV
mana-puni-m
no-CERT-EVD
'By no means.'

(3) *Chay wiqawninchikman**puni** chiri yakuta truranchik.* AMV
chay   wiqaw-ni-nchik-man-puni   chiri   yaku-ta   trura-nchik
DEM.D   waist-EUPH-1PL-ALL-CERT   cold   water-ACC   put-1PL
'We put cold water **right** on our lower backs.'

6 Enclitics

6.2.7 Topic-marking -*qa*

-*qa* indicates the topic of a clause (1–8), including in those cases where it attaches to subordinate clauses (9), (10).

(1) *Madri sultiram kaya: ñuqalla**qa**.* CH
 madri sultira-m ka-ya-: ñuqa-lla-qa
 mother alone-EVD be-PROG-1 I-RSTR-TOP
 'I'm a single mother.'

(2) *Ganawniyki**qa** achkam miranqa.* LT
 ganaw-ni-yki-qa achka-m mira-nqa
 cattle-EUPH-2-TOP a.lot-EVD increase-3.FUT
 'Your **cattle** are going to multiply a lot.'

(3) *Qam**qa** waqakunki sumaqllatam. Ñuqa**qa** quyu quyuta waqayani.* SP
 qam-qa waqa-ku-nki sumaq-lla-ta-m ñuqa-qa quyu quyu-ta
 you-TOP cry-REFL-2 pretty-RSTR-ACC-EVD I-TOP ugly ugly-ACC
 waqa-ya-ni
 cry-PROG-1
 '**You** sing nicely. **I**'m singing awfully.'

(4) *Yatraqnin**qa**; mana yatraqnin**qa** manayá.* AMV
 yatra-q-ni-n-qa mana yatra-q-ni-n-qa mana-yá
 know-AG-EUPH-3-TOP no know -AG-EUPH-TOP no-EMPH
 '**Those** of them who knew; not **those** of them who didn't know.'

(5) *Kanan**qa** mikunchik munasanchik[ta] qullqi kaptin**qa**.* AMV
 kanan-qa miku-nchik muna-sa-nchik[-ta] qullqi ka-pti-n-qa
 now-TOP eat-1PL want-PRF-1-ACC money be-SUBDS-3-TOP
 '**Now** we eat whatever we want when there's money.'

(6) *Llaqtaykipa**qa** ¿tarpunkichu sibadata?* AMV
 llaqta-yki-pa-qa tarpu-nki-chu sibada-ta
 town-2-LOC-TOP plant-2-Q barley-ACC
 'In **your town**, do you plant barley?'

(7) *Urayqa puriq kani trakillawan trakinchikpis nananankama.* AMV
    uray-qa   puri-q   ka-ni   traki-lla-wan   traki-nchik-pis
    down.hill-TOP   walk-AG   be-1   foot-RSTR-INSTR   foot-1PL-ADD
    nana-na-n-kama
    hurt-NMLZ-3-LIM
    'I would walk **down hill** just on foot until our feet hurt.'

(8) *Difindiwanchik malichukunapaqqa.* AMV
    difindi-wa-nchik   malichu-kuna-paq-qa
    defend-1.OBJ-1PL   curse-PL-ABL-TOP
    'It protects us against **curses**.'

(9) *Lluqsila pasiyuman yaykushpaqa manaña puydilaøchu piru.* CH
    lluqsi-la   pasiyu-man   yayku-shpa-qa   mana-ña   puydi-la-chu
    go.out-PST   walk-ALL   enter-SUBIS-TOP   no-DISC   be.able-PST-NEG
    piru
    but
    'They went out for a walk but **when they went in**, they couldn't.'

(10) *Qipiruptinqa … chay kundurqa qipiptin huk turuta pagaykun.* SP
     qipi-ru-pti-n-qa   chay   kundur-qa   qipi-pti-n   huk
     carry-URGT-SUBDS-3-TOP   DEM.D   condor-TOP   carry-SUBDS-3   one
     turu-ta   paga-yku-n
     bull-ACC   pay-EXCEP-3
     '**When he carried her**, after the condor carried her, she payed him a bull.'

6.2.8 Continuative -*Raq*

-*Raq* – realized in CH as -*laq* (1) and in all other dialects as -*raq* – indicates continuity of action, state or quality.

(1) *Kichwallaktam limakuya: kaytraw**laq** manam kastillanukta lima:chu.* CH
    kichwa-lla-kta-m   lima-ku-ya-:   kay-traw-laq   mana-m
    Quechua-RSTR-ACC-EVD   talk-REFL-PROG-1   DEM.P-LOC-CONT   no-EVD
    kastillanu-kta   lima-:-chu
    Spanish-ACC   talk-1-NEG
    'I'm just talking Quechua. Here, **still**, we don't speak Spanish.'

6 Enclitics

It can generally be translated 'still' (2–4) or, negated, 'yet' (5), (6).

(2) *Qamqa flaku**raq**mi. Hawlapam qamtaqa wirayachisayki.* ACH
    qam-qa   flaku-raq-mi   hawla-pa-m   qam-ta-qa
    you-TOP   skinny-CONT-EVD   cage-LOC-EVD   you-ACC-TOP
    wira-ya-chi-sayki
    fat-INCH-CAUS-1>2.FUT
    'You're **still** skinny. I'm going to fatten you up in a cage.'

(3) *Taqsana**raq**tri. Millwata taqsashun.* AMV
    taqsa-na-raq-tri   millwa-ta   taqsa-shun
    wash-NMLZ-CONT-EVC   wool-ACC   wash-1PL.FUT
    'It has to be cleaned **still**. We have to clean the wool.'

(4) *Kamanpi puñukuyaptin**raq** tarirun.* LT
    kama-n-pi   puñu-ku-ya-pti-n-raq   tari-ru-n
    bed-3-LOC   sleep-REFL-PROG-SUBDS-3-CONT   find-URGT-3
    'He found him when he was sleeping **still** in his bed.'

(5) *Runtuwanmi qaquyanmi chaypa **manaraq**mi shakashwan.* AMV
    runtu-wan-mi   qaqu-ya-n-mi   chay-pa   mana-raq-mi
    egg-INSTR-EVD   massage-PROG-3-EVD   DEM.D-LOC   no-CONT-EVD
    shakash-wan
    guinea.pig-INSTR
    'He's massaging with an egg – **not yet** with the guinea pig.'

(6) ***Mana**m mayqinniypis wañuni**raq**chu.* AMV
    mana-m   mayqin-ni-y-pis   wañu-ni-raq-chu
    no-EVD   which-EUPH-1-ADD   die-1-CONT-NEG
    '**None** of us has died yet.'

Marking rhetorical questions, it can indicate a kind of despair (7), (8).

(7) *¿Yawarnintachu? ¿Imata**raq** hurqura chay dimunyukuna?* ACH
    yawar-ni-n-ta-chu   ima-ta-raq   hurqu-ra   chay
    blood-EUPH-3-ACC-Q   what-ACC-CONT   take.out-PST   DEM.D
    dimunyu-kuna
    Devil-PL
    'His blood? **What in the world** did the devil suck out of him?'

6.2 Individual enclitics

(8) *Chay gringukunaqa altukunatash rin. ¿Imaynaraq chay runata wañuchin?* ACH
    chay   gringu-kuna-qa   altu-kuna-ta-sh   ri-n   imayna-raq   chay
    DEM.D   gringo-PL-TOP   high-PL-ACC-EVR   go-3   how-CONT   DEM.D
    runa-ta   wañu-chi-n
    PERSON-ACC   die-CAUS-3
    'The gringos go to the heights, they say. **How on earth** could they kill those people?'

With subordinate clauses, it may indicate a prerequisite or a necessary condition for the event to take place, translating in English as 'first' or 'not until' (9).

(9) *Kisuta ruwashparaq trayamuyan.* AMV
    kisu-ta   ruwa-shpa-raq   traya-mu-ya-n
    cheese-ACC   make-SUBIS-CONT   arrive-CISL-PROG-3
    '**Once** she makes the cheese, she's coming.'

Chay-raq indicates an imminent future, translating in Andean Spanish *recién* (10). Employed as a coordinator, it implies a contrast between the coordinated elements (see §7.3).

(10) *Chayraqmi tapayan. Qallaykuyani chayraq.* AMV
     chay-raq-mi   tapa-ya-n   qalla-yku-ya-ni   chay-raq
     DEM.D-CONT-EVD   cover-PROG-3   begin-EXCEP-PROG-1   DEM.D-CONT
     'He's **just now going to** cap it. I'm **just now** going to start.'

6.2.9 Sequential -*taq*

-*taq* indicates the sequence of events (1).

(1) *Tardiqa yapa listu suyan; yapataqshi trayarun.* AMV
    tardi-qa   yapa   listu   suya-n   yapa-taq-shi   traya-ru-n
    afternoon-TOP   again   ready   wait-3   again-SEQ-EVR   arrive-URGT-3
    'In the afternoon, **again**, ready, he waits. **Then, again,** [the zombie] arrived.'

Adelaar (p.c.) points out that in Ayacucho Quechua -*ña-taq* is a fixed combination. It appears that may be the case here too (2–4). In these examples -*taq* seems to continue to indicate a sequence of events.

(2) *Lliwta pikarushpa, kaymanñataq quturini trurani wakmanñataq.* AMV
 lliw-ta   pika-ru-shpa   kay-man-ña-taq   qutu-ri-ni
 all-ACC   pick-URGT-SUBDS   DEM.D-ALL-DISC-SEQ   gather-INCEP-1
 trura-ni wak-man-ña-taq
 put-1   DEM.P-ALL-DISC-SEQ
 'When I have all these sorted, **then** I gather everything here and **then** store it there.'

(3) *Qaliqa takllawanmi halun. Qipantañataq kulpakta maqanchik pikuwan.* CH
 qali-qa   taklla-wan-mi   halu-n   qipa-n-ta-ña-taq
 man-TOP   plow-INSTR-EVD   turn.earth-3   behind-3-ACC-DISC-SEQ
 kulpa-kta   maqa-nchik   piku-wan
 clod-ACC   hit-1PL   pick-INSTR
 'Men turn over the earth with a foot plow. Behind them, **then**, we break up the clods with a pick.'

(4) *Ñuqapa makiywan aytrichiyanmi. Kanan trakillañataq. Huknin makiwanñataq kananmi.* AMV
 ñuqa-pa   maki-y-wan   aytri-chi-ya-n-mi   kanan
 I-GEN   hand-1-INSTR   stir-CAUS-PROG-3-EVD   now
 traki-lla-ña-taq   huk-ni-n   maki-wan-ña-taq   kanan-mi
 foot-RSTR-DISC-SEQ   one-EUPH-3   hand-INSTR-DISC-SEQ   now-EVD
 'He's stirring it with my hand. Now, the foot. Now with the other hand.'

In a question introduced by an interrogative (*pi-*, *ima-* ...) *-taq* attaches to the interrogative in case it is the only word in the phrase or, in case the phrase includes two or more words, to the final word in the phrase (5–7).

(5) *¡Ishpaykuruwan! ¿Imapaqtaq ishpan?* AMV
 ishpa-yku-ru-wa-n   ima-paq-taq   ishpa-n
 urinate-EXCEP-URGT-1.OBJ-3   what-PURP-SEQ   urinate-3
 'It urinated on me! **Why** does it urinate?'

(6) *¿Ima rikuqtaq karqa sapatillayki?* AMV
 ima   rikuq-taq   ka-rqa   sapatilla-yki
 what   color-SEQ   be-PST   shoe-2
 '**What color** were your shoes?'

6.2 Individual enclitics

(7) ¿Imanashaqtaq? Diosllatañatriki. LT
 ima-na-shaq-taq   Dios-lla-ta-ña-tr-iki
 what-VRBZ-1.FUT-SEQ   God-RSTR-ACC-DISC-EVC-IKI
 '**What am I going to do**? It's for God already.'

In this capacity, -taq may be the most transparent of the enclitics attaching to q-phrases. In a clause with a conditional or in a subordinate clause, -taq can indicate a warning (8).

(8) Kurasunniyman shakashta trurayan. Ñuqa niyani
 "¡Kaniruwaptinñataq!" AMV
 kurasun-ni-y-man shakash-ta   trura-ya-n   ñuqa ni-ya-ni
 heart-EUPH-1-ALL guinea.pig-ACC   put-PROG-3   I   say-PROG-1
 kani-ru-wa-pti-n-ña-taq
 bite-URGT-1.OBJ-SUBDS-3-DISC-SEQ
 'He's putting the guinea pig over my heart. I'm saying, "**Be careful** it doesn't bite me!"'

-taq also functions as a conjunction (9) (see §7.3).

(9) Warmiñataq puchkawan qariñataq tihiduwan. AMV
 warmi-ña-taq   puchka-wan   qari-ña-taq   tihidu-wan
 women-DISC-SEQ   spinning-INSTR   man-DISC-SEQ   weaving-INSTR
 'Women with spinning **and** men with weaving.'

6.2.10 Emotive -ya

-ya indicates regret or resignation. It can be translated 'alas' or 'regretfully' or with a sigh. Not very widely employed.

(1) Hinashpaqaya, "Wañurachishaqña wakchachaytaqa dimasllam
 sufriyan." AMV
 hinashpa-qa-ya   wañu-ra-chi-shaq-ña   wakcha-cha-y-ta-qa
 then-TOP-EMO   die-URGT-CAUS-1.FUT-DISC   lamb-DIM-1-ACC-TOP
 dimas-lla-m   sufri-ya-n
 too.much-RSTR-EVD   suffer-PROG-3
 'Then, **alas**, "I'm going to kill my little lamb already – he's suffering too much," [I said].'

6 Enclitics

(2) *Unay runakunaqa yatrayan masta, mastaya, lliwta ... aaaa.* AMV
unay   runa-kuna-qa   yatra-ya-n   mas-ta   mas-ta-ya
before person-PL-TOP   know-PROG-3   more-ACC more-ACC-EMO
lliw-ta   aaaa
all-ACC   ahhh
'In the old days, people knew more, more, everything, **ahhh**.'

6.2.11 Evidence

Evidentials indicate the type of the speaker's source of information. SYQ, like most[7] other Quechuan languages, counts three evidential suffixes: direct *-mi* (1–3), reportative *-shi* (4–6), and conjectural *-tri* (7–9) (*i.e.* the speaker has her own evidence for P (generally visual); the speaker learned P from someone else; or the speaker infers P based on some other evidence). Following a short vowel, these are realized as *-m, sh,* and *-tr,* respectively (3), (6), (9).

(1) *Taytacha José irransakurqa chaypam.* AMV
tayta-cha   José   irransa-ku-rqa   chay-pa-m
father-DIM   José   herranza-REFL-PST   DEM.D-LOC-EVD
'My grandfather José held herranzas **there**.'

(2) *Trurawarqaya huk ratu. Manayá puchukachiwarqachu.*
Trurawarqam. AMV
trura-wa-rqa-yá   huk   ratu   mana-yá
put-1.OBJ-PST-EMPH   one   moment   no-EMPH
puchuka-chi-wa-rqa-chu   trura-wa-rqa-m
finish-CAUS-1.OBJ-PST-NEG put-1.OBJ-PST-EVD
'They put me in [school] a short while. They didn't have me finish, but they did **put me in**.'

(3) *Qayna puntraw qanin puntrawllam trayamura:.* ACH
qayna   puntraw qanin   puntraw-lla-m
previous   day   day.before.yesterday day-RSTR-EVD
traya-mu-ra-:
arrive-CISL-PST-1
'I arrived yesterday, **just the day** before yesterday.'

---

[7] Note, though, that Huallaga Q counts four evidentials, (*-mi, -shi, -chi,* snd *-chaq*) (Weber 1989:76). South Conchucos Q counts six, (*-mi, -shi, -chi, -cha:,* and *-cher*); Sihuas, too, counts six (Hintz and Hintz 2014).

6.2 Individual enclitics

(4) *Radyukunapa rimayta rimayan. Lluqsiyamun**shi** tirrurista. Tirrurista rikariyamun**shi**.* SP
radyu-kuna-pa rima-y-ta rima-ya-n lluqsi-ya-mu-n-shi
radio-PL-LOC talk-INF-ACC talk-PROG-3 go.out-PROG-CISL-3-EVR
tirrurista tirrurista rikari-ya-mu-n-shi
terrorist terrorist appear-PROG-CISL-3-EVR
'On the radio they talk for the sake of talking. Terrorists **are coming out, they say**. Terrorists **are appearing, they say**.'

(5) *Chay uchukllapa pashñataq uywakuptinñataq**shi** maqtaqa aparqa mikunanta.* AMV
chay uchuk-lla-pa pashña-taq uywa-ku-pti-n-ña-taq-shi
DEM.D small-RSTR-LOC girl-ACC raise-REFL-SUBDS-3-DISC-SEQ-EVR
maqta-qa apa-rqa miku-na-n-ta
young.man-TOP bring-PST eat-NMLZ-3-ACC
'When **he raised** the girl in that cave, the man brought her his food, **they say**.'

(6) *Qarinta**sh** wañurachin mashanta**sh** wañurachin.* AMV
qari-n-ta-sh wañu-ra-chi-n masha-n-ta-sh
man-3-ACC-EVR die-URGT-CAUS-3 son.in.law-3-ACC-EVR
wañu-ra-chi-n
die-URGT-CAUS-3
'She killed her **husband, they say**; she killed her **son-in-law, they say**.'

(7) *Qiñwalman trayarachiptiki wañukunman**tri**.* AMV
qiñwal-man traya-ra-chi-pti-ki wañu-ku-n-man-tri
quingual.grove-ALL arrive-URGT-CAUS-SUBDS-2 die-REFL-3-COND-EVC
'If you make her go all the way to the quingual grove, she **might die**.'

(8) *Suwawan**tri**. Durasnuy kara mansanay kara qanin puntraw.* LT
suwa-wa-n-tri durasnu-y ka-ra mansana-y ka-ra qanin
rob-1.OBJ-3-EVR peach-1 be-PST apple-1 be-PST previous
puntraw
day
'They **may have robbed** me. The day before yesterday I had peaches and apples.'

271

6 Enclitics

(9) *Wasiy rahasa kayan. Saqaykurunqatr.* AMV
wasi-y raha-sa ka-ya-n saqa-yku-ru-nqa-tr
house-1 crack-PRF be-PROG-3 go.down-EXCEP-URGT-3.FUT-EVC
'My house is cracked. **It's going to fall down.**'

The evidential system of SYQ is unusual among Quechuan languages, however, in that it overlays the three-way distinction standard to Quechua with a second three-way distinction. The set of evidentials in SYQ thus counts nine members: *-mI*, *-m-ik*, and *-m-iki*; *-shI*, *-sh-ik*, and *-sh-iki*; and *-trI*, *-tr-ik*, and *-tr-iki*. The *-I*, *-ik*, and *-iki* forms are not allomorphs: they receive different interpretations, generally indicating increasing degrees of evidence strength or, in the case of modalized verbs, increasing modal force. §6.2.11 describes this system in some detail. For further formal analysis, see Shimelman (2012).

In addition to indicating the speaker's information type, evidentials also function to indicate focus or comment and to complete copular predicates (for further discussion and examples, see §7.11 and 7.8 on emphasis and equatives).

Evidentials are subject to the following distributional restrictions. They never attach to the topic or subject; these are, rather, marked with *-qa*. In content questions, the evidential attaches to the question word or to the last word of the questioned phrase (10) (see §7.6 on interrogation).

(10) *¿May**mi** chay warmi?* AMV
may-mi chay warmi
where-EVD DEM.D woman
'**Where** is that woman?'

Evidentials do not appear in commands or injunctions (11); finally, only one evidential may occur per clause (12).

(11) *¡Ruwaruchun*mi/shi/tri!* AMV
ruwa-ru-chun-*mi/shi/tri
make-URGT-INJUNC-EVD-EVR-EVC
'**Let** him do it!'

(12) *¡Vakay wira wiram, matraypi puñushpa, allin pastuta mikushpam.* AMV
vaka-y wira wira-m matray-pi puñu-shpa allin pastu-ta
cow-1 fat fat-EVD cave-LOC sleep-SUBIS good pasture.grass-ACC
miku-shpa-m
eat-REFL-EVD
'My cow is really fat, sleeping in a cave and eating good pasture grass.'

6.2 Individual enclitics

All three evidentials are interpreted as assertions. The first, *-mI*, is generally left untranslated in Spanish; the second, *-shI*, is often rendered *dice* 'they say'; the third is reflected in a change in verb tense or mode (see §6.2.11.3). The difference between the three is a matter, first, of whether or not evidence is from personal experience, and, second, whether that evidence supports the proposition, *p*, immediately under the scope of the evidential or another set of propositions, *P'*, that are evidence for *p*, as represented in Table 6.2.

Table 6.2: Evidential schema: "evidence from" by "evidence for"

	Supports scope proposition *p*	Supports *P'* evidence for *p*
Direct (personal experience) evidence	DIRECT *-mI*	CONJECTURAL *-trI*
Reportative (non-personal experience) evidence	REPORTATIVE *-shI*	CONJECTURAL *-trI*

So, employing *-mI(p)*, the speaker asserts predicate *p* and represents that she has personal-experience evidence for *p*; employing *-shI(p)*, the speaker asserts *p* and refers the hearer to another source for evidence for *p*; and employing *-trI(p)*, the speaker asserts *p* and represents that *p* is a conjecture from *P'*, propositions for which she has either *-mI*-type or *-shI*-type evidence or both. That is, although SYQ counts three evidential suffixes, it counts only two evidence types, direct and reportative; these two are jointly exhaustive. §6.2.11.1–6.2.11.3 cover *-mI*, *-shI*, and *trI*, in turn. §6.2.11.4 covers the evidential modifiers, *-ari* and *-ik/iki*.

6.2.11.1 Direct *-mI*

-mI indicates that the speaker speaks from direct experience. Unlike *-shI* and *-trI*, it is generally left untranslated. Note that in the examples below, with the exception of (1), the speaker's knowledge is *not* the product of visual experience.

(1) *Vakaqa kaypa waqrayuqmiki kayan.* AMV
    vaka-qa   kay-pa   waqra-yuq-m-iki   ka-ya-n
    COW-TOP DEM.P-LOC horn-POSS-EVD-IKI be-PROG-3
    'The cows here **have horns**.'

6 Enclitics

(2) *Piñi**mi** pakarayan wasiypa wak ichuypa ukunpa.* AMV
piñi-y-mi   paka-ra-ya-n   wasi-y-pa   wak   ichuy-pa
necklace-1-EVD hide-UNINT-INTENS-3 house-1-LOC DEM.D straw-GEN
uku-n-pa
inside-3-LOC
'**My necklace** is hidden in my house under the straw.'

(3) *Chaywan**mi** pwirtata ruwayani. Mana**m** achkataq ruwanichu.* AMV
chay-wan-mi   pwirta-ta ruwa-ya-ni   mana-m   achka-taq
DEM.D-INSTR-EVD   door-ACC   make-PROG-1 no-EVD   a.lot-ACC
ruwa-ni-chu
make.1-NEG
'I make doors with this. I don't make a lot.'

(4) *Karrupis ashnakuyan**mi**.* ACH
karru-pis ashna-ku-ya-n-mi
car-ADD   smell-REFL-PROG-3-EVD
'The buses, too, **stink**.'

(5) *Qunirirachishunki. Kaliyntamanchik**mi**.* ACH
quni-ri-ra-chi-shu-nki   kaliynta-ma-nchik-mi
warm-INCEP-CAUS-2.OBJ-2   warm-1.OBJ-1PL-EVD
'It warms you up. **It warms us up.**'

6.2.11.2 Reportative -shI

-shI indicates that the speaker's evidence does not come from personal experience (1–4).

(1) *Awkichanka urupaqa inkantu**sh** – karru**sh** chinkarurqa qutrapa.* AMV
Awkichanka urqu-pa-qa   inkantu-sh   karru-sh   chinka-ru-rqa
Awkichanka hill-LOC-TOP   spirit-EVR   car-EVR   lose-URGT-PST
qutra-pa
lake-LOC
'In the hill Okichanka, there is **a spirit, they say** – a car was lost in a reservoir.'

6.2 Individual enclitics

(2) *Mashwaqa prustatapaqshi allin.* CH
   mashwa-qa   prustata-paq-shi   allin
   mashua-TOP   prostate-BEN-EVR   good
   'Mashua is good for the **prostate, they say**.'

(3) *Chaypash runtuta mikuchishunki.* AMV
   chay-pa-sh   runtu-ta   miku-chi-shu-nki
   DEM.D-LOC-EVR   egg-ACC   eat-CAUS-2.OBJ-2
   'They'll feed you eggs **there, they say**.'

(4) *Lata-wan yanu-shpa-taq-shi runa-ta-pis miku-ru-ra.* ACH
   lata-wan   yanu-shpa-taq-shi   runa-ta-pis   miku-ru-ra
   can-INSTR   cook-SUBIS-SEQ-EVR   person-ACC-ADD   eat-URGT-PST
   'They [the Shining Path] even **cooked** people in metal pots and ate them, **they say**.'

It is used systematically in stories (5), (6).

(5) *Unayshi kara huk asnu.* SP
   unay-shi   ka-ra   huk   asnu
   before-EVR   be-PST   one   donkey
   '**Once upon a time, they say** there was a mule.'

(6) *Chaypaqshi kutirun maman kaqta papanin kaqta.* LT
   chay-paq-shi   kuti-ru-n   mama-n   ka-q-ta   papa-ni-n
   DEM.D-ABL-EVR   return-URGT-3   mother-3   be-AG-ACC   father-EUPH-3
   ka-q-ta
   be-AG-ACC
   'He returned **from there, they say**, to his mother's place, to his father's place.'

6.2.11.3 Conjectural *-trI*

-trI indicates that the speaker does not have evidence for the proposition directly under the scope of the evidential, but is, rather, conjecturing to that proposition from others for which she does have evidence (1–8).

6 Enclitics

(1) *Awayan**triki** kamata.* AMV
    awa-ya-n-tr-iki   kama-ta
    weave-PROG-EVR-IKI blanket-ACC
    '**He must be weaving** a blanket.'

(2) *Wañuypaqpis kayachuwan**triki**.* AMV
    wañu-y-paq-pis   ka-ya-chuwan-tr-iki
    die-INF-ABL-ADD   be-PROG-1PL.COND-EVC-IKI
    '**We could be** also about to die.'

(3) *Kukachankunata aparuptiyqa tiyaparuwanqa**trik**.* AMV
    kuka-cha-n-kuna-ta   apa-ru-pti-y-qa
    coca-DIM-3-PL-ACC   bring-URGT-SUBDS-1-TOP
    tiya-pa-ru-wa-nqa-tr-ik
    sit-BEN-URGT-1.OBJ-EVC-IK
    'If I bring them their coca, **they'll accompany me sitting**.'

(4) *Chayman**trik** ayarikura.* ACH
    chay-man-tr-ik   aya-ri-ku-ra
    DEM.D-ALL-EVC-IK   cadaver-INCEP-REFL-PST
    'She **must** have become a cadaver.'

(5) *Upyachinman**tri**.* CH
    upya-chi-ma-n-tri
    drink-CAUS-1.OBJ-3-EVC
    'She **might** make me drink.'

(6) *Yakuña**tr** rikuyan pampantaqa.* ACH
    yaku-ña-tr   ri-ku-ya-n   pampa-n-ta-qa
    water-DISC-EVC go-REFL-PROG-3   ground-3-ACC-TOP
    '**Water should** already be running along the ground.'

(7) *Allintaqa. Kapas**triki** palabrata kichwapa apakunqa kananpis.* SP
    allin-ta-qa   kapas-tr-iki   palabra-ta kichwa-pa
    good-ACC-TOP   possible-EVC-IKI   word-ACC   Quechua-GEN
    apa-ku-nqa   kanan-pis
    BRING-REFL-3.FUT now-ADD
    'Good. **Maybe** they'll bring Quechua now, too.'

(8) *Ayvis kumpañaw hamuyan – wañuypaqpis kayachuwantriki.* AMV
 ayvis   kumpañaw   hamu-ya-n   wañu-y-paq-pis
 sometimes accompanied come-PROG-3 die-1-PURP-ADD
 ka-ya-chuwan-tr-iki
 be-PROG-1PL.COND-EVC-IKI
 'Sometimes someone comes accompanied – we might be also about to die.'

6.2.11.4 Evidential modification

SYQ counts four evidential modifiers, *-ari* and the set ø, *-ik* and *-iki*. §6.2.11.4.1 and 6.2.11.4.2 cover *-ari* and *-ø/-ik/iki*, respectively. The latter largely repeats Shimelman (2012).

6.2.11.4.1 Assertive force *-aRi* *-aRi* – realized *-ali* in CH (1) and *-ari* in all other dialects – indicates conviction on the part of the speaker.[8]

(1) *Wayrakuyanmari.* AMV
 wayra-ku-ya-n-m-ari
 wind-REFL-PROG-3-EVD-ARI
 'It's windy.'

It can often be translated as 'surely' or 'certainly' or 'of course'. *-aRi* generally occurs only in combination with *-mI* (2), (3), *-shI* (4), (5) and *-Yá* (6–8).

(2) *Manamari llapa ruwayaqhina kayani.* AMV
 mana-m-ari llapa ruwa-ya-q-hina   ka-ya-ni
 no-EVD-ARI   all   make-PROG-AG-COMP be-PROG-1
 '**No, of course**, it seems like I'm making it all up.'

---

[8] The Quechuas of (at least) Ancash-Huailas Parker (1976: 151), Cajamarca-Canaris Quesada Castillo (1976: 158) and Junin-Huanca Cerrón-Palomino (1976a: 238–9) have suffixes *-rI*, *-rI* and *-ari*, respectively, which, like the SYQ *-k* succeed evidentials and are most often translated *pues* 'then'. It seems unlikely that the AHQ, CCQ and JHQ forms correspond to the *-k* or *-ki* of SYQ. First, unlike *-ik* or *-iki*, *-rI* and *-ari* may appear independent of any evidential and they may function as general emphatics. Second, SYQ, too, has a suffix *-ari* which, like *-rI* and *-ari*, functions as a general emphatic, also translating as *pues*. Third, the SYQ *-ari* is in complementary distribution with *-k* and *-ki*. Finally, unlike the AHQ, CCQ and JHQ forms, the SYQ *-ari* cannot appear independently of the evidentials *-mI* or *-shI* or else of *-y*, and, further, always forms an independent word with these.

6 Enclitics

(3) Ñuqa[ta]s firmachiwan**mari**. Piru mana**shari** chay wawi warmiytapis firmachinraqchu. LT
ñuqa[-ta]-s firma-chi-wa-n-m-ari   piru mana-sh-ari chay
I-ACC-ADD sign-CAUS-1.OBJ-3-EVD-ARI but no-EVR-ARI DEM.D
wawi warmi-y-ta-pis   firma-chi-n-raq-chu
baby woman-1-ACC-ADD sign-CAUS-3-CONT-NEG
'**They made me sign**, too. But they **didn't** make my daughter sign yet, **they say**.'

(4) Viñacpaq**shali**. CH
Viñac-paq-sh-ali
Viñac-ABL-EVR-ARI
'From Viñac, she says, then.'

(5) Ripun**shari** umaqa kunkanman. AMV
ripu-n-sh-ari uma-qa kunka-n-man
go-3-EVR-ARI head-TOP neck-3-ALL
'The head **went** [flying back] towards his neck, **they say**.'

(6) ¡Kurriy! Qillakuyanki**trari**. LT
kurri-y qilla-ku-ya-nki-tr-ari
run-IMP lazy-REFL-PROG-2-EVC-ARI
'Run! ... **You must be being lazy**.'

(7) Kidakushun kaypa**yari**. ACH
kida-ku-shun kay-pa-y-ari
stay-REFL-1PL.FUT DEM.P-LOC-EMPH-ARI
'We're going to stay **here**.'

(8) Yatraqninqa mana yatraqninqa mana**yari**. AMV
yatra-q-ni-n-qa   mana yatra-q-ni-n-qa   mana-y-ari
know-AG-EUPH-3-TOP no know-AG-EUPH-3-TOP no-EMPH-ARI
'The ones who knew how. The ones who didn't know how, **no, of course**.'

It is far less often employed than -ik and -iki. It is, however, prevalent in the LT dialect, which supplied the single instance of tr-ari in the corpus (9).

(9) *Chay wayra itana piru rimidyum Hilda. ¡Piru wachikunyari!* AMV
chay wayra itana piru rimidyu-m Hilda piru
DEM.D wind thorn but remedy-EVD Hilda but
wachi-ku-n-y-ari
sting-REFL-3-EMPH-ARI
'The wind thorns are medicinal, Hilda. But **do they ever sting!**'

6.2.11.4.2 Evidence strength -*ik* and -*iki* SYQ is unusual[9] in that each of its three evidentials counts three variants, formed by the suffixation of -ø, -*ik* or -*iki*. The resulting nine forms are direct -*mI*-ø, -*m-ik* and -*m-iki* (1–3); reportative -*shI*-ø, -*sh-ik* and -*sh-iki* (4–6); and conjectural -*trI*-ø, -*tr-ik* and -*tr-iki* (7–9).[10]

(1) *Manam trayamunchu mana**mik** rikarinchu.* ACH
mana-m traya-mu-n-chu mana-m-ik rikari-n-chu
no-EVD arrive-CISL-3-NEG no-EVD-IK appear-3-NEG
'He **hasn't** arrived. He **hasn't** showed up.'

(2) *Limatam rishaq. Limapaqa buskaq kan**miki**. Sutintapis rimayan**miki**.
¿Ichu manachu?* LT
Lima-ta-m ri-shaq Lima-pa-qa buska-q ka-n-m-iki
Lima-ACC-EVD go-1.FUT Lima-LOC-TOP look.for-AG be-3-EVD-IKI
suti-n-ta-pis rima-ya-n-m-iki ichu mana-chu
name-3-ACC-ADD talk-PROG-3-EVD-IKI or no-Q
'I'm going to go to Lima. In Lima, **there are** people who read cards, **then**. They're **saying** his name, **then**, yes or no?'

(3) *Wañuchinakun ima**miki** chaytaqa muna:chu.* SP
wañu-chi-naku-n ima-m-iki chay-ta-qa muna-:-chu
die-CAUS-RECIP-3 what-EVD-IKI DEM.D-ACC-TOP want-1-NEG
'They kill each other and **what-not, then**. I don't want that.'

---

[9] Ayacucho Q also makes use of -*ki*.
[10] In Lincha, -*iki* may modify both -*mI* and -*shI* but not -*trI*; in Tana, -*iki* may modify all three evidentials.

6 Enclitics

(4) *Chayshik chay susyukuna ruwapakurqa chay nichuchanta wañushpa chayman pampakunanpaq.* AMV
chay-sh-ik   chay   susyu-kuna   ruwa-paku-rqa   chay
DEM.D-EVR-IK DEM.D   associates-PL make-JTACC-PST   DEM.D
nichu-cha-n-ta   wañu-shpa chay-man   pampa-ku-na-n-paq
crypt-DIM-3-ACC die-SUBIS   DEM.D-ALL bury-REFL-NMLZ-3-PURP
'That's why, **they say**, before, the members made each other the small crypts, to bury them when they died.'

(5) *Llutanshiki. Llutan runashik kan.* LT
llutan-sh-iki   llutan runa-sh-ik   ka-n
ugly-EVR-IKI   ugly   person-EVR-IK   be-3
'**They're** messed up, **they say**. There are messed up **people, they say**.'

(6) *"¡Mátalo!" nishashiki.* CH
mátalo   ni-sha-sh-iki
[Spanish]   say-NPST-EVR-IKI
'"Kill him!" **she's said, they say**.'

(7) *¿Imapaqraq chayta ruwara paytaqa? Yanqañatrik chayta wañuchira.* ACH
ima-paq-raq   chay-ta   ruwa-ra   pay-ta-qa   yanqa-ña-tr-ik
what-PURP-CONT   DEM.D-ACC   make-PST   he-ACC-TOP   lie-DISC-EVC-IK
chay-ta   wañu-chi-ra
DEM.D-ACC   die-CAUS-PST
'What did they do that to him for? They **must have** killed him **just for the sake of it**.'

(8) *Ablanshiki. "Tragu, vino", nishpatriki ablayamun.* SP
abla-n-sh-iki   tragu vino ni-shpa-tr-iki   abla-ya-mu-n
talk-3-EVR-IKI   drink wine say-SUBIS-EVC-IKI   talk-PROG-CISL-3
'**They talk, they say, for sure**. "Pay me liquor, wine," **they must be saying**, talking.'

(9) *Alkansachin warkawantri. Kabrapis kasusam, piru. Riqsiyantriki runantaqa.* AMV
alkansa-chi-n warka-wan-tri kabra-pis kasu-sa-m piru
reach-CAUS-3 sling-INSTR-EVC goat-ADD attention-PRF-EVD but
riqsi-ya-n-tr-iki runa-n-ta-qa
know-PROG-3-EVC-IKI person-3-ACC-TOP
'She **must make [the stones] reach** with the sling, **for sure**. The goats obey her. They **must know** their master, **for sure**.'

Evidentials obligatorily take evidential modifier (hereafter "EM") arguments; EMs are enclitics and attach exclusively to evidentials. So, for example, *mishi-m [cat-EVD] and *mishi-ki (cat-IKI) are both ungrammatical. The corresponding grammatical forms would be *mishi-m-ø* [cat-EVD-ø] and *mishi-mi-ki (cat-EVD-IKI), respectively. With all three sets of evidentials, the *-ik* form is associated with some variety of increase over the *-ø* form; the *-iki* form, with greater increase still. With all three evidentials, *-ik* and *-iki* – except in those cases in which they take scope over universal-deontic-modal or future-tense verbs – indicate an increase in strength of evidence. With the direct *-mI*, *-ik* and *-iki* generally also affect the interpretation of strength of assertion; with the conjectural *-trI*, the interpretation of certainty of conjecture. In the case of universal-deontic modal and future-tense verbs, with both *-mI* and *trI*, *-ik* and *-iki* indicate increasingly strong obligation and increasingly imminent/certain futures, respectively.

6.2.11.5 Evidentials in questions

In questions, the evidentials generally indicate that the speaker expects a response with the same evidential (*i.e.*, an answer based on direct evidence, reportative evidence or conjecture, in the cases of *-mI*, *-shI*, and *-trI*, respectively) (1–3).

(1) *¿Amador Garaychu? ¿**Imam** sutin kara?* ACH
Amador Garay-chu ima-m suti-n ka-ra
Amador Garay-Q what-EVD name-3 be-PST
'Amador Garay? **What** was his name?'

(2) *¿**Maypish** wasinta lulayan?* CH
may-pi-sh wasi-n-ta lula-ya-n
where-LOC-EVR house-3-ACC make-PROG-3
'**Where did she** say she's making her house?'

6 Enclitics

(3) ¿Kutiramunman**chutr**? ¿**Imatrik** pasan? ACH
    kuti-ra-mu-n-man-chu-tr ima-tr-ik   pasan
    return-URGT-CISL-Q-EVC   what-EVC-IK   pass-3
    '**Could** he come back? **What would have** happened?'

The use of *-trI* in a question may, additionally, indicate that the speaker doesn't actually expect any response at all (4), while the use of *-shI* may indicate not that the speaker is expecting an answer based on reported evidence, but that the speaker is reporting the question.

(4) ¿Kawsan**chutr** mana**chutr**? *No se sabe.* ACH
    kawsa-n-chu-tr mana-chu-tr? No se sabe.
    live-3-Q-EVC   no-Q-EVC   [Spanish]
    '**Would** he be alive or dead? We don't know.'

7 Syntax

This chapter covers the syntax of Southern Yauyos Quechua. The chapter counts fourteen sections covering constituent order, sentences, coordination, comparison, negation, interrogation, reflexives and reciprocals, equatives, possession, topic, emphasis, complementation, relativization and subordination.

7.1 Constituent order

The unmarked constituent order in SYQ, as in other Quechuan languages, is SOV (*Mila-qa vikuña-n-kuna-ta riku-ra* 'Melanie saw her vicuñas'). That said, because constituents are obligatorily marked for case, a change in the order of constituents in an utterance will not necessarily change the sense of that utterance (*Mila-qa riku-ra vikuña-n-kuna-ta* 'Melanie saw her vicuñas'). Change in constituent order does not necessarily change the interpretation of topic or focus. Topic is generally signaled by *-qa*, while the evidentials *-mI*, *-shI*, and *-trI* signal focus (*Carmen-qa llama-n-kuna-ta-sh wañu-chi-nqa* 'Carmen will butcher her llamas, they say' *Carmen-qa llama-n-kuna-ta wañu-chi-nqa-sh* 'Carmen will **butcher** her **llamas**, they say'). In the first case, the focus is on the direct object: she will butcher her llamas and not, say, her goats; in the second case, it is the verb that is marked as the focus: she will butcher her llamas and not, say, pet them. Nevertheless, the verb and the object cannot commute in subordinate clauses, where only the order OV is grammatical (*fruta-cha-y-kuna apa-sa-y-ta* 'the fruit I bring' **apa-sa-y-ta fruta-cha-y-kuna-ta*).

Modifiers generally precede the elements they modify: adjectives precede the nouns they modify (*yuraq wayta* 'white flower'), possessors precede the thing possessed (*pay-pa pupu-n* 'her navel'), and relative clauses precede their heads (*trabaha-sa-yki wasi-pa* 'in the house where you worked'). In case an NP includes multiple modifiers, these appear in the order:

(1)   DEM-QUANT-NUM-NEG-PREADJ-ADJ-ATR-NUCLEUS

7 Syntax

7.2 Sentences

With the exceptions of (a) abbreviated questions and responses to questions (¿*May-pi?* 'Where?' *Chay-pi-(m)* 'There'), and (b) exclamations (¡*Atatayáw!* 'How disgusting!') no SYQ sentence is grammatical without a verb (**Sasa.* 'Hard'). As it is unnecessary in SYQ to specify either the subject or the object, a verb alone inflected for person is sufficient for grammaticality (*Apa-n* '[She] brings [it]'). First- and second-person objects are indicated in verbal inflection: -*wa/-ma* indicates a first-person object, and -*yki*, -*sHQayki* and -*shunki* indicate second-person objects (*suya-wa-nki* 'you wait for me' *suya-shunki* 'She'll wait for you') (see §4.3.2.2 on actor-object reference).

7.3 Coordination

The enclitics -*pis*, -*taq*, and -*raq* can all be used to coordinate NPs (1–2), AdvPs and VPs (3); the case suffix -*wan* can be used with the first two of these three (4). -*pis*, -*taq*, and -*raq* generally imply relations of inclusion, contrast, or contradiction, respectively. Thus, -*pis* (inclusion) can generally be translated as 'and' or 'also' (1), (2).

(1) *walmipis qalipis* CH
walmi-pis   qali-pis
woman-ADD   man-ADD
'women **and** men[1]'

(2) *Uyqapaqpis kanmi alpakapaqpis kanmi llamapaqpis kanmi.* ACH
uyqa-paq-pis   ka-n-mi   alpaka-paq-pis   ka-n-mi   llama-paq-pis
sheep-ABL-ADD be-3-EVD   alpaca-ABL-ADD   be-3-EVD   llama-ABL-ADD
ka-n-mi
be-3-EVD
'There are [some] out of sheep [wool] **and** there are [some] out of alpaca [wool] **and** there are [some] out of llama [wool].'

---

[1] An anonymous reviewer suggests that a better gloss here would be 'not only women, but men, too.' This gloss would be consistent with an analysis of -*pis* as generally indicating contrast. In this case, I am directly translating the Spanish gloss suggested to me by my consultant.

7.3 Coordination

(3) *Ishpani**pis**chu puquchini**pis**chu.* AMV
ishpa-ni-pis-chu puqu-chi-ni-pis-chu
urinate-1-ADD-NEG ferment-CAUS-1-ADD-NEG
'I **neither** urinate **nor** ferment [urine].'

-wan is unmarked and can generally be translated as 'and' (4).

(4) *Mila**wan** Alicia**wan** Hilda trayaramun.* † AMV
Mila-wan Alicia-wan Hilda traya-ra-mu-n
Mila-INSTR Alicia-INSTR Hilda-INSTR arrive-URGT-CISL-3
'Hilda arrived with Mila **and** Alicia.'

-taq and *-raq* (contrast and contradiction) can both be translated 'but', 'while', 'whereas' and so on (5).

(5) *Wawanchikta idukanchik qillakunaqa mana**taq**mi.* ACH
wawa-nchik-ta iduka-nchik qilla-kuna-qa mana-taq-mi
baby-1PL-ACC educate-1PL lazy-PL-TOP no-SEQ-EVD
'We're educating our children; **whereas** the lazy ones aren't.'

Additional strategies employed for coordination in SYQ include (a) the employment of the indigenous coordinating particle *icha* 'or' (6) or any of the borrowed Spanish coordinators *i* 'and' (7), *u* 'or' (8), *piru* 'but' (9), or *ni* 'nor' (10) (*Sp. y, o, pero*, and *ni*) and (b) juxtaposition.

(6) *Mikuramanmantri kara **icha** aparamanmantri.* ACH
miku-ra-ma-n-man-tri ka-ra icha
eat-URGT-1.OBJ-3-COND-EVC be-PST or
apa-ra-ma-n-man-tri
bring-URGT-1.OBJ-3-COND-EVC
'It would have eaten me **or** it would have taken me away.'

(7) *Tushunchik i imahintam kriyinchik ñuqakunaqa **piru** chay ivanhilyukuna sabadistakunaqa mana kriyinchu.* CH
tushu-nchik i   imahin-ta-m   kriyi-nchik ñuqa-kuna-qa piru
dance-1PL and image-ACC-EVD believe-1PL 1-PL-TOP   but
chay ivanhilyu-kuna sabadista-kuna-qa   mana
DEM.D Evangelical-PL Seventh.Day.Adventist-PL-TOP no
kriyi-n-chu
believe-3-NEG
'We dance and believe in the saints **but** those Evangelists and Seventh Day Adventists don't believe.'

7 Syntax

(8) *Kaytaq ishkay puntraw **u** huk puntrawllam ruwa:.* ACH
kay-taq   ishkay puntraw u   huk puntraw-lla-m ruwa-:
DEM.P-SEQ two   day   or   one day-RSTR-EVD make-1
'I make this one in two days **or** just one day.'

(9) *"Ñañaypis, turiypis karqam **piru** wañukunña," nishpa, ¡rimay!* AMV
ñaña-y-pis, turi-y-pis   ka-rqa-m   **piru** wañu-ku-n-ña
sister-1-ADD brother-1-ADD be-PST-EVD but   die-REFL-3-DISC
ni-shpa   rima-y
say-SUBIS   talk-IMP
'Say, "I had a sister and a brother, **but** they died." Talk!'

(10) ***Ni** alpaka **ni** llama. Kanan manam trayamunchu.* ACH
ni   alpaka ni   llama kanan mana-m   traya-mu-n-chu
nor   alpaca nor llama now   no-EVD   arrive-CISL-3-NEG
'**Neither** alpacas **nor** llamas. They don't come here now.'

Juxtaposition is accomplished with the placement of the coordinated elements in sequence (11), (12).

(11) *Sibadakunata kargashpa, triguta rantishpa, sarata rantishpam purira.* ACH
sibada-kuna-ta   karga-shpa   trigu-ta   ranti-shpa   sara-ta
barley-PL-ACC   carry-SUBIS   wheat-ACC   buy-SUBIS   corn-ACC
ranti-shpa-m   puri-ra
buy-SUBIS-EVD   walk-PST
'They walked about, carrying barley and selling wheat **and** selling corn.'

(12) *Walmiqa talpunchik, allichanchikmi.* CH
walmi-qa   talpu-nchik   alli-cha-nchik-mi
woman-TOP   plant-1PL   good-FACT-1PL-EVD
'We women plant **and** fix up [the soil].'

When *-kuna* signals inclusion, it can be used to coordinate NP's (13) (see §3.4.2.1).

(13) *Chayman risa Marleni, Ayde, Vilma, Norma**kuna**.* AMV
chay-man   ri-sa   Marleni Ayde Vilma Norma-kuna
DEM.D-ALL go-NPST Marleni Ayde Vilma Norma-PL
'Marleni went there with Ayde, Vilma **and** Norma.'

The Spanish coordinators are widely employed. Coordinators indigenous to SYQ generally attach to both coordinated elements (14). The coordinators are not necessarily mutually exclusive.

(14) *Ullqush**pis** kayan, ¿aw? Chuqlluqupa**pis** yuraq**pis** puka**pis**.* AMV
 ullqush-pis ka-ya-n aw chuqlluqupa-pis
 ullqush.flowers-ADD be-PROG-3 yes chuqlluqupa.flowers-ADD
 yuraq-pis puka-pis
 white-ADD red-ADD
 'There are *ullqush* flowers, **too**, no? *Chuqlluqupa* flowers, **too** – white and red.'

7.4 Comparison

Comparisons of inequality are formed in SYQ with the borrowed particle *mas* ('more') in construction with the indigenous ablative case suffix, *-paq*, which attaches to the base of comparison (1), (2).

(1) *Huancayopaqa wak mashwaqa papa**paq**pis **mas**mi kwistan.* AMV
 Huancayo-pa-qa wak mashwa-qa papa-paq-pis mas-mi
 Huancayo-LOC-TOP DEM.D mashua-TOP potato-ABL-ADD more-EVD
 kwista-n
 cost-3
 'In Huancayo, mashua costs **more** than potatoes.'

(2) *Qayna puntraw**paq** **mas**mi.* AMV
 qayna puntraw-paq mas-mi
 previous day-ABL more-EVD
 'It's **more** than yesterday.'

mas and *minus* 'less', also borrowed from Spanish, may function as pronouns (3) and adjectives (4), and, when inflected with accusative *-ta*, as adverbs (5) as well.

(3) *Granadakunaktapis, armamintukunaktapis lantiyan **mas**ta.* CH
 granada-kuna-kta-pis armamintu-kuna-kta-pis lanti-ya-n mas-ta
 grenade-PL-ACC-ADD armaments-PL-ACC-ADD buy-PROG-3 more-ACC
 'Grenades and weapons and all, too – they're buying **more**.'

7 Syntax

(4) *Qayna wata pukum karqa. Chaymi **minus** pastupis karqa.* AMV
    qayna   wata   puku-m   ka-rqa   chay-mi   minus
    previous year   little-EVD be-PST   DEM.D-EVD less
    pastu-pis   *ka-rqa*
    pasture.grass-ADD   be-PST
    'Last year there was little [rain]. So there was **less** pasture grass.'

(5) ***Mastaqa** mashtakuyanmi.* LT
    mas-ta-qa   mashta-ku-ya-n-mi
    more-ACC-TOP   spread-REFL-PROG-3-EVD
    'It's spreading out **more**.'

Also borrowed from Spanish are the irregular *mihur* 'better' (6) and *piyur* 'worse' (7), (8).

(6) *Pularpaqpis **mas mihur**tam chayqa ayllukun.* ACH
    pular-paq-pis   mas   mihur-ta-m   chay-qa   ayllu-ku-n
    fleece-ABL-ADD   more better-ACC-EVD   DEM.D-TOP   wrap-REFL-3
    'It's **much better** than fleece – this wraps [you] up.'

(7) *Unayqa manayá iskwilaqa kasa. Unayqa analfabitullaya kayaq. Warmiqa **piyur**.* AMV
    unay-qa   mana-yá   iskwila-qa   ka-sa   unay-qa
    before-TOP   no-EMPH   school-TOP   be-NPST   before-TOP
    analfabitu-lla-ya   ka-ya-q   warmi-qa   piyur
    illiterate-RSTR-EMO   be-PROG-AG   woman-TOP   worse
    'Ah, before, they didn't have schools. Before, they were just illiterate. **Worse** [for the] women.'

(8) *Sapa putraw **piyur piyur**ñam kayani. Mastaña qayna puntraw mana puriyta wakchawta qatiyta atipanichu.* AMV
    sapa   putraw   piyur   piyur-ña-m   ka-ya-ni   mas-ta-ña
    every   day   worse   worse-DISC-EVD   be-PROG-1   more-ACC-DISC
    qayna   puntraw   mana   puri-y-ta   wakchaw-ta   qati-y-ta
    previous   day   no   walk-INF-ACC   sheep-ACC   follow-INF-ACC
    atipa-ni-chu
    be.able-1-NEG
    'Every day it's worse, I'm worse. More yesterday. I couldn't walk or take out my sheep.'

Comparisons of equality are formed with the borrowed particle *igwal* 'equal', 'same' in construction with the indigenous instrumental/comitative case suffix, *-wan*, which attaches to the base of comparison (9).

(9) *Runa**wan** ig**wal**triki vakaqa: nuybi mis.* AMV
    runa-wan   igwal-tr-iki   vaka-qa: nuybi mis
    person-INSTR equal-EVC-IKI   cow-TOP nine month
    'Cows are the **same** as people: [they gestate for] nine months.'

7.5 Negation

This section partially repeats §6.2.2 on *-chu*. Please consult that section for further discussion and glossed examples. In SYQ, negation is indicated by the enclitic *-chu* in combination with any of the particles *mana, ama,* or *ni* or with the enclitic suffix *-pis*. *-chu* attaches to the sentence fragment that is the focus of negation. In negative sentences, *-chu* generally co-occurs with *mana* 'not' (1), (2). *-chu* is also licensed by additive *-pis* (3), (4) as well as by *ni* 'nor' (5), (6).

(1) *Chaytri **mana** suyawarqa**chu**.* AMV
    chay-tri   mana suya-wa-rqa-chu
    DEM.D-EVC   no   wait-1.OBJ-PST-NEG
    'That's why she would**n't** have waited for me.'

(2) *Aa, **mana**ya kan**chu**. **Mana**ya bulayuq kan**chu**.* LT
    aa mana-ya   ka-n-chu mana-ya   bula-yuq ka-n-chu
    ah no-EMO   be-3-NEG no-EMO   ball-POSS be-3-NEG
    'Ah, there aren't any. **No one** has any balls.'

(3) *Kaspin**pis** kan**chu**.* AMV
    kaspi-n-pis   ka-n-chu
    stick-3-ADD   be-3-NEG
    'She **doesn't** have a stick.'

(4) *Manchakushpa tutas puñu:**chu**.* ACH
    mancha-ku-shpa   tuta-s   puñu-:-chu
    scare-REFL-SUBIS night-ADD sleep-1-NEG
    'Being scared, I **didn't** sleep at night.'

7 Syntax

(5) *Apuraw wañururqariki.* **Ni** *apanña***chu***.* AMV
apuraw wañu-ru-rqa-r-iki ni apa-n-ña-chu
quick die-URGT-PST-R-IKI nor bring-3-DISC-NEG
'He died quickly. They **didn't even** bring him [to the hospital].'

(6) ***Manam*** *wayta***chu** *ni pishqu***chu***.* AMV
manam wayta-chu ni pishqu-chu
no-EVD flower-NEG nor bird-NEG
'**Neither** a flower **nor** a bird.'

-chu co-occurs with *ama* in prohibitions (7) and imperatives (8), (9), as well as in injunctions (10).

(7) *¡****Ama*** *manchariy***chu***! ¡****Ama*** *qaway***chu***!* AMV
ama mancha-ri-y-chu ama qawa-y-chu
PROH scare-INCEP-IMP-NEG AMA look-IMP-CHU
'**Don't** be scared! **Don't** look!'

(8) *¡****Ama*** *kutimun***ki****chu!* *Qamqa isturbum kayanki.* AMV
ama kuti-mu-nki-chu qam-qa isturbu-m ka-ya-nki
PROH return-CISL-2-NEG you-TOP nuisance-EVD be-PROG-2
'**Don't** you come back! You're a hinderance.'

(9) *¡****Amam*** *nunka katraykanakushun***chu***!* LT
ama-m nunka katra-yka-naku-shun-chu
PROH-EVD never release-EXCEP-RECIP-1PL.FUT-NEG
'**Let's never** leave each other!'

(10) *¡****Ama*** *wañu***chun****chu!*[†] AMV
ama wañu-chun-chu
PROH die-INJUNC-NEG
'**Don't let** her die!'

-chu does not appear in subordinate clauses. In subordinate clauses negation is indicated with a negative particle alone (11–12).

(11) ***Mana** qali kaptinqa ñuqanchikpis taqllakta hapishpa qaluwanchik.* CH
mana qali ka-pti-n-qa ñuqanchik-pis taqlla-kta hapi-shpa
no man be-SUBDS-3-TOP we-ADD plow-ACC grab-SUBIS
qaluwa-nchik
turn.earth-1PL
'When there are **no** men, we grab the plow and turn the earth.'

(12) ***Mana** qatrachakunanpaq mandilchanta watachakun.* AMV
mana qatra-cha-ku-na-n-paq mandil-cha-n-ta wata-cha-ku-n
no dirty-FACT-REFL-NMLZ-3-PURP apron-DIM-3-ACC tie-DIM-REFL-3
'She's tying on her apron **so** she doesn't get dirty.'

7.6 Interrogation

This section partially repeats §3.2.3 and §6.2.2 on interrogative indefinites and -*chu*. Please consult those sections for further discussion and glossed examples.

Absolute (1) and disjunctive (2), (3) questions are formed with the enclitic -*chu*. When it functions to indicate interrogation, -*chu* attaches to the sentence fragment that is the focus of the interrogation (4).

(1) *¿Chuqamunkiman**chu**?* AMV
chuqa-mu-nki-man-chu
throw-CISL-2-COND-Q
'Can you throw?'

(2) *¿Maytaq chayqa? ¿Apurí**chu** Viñac**chu**?* CH
may-taq chay-qa Apurí-chu Viñac-chu
where-SEQ DEM.D-TOP Apurí-Q Viñac-Q
'Where is that? Apurí **or** Viñac?'

(3) *¿Maniyayan **icha** katrariyan**chu**?* AMV
maniya-ya-n icha katra-ri-ya-n-chu
tie.limbs-PROG-3 or release-INCEP-PROG-3-NEG
'Is she tying its feet **or** is she setting it loose?'

7 Syntax

(4) ¿Chaypa**chu** tumarqanki? AMV
chay-pa-chu tuma-rqa-nki
DEM.D-LOC-Q take-PST-2
'Did you take [pictures] there?'

In disjunctive questions, it generally attaches to each of the disjuncts (5).

(5) ¿Kanastapi**chu** baldipi**chu**? AMV
kanasta-pi-chu baldi-pi-chu
basket-LOC-Q bucket-LOC-Q
'In the basket **or** in the bucket?'

Questions that anticipate a negative answer are indicated by *manachu* (6).

(6) ¿**Mana**chu friqulniki? ¿Puchukarun**chu**? AMV
mana-chu friqul-ni-ki puchuka-ru-n-chu
no-Q bean-EUPH-2 finish-URGT-3-Q
'**Don't** you have any beans? They're finished?'

Manachu may also "soften" questions (7).

(7) ¿**Mana**chu chay wankuchata qawanki? AMV
mana-chu chay wanku-cha-ta qawa-nki
no-Q DEM.D mold-DIM-ACC see-2
'You **haven't** seen the little [cheese] mold?'

Manachu, like *aw* 'yes', may also be used in the formation of tag questions (8).

(8) Wak chimpapaqa yuraqyayan, ¿**mana**chu? ACH
wak chimpa-pa-qa yuraq-ya-ya-n mana-chu
DEM.D front-LOC-TOP white-INCH-PROG-3 no-Q
'There in front they're turning white, **aren't they**?'

Interrogative *-chu* does not appear in questions using interrogative pronouns (9), (10).

(9) *¿Pi haqtrirqa**chu**? AMV
pi haqtri-rqa-chu
who sneeze-PST-Q
'Who sneezed?'

7.6 Interrogation

(10) *¿*Pitaq qurquryara**chu**? *¿*Pitaq**chu** qurquryara? AMV
pi-taq   qurqurya-ra-chu pi-taq-chu qurqurya-ra
who-SEQ snore-PST-Q   who-SEQ-Q snore-PST
'Who snored?'

Constituent questions are formed with the interrogative-indefinite stems *pi* 'who', *ima* 'what', *imay* 'when', *may* 'where', *imayna* 'how', *mayqin* 'which', *imapaq* 'why', and *ayka* 'how much/many' (see Table 3.2). Interrogative pronouns are formed by suffixing the stem – generally but not obligatorily – with one of the enclitics *-taq*, *-raq*, *-mI*, *-shI* or *-trI* (11–13).

(11) *¿**Imay uraraq** chay kunihuqa kutimunqa yanapamananpaq?* SP
imay ura-raq   chay   kunihu-qa kuti-mu-nqa
when hour-CONT DEM.D rabbit-TOP return-CISL-3.FUT
yanapa-ma-na-n-paq
help-1.OBJ-NMLZ-3-PURP
'**What time** is that rabbit going to come back so he can help me?'

(12) *¿**Imatr** kakun?* LT
ima-tr   ka-ku-n
what-EVC be-REFL-3
'**What** could it be?'

(13) *Tapun, "¿**Imapaq** waqakunki, paluma?"* ACH
tapu-n ima-paq   waqa-ku-nki paluma
ask-3 what-PURP cry-REFL-2 dove
'He asked, "**Why** are you crying, dove?"'

Interrogative pronouns are suffixed with the case markers corresponding to the questioned element (14), (15).

(14) *¿Inti pasaruptin **imay urata** munayan?* AMV
inti pasa-ru-pti-n   imay ura-ta   muna-ya-n
sun pass-URGT-SUBDS-3 when hour-ACC want-PROG-3
'**What time** will it be when the sun sets?'

(15) *¿Traklamanchu liyan? ¿**Piwanyá**?* CH
trakla-man-chu li-ya-n   pi-wan-yá
field-ALL-Q go-PROG-3 who-INSTR-EMPH
'Is he going to the field? **With whom**?'

7 Syntax

The enclitic generally attaches to the final word in the interrogative phrase: when the interrogative pronoun completes the phrase, it attaches directly to the interrogative; in contrast, when the phrase includes an NP, the enclitic attaches to the NP (*pi-**paq-taq*** 'for whom' *ima qullqi-**tr*** 'what money') (16).

(16) *Chaypaqa wiñaraptinqa, ¿**ayka puntrawnintataq** riganchik?* AMV
chay-pa-qa   wiña-ra-pti-n-qa   ayka
DEM.D-LOC-TOP grow-UNINT-SUBDS-3-TOP how.many
puntraw-ni-n-ta-taq   riga-nchik
day-EUPH-3-ACC-SEQ   irrigate-1PL
'When it grows, at **how many** days do you water it?'

Enclitics are not employed in the interior of a subordinate clause but may attach to the final word in the clause (*¿Pi mishi-ta saru-ri-sa-n-ta-**taq** qawa-rqa-nki?* 'Who did you see trample the cat?').

7.7 Reflexives and reciprocals

This section partially repeats §4.4.2.3.5 and §4.4.2.3.8 on -*ku*, and -*na* Please consult those sections for further discussion and examples. SYQ employs the verb-verb derivational suffixes -*kU* and -*nakU* to indicate reflexive and reciprocal action, respectively.

-*kU* may indicate that the subject acts on himself/herself or that the subject of the verb is the object of the event referred to, i.e., -*kU* derives verbs with the meanings 'V one's self' (1), (2), and 'be Ved' (3), (4). Note that -*kU* is not restricted to forming reflexives and may also indicate pseudo-reflexives, middles, mediopassives and passives.

(1) *Kikinpis Campiona**ku**run.* AMV
kiki-n-pis   Campiona-ku-ru-n
self-3-ADD   poison.with.Campión-REFL-URGT-3
'They themselves **Campioned themselves** [took Campion rat poison].'

(2) *Kundina**ku**rushpa chay pashña kaqta trayaramun.* AMV
kundina-ku-ru-shpa   chay   pashña ka-q-ta
condemn-REFL-URGT-SUBIS DEM.D girl   be-AG-ACC
traya-ra-mu-n
arrive-URGT-CISL-3

7.7 Reflexives and reciprocals

'Condemning himself [turning into a zombie], he arrived at the girl's place.'

(3) *Manchakunchik runa wañuypaq kaptin.* AMV
    mancha-ku-nchik   runa   wañu-y-paq   ka-pti-n
    scare-REFL-1PL   person   die-INF-PURP   be-SUBDS-3
    'We **get scared** when people are about to die.'

(4) *Pampakurun chayshi.* AMV
    pampa-ku-ru-n   chay-shi
    bury-REFL-URGT-3   DEM.D-EVR
    'He **was buried**, they say.'

-*na* indicates that two or more actors act reflexively on each other, i.e., -*na* derives verbs with the meaning 'V each other' (5), (6).

(5) *Unayqa chay nishpa willanakun.* AMV
    unay-qa   chay   ni-shpa   willa-naku-n
    before-TOP   DEM.D   say-SUBIS   tell-RECIP-3
    'Formerly, saying that, we told **each other**.'

(6) *Valinaku:. 'Paqarin yanapamay u paqarin ñuqakta chaypaq talpashun qampaktañataq', ninaku:mi.* CH
    vali-naku-:   paqarin   yanapa-ma-y   u   paqarin   ñuqa-kta
    solicit-RECIP-1   tomorrow   help-1.OBJ-IMP   or   tomorrow   I-ACC
    chay-paq   talpa-shun   qam-pa-kta-ña-taq   ni-naku-:-mi
    DEM.D-ABL   plow-1PL.FUT   you-GEN-ACC-DISC-SEQ   say-RECIP-1-EVD
    'We solicit **each other**, "Help me tomorrow," or, "Tomorrow me and then we'll plant yours," we say to **each other**.'

-*na* is dependent and never appears independent of -*kU*. -*chinakU* derives verbs with the meaning 'cause each other to V' (7), (8).

(7) *Yuyarichinakuyan.* AMV
    yuya-ri-chi-naku-ya-n
    remember-INCEP-CAUS-RECIP-PROG-3
    'They're **making each other** remember.'

295

7 Syntax

(8) *Kukankunata tragunkunata muyuykachinakushpa.* AMV
    kuka-n-kuna-ta tragu-n-kuna-ta muyu-yka-chi-naku-shpa
    coca-3-PL-ACC   drink-3-PL-ACC   circle-EXCEP-CAUS-RECIP-SUBIS
    '**Making** their coca and liquor circulate **among themselves**.'

Preceding any of the derivational suffixes *-mu, -ykU*, or *-chi* or the inflectional suffix *-ma, -(chi-na)-kU* is realized as *-(chi-na)-ka*.

7.8 Equatives

This section partially repeats §4.2.3 on equative verbs Please consult that section for further discussion and examples. SYQ counts a single copulative verb, *ka-*. Like the English verb *be, ka-* has both copulative (1), (2) and existential (3), (4) interpretations. *ka-* is irregular: its third person singular present tense form, *ka-n*, never appears in equational statements, but only in existential statements. 'This is a llama' would be translated *Kay-qa llama-m*, while 'There are llamas' would be translated *Llama-qa ka-n-mi*.

(1) *Ñuqa-nchik fwirti kanchik patachita, matrkata, trakranchik lluqsiqta mikushpam.* AMV
    ñuqa-nchik   fwirti   ka-nchik   patachi-ta   matrka-ta
    I-1PL   strong   be-1PL   wheat.soup-ACC   ground.cereal.meal-ACC
    trakra-nchik   lluqsi-q-ta   miku-shpa-m
    field-1PL   come.out-AG-ACC   eat-SUBIS-EVD
    'We **are** strong because we eat what comes out of our fields – wheat soup and toasted grain.'

(2) *Qammi salvasyunniy kanki.* AMV
    qam-mi   salvasyun-ni-y   ka-nki
    you-EVD   salvation-EUPH-1   be-2
    'You **are** my salvation.'

(3) *Kanña piña turu.* AMV
    ka-n-ña   piña   turu
    be-3-DISC   angry   bull
    '**There are** mean bulls.'

(4) *Rantiqpis **kan**taqmi.* AMV
    ranti-q-pis   ka-n-taq-mi
    buy-AG-ADD be-3-SEQ-EVD
    '**There are** also buyers.'

Evidentials (*-mI*, *-shI* and *-trI*) often attach to the predicate in equational statements without *ka-n* (5), (6).

(5) *Vakay wira wira**m** matraypi puñushpa, allin pastuta mikushpam.* AMV
    vaka-y wira wira-m   matray-pi puñu-shpa   allin   pastu-ta
    cow-1   fat   fat-EVD cave-LOC   sleep-SUBIS good   pasture.grass-ACC
    miku-shpam
    eat-SUBIS
    'Sleeping in a cave and eating good pasture, my cow **is** really fat.'

(6) *Llutan**sh**iki.* LT
    llutan-sh-iki
    deformed-EVR-IKI
    '**They are** deformed, they say.'

The principal strategy in SYQ for constructing equational statements is to employ the continuous form *ka-ya-n* (7).

(7) *¿Alpakachu wak **kaya**n?* AMV
    alpaka-chu wak   ka-ya-n
    alpaca-Q   DEM.D   be-PROG-3
    '**Is that** alpaca [wool]?'

7.9 Possession

This section partially repeats §3.3.1 on possession. Please consult that section for further discussion and glossed examples. SYQ employs the suffixes of the nominal paradigm to indicate possession. These are the same in all dialects for all persons except the first person singular. Two of the five dialects – AMV and LT – follow the QII pattern, marking the first person singular with *-y*; three dialects – ACH, CH, and SP – follow the QI pattern marking it with *-:* (vowel length). The SYQ nominal suffixes, then, are: *-y* or *-:* (1P), *-Yki* (2P), *-n* (3P), *-nchik* (1PL) (1–5). Table 3.4 displays this paradigm.

297

7 Syntax

(1) *Wiqawniymi nanan.* AMV
    wiqaw-ni-y-mi   nana-n
    waist-EUPH-1-EVD hurt-3
    '**My** lower back hurts.'

(2) *Qusa:ta listaman trurarusa.* ACH
    qusa-:-ta   lista-man trura-ru-sa
    husband-1-ACC   list-ALL   put-URGT-NPST
    'They put **my** husband on the list.'

(3) *Kimsan wambraykikuna takikuyan.* AMV
    kimsa-n   wambra-yki-kuna   taki-ku-ya-n
    three-3   child-2-PL   sing-REFL-PROG-3
    'The three of **your** children are singing.'

(4) *¿Maypish wasinta lulayan?* CH
    may-pi-sh   wasi-n-ta   lula-ya-n
    where-LOC-EVR   house-3-ACC   make-PROG-3
    'Where [did she say she] is making **her** house?'

(5) *Chayna achka wambranchikta familyanchikkunata aparun.* ACH
    chayna   achka   wambra-nchik-ta   familya-nchik-kuna-ta   apa-ru-n
    thus   a.lot   child-1PL-ACC   family-1PL-PL-ACC   bring-URGT-3
    'So they took away lots of **our** children, our relatives.'

In the case of words ending in a consonant, -*ni* – semantically vacuous – precedes the person suffix (6).

(6) *Ganawninta qatikura qalay qalay.* ACH
    ganaw-ni-n-ta   qati-ku-ra   qalay   qalay
    cattle-EUPH-3-ACC   follow-REFL-PST   all   all
    'They herded **their** cattle, absolutely all.'

SYQ "have" constructions are formed SUBSTANTIVE-POSS *ka-* (7).

(7) *Mana **wambrayki kan**chu mana **qariyki kan**chu.* ACH
    mana   wambra-yki   ka-n-chu   mana   qari-yki   ka-n-chu
    no   child-2   be-3-NEG   no   man-2   be-3-NEG
    '**You** don't **have children, you** don't **have a husband**.'

In case a noun or pronoun referring to the possessor appears in the same clause, the noun or pronoun is case-marked genitive with either *-pa*, *-pi*, or *-paq* (8), (9).[1]

(8) *Duyñupa wallqanta ruwan.* AMV
   duyñu-pa   wallqa-n-ta   ruwa-n
   owner-GEN garland-3-ACC make-3
   'They make the owner **his** *wallqa* (garland).'

(9) *Asnuqa hatarishpash ripukun chay runapa wasinman.* SP
   asnu-qa   hatari-shpa-sh   ripu-ku-n   chay   runa-pa
   donkey-TOP get.up-SUBIS-EVR   go-REFL-3   DEM.D person-GEN
   wasi-n-man
   house-3-ALL
   'Geting up, the donkey went to the man's house.'

7.10 Topic

This section partially repeats §6.2.7 on *-qa*. Please consult that section for further discussion and glossed examples. SYQ uses the enclitic *-qa* to mark topic.

(1) *Ganawniyki**qa** achkam miranqa.* LT
   qanaw-ni-yki-qa   achka-m   mira-nqa
   cattle-EUPH-2-TOP a.lot-EVD increase-3.FUT
   'Your **cattle** are going to multiply a lot.'

(2) *Chaynam unay**qa** manam imapis kaptinqa.* AMV
   chayna-m   unay-qa   mana-m   ima-pis   ka-pti-n-qa
   thus-EVD   before-TOP   no-EVD   what-ADD   be-SUBDS-3-TOP
   'That's how it was **before** when there wasn't anything.'

---

[1] An anonymous reviewer points out that possessive constructions are formed differently in QI: "The possessed item takes a possessive suffix and the copula takes -pU followed by an object suffix that agrees with the person of the possessor. In other words, the verbal object suffix and the possessive suffix refer to the same person." The reviewer offers the following examples:
   Ishkay wa:ka-: ka-pa-ma-n. 'I have two cows.'
   Ishkay wa:ka-yki ka-pu-shu-nki. 'You have two cows.'
   Ishkay wa:ka-n ka-pu-n (or ka-n). 'She has two cows.'

7 Syntax

(3) *Kananqa mikun munasanchik qullqi kaptinqa.* AMV
kanan-qa miku-n muna-sa-nchik qullqi ka-pti-n-qa
now-TOP eat-3 want-PRF-1PL money be-SUBDS-3-TOP
'**Now** we eat whatever we want when there's money.'

(4) *Llaqtaykipaqa ¿tarpunkichu sibadata?* AMV
llaqta-yki-pa-qa tarpu-nki-chu sibada-ta
town-2-LOC-TOP plant-2-Q barley-ACC
'In **your town**, do you plant barley?'

7.11 Focus

In SYQ, it is the evidentials, -*mI*, -*shI*, and -*trI*, that, by virtue of their placement, indicate focus or comment. For example, in (1), the evidential attaches to the direct object, *shakash* 'guinea pig', and it is that element that is stressed: it is a **guinea pig** that you are going to butcher tomorrow. In (2) the evidential attaches to the temporal noun *paqarin* 'tomorrow', with the resulting interpretation: it is **tomorrow** that you are going to butcher a guinea pig. Evidentials never attach to the topic or subject. Topic and subject are, rather, marked with -*qa*, as is *qam* in (1) and (2).

(1) *Paqarin qamqa shakashtatr wañuchinki.* † AMV
paqarin qam-qa shakash-ta-tr wañu-chi-nki
tomorrow you-TOP guinea.pig-ACC-EVC die-CAUS-2
'Tomorrow you'll kill a **guinea pig**$_F$.'

(2) *Paqarintri qamqa shakashta wañuchinki.* † AMV
paqarin-tri qam-qa shakash-ta wañu-chi-nki
tomorrow-EVC you-TOP guinea.pig-ACC die-CAUS-2
'**Tomorrow**$_F$ you'll kill a guinea pig.'

7.12 Complementation (infinitive, agentive, indicative and subjunctive clauses)

This section partially repeats §3.4.1 on substantives derived from verbs Please consult that section for further discussion and glossed examples. SYQ forms infini-

7.12 Complementation (infinitive, agentive, indicative and subjunctive clauses)

tive complements with -*y* (1–3), purposive complements with -*q* (4), (5), indicative complements with -*sHa* (6–9), and subjunctive complements with -*na* (10). Infinitive complements often figure as the object of the verbs *muna-* 'want' (1), *atipa-* 'be able' (2), and *gusta-* 'like' (3). Indicative complements are common with the verbs *yatra-* 'know' (7), (8), *qunqa-* 'forget', *qawa* 'see' (9), and *uyari-* 'hear'. Note that infinitive complements are case-marked with accusative -*ta* and that -*q* purposive complements only occur with verbs of movement (-*na*-(POSS)-*paq*, being used for other verb types (11) (see §3.4.1.1)).

(1) ¿*Munankichu sintachiytaqa?* AMV
 muna-nki-chu sintachi-y-ta-qa
 want-2-Q   put.ribbons-INF-ACC-TOP
 'Do you **want to**? To piece their ears with ribbons?'

(2) *Lukuyarun runalla. Manam puñuyta atiparachu.* ACH
 luku-ya-ru-n   runa-lla   mana-m puñu-y-ta
 crazy-INCH-URGT-3 person-RSTR no-EVD sleep-INF-ACC
 atipa-ra-chu
 be.able-PST-NEG
 'My husband was going crazy. He **couldn't** sleep.'

(3) *Algunus turuqa runa waqrayta gustan.* AMV
 algunus turu-qa runa   waqra-y-ta   gusta-n
 some   bull-TOP person horn-INF-ACC like-3
 'Some bulls **like to** gore people.'

(4) *Misa lulaq shamun.* CH
 misa lula-q   shamu-n
 mass make-AG come-3
 'They **come** to hold mass.'

(5) *Pasaruptin qawaq hamuni.* AMV
 pasa-ru-pti-n   qawa-q hamu-ni
 pass-URGT-SUBDS-3 see-AG come-1
 'When that happened, I **came to see**.'

7 Syntax

(6) *Atipasantatriki ruwan.* ACH
atipa-sa-n-ta-tr-iki   ruwa-n
be.able-PRF-3-ACC-EVC-IKI make-3
'They do **what they can**.'

(7) *Ni maypa kasantapis yatra:chu. Waqaku:.* ACH
ni   may-pa   ka-sa-n-ta-pis   yatra-:-chu   waqa-ku-:
nor where-LOC be-PRF-3-ACC-ADD know-1-NEG cry-REFL-1
'I don't even know where **he is**. I cry.'

(8) *Kwirpu: yatran imapaq kayna pulisha:tapis.* CH
kwirpu-:   yatra-n ima-paq   kayna   puli-sha-:-ta-pis
body-1   know-3   what-PURP thus   walk-PRF-1-ACC-ADD
'My body knows **why I walk around** like this.'

(9) *Ñuqaqa wambran **qipikusan**ta qawarqanichu.* AMV
ñuqa-qa   wambra-n   qipi-ku-sa-n-ta   qawa-rqa-ni-chu
I-TOP   child-3   carry-REFL-PRF-3-ACC   see-PST-1-NEG
'I didn't see **that she carried** her baby.'

(10) *Puchuka**nan**ta munani.* AMV
puchuka-na-n-ta   muna-ni
finish-NMLZ-3-ACC   want-1
'I want **them to finish**.'

(11) *¡Uqi pulluyki qawachi**naypaq** kaynam ruwasay!* AMV
uqi   pullu-yki   qawa-chi-na-y-paq   kayna-m   ruwa-sa-y
grey shawl-2   see-CAUS-NMLZ-1-PURP   thus-EVD   make-PRF-1
'[Bring] your grey manta **so I can** show it to her. What I make is like this.'

7.13 Relativization

This section partially repeats §3.4.1 on substantives derived from verbs. Please consult that section for further discussion and glossed examples. SYQ forms relative clauses with the four deverbalizing suffixes: concretizing *-na* (1), agentive *-q* (2), perfective *-sHa* (3), and infinitive *-y* (4). As these structures are

7.13 Relativization

formally nouns, they are inflected with substantive suffixes, not verbal suffixes (*ranti-sa-yki* *ranti-sa-nki 'that you sold') (5).

(1) Asta **wañukunay puntraw**kamatriki chayna purishaq. LT
asta wañu-ku-na-y puntraw-kama-tr-iki chay-na puri-shaq
until die-REFL-NMLZ-1 day-LIM-EVC-IKI thus walk-1.FUT
'Until **the day I die**, I'm going to walk around like that.'

(2) **Rigakuq luna** trabahaya:. CH
riga-ku-q luna trabaha-ya-:
irrigate-REFL-AG person work-PROG-1
'**The people who water**, we're working.'

(3) Ñuqaqa manam rimayta yatrara:chu prufusurni: nimasanta. SP
ñuqa-qa mana-m rima-y-ta yatra-ra-:-chu prufusur-ni-:
I-TOP no-EVD talk-INF-ACC know-PST-1-NEG teacher-EUPH-1
ni-ma-sa-n-ta
say-1.OBJ-PRF-3-ACC
'I didn't know how to say **what my teacher said to me**.'

(4) Chay **vilakuy puntraw** simintiryupa. AMV
chay vila-ku-y puntraw simintiryu-pa
DEM.D candle-REFL-INF day cemetery-LOC
'**The day we lit candles** in the cemetery.'

(5) Rigalakullaq ka: **mana rantikusa:taqa**. ACH
rigala-ku-lla-q ka-: mana ranti-ku-sa-:-ta-qa
give.as.a.gift-REFL-RSTR-AG be-1 no buy-REFL-PRF-1-ACC-TOP
'I used to give away **what I didn't sell**.'

The inflected forms may be reinforced with possessive pronouns (6). *-sHa* may additionally form nouns referring to the location where (7 or time at which (8) an event E occurred. *-sHa* is realized as *-sa* in ACH (5), AMV (9) and SP (11) and as *-sha* in LT (10) and CH. Any substantive constituent – subject (2), object (9), or complement (1) – can be relativized. Nominalizing suffixes attach directly to the verb stem, with the exception that the person suffixes *-wa/-ma* (first person object) and *-sHu* (second person object) may intercede (12), (13).

7 Syntax

(6) *Qampa **rantikurasaykiyá** chay shakash.* AMV
    qam-pa   ranti-ku-ra-sa-yki-yá   chay   shakash
    you-GEN   buy-REFL-UNINT-PRF-2-EMPH   DEM.D   guinea.pig
    'That guinea pig **that you** sold.'

(7) *Chay fwirapi chay vilakuna rantikusan.* AMV
    chay   fwira-pi   chay   vila-kuna   ranti-ku-sa-n
    DEM.D   outside-LOC   DEM.D   candle-PL   buy-REFL-PRF-3
    'That's outside **where they sell** candles.'

(8) *Urqupa kayasanchikpis.* AMV
    urqu-pa   ka-ya-sa-nchik-pis
    hill-LOC   be-PROG-PRF-1PL-ADD
    '**When** we were in the mountains.'

(9) *Pampaykuni **frutachaykuna apasa**yta.* AMV
    pampa-yku-ni   fruta-cha-y-kuna   apa-sa-y-ta
    bury-EXCEP-1   fruit-DIM-1-PL   bring-PRF-1-ACC
    'I bury the fruit **that I bring**.'

(10) *Kalamina **rantishanchikkuna**.* LT
     kalamina   ranti-sha-nchik-kuna
     corrugated.iron   buy-PRF-1PL-PL
     'The tin roofing **that we bought**.'

(11) *Ni mayman yaykusay yatrakunchu.* SP
     ni   may-man   yayku-sa-y   yatra-ku-n-chu
     nor   where-ALL   enter-PRF-1   know-REFL-3-NEG
     'They didn't know even **where I had gone in**.'

(12) *Ampullakta inyikta**man**anchikpaq.* CH
     ampulla-kta   inyikta-ma-na-nchik-paq
     ampoule-ACC   inject-1.OBJ-NMLZ-1PL-PURP
     'Ampoules **to** inject us / **for** injecting us.'

(13) *Filupa paninqa nin, "Maqa**way**tam ñuqata pinsayan".* AMV
Filu-pa pani-n-qa ni-n maqa-wa-y-ta-m ñuqa-ta
Filu-GEN sister-3-TOP say-3 hit-1.OBJ-INF-ACC-EVD I-ACC
pinsa-ya-n
think-PROG-3
'Filomena's sister said, "He's thinking about hitting [wants to hit] **me**."'

7.14 Subordination

This section partially repeats §4.3.7 on subordination. Please consult that section for further discussion and glossed examples. SYQ counts three subordinating suffixes – *-pti, -shpa,* and *-shtin* – and one subordinating structure – *-na-*POSS-*kama*. Additionally, in combination with the purposive case suffix, *-paq, -na* forms subordinate clauses that indicate the purpose of the action expressed in the main clause (*qawa-na-y-paq* 'so I can see') (see §3.4.1.1).[2]

-pti is employed when the subjects of the main and subordinate clauses are different (*huk qawa-**pti**-n-qa, ñuqa-nchik qawa-nchik-chu* 'Although others see, we don't see') (1); *shpa* and *-shtin* are employed when the subjects of the two clauses are identical (*tushu-**shpa** wasi-ta kuti-mu-n* 'Dancing they return home') (2), (3). *-pti* generally indicates that the event of the subordinated clause began prior to that of the main clause but may also be employed in the case those events are simultaneous (*urkista-qa traya-mu-**pti**-n tushu-rqa-nchik* 'When the band arrived, we dansed').

(1) *Qaway**kuptin**qa sakristan wañurusa.* AMV
qawa-yku-pti-n-qa sakristan wañu-ru-sa
see-EXCEP-SUBDS-3-TOP sacristan die-URGT-NPST
'**When he** looked, the care-taker had died.'

(2) *Chitchitya**kushpa** rikullan kabrakunaqa.* LT
chitchitya-ku-shpa riku-lla-n kabra-kuna-qa
say.chit.chit-REFL-SUBIS go-RSTR-3 goat-PL-TOP
'"**Chit-chitting**," the goats just left.'

---

[2] An anonymous reviewer points out that all of the case-marked deverbal NPs – not just *-kama* and *-paq* – can form subordinate/adverbial clauses.

7 Syntax

(3) *Yantakunata qutu**shtin** lliptakunata kaña**kushtin**, hanay* ... AMV
yanta-kuna-ta   qutu-shtin   llipta-kuna-ta   kaña-ku-shtin
firewood-PL-ACC gather-SUBAVD ash-PL-ACC   burn-REFL-SUBADV
hanay
up.hill
'**Gathering** wood, **burning** ash, [we lived] up hill.'

-shpa generally indicates that the event of the subordinated clause is simultaneous with that of the main clause (*sapu-qa kurrkurrya-**shpa** kurri-ya-n* 'The frog is running going *kurr-kurr!*') (4) but may also be employed in case the subordinated event precedes the main-clause event (5).

(4) *Traguwan, kukawan tushuchi**shpa**llam kusichakuni.* AMV
tragu-wan   kuka-wan   tushu-chi-shpa-lla-m   kusicha-ku-ni
drink-INSTR coca-INSTR dance-CAUS-SUBIS-RSTR-EVD harvest-REFL-1
'With liquor and coca, **making** them dance, I harvest.'

(5) *Familyanchikta wañurichi**shpa**qa lliw partiyan.* SP
familya-nchik-ta wañu-ri-chi-shpa-qa   lliw parti-ya-n
family-1PL-ACC die-INCEP-CAUS-SUBIS-TOP all distribute-PROG-3
'**After** they killed our relatives, they distributed everything.'

-shtin is employed only when the main and subordinate clause events are simultaneous (*Awa-**shtin** miku-chi-ni wambra-y-ta* '(By) weaving, I feed my children') (6).

(6) *Yatrakunchik imaynapis maski waqaku**shtin**pis ... asiku**shtin**pis ... imaynapis.* ACH
yatra-ku-nchik   imayna-pis maski waqa-ku-shtin-pis
live-REFL-1PL   how-ADD   maski cry-REFL-SUBADV-ADD
asi-ku-shtin-pis   imayna-pis
laugh-REFL-SUBIS-ADD how-ADD
'We live however we can, although **we're crying** ... **laughing** ... however we can.'

-pti subordinates are suffixed with allocation suffixes (*tarpu-**pti**-nchik* 'when we plant') (7); *-shpa* and *-shtin* subordinates do not inflect for person or number (**tarpu-shpa-nchik*; **tarpu-shtin-yki*). Subordinate verbs inherit tense, aspect and conditionality specification from the main clause verb (*Ri-shpa qawa-y-man karqa* 'If I **would have** gone, I **would have** seen').

(7) *Manam pagawa**pti**kiqa manam wambraykiqa alliyanqachu.* LT
mana-m paga-wa-pti-ki-qa   mana-m wambra-yki-qa
no-EVD pay-1.OBJ-SUBDS-2-TOP   no-EVD child-2-TOP
alli-ya-nqa-chu
good-INCH-3.FUT-NEG
'**If** you don't pay **me**, your son isn't going to get better.'

Depending on the context, *-pti* and *-shpa* can be translated by 'when' (1), 'if' (8), 'because' (9), (10) 'although' (11) or with a gerund (2). *-shtin* is translated by a gerund only (3), (6).

(8) *Kuti**shpa**qa kutimushaq kimsa tawa watata.* AMV
kuti-shpa-qa   kuti-mu-shaq   kimsa tawa   wata-ta
return-SUBIS-TOP return-CISL-1.FUT three four   year-ACC
'**If** I come back, I'll come back in three or four years.'

(9) *Priykupaw puriyan siyrtumpatr warmin mal ka**ptin**.* AMV
priykupaw puri-ya-n   siyrtumpa-tr   warmi-n   mal ka-pti-n
worried   walk-PROG-3   certainly-EVC   woman.3   bad be-SUBDS-3
'Certainly, he'd be wandering around worried **because his wife** is sick.'

(10) *Payqa rikunñash warmin saqiru**ptin**.* AMV
pay-qa   ri-ku-n-ña-sh   warmi-n   saqi-ru-pti-n
he-TOP   go-REFL-3-DISC-EVR   woman-3   leave-URGT-SUBDS-3
'He left **because** his wife abandoned him, they say.'

(11) *Qullqita gana**shpas** bankuman ima trurakunki* ACH
qullqi-ta   gana-shpa-s   banku-man   ima   trura-ku-nki
money-ACC   earn-SUBIS-ADD   bank-ALL   what   put-REFL-2
'**Although** you earn money and save it in the bank'

-na-POSS-*kama* is limitative. It forms subordinate clauses indicating that the event referred to either is simultaneous with (12) or limits (13) the event referred to in the main clause (*puñu-**na**-y-**kama*** 'while I was sleeping'; *wañu-**na**-n-**kama*** 'until she died').

(12) *Mana vilakuranichu puñu**naykaman**.* AMV
mana   vila-ku-ra-ni-chu   puñu-na-y-kaman
no   watch.over-REFL-PST-1-NEG   sleep-NMLZ-1-LIM
'I didn't keep watch **while** I was sleeping.'

307

7 Syntax

(13) *Traki paltanchikpis pushllu**nankama** purinchik.* AMV
 traki palta-nchik-pis pushllu-na-n-kama puri-nchik
 foot soul-1PL-ADD blister-NMLZ-3-LIM walk-1PL
 'We walked **until** blisters formed on the souls of our feet.'

Appendix A: Analysis of the Southern Yauyos Quechua lexicon

What follows is an analysis of lexical differences among the five dialects. This analysis is excerpted from the introduction to the lexicon that accompanies this volume.

The lexicon counts 2537 Quechua words. Most were gleaned from glossed recordings collected in the eleven districts over the course of four years, 2010–2014; additional terms were identified by eliciting cognate or correlate terms for various items in Cerrón-Palomino (1994)'s unified dictionary of Southern Quechua as well as his dictionary of Junín-Huanca Quechua (Cerrón-Palomino (1976b)). The recordings and annotated transcriptions have been archived by The Language Archive of the Dokumentation Bedrohter Sprachen/Documentation of Endangered Languages (DoBeS) archive at the Max Planck Institute (http://corpus1.mpi.nl/ds/imdi_browser/?openpath=MPI1052935%23) and the Archive of the Indigenous Languages of Latin America (AILLA) at the University of Texas at Austin (http://www.ailla.utexas.org/site/welcome.html). All documents – including the unformatted .xml lexical database – can be consulted via those institutions' web sites. All terms were reviewed with at least two speakers of each dialect: Benedicta Lázaro and Martina Reynoso (AH); Mila Chávez, Delfina Chullunkuy, Esther Madueño, Hilda Quispe, and Celia Rojas (MV); Iris Barrosa, Gloria Cuevas, Senaida Oré, Hipólita Santos, and Erlinda Vicente, (CH); Ninfa Flores and Sofía Vicente (LT); and Santa Ayllu, Elvira Huamán, Sofía Huamán, and Maximina P.

As stated in the Introduction, Yauyos is located on the border between the two large, contiguous zones where languages belonging to the two great branches of the Quechua language family are spoken: the "Quechua I" (Torero) or "Quechua B" (Parker) languages are spoken in the regions immediately to the north; the "Quechua II" or "Quechua A" languages, in the regions immediately to the south. Both grammatically and lexically, the dialects of southern Yauyos share traits with both the QI and QII languages. Critically, however, the dialects which sort with the the QI languages grammatically do not necessarily also sort with them lexically; nor do the dialects which sort with the QII languages grammatically necessarily sort with them lexically. That is, grammatically and lexically, the dialects cleave along distinct lines.

Grammatically, two of the five dialects – those of Madeán-Viñac and Lincha-Tana – sort together, as these, like the QII languages, indicate the first-person subject with *-ni*, the first-person possessor with *-y*, and first-person object with *-wa*. The remaining three – Azángaro-Huangáscar, Cacra-Hongos, and San Pedro – sort together, as these, like the QI languages, indicate the first person subject and possessor with vowel length and the first-person object with *-ma*.[1]

Lexically, however, the dialects cleave along different lines, lines defined not by morphology but by geography. Lexically, the two more northern dialects – the "QI" CH and the "QII" LT – sort together while the three more southern dialects – the "QI" AH and SP together with the "QII" MV – sort together. Below, I detail an analysis of the lexicon that I performed using a subset of 2551 terms. The dialects generally agree in the terms they use to name the same referent: I could identify only 37 instances in which the dialects employed words of different roots. In 32 of these instances the dialects cleaved along north-south lines and in 22 of the relevant 28 cases for which correlate terms could be identified from Junín-Huanca Quechua and Ayacucho Quechua (the former a "QI" language spoken immediately to the north of Yauyos, the second, a "QII" language spoken very nearby, to the south), the northern dialects employed the term used in Junín-Huanca, while the southern dialects employed the term used in Ayacucho.[2]

This does not mean that the dialects employed identical terms in all the remaining 2387 cases (subtracting 75 for 36 pairs and one triplet). Far from it. All dialects employed identical terms in only 1603 instances. Included among these are all but 20 of the 522 words in the corpus borrowed from Spanish (examples

---

[1] Yauyos counts three additional dialects, spoken in the districts of Alis and Tomas; Huancaya and Vitis; and Laraos, all located in the north of the province. The lexicon, like the grammar, makes abstraction of these dialects.

[2] No pair was counted more than once. The lexicon includes both roots and derived terms. Thus both the pairs *sumaq* (MV, AH, SP) and *tuki* (CH, LT) 'pretty' and *sumaq-lla* (MV, AH, SP) and *tuki-lla* (CH, LT) 'nicely' appear in the corpus. Only the root pair, *sumaq* ~ *tuki*, was entered in the catalogue of those cases where dialects differed in root terms employed. There were 116 cases of this type. These were excluded from the count and account given here. Examples are given immediately below.

 qawa- (MV, AH, SP) ~ *rika-* (CH, LT) 'see'
  → *qawa-chi-* ~ *rika-chi-* 'show',' make and offering'
 chakwash (MV, AH, SP) ~ *paya* (CH, LT) 'old woman'
  → *chakwash-ya-* ~ *paya-ya-* 'become an old woman'
 qishta (MV, AH, SP, LT) ~ *tunta* (CH, LT) 'nest'
  → *qishta-cha-* ~ *tunta-cha-* 'build a nest'

in 1.[3] Once terms of Spanish origin are eliminated, we are left with a corpus of 1940 items. All dialects agreed perfectly in their realizations of these items in 1081 cases (56%) (examples in 2). The remaining 755 items are accounted for as follows. In 154 cases a Quechua-origin term was realized identically in all dialects in which it was attested but remained unattested in one or more dialects, as in 3. Given the current state of the language – classified as "moribund" in the 2013 edition of Ethnologue Lewis, Simons & Fennig (2015)() – nothing can be concluded from these gaps, neither that the dialects originally employed the same term, nor that it was necessarily different. In 630 cases, the dialects employed terms of the same root but with different realizations, as in 4. Included among these are 236 cases where these differences can be attributed to differences in the phonology between Cacra-Hongos and the other four dialects: the realization of *[r] as [l], for example (151 cases, examples in 5) or */s/ as [h] (45 cases, examples in 6). Also counted among these 745 cases are terms affected by metathesis and other phonological processes (vowel lowering (/i/), velarization (/q/), depalatization (/sh/), and gliding (/y/), among others) (207 cases, examples in 7 and 8). Finally, the sample counts terms affected by variation in verbal or nominal morphology (62 cases, examples in 9). Principal among these are instances of words derived with past participles – formed with -*sha* in the north and -*sa* in the south – and others that also differ by virtue of the fronting of /sh/ (40 cases, examples in 10 and 11).

1. Spanish-origin terms identical in all dialects

tuma-	(ALL)	(*Sp. tomar*)	'take'
kida-	(ALL)	(*Sp. quedar*)	'stay'
papil	(ALL)	(*Sp. papel*)	'paper'

---

[3] Virtually any term of Spanish origin in current use in the area may be borrowed into SYQ. I have included Spanish- origin words in the lexicon just in case they were either 1 of extremely high use (*tuma-* 'take', 'drink' (*Sp. tomar* 'take', 'drink')); 2 had no corresponding indigenous term (in contemporary usage) (*matansya* 'massacre' (*Sp. matanza* 'massacre')); or 3 had altered substantially either in their pronunciation or denotation (*firfanu* 'orphan' (*Sp. huérfano* 'orphan'); *baliya-* 'shoot' (*Sp. bala* 'bullet')).

A Analysis of the Southern Yauyos Quechua lexicon

2. Quechua-origin terms identical in all dialects

sapi	(ALL)	'root'
sasa	(ALL)	'hard'
yanapa-	(ALL)	'help'
ishpay	(ALL)	'urine'
ayqi-	(ALL)	'escape'
chaqchu-	(ALL)	'sprinkle, scatter'

3. Terms with no Quechua-language correlate in one or more of the dialects

Quechua-origin term		Spanish-origin term		Gloss
chaskay	(MV, AH, SP)	*lusiru* (*Sp. lucero*)	(CH, LT)	'morning star'
tapsipa-	(MV, AH, SP)	*balansya* (*Sp. balancear*)	(CH, LT)	'rock'
uya	(MV, AH, SP)	*kara* (*Sp. cara*)	(CH, LT)	'face'

4. Terms of the same root but with different realizations in different dialects

warmi	(MV, AH, SP)	~ *walmi*	(LT, CH)	'woman'
sapa	(MV, AH, SP)	~ *hapa*	(LT, CH)	'alone'
aqsa	(MV, AH)	~ *asqa*	(SP)	'bitter [potato]'
qaracha	(MV, AH, SP, CH)	~ *karacha*	(LT)	'scabies', 'mange'
*alli-**paq***	(MV, AH, SP)	~ *alli-**lla***	(LT, CH)	'slowly'
*kitra-**sa***	(MV, AH, SP)	~ *kitra-**sha***	(LT, CH)	'open'

5. Terms where *[r] is realized as [l] in CH

raki-	→ [*laki*]	'separate'
quru	→ [*qolu*]	'mutilated'
trura-	→ [*ĉula*]	'put'

6. Terms where */s/ is realized as [h] in CH

/*sara*/	→ [*hala*]	'corn'
/*sama*/	→ [*hama*]	'rest'
/*sati*/	→ [*hati*]	'insert'

7. Terms affected by metathesis

chaksa-	(MV, AH, CH) ~ *chaska-*		(LT, SP)	'air out'
shanta-	(AH, CH, SP) ~ *tansha-*		(MV, LT)	'choke'
shipti-	(MV, AH, LT) ~ *tipshi-*		(CH, SP)	'pinch'

8. Terms affected by other phonological processes

allpi (MV, AH, LT, CH)	~ *allpa* (SP)	'dust', 'dirt'	(vowel lowering)
chillqi (MV, AH, LT, SP)	~ *chillki* (CH)	'bud'	(develarization)
malshu (LT, CH)	~ *mayshu* (MV, AH, SP)	'breakfast'	(gliding)

9. Terms affected by variation in verbal or nominal morphology

utrku-	(MV, AH, LT, SP) ~ *utr'ku-cha-*	(CH)	'dig a hole'
tardi-ku	(MV AH, CH, LT) ~ *tardi-ya-*	(SP)	'get late'
aytri-na	(MV, CH) ~ *aytri-ku*	(AH, LT)	'stick for stirring'

10. Terms derived with past participles

paki-sa	(MV, AH, SP) ~ *paki-sha*	(CH, LT)	'broken'
punki-sa	(MV, AH, SP) ~ *punki-sha*	(CH, LT)	'swolen'
yaku-na-sa	(MV, AH, SP) ~ *yaku-na-sha*	(CH, LT)	'thirsty'

11. Terms that differ by the exchange s/sh

suytu	(MV, AH, SP)	~ *shuytu*	(CH, LT)	'oval', 'oblong'
siqsi-	(MV, AH, SP)	~ *shiqshi-*	(CH, LT)	'itch'
wiswi	(MV, AH, SP CH)	~ *wishwi*	(LT)	'greasy'

A clear pattern emerges both with regard to the cases where the dialects employed terms of different roots and those in which they varied in their realizations of the same root term. In 32 of the 37 instances in which root terms differed, the dialects cleaved along north-south lines, with the northern dialects – CH and LT[4] – sorting together and the southern dialects – MV, AH, and SP – sorting together, as in 1.

---

[4] With the exception of two and a half cases: one where LT sorts with the southern dialects ('make an offering'), one where LT recorded no Quechua-origin term ('bitter'), and one where Cacra and Hongos split, Cacra alone recording a second term ('rain').

A Analysis of the Southern Yauyos Quechua lexicon

In four of the five remaining instances San Pedro supplied the outstanding term. In 32 of the 37 cases, cognate terms could be identified for Junín and Ayacucho (Yauyos' "QI" (northern) and "QII" (southern) neighbors, respectively). In 23 of the relevant 28 of these 32 cases, the northern dialects – "QI" CH and "QII" LT – employed the term used in Junín, while the southern dialects – the "QI" AH and SP and the "QII" MV – employed the term used in Ayacucho, as in 2.[5]

The full list appears in Table A.1.

1. Root terms varying along north-south lines

South MV, AH, SP		North LT, CH		Gloss
chumpi	(MV, AH, SP)	watrakuq	(CH, LT)	'sash'
anu-	(MV, AH, SP)	wasqi-	(CH, LT)	'wean'
sumaq	(MV, AH, SP)	tuki	(CH, LT)	'pretty'

2. North/south differences in root terms alligning with Junín and Ayacucho.

South MV, AH, SP	North LT, CH	Ayacucho	Junín	Gloss
puyu	pukatay	puyu	pukatay	'cloud', 'fog'
qishTa	tunta	qisha	tunta	'nest'
rakta	tita	rakta	tita	'thick'

3. Synonyms employed in southern but not northern dialects

Employed in all		Employed just in the south		Gloss
wallwa-	(ALL)	uqlla(n)cha-	(MV, AH, SP)	'carry under the arm'
patrya-	(ALL)	tuqya-	(MV, AH, SP)	'explode'
alalaya-	(ALL)	chiriya-	(MV, AH, SP)	'be cold'

I have taken it as my task here only to present the data; I leave it to other scholars to come to their own conclusions. The raw data are available in the form of an .xml document that can be accessed by all via the DoBeS and AILLA websites.

---

[5] In at least two of these 32 cases, the Junín term had a cognate correlate in Jaqaru, an Aymaran language spoken in Tupe, Cacra's closest neighbor to the north. The terms are *kallwi-* 'cultivate' and *liklachiku* 'underarm'.

Table A.1: Differences among dialects in root terms used to refer to the same referent

gloss	root$_A$	dialect	root$_B$	dialect	Ayacucho root	Junín root
'old man'	machu	MV, AH, SP	awkish	LT, CH	machu	awkish
'old woman'	chakwash	MV, AH, SP	paya	LT, CH	chakwash	paya
'nettle'	llupa/itana	MV, AH, SP	chalka	LT, CH	itana	itana
'germinate'	shinshi-	MV, AH, SP	chilQi	LT, CH	NC	?
'close eyes, blink'	qimchiku-	MV, AH, SP	chipupa-	LT, CH	chipu- (close hand) qimchikatraa-	qimlla-/ qimchi-
'sash'	chumpi	MV, SP	watraku	LT, CH	chumpi	watrakuq
'sneeze'	hachiwsa-	MV, AH, CH, LT	haqchu-	SP	hachi-	haqchwsa-, achiwyaa-
'cultivate, hoe'	hallma-	MV, AH, SP	kallwa-	LT, CH	hallma-	kallwa-
'scratch'	rachka-	MV, AH, SP	hata-	LT, CH	hata-	rachka-
'add fuel'	lawka-	MV, AH, CH, LT	huya-	SP	?	?
'sickly'	iqu	MV, AH, SP	latru	LT, CH	iqu	?
'thorn, bramle'	kichka	MV, AH, SP	kasha	LT, CH	kichka	kasha
'stick'	kaspi	MV, AH, SP	shukshu	LT, CH	kaspi	shukshu
'splinter'	killwi	MV, AH	qawa/ waqcha	LT, CH/SP	killwi	waqcha ('log', 'timber')
'make an offering return'	qawachi-	MV, AH, LT	likachi-	CH	qawa- ('see')	lika- ('see')
'underarm', 'armpit'	wallwachuku	MV, AH, SP	liklachku	LT, CH	wallwa	liklachiku
'all'	lliw	MV, AH, SP	limpu	LT, CH	lliw	lliw
'avalanche', 'mudslide'	lluqlla	MV, AH, SP	tuñiy	ALL	tuñi- ('tumble down')	lluqlla ('waterfall')
'coagulate'	tika-	MV, AH, CH, LT	marki-	SP	tikaya-	tika- ('make adobe bricks')
'knee'	muqu	MV, AH, SP	qunqur	ALL	muqu, qunqura- ('kneel')	muqu (joint)
'comb' (v.)	ñaqcha-	ALL	qachaku-	LT, CH	ñaqcha-	ñaqcha-
'cloud', 'fog'	puyu	MV, AH, SP	pukutay	LT, CH	puyu	pukutay
thorn bush variety	ulanki	MV, AH, SP	qaparara	LT, CH	?	?
'sick'	unqu	MV, AH, SP	qisha	CH	unqu	qishya
'nest'	qisTa	MV, AH, SP	tunta	LT, CH	qisTa	qisha
'thick'	rakta	MV, AH, SP	tita	LT, CH	rakta	tita
'snow', 'sleet'	riti	MV, AH, SP	rasu	LT, CH	riti	lasu
'eaten by birds'	shuqli	MV, AH, CH, LT	wishlu	SP	?	?
'beautiful'	sumaq	MV, AH, SP	tuki	LT, CH	sumaq	tuki
'sheep'	uyqa	MV, AH, SP	usha	LT, CH	NC	(uwish)
'roll'	sinku-	ALL	trinta-	LT, CH	NC	NC
'explode'	tuqya-	MV, AH, SP	patra-	ALL	tuqya-	patra-
'bitter' [potato]	aqsa	MV, AH, SP	qatqi	CH	qatqi	?
'rain'	para-	MV, AH, SP, CH	tamya-	Cacra	para-	tamya-

NC= not cognate; ?= not found

Appendix B: Further analysis of evidential modifiers

This appendix presents a further analysis of the interpretation of propositions under the scope of the various permutations of the direct and the conjectural evidentials – *-mI* and *-trI* – in combination with the three evidential modifiers – *-ø*, *-ik*, and *-iki*.

B.1 The EM's and the interpretation of propositions under direct *-mI*

In the case of the direct *-mI*, all three forms, *-mI-ø*, *-m-ik*, and *m-iki*, indicate that the speaker has evidence from personal experience for the proposition immediately under the scope of the evidential. The *-ik* and *-iki* forms then indicate increases in the strength of that evidence, generally that it is increasingly immediate or definitive. For example, consultants explain, with *wañu-rqa-ø* [die-PST-3] 'died', a speaker might use *-mI-ø* if she had seen the corpse, while she would use *-m-iki* if she had actually been present when the person died. Or with *para-ya-n* [rain-PROG-3] 'it's raining', a speaker might use *-mI-ø* if she were observing the rain from inside through a window, while she would use *-m-iki* if she were actually standing under the rain. (1) and (2) give naturally-occurring *-m-iki* examples. In (1) the speaker reports her girlhood experience working as a shepherdess in the *puna* (high, cold, wet pasture grounds). What would run out on her was her matches. In (2) the speaker reports her experience with the Shining Path, an armed Maoist group that terrorized the region in the 1980's with its robberies, kidnappings and public executions. The fight she refers to is the battle between the Shining Path and the government *Sinchis* (commandos). In both examples, the speakers are reporting events they experienced with painful immediacy and with regard to which there are no more authoritative sources than themselves.

B Further analysis of evidential modifiers

(1) *Ariyá urqupaqa puchukapakunchik**miki**.* AMV
 ari-yá urqu-pa-qa puchuka-paku-nchik-m-iki
 yes-EMPH hill-LOC-TOP finish-MUTBEN-1PL-EVD-IKI
 'Yes, in the hills **we ran out**.'

(2) *Huk visislla piliyara chaypaq chinkakuraña**miki**.* AMV
 huk visis-lla piliya-ra chay-paq chinka-ku-ra-ña-m-iki
 one times-RSTR fight-PST DEM.D-ABL lose-REFL-PST-DISC-EVD-IKI
 'They fought just once and then **they disappeared**.'

In addition to indicating increases in evidence strength, *-ik* and *-iki*, in combination with *-mI*, generally correspond to increases in strength of assertion. A *-m-ik* assertion is interpreted as stronger than a *-mI-ø* assertion; a *-m-iki* assertion as stronger still. In Spanish, *-mI-ø* generally has no reflex in translation. More than anything else, it serves to mark comment or focus (see §7.11) or else to stand in for the copular verb *ka*, defective in the third-person present tense (see §4.2.3). In contrast, *-m-iki* does have a reflex in Spanish: it translates with an emphatic, either *pues* 'then' or *sí* 'yes'. So, *quni-**m**-ø* [warm-EVD-ø] receives the Spanish translation '*es caliente*' 'it's warm'; in contrast, *quni-**m**-iki* [warm-EVD-KI] receives the translations, '*es caliente, pues*' 'it's warm, then' or '*sí, es caliente*' 'yes, it's warm'. Example (3) is taken from a story. An old lady has sent two boys for wood – "so I can cook you a nice supper," she said. Two doves appear at the wood pile to warn the boys. *Miku-shunki-**m**-**iki*** 'she's going to eat you', they warn. Using the *-iki* form, the birds make the strongest assertion they can. They need to convince the boys that they are indeed in trouble – their very lives are in danger.

(3) *Kananqa wirayaykachishunki mikushunki**miki**.* AMV
 kanan-qa wira-ya-yka-chi-shunki miku-shunki-mi-ki.
 now-TOP fat-INCH-EXCEP-CAUS-3>2.FUT eat-3>2.FUT-EVD-IKI
 'Now she's going to fatten you up and **eat you**!'

In those cases in which *-mI* takes scope over universal-deontic-modal or future-tense verbs, *-k* and *-ki* do not generally indicate an increase in evidence strength; rather, they indicate increasingly strong obligations and increasingly immediate futures, respectively. So, for example, under the scope of *-mI-ø*, *yanapa-na-y* [help-NMLZ-1] receives a weak universal deontic interpretation, 'I ought to help'. In contrast, under the scope of *-m-ik* or *-m-iki*, the same phrase receives increasingly strong universal interpretations, on the order of 'I have to help' and 'I must

B.2 The EM's and the interpretation of propositions under conjectural -trI

help', respectively. Under the scope of *-mI-ø*, the phrase is understood as something like a strong suggestion, while under *-m-iki*, it is understood as a more urgent obligation. That is, here, *-ik* and *-iki* seem to do something like increase the degree of modal force, turning a weak universal modal into a strong one. This is the case, too, where *-mI* takes scope over future-tense verbs. For example, explain consultants, in the case of the future-tense *ri-shaq* [go-1.FUT] 'I will go', a speaker might use *-mI-ø* if she were going to go at some unspecified, possibly very distant future time. In contrast, she might use *-m-ik* if her going were imminent, and *-m-iki* if she were already on her way. The speaker of (4), for example, urgently needed to water her garden and had been on her way to do just that when she got caught up in the conversation. When she uttered (4) she was, in fact, already in motion.

(4) *Rishaq yakuta**miki** qawashaq.* AMV
 ri-shaq yaku-ta-mi-ki qawa-mu-shaq
 go-1.FUT water-ACC-EVD-IKI look-CISL-1.FUT
 'I'm **going to** go. I'm **going to** take care of the water now.'

B.2 The EM's and the interpretation of propositions under conjectural *-trI*

In the case of the conjectural *-trI*, all three forms, *-trI-ø*, *-tri-k*, and *-tri-ki*, indicate that the speaker has either direct or reportative evidence for a set of propositions, *P*, and that the speaker is conjecturing from *P* to *p*, the proposition immediately under the scope of the evidential. The *-ik* and *-iki* forms then indicate increases in the strength of the speaker's evidence and generally correspond to increases in certainty of conjecture.

In case a verb under its scope is not already modalized or not already specified for modal force or conversational base by virtue of its morphology, *-trI* assigns the values [universal] and [epistemic], for force and base, respectively. So, for example, the progressive present-tense *kama-ta awa-ya-n* [blanket-ACC weave-PROG-3] 'is weaving a blanket' and the simple past-tense *wañu-rqa-ø* [die-PST-3] 'died', both unmodalized and therefore necessarily not specified for either modal force or conversational base, receive universal epistemic interpretations under the scope of *-trI*: 'he would/must be weaving a blanket' and 'he would/must have died', respectively. Speakers bilingual in Yauyos and Spanish consistently translate and simple-present- and simple-past-tense verbs under the scope of

B Further analysis of evidential modifiers

-trI with the future and future perfect, respectively. The *awa-ya-n* 'is weaving' and *wañu-rqa-ø* 'died' of the examples immediately above are translated *estará tejiendo* and *habrá muerto*, respectively. In English, 'would' and 'must' will have to do the job.

Present-tense conditional verbs in SYQ may receive at least existential ability, circumstantial, deontic, epistemic and teleological interpretations. Past-tense conditional verbs may, in addition to these, also receive universal deontic and epistemic interpretations. That is, present-tense conditionals are specified for modal force [existential], but not modal base, while past-tense conditionals are specified for neither force nor base. *-trI* restricts the interpretation of conditionals, generally excluding all but epistemic readings. In the case of past-tense conditionals, it generally excludes all but universal readings, as well. For example, although the present-tense conditional of (1), *saya-ru-chuwan* 'we could stand around', is normally five-ways ambiguous, under the scope of *-trI*, only the existential epistemic reading available: 'it could happen that we stand around'. Similarly, although the past-tense conditional of (2), *miku-ra-ma-n-man ka-rqa-ø* 'could/would/should/might have eaten me', is normally seven-ways ambiguous, under the scope of *-trI*, only the universal epistemic reading is available: 'the Devil would necessarily have eaten me'. The context for (1) – a discussion of women and alcohol – supports the epistemic reading. The speaker, a woman who in her eighty-odd years had never taken alcohol, was speculating on what would happen if women were to drink. Her conclusion: it's possible we would stand around naked, going crazy.

(1) *Qalapis sayaruchuwan-**tri** lukuyarishpaqa.* AMV
     qala-pis   saya-ru-chuwan-tri   luku-ya-ri-shpa-qa
     naked-ADD   stand-URGT-1PL.COND-EVC   crazy-INCH-INCEP-SUBIS-TOP
     'We could also stand around naked, going crazy.'

(2) *Mana chay kaptinqa mikuramanman**tri** karqa chay dimunyukuna.* AMV
     mana chay   ka-pti-n-qa   miku-ra-ma-n-man-**tri**   ka-rqa
     no   DEM.D   be-SUBDS-3-TOP   eat-URGT-1.OBJ-3-COND-EVC   be-PST
     chay   dimunyu-kuna
     DEM.D   devil-PL
     'If not for that, the Devil **might have** eaten me.'

If it is the case, as Copley (2009) argue, and Matthewson, Rullmann & Davis (2005) that the future tense is a modal specified for both force, [universal], and

B.2 The EM's and the interpretation of propositions under conjectural -trI

base, [metaphysical] or [circumstantial], *-trI* should have no effect on the interpretation of mode in the case of future-tense verbs. This is indeed the case. For example, both the *tiya-pa-ru-wa-nga* of (3) and *ashna-ku-lla-shaq* of (4) receive exactly the interpretations they would have were they not under the scope of *-trI*: 'they will accompany me sitting' and 'I'm going to stink', respectively. This does not mean that *-trI-ø/ik/iki* has no effect on the interpretation of future-tense verbs, however. Although it leaves TAM interpretation unaffected, *-trI* continues to indicate that the proposition under its scope is a conjecture. And *-ik* and *-iki*, as they do in conjunction with *-mI*, indicate increasingly immediate or certain futures. So, although the TAM interpretations of (3)'s *tiya-pa-ru-wa-nga* 'will accompany me sitting' and (4)'s *ashna-ku-lla-shaq* 'I'm going to stink' are unchanged under the scope of *-trI*, the *-ik* of the first and the *-iki* of the second signal immediate and certain futures, respectively. In (3), that future was about an hour away: it was 6 o'clock and the those who were to accompany the speaker were expected at 7:00 for a healing ceremony. The context for (4), too, was a healing ceremony. The speaker was referring to the upcoming part of the ceremony in which she would have to wash with putrid urine – certain to make anyone stink!

(3) *Kukachankunata aparuptiyqa tiyaparuwanqa**trik***. AMV
     kuka-cha-n-kuna-ta   apa-ru-pti-y-qa
     coca-DIM-3-PL-ACC   bring-URGT-SUBDS-1-TOP
     tiya-pa-ru-wa-nqa-tri-k
     sit-BEN-URGT-1.OBJ-3.FUT-EVC-IK
     'When I bring them their coca, **they will accompany me sitting**.'

(4) *¡Ashnakullashaq**triki**!* AMV
     ashna-ku-lla-shaq-tri-ki
     smell-REFL-RSTR-1.FUT-EVC-IKI
     'I'm going to stink!'

In those cases in which *-ik* and *-iki* modify *-trI*, they generally correspond to increases in certainty of conjecture: a *-tr-ik* conjecture is interpreted as more certain than a *-trIø* conjecture; and a *-tr-iki* conjecture is interpreted as more certain still. Recall that under the scope of *-trI*, present-tense conditional verbs generally receive existential epistemic interpretations while past-tense-conditional as well as simple-present- and simple-past-tense verbs generally receive universal epistemic interpretations. In the case of the first, *-k* and *-ki* yield increasingly

B Further analysis of evidential modifiers

strong possibility readings; in the case of the second, third and fourth, increasingly strong necessity readings. So, under the scope of *trI-ø*, the present-tense conditional *wañu-ru-n-man* [die-URGT-3-COND] 'could die' receives something like a weak possibility reading; under *-tr-iki*, in contrast, the same phrase receives something like a strong possibility reading. Consultants explain that the -ø form might be used in a situation where the person was sick but it remained to be seen whether he would die; the *-iki* form, in contrast, might be used in a situation where the person was gravely ill and far more likely to die. Similarly, under the scope of *-trI-ø*, the simple past tense *wañu-rqa-ø* [die-PST-3] 'died' would receive something like a weak necessity reading: it is highly probable but not completely certain that the person died. In contrast, under the scope of *-tr-iki*, the same phrase would receive something like a strong necessity reading: it is very highly probable, indeed, virtually certain, that the person died. Consultants explain that a speaker might use -ø form if she knew, say, that the person, who had been very sick, still had not returned two months after having been transported down the mountain to a hospital in Lima. In contrast, that same speaker might use the *-iki* form if she had, additionally, say, heard funeral bells ringing and seen two of person's daughters crying in the church. (5) and (6) give naturally-occurring examples. In (5), the speaker$_i$ makes a present-tense conditional *-trI-ø* conjecture: She$_j$ could possibly be with a soul (*i.e.*, accompanied by the spirit of a recently deceased relative). The speaker made this conjecture after hearing the report of a single piece of evidence – that a calf had spooked when she$_j$ came near. Surely, whether or not a person is walking around with the spirit of a recently dead relative hovering somewhere close by is a hard thing to judge, even with an accumulation of evidence. In this case, only the weak -ø form is licensed. In (6), in contrast, the speaker makes a simple-present-tense *-tr-iki* conjecture: A certain calf (a friend's) must be being weaned. The speaker, having spent all but a half dozen of her 70-odd years raising goats, sheep, cows and alpacas, would not just be making an educated guess as to whether a calf was being weaned. She knows the signs. In this situation, the strong *-iki* form is licensed.

(5) *Almayuqpis kayanman**tri**.* AMV
 alma-yuq-pis ka-ya-n-man-tri
 soul-POSS-ADD be-PROG-3-COND-EVC
 'She **might be** accompanied by a soul.'

(6) *Anuyannatriki.* AMV
 anu-ya-n-ña-tr-iki
 wean-PROG-3-DISC-EVD-IKI
 'She **must** be weaning him already, for sure.'

In sum, Yauyos' three evidentials, -*mI*, *shI*, and -*trI*, each has three variants, formed by the affixation of three evidential modifiers, -ø, -*ik*, and -*iki*. The EM's are ordered on a cline of strength, with the -*ik* and -*iki* forms generally indicating progressively stronger evidence. With the direct -*mI*, this then generally corresponds to progressively stronger assertions; with the conjectural -*trI*, to progressively more certain conjectures. In the case of verbs receiving universal-deontic-modal or future-tense interpretations, -*k* and -*ki* indicate stronger obligations and more imminent futures, respectively. -*trI* has the prior effect of changing the modal interpretation of the verbs under its scope. In case a verb under its scope is not already already specified for modal force or conversational base by virtue of its morphology, -*trI* assigns the default values [universal] and [epistemic] for force and base, respectively.

B.3 A sociolinguistic note

In a dialogue, -ø(φ) will often be answered with -*ik*(φ) or -*iki*(φ), where φ is a propostition-evidential pair. Thus, *Karu-m-ø* 'it's far' may be answered with *Aw, karu-mi-ki* 'Yes, you got it/that's right/you bet you/ummhunn/, it's far'. In (1), the first speaker makes a -*trI-ø* conjecture, 'They must have left drunk'. The second answers with -*tr-ik*, echoing the judgement of the first, 'Indeed, they must have gotten drunk'.

(1) Spkr 1: *"Chay kidamuq runakuna shinkañatr lluqsimurqa."*
 Spkr 2: *"Shinkaruntri-k."* AMV
 chay   kida-mu-q   runa-kuna shinka-ña-tr   lluqsi-mu-rqa
 DEM.D stay-CISL-AG person-PL drunk-DISC-EVC exit-CISL-PST
 shinka-ru-n-tri-k
 get.drunk-URGT-3-EVC-IK
 'Spkr 1: "Those people who stayed must have come out drunk already." Spkr 2: "**Indeed**, they must have gotten drunk."'

References

Adelaar, Willem F. H. 1977. *Tarma Quechua: Grammar, texts, dictionary*. Lisse: Peter de Ridder (distributed by E.J. Brill, Leiden).
Adelaar, Willem F. H. 1986. *Morfología del Quechua de Pacaroas*. Lima: Universidad Nacional Mayor de San Marcos, Centro de Investigación de Lingüística Aplicada.
Adelaar, Willem F. H. 1988. Categorías de aspecto en el Quechua del Perú central. *Amerindia* 13. 15–42.
Adelaar, Willem F. H. 2006. The vicissitudes of directional affixes in Tarma (Northern Junín) Quechua. In Grażyna J. Rowicka & Eithne B. Carlin (eds.), *What's in a verb? studies in the verbal morphology of the languages of the americas*. Utrecht: LOT.
Adelaar, Willem F. H. 2008. Toward a typological profile of the Andean languages. In Frederik Herman Henri Kortlandt, Alexander Lubotsky, Jos Schaeken & Jeroen Wiedenhof (eds.), *Evidence and counter-evidence: essays in honour of frederik kortlandt*. Amsterdam & New York: Editions Rodopi, B.V.
Adelaar, Willem F. H. & Pieter C. Muysken. 2004. *The languages of the Andes*. Cambridge: Cambridge University Press.
Brougère, Anne-Marie. 1992. *Y por qué no quedarse en Laraos? Migración y retorno en una comunidad altoandina* (Travaux de l'IFEA 61). Lima: Institut Français d'Études Andines.
Bybee, Joan, Revere Perkins & William Pagliuca. 1994. *The evolution of grammar: tense, aspect, and modality in the languages of the world*. Chicago: University of Chicago Press.
Castro, Neli Belleza. 1995. *Vocabulario jacaru-castellano castellano-jacaru: aimara tupino*. Vol. 3. Centro de Estudios Regionales Andinos "Bartolomé de Las Casas".
Catta, Javier. 1994. *Gramática del quichua ecuatoriano*. Quito: Editorial Abya Yala.
Cerrón-Palomino, Rodolfo M. 1976a. *Gramática quechua Junín–Huanca*. Lima: Ministerio de Educación, Instituto de Estudios Puruanos.
Cerrón-Palomino, Rodolfo M. 1976b. *Diccionario quechua Junín–Huanca*. Lima: Ministerio de Educación, Instituto de Estudios Puruanos.

References

Cerrón-Palomino, Rodolfo M. 1987. *Lingüística quechua*. Cuzco: Centro Bartolomé de las Casas.

Cerrón-Palomino, Rodolfo M. 1994. *Quechumara: estructuras paralelas de las lenguas quechua y aimará*. La Paz: Centro de Investigación y Promición de Campesinato.

Cerrón-Palomino, Rodolfo M. 2000. *Lingüística aimara*. Cuzco: Centro Bartolomé de las Casas.

Cerrón-Palomino, Rodolfo M. & Gustavo Solís-Fonesca (eds.). 1990. *Temas de lingüística amerindia: Actas del Primer Congreso Nacional de Investigaciones Lingüístico–Filológicas*. Lima: Consejo Nacional de Ciencia y Tecnología (CONCYTEC) & Deutsche Gesellschaft für technische Zusammenarbeit (GTZ).

Chirinos-Rivera, Andrés. 2001. *Atlas lingüístico del Perú*. Cuzco, Lima: Centro Bartolomé de las Casas & Ministerio de Educación.

Cole, Peter. 1982. *Imbabura Quechua*. Amsterdam: North-Holland.

Cole, Peter, Gabriella Hermon & Mario D. Martín. 1994. *Language in the Andes*. Newark, DE: Latin American Studies Program, University of Delaware.

Coombs, David, Heidi Coombs & Robert Weber. 1976. *Gramática quechua San Martín*. Lima: Ministerio de Educación, Instituto de Estudios Puruanos.

Copley, Bridget. 2009. *The semantics of the future*. New York: Routledge.

Cusihuamán Gutiérrez, Antonio. 1976. *Gramática quechua Cuzco–Collao*. Lima: Ministerio de Educación, Instituto de Estudios Puruanos.

Echerd, Stephen M. 1974. *Sociolinguistic data on Quechua of Yauyos and Northern Lima*.

Faller, Martina. 2003. Propositional- and illocutionary-level evidentiality in Cuzco Quechua. In *Semantics of understudied languages of the americas (sula)*, 19–33. Amherst, MA: GLSA.

Floyd, Rick. 1999. *The Structure of evidential categories in Wanka Quechua*. Dallas: SIL & The University of Texas at Arlington Publications in Linguistics.

Hardman, Martha J. 1966. *Jaqaru: Outline of phonological and morphological structures*. The Hague: Mouton.

Hardman, Martha J. 1983. *Jaqaru: Compendio de estructura fonológica y morfológica*. Lima: Instituto de Estudios Peruanos.

Hardman, Martha J. 2000. *Jaqaru*. Munich: LIMCOM Europa.

Heggarty, Paul. 2007. Linguistics for archeaologists: Principles, methods, and the case of the Incas. *Cambridge Archaeological Journal* 17(3). 311–340.

Herrero, Joaquín & Federico Sánchez de Lozada. 1978. *Gramática quechua: Estructura del quechua boliviano contemporaneo*. Editorial Universo.

Hintz, Daniel. 2011. *Crossing Aspectual Frontiers: Emergence, Evolution, and Interwoven Semantic Domains in South Conchucos Quechua Discourse.* Berkeley, CA: UC Publications in Linguistics.

Hintz, Daniel & Marlene Ballena Dávila. 2000. Características distintivas del quechua de corongo: perspectivas histórica y sincrónica.

Hintz, Daniel & Diane Hintz. 2017. The evidential category of mutual knowledge in Quechua. *Lingua* 186–187. 88–109.

Landerman, Peter N. 1991. *Quechua dialects and their classification.* University of California, Los Angeles PhD thesis.

Lewis, M. Paul, Gary F. Simons & Charles D. Fennig (eds.). 2015. *Ethnologue: Languages of the world.* 18th edn. http://www.ethnologue.com/. Dallas, TX: SIL International.

Matthewson, Lisa, Hotze Rullmann & Henry Davis. 2005. Modality in St'át'imcets. In *40th International Conference on Salish and Neighbouring Languages.*

Muysken, Pieter C. 1977. *Syntactic developments in the verb phrase of ecuadorian quechua.* Lisse: The Peter De Ridder Press.

Parker, Gary J. 1969. *Ayacucho Quechua grammar and dictionary.* The Hague: Mouton.

Parker, Gary J. 1976. *Gramática quechua Ancash–Huailas.* Lima: Ministerio de Educación, Instituto de Estudios Peruanos.

Peterson, Tyler. 2014. Rethinking mirativity: The expression and implication of surprise. unpublished ms., University of Toronto.

Quesada Castillo, Félix. 1976. *Gramática quechua Cajamarca-Cañaris.* Lima: Ministerio de Educación, Instituto de Estudios Peruanos.

Shimelman, Aviva. 2012. Yauyos Quechua evidentials: Interactions with tense, aspect and mode. In *Conference on Endangered Languages and Cultures of Native America (CELCNA).*

Shimelman, Aviva. 2014. Yauyos Quechua evidentials and the interpretation of mode. Unpublished ms. https://doi.org/10.5281/zenodo.345419. DOI:10.5281/zenodo.345419

Soto Ruiz, Clodoaldo. 1976a. *Gramática quechua Ayacucho–Chanca.* Lima: Ministerio de Educación, Instituto de Estudios Peruanos.

Swisshelm, Germán. 1972. Un diccionario del quechua de huaraz. *Estudios Culturales Benedictinos* 2.

Taylor, Gerald. 1984. Yauyos: Un microcosmo dialectal quechua. *Revista Andina* 2. 121–146.

References

Taylor, Gerald. 1987a. Algunos datos nuevos sobre el quechua de Yauyos (Vitis y Huancaya). *Revista Andina* 9. 253–265.

Taylor, Gerald. 1987b. Atuq: Relatos quechuas de Laraos, Lincha, Huangáscar y Madeán. *Allpanchis phuturinqa* 29/30.

Taylor, Gerald. 1987c. Relatos quechuas de Laraos, Lincha, Huangáscar y Madeán, provincia de Yauyos. *Allpanchis* 29.

Taylor, Gerald. 1990. Le dialecte quechua de Laraos, Yauyos. Étude morphologique. *Bulletin del'Institut Français d'Études Andines* 19. 293–325.

Taylor, Gerald. 1991. Textes quechua de Laraos (Yauyos). *Journal de la Société des Américanistes* 76. 121–154.

Taylor, Gerald. 1994. *Estudios de dialectología quechua (Chachapoyas, Ferreñafe, Yauyos)*. Lima: Ediciones Universidad Nacional de Educación, La Cantuta.

Taylor, Gerald. 1994b. *El quechua de Laraos. Esbozo morfológico, breve léxico, texto.* Paris: *Chantiers Amerindia.*

Taylor, Gerald. 2000. *Camac, camay, y camasca y otros ensayos sobre el Huarochirí y Yauyos.* Lima: L'Institut Français d'Études Andines.

Torero, Alfredo. 1964. *Los dialectos quechuas.* Univ. Agraria.

Torero, Alfredo. 1968. Los dialectos quechuas. *La Molina: Anales Científicos de la Universidad Agraria* 2.

Torero, Alfredo. 1974. *El quechua y la historia social andina.* Lima: Universidad Ricardo Palma, Dirección Universitaria de Investigación.

Varilla Gallardo, Brígido. 1965. *Apuntes para el folklore de Yauyos: Mitologías, leyendas, cuentos y fábulas, canciones populares, danzas, costumbres y fiestas, comidas y bebidas, creencias, supersticiones, medicina popular, y adivinanzas de la región de Yauyos.* Lima: Litografía Huascarán.

Weber, David. 1989. *A grammar of Huallaga (Huánuco) Quechua.* Berkeley: University of California Press.

Name index

Adelaar, Willem F. H., 4, 11, 13, 18, 154, 165, 190

Brougère, Anne-Marie, 5
Bybee, Joan, 233

Castro, Neli Belleza, 23
Catta, Javier, 13
Cerrón-Palomino, Rodolfo M., 8, 9, 13, 19, 21, 22, 154, 210, 277, 309
Chirinos-Rivera, Andrés, 3
Cole, Peter, 13
Coombs, David, 13
Coombs, Heidi, 13
Copley, Bridget, 320
Cusihuamán Gutiérrez, Antonio, 13, 24

Davis, Henry, 320
Dávila, Marlene Ballena, 10

Echerd, Stephen M., 5

Faller, Martina, 18, 165
Fennig, Charles D., 3, 5, 311
Floyd, Rick, 18

Hardman, Martha J., 19
Heggarty, Paul, 5
Hermon, Gabriella, 13
Herrero, Joaquín, 13
Hintz, Daniel, 9, 10, 13, 18, 154, 188

Hintz, Diane, 18

Landerman, Peter N., 5, 7, 21
Lewis, M. Paul, 3, 5, 311
Lozada, Federico Sánchez de, 13

Martín, Mario D., 13
Matthewson, Lisa, 320
Muysken, Pieter C., 4, 18, 165

Pagliuca, William, 233
Parker, Gary J., 13, 22, 56, 97, 277
Perkins, Revere, 233
Peterson, Tyler, 165

Quesada Castillo, Félix, 13, 277

Rullmann, Hotze, 320

Shimelman, Aviva, 18, 272, 277
Simons, Gary F., 3, 5, 311
Solís-Fonesca, Gustavo, 13
Soto Ruiz, Clodoaldo, 13
Swisshelm, Germán, 24

Taylor, Gerald, 2, 5, 7, 8, 11, 13
Torero, Alfredo, 5, 6, 22

Varilla Gallardo, Brígido, 5

Weber, David, 13, 18, 23, 188
Weber, Robert, 13

Language index

Alis, 6
Alto Huallaga, 6, 12
Alto Marañón, 6, 12
Alto Pativilca, 6, 12
Amazonas, 6, 12
Ancash, 4, 10, 13, 22–24, 28, 277
Ap-am-ah, 6, 12
Apurí, 6
Argentinan Quechua, 6, 12
Ayacucho, 4, 6, 8–10, 12, 13, 24, 267, 279, 310, 314
Aymara, 18
Azángaro, 6

Bolivian Quechua, 4, 6, 12, 13

Cacra, 6
Cajamarca, 6, 12, 13, 21, 24, 277
Cañaris, 6, 12
Chinchay, 6, 12
Chocos, 6
Colombian Quechua, 6, 12
Conchucos, 6, 12, 13, 18, 24, 154, 188, 233, 270
Corongo, 9, 10, 24
Cuzco, 4, 6, 12, 13, 18, 24, 165, 233

Ecuadorian Quechua, 6, 12, 13

Ferreñafe, 13

Hongos, 6
Huaihuash, 6, 12

Huailas, 6, 12
Huailay, 6, 12
Huallaga, 10, 13, 18, 23, 24, 188, 233, 270
Huampuy, 6, 8, 12
Huanca, 6, 12, 13, 24, 277, 309, 310
Huancayo, 1, 3, 46, 287
Huangáscar, 6
Huanuco, 10, 13, 22, 23
Huaylas, 10, 24, 253

Imbabura, 13
Incahuasi, 6, 12

Jaqaru, 18, 19, 23
Jauja, 6, 12
Junín, 8–10, 22, 24, 309, 310, 314

Kawki, 18

Laraos, 6, 12
Lincha, 6
Loreto, 6, 12

Madeán, 6

Pacaraos, 6, 12, 13, 22, 24, 154
Proto-Quechua, 6, 12
Puno, 6, 12

San Martín Quechua, 6, 12, 13, 22
Sihuas, 9, 18, 21, 22, 270

Tana, 6

Language index

Tarma, 13, 21, 154, 190, 233
Tomas, 6
Topará, 6, 9

Vitis, 6
Víñac, 6

Yaru, 6, 12
Yungay, 6, 12

Subject index

ablative, 82
accompaniment, 234
accusative, 89
actor and object reference, 138
adjectives, 55
    adverbial, 55, 56
    gender, 55, 57
    preadjectives, 58
    regular, 55, 56
adverbial, 199
adverbs, 245
AILLA, 14, 309
allative, 77
alternative conditional, 176
assenters, 243
Aysa, 18

benefactive, 84

Cachuy, 18
case
    combinations, 96
causative, 88, 215
certainty, 263
Chavín, 9
cislocative, 222
classification, 7
comitative, 94
comparative, 72
conditional, 168
constituent order, 283
continuitive, 265

conventions, xi

dative, 77
different subjects, 192
diminutive, 214
discontinuitive, 259
disjunction, 254
DoBeS, 14, 309
dummy noun, 64
durative, 189

emotive, 269
emphatic, 252
enclitic, 249
    sequence, 250
endangerment, 3
evidentials, 270
    assertive force, 277
    conjectural, 275
    direct, 273
    evidence strength, 279
    modification, 277
    questions, 281
    reportative, 274
exceptional, 237
exclusive, 88

factive, 203
fourth person, 36
frequentive, 217
future, 151

genitive

Subject index

-pa, 79
-pi, 87
greetings, 244

imperative, 181
inceptive, 232
inchoative, 206
inclusion, 260
injunctive, 184
instrumental, 94
intensive, 236
interjections, 241
interrogation, 291
   -chu, 254
irreversible change, 235
iterative past, 166

joint action, 147, 209, 228

limitative, 75, 201, 220
loan words, 26
locative
   -pa, 80
   -pi, 86

modal system, 169
modals, 168
morpheme codes, xi
   sorted by code, xi
   sorted by morpheme, xiv
morphophonemics, 24, 26, 213
mutual benefit, 229

negation, 289
   -chu, 254
nouns, 32
   gender, 34
   locative, 35
   regular, 32
   time, 33

numerals, 59
   huk, 63
   cardinal, 59
   ordinal, 60
   time, 61
   with possessive suffixes, 62
ñuqakuna, 8, 37
ñuqanchikkuna, 37
ñuqayku, 8

orthography, 28

particles, 241
parts of speech, 31
passive, 218
passive/accidental, 216
past, 153
past conditional, 179
perfect, 162
perfective
   -ku, 190
phonemic inventory, 24
   consonant, 24, 25
   vowel, 24, 25
precision, 263
prepositions, 244
progressive, 186
pronouns, 36
   demonstrative, 36, 40
   dependent, 36, 43
   determiners, 42
   indefinite, 46
   interrogative, 46
   negative indefinite, 46
   personal, 36
psychological necessity, 225
purposive, 84

reciprocal, 223

Subject index

recordings, 14
reflexive, 204, 218
repetitive, 226
restrictive, 257

same-subjects, 196
sensual necessity, 225
sensual or psychological necessity, 208
sentence, 284
    comparison, 287
    complementation, 300
    coordination, 284
    emphasis, 300
    equatives, 296
    interrogation, 291
    negation, 289
    possession, 297
    reciprocals, 294
    relativization, 302
    subordination, 305
    topicalization, 299
sequential, 267
Shining Path, 4, 317
simple past, 154
    quotative tense, 159
simple present, 148
simulative, 72, 205
subordination, 191
substantive
    accompaniment, 113
    agentive, 102
    case, 72
    classes, 32
    concretizing, 99
    derivation, 98
    derivation from substantives, 112
    derivation from verbs, 98

infinitive, 108
inflection, 66
multi-possessive, 113
non-exhaustivity, 112
number inflection, 70
partnership, 116
perfective, 105
possessive, 67, 114
restrictive suffix, 117
syntax, 283

to do, 207
topic marker, 264
translocative, 227
Tupe, 2, 18

uninterrupted action, 230
urgency/personal interest, 233

verb derivation, 202
verbs, 121
    copulative, 124
    inflection, 129
    intransitive, 123
    onomatopoetic, 126
    transitive, 121

www.ingramcontent.com/pod-product-compliance
Lightning Source LLC
Chambersburg PA
CBHW081202170426
43197CB00018B/2897